Witness to War

The Story of the Civil War Told by Those Who Lived It

J. Mark Powell

STACKPOLE BOOKS

Essex, Connecticut

STACKPOLE BOOKS

An imprint of The Globe Pequot Publishing Group, Inc.
64 South Main St.
Essex, CT 06426
www.GlobePequot.com

British Library Cataloguing in Publication Information available

Library of Congress Cataloging-in-Publication Data available

ISBN 978-0-8117-7769-8 (paperback)
ISBN 978-0-8117-7770-4 (ebook)

To Dr. John and Sara Carter,
who personify Southern graciousness and charm

and

Robert Serio,
without whose friendship this book would not exist

Soli Deo Gloria

"I wish I could tell you more of it. Maybe I will one day."
UNKNOWN OFFICER IN THE 12TH ALABAMA INFANTRY
AFTER THE BATTLE OF FIRST BULL RUN/MANASSAS

CONTENTS

The Beginning

Pause for a moment and picture an auditorium where 432 people are seated. It's an eclectic group. Although the rows are filled mostly with men, nearly 50 women are scattered among them. There are nine teenagers, plus a smattering of college students as well.

Their voices run the gamut of America's geography, from the tight nasal tone of Yankee New England to the slow, deep drawl of the Mississippi Delta to the flat twang of the Midwest and Great Plains. Theirs is a folksy, casual English, frequently garnished by adding an "a" before words, as in "I'm a going tell you."

They are middle-class yeomen farmers and wealthy plantation owners, lawyers and loafers, doctors and day laborers, shopkeepers and public officials. There is a Baptist preacher, a Presbyterian minister, and a woman missionary to the West Indies.

And soldiers. Lots and lots of soldiers.

More than half of them wear a uniform, be it blue or gray. Two will go on to receive the Medal of Honor. Only a handful of West Point–trained professional military men are sprinkled among them; the overwhelming majority are volunteers who stepped forward when called. A few are draftees compelled to serve at the point of a bayonet. Apart from them, the rest are citizen soldiers who willingly left their families and homes, guided by a sustaining conviction in the rightness of their cause.

This disparate group also shares something special in common.

These 432 people are the *witnesses*. They all experienced the Civil War.

There are no famous figures from history in their ranks, no legendary generals or statesmen. Yet it is their everyday ordinariness that makes them extraordinary. Because they give us the rare opportunity to experience the war exactly as they did: through their eyes and hearts and told in their own words as events unfolded. Whether on the front lines or the home front, theirs is a real-time account of not only what happened but also how it felt as they lived through it.

In some cases, they participated in epic events. In others, they expressed their reaction to them. Together, they open a unique window into the period, allowing us to view the conflict as they did while it was actually happening.

The purpose of this book is not to judge which side was "right" and which was "wrong." Rather, it is intended to hold a mirror to that remarkable time and allow its people to reveal themselves to us.

These are not memoirs or recollections set to paper decades later. They are in-the-moment accounts where idealism mingles with fear, where heroism, confusion, and uncertainty all dwell alongside each other. There is also hope, courage, moments of laughter, and a sustaining sense of optimism. No matter how painful the road, no matter how horrendous the toll, the witnesses carry on with the firm belief that something good, something worthy, will ultimately emerge.

Over the next few hundred pages, the witnesses will share the same breath of time with us, the people of the twenty-first century. We will discover a remarkable moment when the nation's fate hung in the balance—with no guarantee of how it would turn out. And we will gain not only a better knowledge of what occurred and how it felt to live during it but also a richer, fuller understanding of these equally remarkable men, women, and children.

So how did this assemblage of the 432 witnesses come about?

It was the offspring of happenstance. Because sometimes, a very big thing can result from the smallest whim.

One weekend in early 1970, my father took my Missouri family on a day trip to nearby Pea Ridge National Military Park in northwestern Arkansas. I fell in love with the Civil War on the spot. I discovered my life's passion that day at the age of nine, and it still burns within me as strongly today as ever.

Things only intensified when, one day in fifth grade, a classmate showed me a Civil War letter written by his great-great-grandfather. Holding that paper in my hand was mesmerizing. I knew I was a writer even at that young age, and so I connected with people of the period through their written words. I recognized the letter was, quite literally, a time machine. It had been in an actual army camp in the 1860s, and there it was in my 1970s classroom, connecting us across more than a century.

During my high school and college years, I participated in Civil War reenacting. That experience stirred within me a desire to understand what the war felt like on a personal level. I didn't want to just know what had happened so long ago; I yearned to experience it for myself.

Ever so slowly, commencing in 1989, I began acquiring original Civil War letters, buying one whenever I could afford it. One spring day in 2014, I went to the post office to collect an acquisition that had just arrived. Reflecting on its contents while driving home, it occurred to me that this newest letter directly related to the content of another letter I owned. I experienced an epiphany at that moment. What if I could assemble a collection that told the story of the war completely through letters, moving from one major event to another—a narrative that would allow the reader to follow the war's full arc and sweep as it unfolded in real time?

I identified major battles, issues, and developments and drafted an outline. From that point on, I approached all letters I encountered on the market with a simple question: Does this piece fill a hole in the outline and keep the narrative moving forward?

I also discovered something else. For decades, museums, libraries, and archives have housed collections of letters written by famous figures. Those letters have long been in print. Additionally, there are hundreds of books comprising the correspondence of generals and letters exchanged between husbands and wives and those written by soldiers in particular regiments or brigades, among others.

Yet what about the full array of voices from average, everyday people—Union and Confederate, military and civilian, men and women? Where were they?

Indeed, excerpts from diaries and letters have been featured in books for many years. But all too frequently, the same quotes from the same sources were repeatedly used. Or the excerpts were compiled into a volume focusing on a single specific battle or campaign. Or they were letters from soldiers alone. Very often, memoirs and recollections written decades after the war's end were also included. Despite my search, I was unable to find a book that covered the war's full scope entirely from the unique narrative perspective of the period's populace.

More than 30 years and 550 letters later, the conflict's story is now told through the words of the witnesses who lived through one history-making episode after another, shared as those events took place.

My timing turned out to be ideal. For many years, original letters were chiefly available for purchase only from established relics dealers. Like any business, they had limited inventory and so naturally focused on pieces from famous figures that commanded high prices. Few bothered carrying materials from obscure everyday people, the very folks whose voices I wanted to resurrect.

However, the arrival of eBay and other online retail outlets changed everything. Suddenly, there was a new way to sell the material many established dealers didn't handle. As a result, letters that had sat untouched in Great Aunt Thelma's dresser drawer began seeing the light of day for the first time in 75 years. Consequently, this is the first time the material you are about to read has ever been published.

This fresh content, in turn, helps flesh out our understanding of the period. For example, my reading revealed that the one piece of equipment hated above all else by both Northern and Southern soldiers alike was the knapsack. They ceaselessly griped about them in their correspondence. The one thing they longed for above all else? A wooden box from home filled with goodies that they couldn't obtain in the field (sometimes including, surprisingly, ketchup). By far, the most often requested single item was simple postage stamps so that soldiers could continue staying in touch with their loved ones. "Love nor money cannot get them here," one lamented.

This book is the result of my reading more than 20,000 original letters (and acquiring far too many of them!) over four decades. It is based solely on the 550 pieces contained in the *J. Mark Powell Specialized Collection of Civil War Letters* (with the exception of three letters jointly shared with my dear friend and fellow collector Scott Senft). It isn't just a "bunch of Civil War letters." Rather, it is a grouping specifically curated with the intention of telling the war's story in its entirety through original correspondence.

The witnesses who wrote these letters never imagined anyone else would ever read them. (At least one writer requested the recipient burn his letter after having read it, which, thankfully for us, she did not do.) So they poured out their hearts without reservation. Reading their words now is like peeking over their shoulder as they were penning each line. It's as close as we can get to actually asking them, "What was the war really like?"

It is important to understand that this book is not a military history. It does involve a war, after all, so much space is devoted to soldiers' descriptions of combat, camp life, and army movements. Most of the major campaigns are chronicled here, though not always in as great detail as I would have wished since collecting is all too often a matter of catch as catch can. Yet the essence and spirit of the war's biggest battles and movements are fully captured.

It should be pointed out that there are far more surviving Federal letters than Confederate ones. Due to that scarcity, the Southern perspective is not as fully presented as I would have wished.

Also, some excerpts contain material that is considered offensive today. Most prominent is the so-called N-word. I do not use or condone that word. Yet if we sanitize history by expunging details to suit contemporary standards, we lose the ability to learn from it. Removing milestones undermines our ability to discern the progress society has made while simultaneously diluting our understanding of earlier eras. (For example, it will be disturbing for many modern readers to see how often and how casually that slur was tossed around and to discover that it appears in far more Northern letters than Southern ones.)

A note now about format and presentation. It was very important to me that these excerpts remained as close to the original version as possible. However, a few changes were unavoidable.

I adopted a standardized dateline at the top of each excerpt. It is the type most frequently seen in the original letters. Additionally, punctuation was highly individualized at the time. (It appears that educators' major emphasis in the first half of the nineteenth century was on penmanship. Spelling was second, and punctuation was almost left to "figure it out for yourself.") As a result, I have modernized it to make it easier for today's reader to follow. I also corrected spelling whenever necessary, although I retained much incorrect grammar to maintain the period's tone.

Mid-Victorians tended to ramble in their letters. They sometimes started to relate an experience, meandered to ask about things at home, and then returned to the subject at hand. They also often casually buried significant details that are fascinating to modern readers deep in the body of their correspondence. (For example, it is common to encounter in Union soldiers' letters, "I saw President Lincoln today," tacked on almost as an afterthought.) Consequently, I have moved content whenever necessary, but I have done so sparingly.

They underlined the oddest words for emphasis, which I have mostly removed; the few instances that remain were written that way originally. Unlike today, they used exclamation points with exceeding rarity; all contained here are original. I also added the first names of generals (and other historical figures) to assist modern readers, referring to all of them simply as "general" to avoid confusion over those who rose in rank as the war progressed. (For this, I ask for understanding from serious students of history.)

At times, it was necessary to clarify a word's meaning or add a brief explanation. Whenever I did so, it appears in square brackets. All comments appearing in parentheses were put that way by the letter's writer. I added brief biographical details about each correspondent whenever possible. In some cases, the writer's identity is unknown because they didn't sign their full name. Traditionally, academia has slighted such pieces. Yet I utilized them when the letter's content merited it.

As you read these words, I urge you to keep a crucial point in mind. America had never experienced a war of such sweeping magnitude before. It covered nearly one-quarter of a continent, introduced new weaponry and technology, and produced extensive casualties that were utterly unimaginable when the conflict began. Even people watching from afar in Europe, which was no stranger to large-scale warfare, were horrified by the extent of the bloodshed here.

What emerges from the witnesses is a picture of people sincerely trying to understand what was occurring. They were keenly aware that they were living in a decisive moment in American history, and they earnestly tried to make sense of it all as it was happening.

A final thought. One line contained in a letter written by a war widow in the summer of 1865 has haunted me ever since the first time I read it: *"Now that the cruel war is over, and I look back and see the many lonely homes, I wonder what it all meant."*

In this book, the people of that time tell us the answer in their own words.

Any faults, be they literary or factual, are mine alone.

J. Mark Powell
Gilbert, South Carolina
March 3, 2025

1861

"Our glorious union is now about to be severed."

IT HAD FINALLY ARRIVED.

The crisis had been brewing since America's earliest days, rumbling for decades beneath the surface the way volcanic pressure builds, out of sight but never out of mind. From the minute the first English settlers reached the Atlantic shore in the early seventeenth century, the country was pulled in opposite directions. Two distinct cultures developed. Slavery put a human face on the problem because one group permitted the practice and the other did not. But the differences that separated them ran far deeper than slavery alone.

By the middle of the nineteenth century, America had, for all practical purposes, become two separate societies. Like a couple who had reached a crisis point in their marriage, they had to either find a way to move on together or permanently go their separate ways.

One section chose the latter option. The other would not permit it to do so. Abraham Lincoln succinctly summed up what happened next.

"And the war came."

We begin in the final months of 1860. As that year's presidential election drew near, people everywhere sensed that a monumental moment was at hand, making it one of history's most dramatic political contests.

The infant Republican Party, whose nominee was Abraham Lincoln, capitalized on several innovative attractions. They included marches by Wide Awake clubs consisting of uniformed and enthusiastic young male Lincoln supporters, mostly in their twenties, and raising Liberty Poles—sometimes called Lincoln Poles—topped by a U.S. flag (often emblazoned with the GOP ticket "Lincoln and Hamlin" in large letters) and followed by a picnic or other social gathering.

A letter written by a young man identified only as **Cornelius (unknown)** to a friend captured the excitement of the campaign's closing weeks.

North Bloomfield, New York
October 8, 1860

Hurrah for Lincoln. I suppose you are a Lincoln man. I hope so, and a Wide Awake, too. We have a [Wide Awake] company of about 75 at this place. There is a company in every place where there is a dozen houses around here. Our club went to a pole raising yesterday about four miles from here. There was three companies there, about 200 people. We raised a pole 140 feet out of the ground. Put it eight feet in the ground. We had a gay old time. It is getting late and I do not know what to write more, so I will bid you goodbye with three cheers for Old Abe. Hurrah, Hurrah, Hurrah. From your humble servant and a Wide Awake, Cornelius

Lincoln's victory on November 6, 1860, was the tipping point.

South Carolina had declared in advance that if Lincoln emerged victorious in the four-candidate contest, it would secede from the Union. It was widely believed that other Deep South states would quickly follow.

Twelve days after the election, a man who signed himself simply **Frank (unknown)** wrote to a friend living in the South. He mentioned the Minutemen, a pro-secessionist paramilitary group founded in St. Louis earlier that year to counter the pro-Union Wide Awakes.

St. Louis, Missouri
November 18, 1860

Have just this moment received news from California. Far as heard from 70,000 votes cast of which—Abraham Lincoln 27,000—Stephen A. Douglas 24,000—John C. Breckinridge 20,000 and John Bell 2,000. Awful, ain't it? Every free state likely gone Lincoln. Well, I expect we will have to put up with it.

Lincoln being elected, the Union may be dissolved. You, of course, would join the Minutemen and march on to glory and independence. Hurrah for the South, take off your hat and throw it up. Will you be so cowardly as to permit them to preside over this nation? No—you must go on there to Washington and help prevent his inauguration, do you hear? Do you hear?

You who are away down South among strangers, you must expect to feel lonesome and homesick for a while, but it will wear away and only come over you at times. I think it will be a good thing for you, having had a long experience with the North, this living South will finish your education. And while educating yourself, you must educate others by writing us long letters, and, as you get better acquainted, tell us of their customs, their sociability, and hospitality. Also, of that "peculiar institution slavery" as seen by yourself. Your opinions would be worth having. Tell us what church you attend; Episcopal, of course.

The usual postelection finger-pointing by the losing party followed. Democrats realized that their two-way split had made it possible for Lincoln to eke out a win with a scant just under 40 percent of the popular vote. **Austin Lamonte (1837–1918)** had voted for Democrat Stephen Douglas. The University of Michigan medical student scolded a friend, believing that Republicans were responsible for whatever came next.

Ann Arbor, Michigan
November 27, 1860

You speak of the result of the election and of politics. I think it poorly becomes you and your party to glory over the victory which you have won. When you look at what the expense has been and what disaster it has brought on the land—and what greater disaster it is so very likely to bring. It is your party who have done this by the promulgation of their doctrines, who have irritated the South until they are ready to sever the ties of this Union.

You cannot get rid of it, George; your party have done all this. You may try and throw it off on our party, but history and truth will do the Democratic Party justice. What it will come to, the future only can tell. I hope it will not prove to be as bad as now to all appearances it will be. We all think too much of our country to have it broken for a nigger. I have no doubts but that there are patriots who vote with the Republican Party who, when they come to think soberly at what they have done, will repent and will turn around and do all they can to remedy the matter, but it may be too late.

It was, in fact, too late. Just days later, South Carolina followed through on its promise to secede from the Union. A special secession convention opened on December 17, with Americans in both the North and the South closely monitoring developments. That was especially true in the Deep South, as an **unknown young teacher** indicated to a friend in North Carolina.

Selma, Alabama
December 20, 1860

We are looking every day for news from South Carolina. By this time, it is likely she has seceded. Alabama will follow her as soon as her convention meets unless something unexpected turns up. The election for delegates to the convention takes place next Monday.

The ladies commenced today to make wreaths to dress up the church for Christmas. They turned out in full force, and to judge by the way they worked this morning, they will make quick work of it. I was reminded of old times in Fayetteville [North Carolina] when I used to help there.

Indeed, South Carolina seceded the very day that letter was written. (Alabama followed 22 days later.)

Things rapidly escalated. A week later, on the night of December 26, the commander at Fort Moultrie at the entrance to Charleston Harbor quietly transferred his small garrison to the bigger and still unfinished Fort Sumter, located on a manmade island. Charlestonians were livid when they awoke the next morning to see the U.S. flag flying from atop the massive brick fort.

In an instant, the situation transformed from a political crisis into a military one. Many people, including **George Tracy (unknown)**, concluded that war was now inevitable, as he wrote to his mother.

[Maryland; location unknown]
December 30, 1860

We are in the midst of considerable excitement. There is but one topic, and that is the trouble in and with South Carolina. Yesterday, the excitement was somewhat increased by a dispatch from Charleston announcing the evacuation of Fort Moultrie (situated at the mouth of Charleston Harbor) by the U.S. troops and the partial burning of the fort. Major Robert Anderson has been in command for nearly four weeks. Today's telegraph says that he evacuated Fort Moultrie to take possession of Fort Sumter. The latter is a new fort but recently finished, said to be the strongest fort for its size in the U.S.

This evening's dispatch says that the citizens, together with the military, have taken possession of Fort Moultrie, the Custom House, and post office.

It is impossible to conceive what will be the result of the present trouble. South Carolina proclaims herself to be out of the Union, an independent state, and is exerting herself to the utmost to drag the rest of the Cotton States with her. Our own state of Maryland is for Union on reasonable terms. But if the North makes no move to repeal their personal liberty bills nor make any concessions to the South, then Maryland will go with the South.

The present trouble has been weighing heavily upon me. The financial trouble has caused a general stoppage in all kinds of business. Some of our largest bankers and merchants have been compelled to stop, and yet these troubles are passed by hardly noticed in consequence of the Southern trouble.

Our politicians, both North and South, are bringing all this trouble upon us. It is sad to contemplate the result which must follow the breaking up of this glorious Union of states. If civil war must come, which all I think feel sure, the horrors of war can be but feebly estimated. Father against son and brother against brother—hands raised against our dearest friends.

As 1861 dawned, America faced stark new realities. North and South were clouded in dark billows of uncertainty.

As other Deep South states prepared to follow South Carolina into secession, Northern ire was focused on the state that had initiated the split. **Dr. James Vandervort's (1834–1911)** reaction typified the feelings of many Unionists.

Clarksville, Ohio
January 7, 1861

People about here talk of nothing now but pork and politics. Pork, however, will soon all be sold, and then we'll hear of nothing but secession. South Carolina needs a good mauling. Nothing will bring her to her senses quicker than a little wholesale discipline of that kind. Although one of the least, poorest, and most contemptible of all the states, she has created more destruction than any other state in the Union. She is completely under the thumb of a few unprincipled men who think it better to "reign in Hell than to serve in Heaven" and consequently want to set up for themselves. If I think my services are required, I shall not hesitate to shoulder my musket "to maintain etc." [the Union]. Would you?

(Vandervort, whose wife died later that year after giving birth to their daughter, eventually served as an assistant surgeon in the 16th Ohio Infantry.)

The situation was especially precarious for people living in the Border States of Maryland, Missouri, and Kentucky. Many had strong cultural and family ties to the South and equally strong financial ties to the North.

Consider the perilous position of Baltimore's Balderston, Ward & Co., "Commission merchants for the sale of Boots and Shoes." Northern footwear manufacturers contracted with it to sell their products to shops and retailers around the country. Suddenly, the Southern market was in jeopardy. Uncertainty froze business in its tracks, as an **unknown clerk** revealed in a letter to Captain Clark Partridge, a boot maker in Medway, Massachusetts.

Baltimore, Maryland
January 12, 1861

Our policy is to keep within bounds until things change for the better. Should there be civil war, there must follow a general suspension in trade. Should this be averted, things may continue unsettled, for the South will not come into the arrangement with kindly feelings for some time. There are no goods being sold. Our sales since the 1st of January only amount to $400. T&A have not sold $1. The jobbers [suppliers] are doing nothing either by orders or otherwise, and they do not know if their customers can pay up and will want spring goods. Those who go east will buy but very little indeed, and it would be the very worst thing for us to go on to make goods in the face of the present troubles.

As to you saying we will have a better trade in consequence of the political troubles, it is all nonsense. Yankee boots will be damned in Baltimore just as much as they are in New York. Hill and Pastor and the Southern trade on them will be light. Do not make over 20 cases a week at the outside [most].

Uncertainty dominated politics as well. Lincoln would not become president until March 4. The outgoing president, James Buchanan, sat in the White House and did nothing, allowing events to unfold without federal interference. For that, historians rate him as one of the worst of all presidents.

Lewis S. Coryell (1788–1865) saw it differently. A wealthy businessman and fellow Pennsylvanian, he was Buchanan's close friend and staunch supporter. A correspondent had asked Coryell's opinion about what would happen next.

His reply demonstrates that nobody could predict with certainty how events would play out.

New Hope, Pennsylvania
January 14, 1861

Mr. Buchanan is the President of the whole people. They are the sovereigns. He holds the veto power for their equalized benefits, and most commendably, he has exercised that power. In fact, he is the "Noblest Roman" of them all. He has, with a view to conciliation to avoid violence, practiced the most masterly inactivity. Now, when no other alternative is left, he demonstrates to execute his duties, as in accordance to his oath of office, and history will assign a proud page to his merits.

If the South will become prudent, what a glorious result might, perhaps, may be since we are to be divided. If they of the South adopt our present Constitution and peacefully unite in an administration as is now in practice, they would soon include southern New York, New Jersey, North Carolina, Louisiana, Delaware, South Carolina, Texas, Maryland, Georgia, Mississippi, Virginia, Florida, Arkansas, Kentucky, Florida, California, Missouri, and subsequently at least Pennsylvania, perhaps.

This reconstruction would attach all, except those of western New York and the New England states, which might slide to Canada.

All hope is now at an end for permanent future reconciliation, and we are now compelled to conjuncture [envision] the future in some changed aspect.

South Carolina's departure from the Union was swiftly repeated in 1861's opening weeks. By January 21, four other states had also seceded. On that day, five U.S. senators—including Mississippi's Jefferson Davis—resigned their seats. It was also when **Mary A. Little (1817–1873)** penned this observation to her cousin in Washington, D.C.

Woodstock, Virginia
January 21, 1861

I suppose no one writes now without making the deplorable situation of our country their theme. Where it will end, God only knows. I find the people around us daily getting more excited by the refusal of the Republicans to move one inch in measures to satisfy the South. And I fear if something is not quickly done, the Border States will follow the Cotton States out [of the Union]. Persons who are calm and moderate in their opinions and who at first were warm to the Union now say that without some guarantees from the North, they are for dissolving the Union. That the course of Congress has destroyed the confidence they felt in it. Many persons feel there will be trouble in the District of Columbia on the fourth of March [Inauguration Day], and I think all who can better get out of harm's way.

Mamma and I have been wishing for a long time we could urge some plea you could not resist to induce you to come and see us. I think now we have every inducement to urge you all to stay with us until the matter is settled one way or the other, so come. I will have the carriage in Warrenton any day you will desire.

The Cotton States of Alabama, Georgia, Florida, Louisiana, Mississippi, South Carolina, and Texas sent delegates to Montgomery, Alabama. On February 4, they set about creating the Confederate States of America, with Davis as its president.

While one new government was being formed, the other was waiting in the wings. Lincoln left his home in Springfield, Illinois, on February 11 for a three-week procession to his inauguration in Washington. There were speeches and receptions in major cities along the way, including a stop in Albany, New York, on February 18. Druggist **William A. Rice (1820–1906)** mentioned it to his elderly mother in Massachusetts.

Albany, New York
February 22, 1861

Lincoln passed through here on his way to Washington and gave us an opportunity to see him. He is better-looking than has been represented. I hope he will prove wise enough to do right. He has a hard task before him, and I fear he is not equal to the emergency. If he trusts to moderate prudent men for advice, we may yet be saved. A few more days will decide, for well or for woe, the future prospects of our country.

As Northerners and Southerners alike prayed for peace and hoped for the best, many accepted coming bloodshed as a forgone conclusion. Some even believed that they were living in the path of looming warfare, as this **unknown**

Northern woman did. She also revealed how the mounting crisis was straining relationships, both personal and political.

Blandinsville, Illinois
February 16, 1861

If this war goes on—and it no doubt will from the news brought last night—I'll not stay in Illinois. I want you to hold yourself in readiness to send for me. We are right in the midst of traitors, and it is said that the war will be transferred from the South to Illinois, and blood will yet be seen running down the streets of Chicago. There are more people here and in Macomb for disunion than for the Union.

They say that the Republicans don't, or are afraid, to say anything anymore and that some of the Democratic storekeepers won't stay in the store at night for fear he will hear something against the South. Some men got talking on the subject in Hardin's barroom. Pap said something, and Hardin slipped up to him and whispered that his time was coming. Pap did not know what he meant, but he is going to ask him for an explanation.

The intention and determination of the South is to bring the North under subjection to them. They are going to have an aristocratic form of government or have royalty, and enslaving the North is their aim. But I would a thousand times be subject to a foreign power than to such Rebels and traitors as the South.

While America's fate was being decided, the business of slavery went on as usual in the places where it was legal. **J. C. Cross (unknown)** was a partner in Price, Birch & Co., one of the biggest slave-trading firms in the country. In a business letter, he offered the equivalent of more than $36,000 in modern dollars to purchase one slave.

Washington, D.C.
February 28, 1861

Mr. B. O. Sheckell had me a letter from you this morning that he got from you about a Negro man that you have got for sale. He gave me your letter thinking I could give a little more for your Negro at this time than he would like to pay as I shall start with a lot of Negroes out South in some few days from this. I shall have to take my Negroes South, as I can't sell them this side of the South, and as I have got to go South, I will buy some few more than I have at this time. If the Negro you speak of is a good No. 1 boy, I will give you One Thousand Dollars for him. You will please answer this as soon as you get it.

With emotions growing increasingly frayed daily, people became very careful about what they said. That was especially true for those from one section of the country while traveling in the other. An **unknown woman** from Philadelphia was keenly aware of that as she and her husband left to spend the winter in Florida. Describing their travels to a friend back home, she made it clear that the couple took special pains to think before they spoke.

Magnolia, Florida
March 23, 1861

We went to Washington the first place and spent a week, which I enjoyed very much, there being so many places of interest to visit. We then went to Goldsboro, North Carolina, by way of Richmond and Petersburg, Virginia, spending a few days at each place.

We spent more than a week at Goldsboro with Mr. Latta's family. It is a pretty little place, larger than I expected to see. There are several families from the North, which makes it pleasant for the Lattas. It is the greatest secession place you ever saw. We dare not express our opinions publicly, but when we got with Mr. Latta in a room, we would close the door, look in the corners, under the chairs, etc., and then have a little talk on national affairs, but always fearful of someone hearing us.

When we arrived in Charleston, South Carolina, we found the weather quite cold and concluded to go directly to Florida. As we were coming out of Charleston Harbor, in passing Fort Sumter, Mr. Stephenson and I got behind our umbrella so no one on the boat could see us and waved our handkerchiefs to some officers we saw on the fort. They acknowledged it by waving theirs in return. Of course, we imagined one of them to be the gallant Major Anderson.

Arriving in Magnolia last Monday, we found the hotel quite full, but we have a very pleasant room in Dr. Benedict's house. The boarders are all Northerners, and several families are from Philadelphia, which makes it very pleasant. We are not afraid to speak as we are when in the company of Southerners.

Conditions were even more volatile where North and South met in the Border States. As bad as business conditions had been at the start of the year, they were now getting worse. An **unknown clerk** at the Balderston, Ward & Co. in Baltimore updated boot maker Partridge in Massachusetts on the latest.

Baltimore, Maryland
April 6, 1861

Our opinion is that you had better not increase the boot manufacturing for this month. Keep on at 25 cases a week until May, and by that time, we may be able to form some idea of what it will be best to do. Business is almost ruined. The aspect of affairs is very gloomy, and we do not know what a day may bring forth.

By the time spring arrived, everyone—Union, Confederate, and undecided alike—realized that the war would soon commence at Fort Sumter. The Confederacy insisted that all Federal troops be withdrawn from fortifications located within its territory, especially those near major ports. There was much debate within the cabinet of the newly inaugurated Lincoln about whether they should be abandoned or resupplied. Lincoln ultimately adopted the latter course.

However, things didn't go exactly as planned, prompting presidential irritation, as naval Captain **Hiram Paulding (1797–1878)** wrote to his wife.

Washington, D.C.
April 7, 1861

The order was sent from the War Department to the officer commanding the artillerists on board the [USS] Brooklyn *to land with his men at Fort Pickens [at Pensacola, Florida]. But as no order was sent to the captain of the* Brooklyn, *he would not land them. The President was much chagrined and will send a messenger overland and orders by water.*

I suppose the expedition that sailed yesterday from New York is destined for the relief of Fort Sumpter [sic]. I fear they have waited so long that they [the fort's garrison] are not strong enough. The government should risk nothing but always strike with an irresistible hand. I think we may now consider that peace is at an end. The people of the North have compelled the President to go forward and are ready to march with a host whenever the first blow is struck. There will be a new era in the future, which is sad enough to contemplate. The Navy—with the exception of the African Squadron—will be withdrawn except here and there a ship, and all will be employed at home if necessary.

Great secrecy is observed, but almost everything seems to leak out. I will try and bring about a new order of things as soon as I am acknowledged as one of the [president's] kitchen cabinet.

As noted above, Lincoln ordered supplies to be sent to Anderson's 85-man garrison but did not send actual reinforcements. Davis then called for the fort's surrender. When Anderson refused, Confederate batteries opened fire shortly before dawn on April 12. In faraway New England, teenager **Almon Gowing Pierce (1843–1864)** was closely following the first combat. (He would later die of disease while serving in the Union army.)

Dublin, New Hampshire
April 14, 1861

They are having queer times at the South. I think they will find out soon if they are not careful. They have demanded a surrender of Fort Sumter. But Anderson refused to surrender. They have begun to fight. So father heard at Peterborough Friday. The news came on the telegraph.

I guess they will find out before long whether they can do as they are a mind to or not. Lincoln said on April 3rd that they would see whether we have any government or not before this month was out. I believe Lincoln is the best man we could have for this time.

The reaction was equally impassioned below the Mason-Dixon line. **Henry Stoner Kupp (1821–1866)** was a Pennsylvanian engaged in constructing a railroad in Virginia. Writing the same day as the previous letter, he described the situation to his wife.

Spotswood House [Hotel]
Richmond, Virginia
April 14, 1861

Here I am surrounded by all the excitement imaginable—the result of the fight and firing at Charleston on Fort Sumpter [sic]. This is a war of brothers, and I cannot say when it will end. I would not be surprised from the excite-

ment here that Virginia will join the Southern armies and at once march upon Washington this week. All business is prostrated here. Mr. Fish has not reached here yet, and so I cannot say what will be the result of our railroad and my work.

As both those letters were being penned, Fort Sumter was being evacuated, having surrendered the day before. The very next day, April 15, Lincoln called for 75,000 volunteers to serve 90 days to put down the rebellion. The response was immediate and intense. In the North, men flooded recruiting offices. Rallies were held to mobilize support for the war effort by encouraging men to enlist. **R. J. Willevy (unknown)** mentioned one of them to an acquaintance.

East Saginaw, Michigan
April 20, 1861

There is to be a Union street meeting this afternoon. Many express sympathy for the South but are bound to stick to the Union. There is a company of seventy getting ready to go south. Hiram, we witness the commencement of a war between brothers and coworkers in government. But I fear it will be left to other generations to record the close.

Lincoln's call for troops created an instant backlash in the Mid-South. In the Upper South, vitally important Missouri, Kentucky, and Maryland dangled in the balance. All were slave states, and all were led by pro-secessionist governors. Consider Missouri Governor Claiborne Fox Jackson's reply to Lincoln: "Your requisition, in my judgment, is illegal, unconstitutional, and revolutionary in its objection, inhuman, and diabolical and cannot be complied with. Not one man will the State of Missouri furnish to carry on any such unholy crusade."

Yet there were also thousands of equally fervent Union supporters in those three terribly divided states, such as **John McGee (unknown)** in St. Louis, who wrote to a friend with close ties to Union Secretary of War Simon Cameron.

St. Louis, Missouri
April 19, 1861

I have just written to Cameron requesting him to use his influence or to accept one hundred men as a company I have enrolled. They are now ready to march under the Stars and Stripes as our Gov. Jackson has refused to respond to the call of Pres. Lincoln for troops to put down the present rebellion. We wish Gov. Jackson and the balance of his section coadjutors to know that there is still a Union spirit that exists in Missouri, and we are ready and determined to serve the Union. If the government will accept us our services we freely offer. We wish arms and equipments, and for this reason, I write to you to use your influence to have us accepted. We are ready at ten days' notice after receiving proper orders to march to any point the government may order. The war spirit is assuming a high feeling in St. Louis in favor of the South, and a riot is expected hourly.

A second wave of secession followed Lincoln's call for troops. It commenced on April 17, when Virginia severed its ties to the United States. Just like their counterparts in the North, women of the Old Dominion eagerly showed their support, as seen in this letter written a few days later by Richmond pastor **Lyman W. Seely (1815–1884)** to Governor John Letcher.

Richmond, Virginia
April 22, 1861

I have the pleasure to inform you that at a meeting of the ladies of the congregation of 2nd Baptist Church this morning, a Soldiers Relief Association was formed whose services are hereby respectfully tendered to you for the aid of our country in this crisis. Eighty-five names were handed to me, and as the association is patriotic and not denominational, I am confident that the number will soon be doubled, not only from members of my own congregation but from others in this vicinity.

I hope that their labors will not be confined to the preparation of lint bandages, clothing, etc., and although we may not furnish you with a Florence Nightingale, there will be many emulations of her example.

Secessionists swarmed around the Gosport Navy Yard near Norfolk, Virginia. It held several Federal warships, critically important dry docks, and a treasure trove of artillery. Washington ordered naval Captain **Hiram Paulding (1797–1878)** to rush there. He updated his wife on the situation.

Barnum's Hotel
Baltimore, Maryland
10 a.m., Thursday, April 18, 1861

I arrived here this morning. Great excitement prevails at Norfolk and about Portsmouth, and it was reported as I heard on the boat that an attack would be made last night on the [Navy] Yard. The [USS] Cumberland's heavy battery was bearing upon it, and full authority was given to defend it. We want [lack] sailors and soldiers there to secure the ships and other property. I have just telegraphed that no time may be lost. They have blocked the channel with vessels sunk, but that can be removed later.

There is from a thousand to fifteen hundred guns [cannons] and immense quantities of stores at the Yard. We may have to fight for them. Virginia is going out. The Southern officers will nearly all go with their states because, in many instances, their friends and families are there. They express regret and wish they could stand by the flag. Sinclair and another lieutenant resigned yesterday whilst I was at the Yard. He came to the boat before I left to see me with his wife and child. He says he loves Virginia better than his wife, and his wife loves Virginia better than she does him. He expects to join the Southern army at the head of a battery of flying artillery.

I have told [Post Captain Charles] McCauley to burn what he cannot defend at the Yard.

McCauley did just that on April 20. After having the powerful *Cumberland* towed to safety, he then ordered everything else put to the torch, as Paulding described in another letter to his wife.

Washington City
April 24, 1861

I returned from Norfolk yesterday, having with the [USS] Pawnee burnt the buildings and ships at the Navy Yard there. We sent a steamer to New York today for provisions—nothing comes through by mail and has not for four days.

The city [Washington] is very quiet under martial law. We have four or five thousand soldiers at last, and more are coming, but they advance slowly. We have a feeble government of feeble men—feeble for want of knowledge— perhaps they will improve as they get wiser. How fortunate it is that you are all at home and away from the scenes of confusion and violence.

Losing the Navy Yard was a major setback for the Federals. Nearly one dozen vessels were left behind, burned and sinking. One, the USS *Merrimack*, would be rebuilt as the ironclad CSS *Virginia* and would make naval warfare history the following March. Also abandoned were more than 1,000 cannons, some of which ultimately made their way as far west as Vicksburg, Mississippi, and Little Rock, Arkansas, along with various coastal forts and defenses.

In Baltimore, tensions finally turned into deadly street violence. On April 19, protestors attacked the 6th Massachusetts Infantry as it passed through city streets en route to Washington. Bricks and rocks were thrown. The troops opened fire on the crowd. When the smoke had cleared, four soldiers were dead and 36 others wounded; 12 civilians had been killed, with more than a hundred others injured. **Amy Galusha (1825–1869),** a textile millworker in New England, was swept up in the excitement as she wrote to her mother and sister.

Lowell, Massachusetts
April 19, 1861

Today noon, a dispatch came that the Baltimoreans were fighting among themselves, and great fears are entertained that Maryland will secede. If she does, it will be the "unkindest cut of all," but we can do nothing but pray.

All our worst fears are more than realized concerning the immoral and unChristian character of the people of the Southern states and the inevitable prospect of an entire suspension of business at the North. I do not know how long the Merrimack River mills will run, but do not think long. I don't know whether I shall stay here or go south as a nurse. I told Charlie that if they had hard battles and so many got wounded so as to need my assistance, I would go with all my heart, but I hope and trust they will not need me for any such purpose. But it is hoping against hope, for if it was true Jeff Davis was within 24 hours of Washington last night, there has probably been fighting there before now. I never deplored the incompatibility of my sex for war until now, but I feel as though a woman was a worthless being in such a time as this.

The red, white, and blue is the order of the day here. It is worn blended in many fanciful ways, and I have even seen it twisted in the inside of bonnets of our beautiful national flag. The streets and shops present a very gay appearance. There are flags waving from every public building, and the shops have red, white, and blue in every variety of shade intertwined and hanging in graceful folds over the fronts of the shops and reaching the whole length of the street. The city has a much more gay appearance than on the Fourth of July, but countenances are sad, and eyes are tearful.

Write as soon as you can and tell me if L. has any idea of going to the war. I hope to have you here this summer, but hopes are like flowers beneath the iron wheel of war.

"The first gun is fired," newspapers proclaimed after the fighting at Fort Sumter. People on both sides were driven to a level of intensity bordering on hysteria in the war's opening weeks. Misinformation that sounds wildly absurd in hindsight was passed on as gospel truth. Consider the "news" that **Polly Giddings (1822–1864)** related to her son in Pittsburgh.

Maple Grove Farm
Cherry Valley, Ohio
April 22, 1861

There is so much excitement all over the country. Yesterday, while at church, Esq. Abel Krum, our representative in Columbus [the state capital], entered the church direct from that city with exciting war news. He went into the pulpit to announce that when he left Columbus, Jeff Davis was marching to take Washington and probably now they were engaged with the Federal troops fighting. He then requested that our citizens would call a meeting and see who would volunteer for the defense of the southern part of our state, where they had already been skirmishing. Tomorrow evening, the citizens meet.

The cannons have been heard here this morning and again since three o'clock, the wind very strong in the east and the air filled with smoke ever since sunrise. Shouldn't be surprised if it's from the fire of our public buildings. And so, the antagonist factions have succeeded in drawing us conservatives into the perils and horrors of civil war. If the fire eaters [secessionists] of the South and ultraists [abolitionists] of the North alone could meet and both get whipped, it might cool off their excited blood. But here we are in a family quarrel like naughty children trying to break the will of a deceased parent. So we of the South and North, trying to break the Constitution, having lost in a manner respect for the opinions of the Fathers who, with wisdom, framed it and adopted the motto, "United we stand, divided we fall." Well, politicians have their plans, military men theirs, and Jeff Davis his. But above all, God will reign.

Your Grandma fears you may be so enthusiastic that you may be persuaded to volunteer. I trust not. I should not be willing except you have first given your heart to God and then, if prepared to die and it was necessary to thus take your life in your hands and go to defend your country's honor, I should not object.

John Brown, Junior is in Canada. Has been all winter drilling the colored people (for active service somewhere—so say the abolition friends here). The professed purpose has been to help and persuade them to emigrate to Haiti.

Misinformation wasn't limited to the North, as **Reverend William H. Vernor (1829–1890)**, a Presbyterian minister who later became a Confederate chaplain, passed along in a letter to a parishioner written in the style of newspaper headlines of the era.

Shelbyville, Tennessee
April 25, 1861

Great Excitement
War News
The Coercer Lincoln
Jeff Davis

The greatest excitement prevails in Middle Tennessee since the war fever has commenced raging. A dispatch says that the Confederacy has taken Fort Pickens with great loss. Doubtful. It is said Jeff Davis intends being in New York City in 15 days and will conquer the United States and the balance of mankind.

Lincoln has done for the Secessionists what they could not do for themselves.

The legislature meets today. The state will go out [of the Union].

Events were now escalating even faster as the country came apart. **Hetty A. Barclay (1801–1881)**, a spinster living with relatives, recounted the breathtaking speed at which developments were unfolding to her nephew, a young lawyer in Iowa.

Bedford, Pennsylvania
April 23, 1861

The telegraph daily announces to us some startling event such as "Virginia is out—All the border slave states refuse volunteers—Harpers Ferry Armory

Arsenal blown up and its small force withdrawn almost in the presence of 2,500 Virginians advancing to demand its surrender." These and similar [news] dispatches are constantly passing.

The Free State volunteers are rushing to Washington, some fighting their way through Baltimore. Others (unarmed Massachusetts regiment) attacked and driven back by a vile mob. All troops are now ordered round by Annapolis. I suppose that route will be guarded. Devoted Maryland! She will follow Virginia in [secession] despite of her patriotic citizens, and her soil will be the battleground. It is not known where the Southern army will make the first attack—reports are conflicting. [State Representative John] Cessna and Tate are out calling on the Democrats to support the government.

I suppose you enjoyed the description of the reception of the heroes of Ft. Sumter [in New York City after the surrender], and we have ours paid to the gallant Major Anderson. How they fought and suffered—every man is a hero.

I am glad you are so far north of this excited border. The Border and Slave States have played a deep game with their pretended compromises, all intended to lull the unsuspicious Free States into a false security. We have so honored them that this war seems to be with dear friends and is truly terrible. But they have chosen for themselves. "The die is cast," and the government must be supported.

People originally from one section of the country who lived in the other suddenly found themselves behind enemy lines. The experience was often unpleasant. Consider **Katherine Pinckard Greenleaf (1835–1905)**. A distant relative of President James Monroe and a Southerner, she and her toddler daughter were living with her in-laws in Indiana when the war began. As she wrote to her sister in New Orleans, hers was a miserable situation.

Out at Mrs. Greenleaf's
[Near Indianapolis, Indiana]
April 23, 1861

Oh, how thankful I am you are not here. Never in my life put together did I ever suffer such exquisite torture as I have since the news from Fort Sumter came; for I am living among a set of hungry wolves—I can call them nothing better, who are actually thirsting for the blood of those who are dearer to me than all the world beside, and they all take the greatest delight in letting me know the state of their feelings and insulting me in every possible way. The people have gone perfectly mad. I never imagined savages could be so bloodthirsty—Cousin Annie and Will as bad, if not worse than any. All our relations and all the Greenleafs and Espys. So you see, I am in the midst of a hornet's nest, and the worst of it is, here I have to stay, and all whom I once cared for here have taken every means to let me know they stood in that position. Anyone would be in danger of their life who was known to have any sympathy with the South and is a true Southerner in every feeling.

Oh! it would make the blood boil in your very veins to hear some of them talk. Others are so deplorably ignorant, it only awakens a feeling of perfect contempt. No one is allowed to even wish for peace without danger of being mobbed, and if we dare say a word in favor of the South, we are to be hung. There are said to be 9,000 men (I cannot call them soldiers) here now encamped on the fairgrounds, and I have heard several say they never in their lives saw such a godless set of men congregated together. You know they ran the first battle in the Mexican War, but they can bluster and braggart. That is about as much as the people here know about bravery. They have no idea of true, manly courage. The Southerners have that yet to teach them. May the lesson be one they will never forget.

I feel when the struggle comes, I must be with you all down there, for if you suffer, I must suffer. And if need be, die with you. I just feel like going right to see everyone I hear favors the South, for my heart goes right out to them.

Someone gave Katie [age four] a Union flag the other day, and I told her she should not have it. But she begged so hard, and I could not explain to her then why I did not wish her to carry it, so I let her have it. As we were going home, she was running along before me. I noticed some lady stop Katie. She says, "So, little girl, you are for the Union, are you?" "No ma'am," says Katie, "My mamma said I should not carry this flag at first, but a little girl gave it to me and I begged her to let me keep it, but I am a Southerner." "I ain't for Lincoln," she always says whenever she hears his name mentioned.

There was an immediate rush to the colors on both sides as men volunteered to serve. Military life required an adjustment for some volunteers, as **David M. Simpson (1844–unknown)**, a teenage private in 4th South Carolina State Troops, wrote to a friend at home.

Headquarters
Columbia, South Carolina
April 25, 1861

My mind is full of war. We hear nothing but war. I have not much of a chance to write as there are so many men walking about and talking—it confuses me. Some of our men are eating, drinking, smoking, talking war, playing the fiddle, dancing, and doing something of anything you could think of.

It would do you good to see some of the boys cooking—Jude McLees for instance. We are all divided off in messes. Tom Holland, Isaac Shirah, S. Horton, and John Clinkscales are in a mess and have a Negro to cook for us, but he is going home, and then we will see sights for not one of us can cook a bit.

The general opinion is that the fighting will now be in Virginia, and we are only state volunteers and are not bound to go. There is, at this time, two regiments in this place numbering 2,200. There was a call made today for volunteers from here for the Confederate army, but they only got one entire company. How many more they will get, I can't tell. The call is for 8,000, but I don't think they will get 300, and if they fail, you men who are not volunteers may look out. Jeff Davis is bound to have troops for his army. Don't you volunteer.

A rush of fierce nationalism swept over both North and South. In both sections, people made public displays of their patriotism. A young woman identified only as **Dalia (unknown)** described the atmosphere in New England to a friend.

Dover, New Hampshire
April 27, 1861

Oh, is it not dreadful Allie, to have our country in such a confusion? Here in Dover, there is very great excitement. All are bound that our flag shall not be taken down if they can help it. Most all of the ladies and gentlemen wear the red, white, and blue badge. I have a very pretty one. Many say it is as handsome as any in the city. Flags are upon every pole hung from people's windows and festooned over their doors. We have to have our flag on our newspaper also. There is a company to leave Dover on Monday, and another company is about ready to go. The ladies have been at work the past week fitting the soldiers out [with uniforms]. Tomorrow morn, they are each to be presented with a Testament. They go with good courage, and say they will fight for the Union as long as they have life enough to do so. And if they die, it will be for their country.

I hope the battle will come soon. Most people think that it will be a hot and quick war. All I hope is that the Southerners will get a good whipping, which I think they will. I suppose you know that they have got a great many men to work on the Navy Yard now fitting out vessels, also to command the forts. I think they are right in arming the forts there. It seems too bad that those men in Kittery, Maine, have got to go away now when they could be at work on the Navy Yard and be with their friends at home. But enough of war. I think of it as little as possible, always hoping for the best.

Arkansas followed in secession on May 6. Three days later, young attorney **John W. Hodges (1838–1862)** wrote about it to his sister in Maryland.

Benton, Arkansas
May 9, 1861

Everything is excitement here. Our state has gone out of the Union. One thousand men expect to start from Little Rock today for Virginia for the purpose of assisting them in their struggle with the fanatics of the North guided by that prince of impious double-dealing scoundrels Lincoln. I hope that he may utterly fail in his attempts to gain honor and applause by making war upon the South and to deprive us of our equal rights. Arkansas is all "up in arms." About 400 soldiers have passed through here on their way to Little Rock to serve their country, however, duty calls them. My name is down on a list to form a cavalry company. I will not go unless there is a certainty that our state will be invaded. If I go, I think I can get a good office and have a chance to serve my country and distinguish myself at the same time. I have made several speeches for Southern rights and Southern honor which were received with great applause.

People living on the West Coast were frustrated by the long delay in keeping up with rapidly escalating events back east. The first transcontinental telegraph line would not be completed for another six months. The fastest news came on horseback and took 10 days of nonstop relay riding across the Great Plains, as **B. R. Horton (unknown)** explained to a friend in Michigan.

San Francisco, California
May 9, 1861

We have no news of importance except that sent by Pony Express. Have dates up to the 28th of April. I will not attempt to draw any pictures of our once glorious Union now about to be severed by a band of traitors. Suffice it to say my feelings are as yours and all true lovers of the Stars and Stripes. The traitors in this city sometimes get very noisy. It generally ends in their going home with sore heads. There was some dozen or more of the above-named that went from Montgomery Street a few nights ago, so a report says. Union clubs are forming throughout the state. To what extent it will affect California time alone can tell.

The explosion of patriotism made some people go to great lengths to show their support for the troops, even when it involved getting up in the middle of the night, as **Elizabeth A. Foster (1814–1883)** wrote to a friend.

Meriden, Connecticut
May 11, 1861

We have been in the most intense excitement here since the President called for troops to sustain the federal government and protect the capital. For about a week, we did not eat, sleep, nor work with any regularity. Troops passed through here about five thousand in four days. The trains mostly passed in the night so as not to interfere with the regular trains in the daytime, but it made no difference. People went to the depot at midnight by hundreds to await the arrival of the train, which sometimes would not come till four o'clock. People all along the line of the road would rise from their beds and cheer the brave men who voluntarily offered their lives for the country.

Two hundred have gone from this place, and more are enlisting. Two regiments from this state started for Washington last week. They carried off the last male boarder I had. We women are all engaged in making clothes for the volunteers. Some 129 are at work at the town hall, and many work at their homes. Have either of your sons enlisted, and if so, do you feel willing to offer them up on the shrine of patriotism?

Uncle Albert is in Salem. He is full of war. Attended the inauguration of President Lincoln. Stopped here, both going and returning. Had a number of relics from the tomb of Washington.

The violence that had rocked Baltimore now shifted to St. Louis. An **unknown student** at nearby Shurtleff College across the Mississippi River in neighboring Illinois saw it happen. The pro-secessionist Missouri Volunteer Militia was camped outside the city for its annual muster and drill. It was widely suspected its leaders were secretly planning to seize the St. Louis Arsenal and its extensive stores of guns and ammunition.

Shurtleff College, Illinois
May 15, 1861

There is quite an excitement here in relation to war news. Situated as we are so near St. Louis, the present seat of war, you no doubt ere this have heard of the surrender of the Secession forces at St. Louis and the great excitement therefore. I chanced to be in the city on that day and had the unspeakable pleasure of seeing the whole Secession army taken prisoners of war.

The United States forces presented a grand appearance. They marched out of the Arsenal, some 6,000 to 8,000 of them, then formed in 3 columns and marched to the Secession encampment. The artillery was at the head of the columns while the long line of soldiers stretched back as far as the eye could reach, and the bright muskets and bayonets as they glistened in the sun at once presented a sublime and imposing scene. They drew up in line around the encampment with two divisions farther back as a reserve, the artillery was placed on a little knoll where they could rake the whole ground occupied by the Secession encampment.

While the U.S. troops were thus forming, I went down into the park where I could get a good view of the enemy's encampment and the position of their troops. They were in great confusion, but the cannoneers were standing at their guns, ready to apply their wrath whenever the word was given. Some of the many spectators that came out of the city were expecting to see a battle fought before their friends, the Secessionists, would surrender. I had no such expectation. Although one of the Secession officers had told me in the forenoon while I was on a visit to their encampment that they would not give up their arms without a fight, yet I had no idea that they would offer resistance.

General Nathaniel Lyon, the commander of the U.S. troops, sent in his demand for an unconditional surrender, allowing General Daniel Frost 15 minutes in which to make up his mind. After a brief consultation with his officers, Frost complied, and the whole force stacked their arms and marched

out prisoners of war preceded by one division of the U.S. army. The surren-
dered troops came out cheering Jeff Davis and General Frost at the top of their
lungs. The U.S. troops were abused in the most violent manner by the Seces-
sion citizens in the crowd, and finally, one more reckless than the rest stepped
forward and shot one of the soldiers, killing him instantly. Then, others
of the mob commenced to throw stones and fire pistols into the ranks, killing
some and wounding others. Then, some 5 or 6 of the soldiers opened fire.

Almost 30 people—including a baby and its mother—were killed, and
nearly 100 others were seriously injured.

An **unknown clerk** at the Balderston, Ward & Co. in Baltimore detailed
the deteriorating business situation in a final letter to boot supplier Partridge in
Massachusetts.

Baltimore, Maryland
May 13, 1861

Tucker and Smith stopped working on Friday last. This leaves Carroll and
Adams alone among jobbers [suppliers] as paying, but they say they cannot
tell how long they can go on. All communications are now cut off from
Virginia. We had a letter that took 8 days getting to Richmond. The express
company will not take money except at the risk of the owner [sender], and
of course, the jobbers are getting no money. Banks only direct to take paper
[cash].

Emotions were nearing the breaking point. Colonel Elmer Ellsworth, a
24-year-old Federal officer and close friend of the Lincoln family, was fatally
shot on May 24, minutes after removing a Confederate flag from a hotel rooftop
in Alexandria, Virginia. His assailant, the hotel owner, was immediately shot,
though not in the grisly manner described the next day by this **unidentified
soldier** in the 8th Massachusetts Infantry (nor was the city burned).

Elkridge Landing, Maryland
May 25, 1861

Yesterday, we received news of the assassination of Colonel Ellsworth of the
New York Zouaves in Alexandria and that his regiment had set the town
on fire and that they put twenty bullets through James Jackson, the one that

shot him. Next came the news that we were ordered to hold ourselves in readiness to start at a moment's notice. Last night, at ten o'clock, we were all turned out, all ready for a march and inspected. They gave us thirteen rounds of cartridges each and then came the orders to lay down until morning with our equipments on, as we were liable to be called any moment. Last evening, there were forty-three cars full of troops passed here on their way to Washington.

We are encamped within a hundred yards of the Sixth Massachusetts Infantry. They done guard duty yesterday. There is a Baltimore regiment encamped close to us. They are the hardest set of men that I ever saw. The Baltimore folks tell us that they could get nothing to do, so they had to enlist. They say that there is between fifty and sixty thousand troops in Washington and three thousand marched on to Alexandria Thursday night at one o'clock. It is rumored here that there is a large force going to march on to Richmond and that the Massachusetts troops will have to take the lead, as they were the first that arrived South. The boys are all pleased with that news, but I do not credit it. There is so many reports going the rounds of the encampment that there is nothing to rely on.

Things were likewise difficult for Marylanders who supported the South, though their circumstances were different. Many went to neighboring Virginia and joined Confederate ranks, knowing that meant their families and friends were now behind enemy lines. Simply getting a letter to them was challenging, as Baltimorean **Henry W. Arnold (unknown–1861)**, a private in 13th Virginia Infantry, related to a friend back home. (Arnold was seriously wounded at Munson's Hill, Virginia, on August 27; he died three weeks later.)

Harpers Ferry, Virginia
May 28, 1861

When the news of Ellsworth's death was received, the very mountains rang with shouts of joy. The Kentucky boys want to take the Baltimoreans and go to Balto; they say they will do all the fighting if our boys will show them the way and where it is to be done at.

You will see by this that we have not yet gone to Richmond, and at present, it is not probable that we will go soon. All our company are here now, and we completed our organization and were mustered into the service of Virginia this morning. All the other companies here are in the service of the Confederate States for three years; we for one only, or less in case of peace. We occupy the upper story of one of the machine shops, cook for ourselves, and sleep on planks wrapped in blankets. Our uniforms, which consist of a gray blouse or hunting shirt, gray pants with black stripe, and gray slouch hat, will be ready in a few days. Although we suffer many inconveniences, no grumbling is heard except from those that came more for pleasure than to serve the South, but they are scarce.

The health of the troops is good, except a touch of the diarrhea, which is brought on by drinking the water, and in some instances the whiskey, which is the most abominable damned stuff I ever tasted. You must know it is bad when I can't drink it. A man died last week in less than an hour after taking one drink. All that could be found was yesterday poured out in the river.

Ned is well and likes the life exceedingly. If you see Hoover, tell him I would like to have him in our company, but not to start unless he makes up his mind to be a soldier in the strict sense of the word. You can see everyday merchants and clerks washing their own clothes, cooking their own meat, and cleaning their tin cups and plates after eating, but you can't see any back-out in them.

Tell Papa of the step I have taken, that I did so from a sense of duty, that I am well and expect to return sooner or later. Tell Davy Cooper to come out [enlist]. If you can, send anything you have for me by some of the railroad men. The mail is not secure. If this is delivered by a friend, answer by him. Send some money if you can spare it. I hope, before my time is out, to march into Baltimore under the flag of the Southern Confederacy.

Political and military conditions continued their crippling stranglehold on trade. This letter from businessman **Frank C. Brownell (unknown)** to his father in Connecticut captures both the excitement of the moment and its impact on commerce.

New York City
May 27, 1861

Business is at a standstill since the war began with everyone, me included. As I don't expect to sell much from April to July or August any year, it will be of less consequence than if it were the busy season. So far as now appears, we are to have hard times until the Southern traitors are hung and matters settled.

I can get no funds from Chicago now without paying 15 to 20 percent exchange [interest], which would take off more profit than we can afford to lose, so we hold back.

We have made up our minds this way for a grand fight till the Southern traitors are hung up and rebellion comes under.

The girls will give you all the news we have of Baltimore friends. The feeling in Maryland now will prevent fighting in that state, but Baltimore was only just saved [for the Union]. Uncles at Baltimore will probably fare better than they feared a week ago but must find some trouble.

Passions were equally intense in the South, where an **unidentified young woman** in Tennessee wrote to a Northern friend the night before her state affirmed in a referendum joining the Confederacy.

Madisonville, Tennessee
June 7, 1861

Tomorrow, Tennessee will shake off the shackles that bind her to that government which has been (but alas! has fallen) the best government ever bequeathed to posterity, but which has become the most tyrannical. Look at Maryland. The tyrant's heel is on her neck. Is hers the liberty of your glorious Union? Also, St. Louis—are her people free and independent? Protected by Federal troops! Protection indeed! Killing innocent, helpless children, unoffending women, and peaceable men? We want no such protection, and Tennessee will resist it to the death.

I disclaim being a Secessionist but boast myself (though a Rebel) a loyalist—loyal to my state, to my home, and to my own interests. Southern Rebels, yes! And were not our grandfathers, to whom you refer Rebels also? Though Rebels, they fought for a just cause, for homes, friends, country, and liberty, and so will the "Southern Rebel." Blot them out if you will; subjugate them if you can; what great end will you have attained? Crush them you may, subdue them never! Like the smothered volcanic fire, it will still burn and burst forth fiercer than before.

Among the many innovations seen for the first time during the war was the widespread use of photography. Although the art form was still in its infancy, hundreds of photographers (who also promoted themselves as "photographists" and "photographic artists") took hundreds of thousands of images of men in uniform as they hurried off to war and of the families they left behind. They were often shared with each other. **James S. Shaw (unknown)**, an engineer in the 8th New York State Militia, mentioned seeing the era's most famous photographer of all taking pictures in the field.

Arlington Heights, Virginia
June 25, 1861

Today, the Engineer Corps on the field in different positions were photo-graphed by Professor Mathew Brady from New York. I will present you with a copy on my return to decorate your gallery of fine arts and give you an imperfect view of my position as a soldier.

Camp life after a time becomes very monotonous and wearisome, par-ticularly having to undergo so much exposure and warm weather. We all feel it very much. As I have told you before, a soldier is but a machine and must wait to be put in motion. Yesterday, I visited the 69th New York Infantry's camp. I was well received and treated well. We had five baskets of champagne with the officers.

One of the first clashes of arms came on June 10 at Big Bethel in Virginia. Its small scale would soon be considered a skirmish, but in the war's early days, the minor engagement took on an importance far beyond its actual significance. Only a combined 4,900 men on both sides were engaged, with a total of 86 casualties. Several of the 18 Federals who died were killed by friendly fire. Still, with the press starved for actual combat, the Confederate victory was reported in minute detail (with many Northern papers erroneously calling it "Great Bethel") and was a propaganda bonanza for the South. **Francis Teear (1834–1862)**, a private in the 24th New York Infantry, wrote about it to his wife.

Elmira, New York
June 13, 1861

It appears by recent accounts that our boys are determined to fight somebody and, not finding any Rebels, fought among themselves. But then, mistakes will happen sometimes, and it will give the Rebels something to talk about. The defeat at Great Bethel is more to be lamented; a great blunder must have been made somewhere, a second Balaclava [the 1854 Charge of the Light Brigade in the Crimean War]. General Benjamin Butler swears he will wipe out the disgrace by taking the batteries in less than 24 hours, and according to an extra [newspaper edition] that was issued last night, he has fulfilled his word. It stated that he had taken the battery and also 1,000 prisoners.

I must see you before we move south, which will probably not be before September, without there is much fighting around Washington. A great battle must be fought there before long; that's the opinion of military men here.

Even at this late date, some people still naively believed that there would be no bloodshed. The war seemed like a lark to new recruits undergoing training, as Orderly Sergeant **Isham C. Paine (unknown)**, 4th Virginia Infantry, described to his sister.

Camp Stephens or Victory, Virginia
June 25, 1861

If James has not started to join our company yet, tell him my advice is not to come at present, as I think the disturbances will be settled without any fighting.

The Yankees have all run across the Potomac River and are camping. I think they are waiting for more troops to come to their assistance. We traveled two or three days and got to this place, four miles from the river and eight from Williamsport. We are just ready and waiting for them. We are stationed here on a ridge with woods all around us and no house near us, just roosting in the leaves and getting fat on bread and meat. As to myself I have been amusing myself drilling a squad of new recruits.

So many men rushing to join the armies put a sudden and severe strain on the civilian workforce, especially among farmhands preparing for the harvest season. That was noted by **T. J. Scott (unknown)**, a young student who was writing to a classmate in Massachusetts during summer break and was fascinated by watching the mobilization.

Marlton, New Jersey
June 29, 1861

Have you got a camp in Sharon? I was in Philadelphia four times this week. It is full of soldiers. There is another camp at Trenton, New Jersey. I was there three times last week. The camp at Easton only had three organized regiments when I left.

The foremen here are rushing the harvest. The grain harvest will commence as soon as this [the war] is done. You have never seen a grain field yet. Just wait until you have seen a field of 50 acres—nearly level—just the color of an orange, swaying in the wind. This is farming country. Such cherries as I used to pay ten cents a quart for, I can go out and pick by the bushel for nothing; they grow wild here. Just ripe now; as many as you want by picking them.

The Confederate capital was moved to Richmond, Virginia, in late May as both governments set about preparing for war. Thousands of Southern troops rendezvoused in Richmond. Among their ranks was **John William Hamlett (1841–1862)**. He had enlisted in the 21st Virginia Infantry just 10 days earlier and wrote about his new life to his father.

Richmond, Virginia
June 30, 1861

President Davis and General Robert E. Lee came out to the dress parade yesterday evening, and I had a good look at both. The President has a very pleasing look and conversed with a good many of the soldiers, shook hands with as many as could get to him, and bowed to all companies that passed him, while General Lee looked as savage as a meat ax and appeared in finer style than the President.

We received our arms several days ago. They are smoothbore muskets, and we drill with them twice a day.

Our quarters are very good. We have not received our tents yet but are in a house about the middle of the fairgrounds. Our fare consists of light bread, bacon or beef, peas, rice, and coffee. The Appomattox Invincibles are close by us in sheds, open in the front.

The North was sending as many soldiers southward as possible. **John Holt (1837–1902),** a newly recruited musician in the 13th Massachusetts Infantry, told an unidentified friend what the experience was like.

[Location unknown]
July 29, 1861

I got into the cars with the rest and went with them. When we arrived at Philadelphia, we were provided with a bountiful collation [a light meal] by the Union Committee, and it was very acceptable indeed. On our march through the city, we saw the 6th Massachusetts Infantry returning from their 3-month campaign. They were a sorry-looking set, being without caps in some instances and ragged, dirty, and huddled together in cattle cars like so many cattle.

About 3 p.m., started for Harrisburg, Pennsylvania. The reason that was given for our going this way has never been explained to our satisfaction, but we always supposed it was for the purpose of giving patronage to this railroad, which is almost entirely owned, it is said by Sec. of War Simon Cameron. We started for Hagerstown, Maryland, at about daybreak in a soaking rainstorm and landed in a perfect puddle of mud, of which we got plenty before we left that godforsaken state. Here, we were treated to cold water, crackers, and cheese. Then, we were marched out of the town and pitched our tents for the first time.

At night, after the guards were posted commenced our first experience of soldiering. After Taps, say an hour or two, we were startled by the alarm of firearms and, in an instant, the whole camp was aroused and turned out. But it proved to be a false alarm. Someone of the guard imagined he saw something and fired without challenging. Just before reaching Philadelphia, the boys had begun to growl at the officers for not giving out cartridges. They had an idea that as we were approaching enemy country, we were liable for an attack like that of Baltimore on the 19th of April last, and this growling continued until we reached Hagerstown. When we arrived at that place, it almost amounted to open rebellion. If the boys saw a person look cross at them, they said he was Secesh, and we were very much in constant fear of an attack. So, anyone may judge how easily a guard may be frightened at nothing when he has just entered upon a new business. When I look back and see what asses both officers and men made of themselves at that time, I am encouraged to hope we have learned one thing: "That all the fools are not dead yet."

(The "Taps" Holt referred to wasn't the familiar bugle call we know today; it wouldn't be written until the following year. The earlier version ordering lights out in camp, also called "Taps," was a drumbeat.)

All those troops streaming into Washington created a pressing housing problem. Available space was so severely limited that even government buildings such as the White House and U.S. Capitol were temporarily pressed into military service, as this **unidentified Federal soldier** described to a friend.

Washington, D.C.
[circa June 1861]

Soon after my arrival here I was recommended as being qualified to act as clerk and storekeeper for the Commissary of the U.S. Army. In this situation, I was placed and have been employed here. I like this business very much. I have charge of the storeroom in the Capitol Building, where I have quite a grocery. I here deal out the provisions for a large portion of the army concentrated around here. I have one clerk and four assistants to do the work while I oversee the work and keep the accounts. I have a splendid little office situated immediately under the dome of the Capitol. It is carpeted with a nice Brussels carpet, supplied with the necessary furniture including my bed. Don't you think I enjoy being a soldier?

Now, I must give you a brief description of Washington. I was very much disappointed in the appearance of a city of as much note as this. I expected to see a large collection of splendid buildings, both public and private; instead of this the buildings, save on a few streets and avenues, are scattered and low. Still, the streets are very wide, which makes it the more healthy and gives it a grand appearance where it is filled up with buildings on both sides. The public grounds, garden, and parks are beautiful, and in these I pass a great deal of my time.

I think, after all, it is pleasant on account of the extensive public grounds, and the Potomac is a delightful river. I sometimes take a boat and sail down to Alexandria and view the river as it winds its way along between the hills. It seems too bad that such a splendid country as 'tis here should be the seat of this, what I fear will be a bloody war.

Meanwhile, the race was on for control of Missouri. Union General Nathaniel Lyon divided his small force in a two-pronged attack. He headed with the bulk of it up the Missouri River, driving off pro-Southern forces and sending them, along with Governor Claiborne Fox Jackson, retreating from the state capital in Jefferson City.

Lyon pressed on, and a few days later, his 2,200-man command met a smaller group of raw recruits to the newly created Missouri State Guard at the river town of Boonville. As **John Danforth Wilkinson (1840–1918),** a private in the 1st Missouri Infantry (Federal), recounted to his brother, the secessionists were quickly sent fleeing.

Boonville, Missouri
June 22, 1861

We met the enemy at this place last Monday and routed them. There was 3,000 of them under General Sterling Price and Governor Claiborne Jackson. There was about 2,200 of us, being the 1st and 2nd Missouri regiments and a company of Regulars with Captain James Totten's Flying Artillery. Our own company captured Camp Adams of 400 men. Our officers could not keep us back. We rushed on to them and drove them before us like chaff. I made about 30 dollars and if I had any place to put plunder I could have made two or three hundred.

We have waited here for reinforcements. They have come and we start soon for Lexington, Missouri, above here. The secessionists are concentrated there, and General Ben McCulloch with his horde of Texas roughs are there to oppose us, but we are not afraid of them. We probably will have a bloody battle there. I shall send this to St. Louis by a steamer that is going to carry the wounded down [the Missouri River]. The killed were wrapped in the Stars and Stripes and buried with honors.

At the same time, a smaller contingent with several German American regiments under the command of German-born Colonel Franz Sigel moved across the southern part of the state to keep Jackson's troops from linking up with General Ben McCulloch's Confederates in northwestern Arkansas. Sigel first captured Neosho, where he left a company to guard the little county seat, then swung his command north. On July 5, he was defeated by the pro-Southern Missourians about 25 miles away at Carthage—just as McCulloch's command was advancing out of Arkansas. Private **Friedrich William Charles Heldman (1840–1912),** a young German immigrant in the Union's 3rd Missouri Volunteers, later wrote to his brother what happened.

St. Louis, Missouri
August 13, 1861

You have heard about all our bad luck we have had. You heard we have been taken prisoners at Neosho in Newton County. We first started from Rolla at nine o'clock in the night, and we kept on marching almost day and night till Springfield. There, we stopped one day, and then we went on 85 miles to Neosho. There, our company was left behind, and Sigel went on to Carthage with about 800 men. There was a great many left in Mt. Vernon [Missouri] who could not walk any further and near Carthage.

Sigel found Jackson on a large prairie where he found him with about 5,000 men, but they were not very good armed. Sigel attacked one or two o'clock in the evening. We heard the cannons at Neosho, and at three o'clock there came a man from Sigel and brought the orders for us to go back. We were all ready to go when there came about 1,500 Secessionists from Arkansas and Texas commanded by McCulloch.

We were all in the courthouse, where we had our place to stay. As soon as we seen them come, we knocked out all the windows and shut the doors, got ready to shoot through the windows. The Secessionists stopped, and two men came up to the fence with a white handkerchief and asked our captain to surrender, and our captain came in to us and told us. We told him we would sooner die. Our captain told us we could not fight against so many and our captain asked them if they would treat us just [fairly] we would surrender to them and they promised by their honor, and so we give up. They kept us three days, and then we had 85 miles to go without anything to eat.

"On to Richmond!" Horace Greeley's *New York Tribune* urged in each day's edition, and the phrase quickly became a Northern rallying cry. Summer's arrival also brought a new deadline for the Federals. Enlistments for thousands of the 90-day volunteers who had joined up in April were due to expire in late July.

With public pressure for action growing and the days until soldiers would return home dwindling, Lincoln spurred his officers in Virginia to move. The Union's Commanding General of the Army, aged, ailing, and morbidly obese Winfield Scott (the victor of the Mexican War who had served in uniform since before the War of 1812), was also feeling pressure from on high.

In Boston, 17-year-old **Cyrus Bates (1844–1928)** kept his father, a New England sea captain, updated on developments, including the passing of a major national figure.

Boston, Massachusetts
July 13, 1861

We have recently lost one of our noblest statesmen, Stephen A. Douglas, a true friend to the Constitution and a man of whom no one can say ought of injury and the idol of his party. We can ill spare such a man and at such a time as this, for it is such men we want to teach our President his duty, for I do not think he knows it himself. The President has issued his message and calls for 400,000 men and four hundred millions of dollars. He cannot get the men, I do not think, without drafting, although some think he can.

These are exciting times. War is the all-absorbing topic. "Large bodies move slowly" is the old saying, and it seems as if General Winfield Scott is slow enough to suit the slowest. I think things are approaching a crisis within two or three days. The two grand divisions of the army will meet, and there will be a great loss on both sides. General Scott will superintend the battle in person in his carriage with his aides. I am afraid the old hero will not live long enough to see the end of this contest, as he has the gout very bad, and he is so old.

Some of the three-month volunteers who went out first have returned. A friend of mine who was in the Battle of Great Bethel had his comrade killed beside him, and he saw a soldier getting into a baggage wagon when it ran against a cannonball and smashed both wagon and man to pieces. So much for war. I think it is impossible to conquer the South. They are determined to fight till the last.

This morning the news is that the Southern privateers are within a short distance of Nantucket. They have captured three Boston vessels. Two of them were bound from New York to Montevideo. The privateers show English, Dutch, and American colors hoisted as signals of distress and thus lure their prey. They do not take the vessels with them. They compel the crew to join their army and let the captains run. If I was you and coming on this way, I should place a twelve-pounder [cannon] amidship. It is a good thing for an argument.

In the war's first bloom, while its newness was still fresh before there was serious fighting, the enthusiasm of newly minted soldiers knew no bounds, as Private **Francis Faurot (1836–1897)**, 16th Indiana Infantry, wrote to his sweetheart. (The early war camaraderie he described would vanish within a few weeks.) The enlistees were also growing accustomed to a new fact of their daily life: uncertainty.

Camp Wayne
Richmond, Indiana
July 19, 1861

Mary, you ought to have been in the camp when we arrived to see us shaking hands. They made as much noise over us as though we had been absent brothers for years. We had 70 men to shake hands with before we got to bed after traveling all day and shaking hands with so many. After I got to bed, I slept so sweet on my bunk of boards.

This morning, our colonel received a dispatch from Governor O. P. Morton that this regiment was accepted in the United States service for one year from last May. I do not know when we will be ordered away or whither do I know where. I expect we will either go to Missouri or Virginia. We will not know until we get ready to start. Nobody will know it but our officers. We may not know where we go until we get there.

This happens to be my day to go on guard. It is easier than drilling. Well, Mary, it is almost time for me to go on guard. So, I will quit writing for the present. When you want to write, just go ahead and write. Don't pay any attention if you hear that this regiment is gone. When it starts, I will write immediately and let you know.

As incredible as it sounds today, even as major military operations were getting underway that summer, many people clung to the belief that it would be a short war. Among them was **Charles M. Shipley (unknown)**, a private in the 29th Pennsylvania Infantry, who wrote to his wife from a camp of instruction outside Philadelphia.

Camp Washington
Hestomville, Pennsylvania
July 25, 1861

I still cherish a hope and believe that the hour of our country's peril will soon end. At the expiration of six months, I expect to see all our volunteers free.

I shall be glad when we leave Philadelphia. For some of our camp visitors are very immodest and disgusting. While others are some of the most

influencialist [sic] class possessed of great riches and have sons and other
relation who have enlisted in this glorious cause.

On the home front, Northerners were preparing to welcome home the original 90-day volunteers as heroes. This letter written by someone who signed their name simply **"Con" (unknown)** to neighbors serving in a New Jersey regiment stationed at Washington showed a big homecoming was in the works.

Long Branch, New Jersey
July 20, 1861

I want you to inform me at first opportunity what is the name of anyone in
your company who is killed or wounded or anything of that kind; what day
you will be home, and whatever you can propose to make the return home
agreeable and patriotic.

> *This has been the course thought of: To meet you, as [the town of] Free-*
> *hold is trying to bring you home. The soldiers to meet you at Elisha Lippin-*
> *cott's and escort you into the village where the company would be received*
> *with speeches, etc., and proceed to the orchard of L. Shinpits where the dis-*
> *charge would take place, and also have a picnic dinner provided for all hands*
> *of the military and interested guests. A meeting will be held on Saturday*
> *evening to make the necessary arrangements. Telegraph the day you will come*
> *and write particulars by fast mail. I have written two times to Washington*
> *on the same business but have received no answer yet.*

Despite repeated protests to Lincoln and Scott from General Irvin McDowell, the Union's first commander in Virginia, that his men weren't ready yet for action, Northern forces headed off to fight the Confederate troops concentrated near Bull Run and Manassas Junction, Virginia, on a brutally hot Sunday, July 21.

It was both the first major battle of the war and the largest Americans had ever fought up to that time. The engagement began early in the morning. What initially looked like a Union victory turned into a Confederate triumph by day's end.

The changing tide of battle led to great confusion for both sides watching from afar. Some 850 miles away from the fighting, Private **William H. Bennett (1837–1864)** of the 5th Wisconsin Infantry was eagerly following the seesaw news by telegraph. (He would die from wounds received in fighting near Atlanta three years later.)

Camp Randall
Madison, Wisconsin
July 22, 1861

Telegraph dispatch has just been received stating that one of the greatest battles, as far as heard from—up to eight o'clock Sunday evening—is being fought that has been fought on this continent.

The fight commenced yesterday morning—Sunday—at 3 o'clock a.m. Official reports have been received up to 5:30 p.m. Action commenced six miles north of Manassas Junction. The Rebels, although far superior in number, have been driven back to the Junction and are still retreating. Our Fire Zouaves and 69th Regiment carry off the palm [victory]. Ours met a regiment of Southern Zouaves, routed them, and captured their colors. The 69th stripped everything but their pants and pitched into the thickest of the fight without regard to the terrible slaughter that was made among them. The loss on both sides is very great. It is estimated that upwards of 3,000 men have been killed and twice or three times that number wounded. The Secessionists seem to be universally panic-stricken. Their forces are driven back in every part of the field—completely cut off from water and their men discouraged.

How a very short period will sometimes change the hopes of a nation.

A new dispatch has just been received stating that our troops have been completely routed from Manassas and driven back with terrible losses. Our whole army is struck with the greatest consternation. Disorder and confusion reign supreme.

It is feared that the Rebels are marching on to Washington; in the present state of affairs, they would make an easy conquest. The loss on our side alone is estimated 3 or 4,000. One regiment, the Fire Zouaves, came out of battle with but 200 living. We start for Washington on Wednesday.

By sundown, the Yankees were running in wild confusion back to Washington. Days later, Private **Warren A. Friend (1842–1868)** of the 3rd Maine Infantry recounted details of the fight.

Fairfax County, Virginia
August 1, 1861

I suppose you have heard of that battle that was fought on the 21st on the Sabbath. It was, without doubt, the toughest battle that was ever fought on

American soil. I was not an eyewitness myself of that dreadful battle, but I was near enough to hear the roar of the cannons to my heart's content. The boys all say it was a dreadful time.

The Maine boys had a hard time of it. When they was a marching on to the battle the last four miles, they went on a double quick after they had been living on hard bread and beef and such water as they could get. The boys say they never experienced such a sun before in their life. They had such a gant [exhaustion] that there was but only seven out of our company that could stand it to get on the field with the regiment. There was some that got on afterwards. The water was so scarce that they was glad to get the muddy water that had been trampled in by the horses.

They fought nine hours without any fresh troops to relieve those that were in the engagement. Our men, at last, had to retreat and ran for life. Our men retreated from that horrible place called Bull Run to Alexanderry [Alexandria] the distance of about 30 miles. You can't think how much they suffered for the want of water. They was as tired a lot of fellows as you ever saw.

The Federal defeat sent shock waves through Washington, D.C. **Daniel Lamb (1810–1894),** a prominent banker, lawyer, and Unionist from western Virginia, told a friend how the capital was gripped by panic.

Washington City
July 30, 1861

Washington is now as quiet as usual. The people have, for the present, got over their fright. There never was a worse scared set than the folks here, including Senators and Representatives in Congress, were a week ago yesterday, the day after the fight at Bull's Run [sic]. Everybody was frightened out of his senses. They all thought General Pierre G. T. Beauregard would be on them before nightfall. They have now discovered they were worse scared than hurt. The number of killed, wounded, and missing has dwindled down to a small affair. The number of frightened was very large. The defeat will do no harm. The lesson was needed, and will, I doubt not, be in every way of advantage to us.

We have news here today. Yesterday, it was reported that Generals Robert E. Lee and Joseph E. Johnston of the Confederate Army had crossed the Potomac from Leesburg, Virginia with 40,000 troops. I was in hopes it was true, for it would have given us a chance for a fair fight. But today it is said there is no foundation for the rumor.

Mr. Carble is very apprehensive respecting western Virginia. He says Lee and General Albert Sidney Johnston (the Utah Campaign Johnston) are both marching for our country. If this be so, we must look out for squalls. But while I think such a thing is possible, there is not, so far as I can make out, any reliable information to that effect as yet.

Our business here is still unfinished. Washington is a terribly slow place to get anything done. Everybody seems to be in a desperate hurry, the quantity of talking done is prodigious, but the result is nothing, or very little, is accomplished. When they make me dictator, I will retrench and reform [move the capital] with a vengeance. I believe, however, we will get through with all we can do here and start for New York tomorrow.

The victory electrified the Confederacy. Writing to his wife six days later, this **unidentified Southerner** heard the news while traveling by train from Georgia to Richmond and captured the popular feeling.

Richmond, Virginia
July 27, 1861

Then came booming along the news of the great Manassas victory. And I was on the cars and hurrying along towards the great theater of agony and ecstasy, of anguish and rejoicing. We had an immense train of cars, and they were crowded to suffocation. Soldiers on furlough hastening back to their posts, anxious fathers, brothers, and friends wending their way to the scene of action, most of them uncertain of the fate of their loved ones, excited unpatient citizens unable longer to content themselves so far from scenes of so much interest, all were crowded together and sharing one common impatience to be on the soil of "old Virginia."

The cars were crowded and such a mass of excited, one-minded people you never saw. Turn your ear which way you would, and the sounds came mingling the names of "Beauregard, Johnston, Jeff Davis, Zouaves killed, wounded Yanks, Confederates," our boys, pet lambs, and the name of regiments, of colonels and captains in whom each speaker felt some especial interest were the sole topics of an excited discussion for three days and nights. All along as we passed, the outdoor scene was equally, often more, exciting. Large Confederate banners floated at every prominent place, and little tiny ones in the hands of tiny children waved from every cabin door. Shout answered to shout as we approached and left each stopping place. Even in East Tennessee, the lurking place of treason and base submission, the Union flag is no longer seen, but in its place, the Stars and Bars float and seem to promise a lasting protection to all who put their trust in them.

With a major engagement now fought, the custom of seeing the battlefield in person began. Sites of significant fighting became early tourist destinations, with soldiers and civilians alike visiting them.

Consider a trip to the Manassas battleground described by a Confederate officer identified only as **William (unknown)**. Most of his newly formed 12th Alabama Infantry arrived the day after the battle (and was quickly given the unpleasant task of burying dead Federals from the Brooklyn Zouaves). When the remainder of the regiment joined three weeks later, the new arrivals immediately went to see where the action had taken place.

Camp Walker, 2 miles from Manassas, Virginia on the railroad
August 20, 1861

The opportunity presented of visiting the battlefield. Lt. Goodwin and Lt. Jones, with myself, mounted our horses and left the camp. We rode about five miles over an uneven country, sometimes in open fields and again in thick pine woods until we reached the famous ground. I especially and with pride examined that portion of the field upon which the 4th Alabama Infantry saw for themselves an undying fame. I saw where they entered, where they lay behind the hill, where they charged the battery, where Col. Egbert Jones and Maj. Charles Scott were disabled, where General Bernard Bee fell, and Col. Francis Bartow died, where [Union then-Colonel] William Sherman's battery was taken, where Ellsworth's Zouaves bit the dust. I traveled for several miles along the route over which the grand Federal army that morning marched in all the pride and pomp of glorious war, and along which that same day they ingloriously and incontinently fled, strewing the road with their guns, accouterments, and clothing. I saw where, at Stone Bridge over Bull Run and at Cub Run further on towards Centerville, the enemy was mown down like grass by the pursuing artillery and cavalry. I gathered several old canteens, a piece of bomb, an old muster roll, and a haversack as reminiscences.

I wish I could tell you more of it and better. Maybe I will one day.

There were swift consequences for the Federals following the defeat. McDowell was quickly reassigned. In his place, Lincoln appointed 34-year-old General George B. McClellan as head of the Military Division of the Potomac on July 26. He had led the successful occupation of Virginia's pro-Union western counties (which became the state of West Virginia two years later), one of the North's few bright spots that summer.

Called the "Young Napoleon," the charismatic and confident McClellan quickly merged another command with his to create the Army of the Potomac. A superb organizer and administrator, he set about forging what would become the Union's premier fighting force for the rest of the war. The following month, Private **Joseph W. Shaw (1834–1909)** of the 5th Pennsylvania Reserves passed in review before his new general and the commander in chief, which he described to his brother.

Camp Tinley
Washington, D.C.
August 22, 1861

On the 20th, all of the Pennsylvania troops was drawn up about 2 miles from here in some large fields, and a grand review of all the Penn. troops by General McClellan and President Lincoln. One regiment cavalry, looked splendid. One regiment artillery (Campbell's Batteries). 12 regiments infantry. 14 thousand, big lot of soldiers. General McClellan is a splendid-looking man, and his staff are nice-looking men. The President is tall, he looks a great careworn. President and all the rest passed along the lines and reviewed us and then took his stand at the flag staff, and we all passed in front of him and all the bands playing. It looked nice, you better bet, and here is where there is good bands. The soldiers felt proud. How straight they marched.

We cannot get out of Washington. We are not allowed to leave camp. They are throwing up entrenchments close to where we are, 2 thousand men at work every day, and we expect Washington will be attacked every day and we will have a grand fight. We are ready for them.

As Shaw indicated, another result of the debacle at Bull Run for the North was that it revealed the Federal capital's vulnerability due to its proximity to the front. McClellan immediately remedied the problem by having Union forces commence building a ring of strong fortifications to safeguard it. By 1862, Washington would be the most heavily fortified city in the world.

Sylvester H. Brown (1816–1862), a captain in the 22nd New York Infantry, was helping construct one such bastion, as he described to his wife. It was located across the Potomac River in northern Virginia on land that was part of the Arlington estate owned by Mary Custis Lee, wife of General Robert E. Lee. (Brown would die in battle eight months later.)

Lee's Farm
Near Arlington, Virginia
September 3, 1861

We are now engaged in building a large fort near our camp to be called Fort Franklin in honor of our Chief of Division, General William Franklin. About 500 men are at work on the entrenchments. Yesterday, we mounted four rifled cannons, and today shall mount four more. As fast as the works are completed, guns are mounted. We shall have a formidable battery in a few days. We shall soon have completed a chain of fortifications from Alexandria to Washington, commanding this line of the Potomac from any force the Rebels can bring against us.

At 2.5 miles, the Rebel battery in the process of erection on Munson's Hill can be distinctly seen. To their right, about two miles is Fort Corcoran, and on another line is Fort Albany [both Union]. Fort Albany commands the whole country for miles around. After all the sensation inaugurated by the press, I see no prospect of a battle at present. I think after we complete our work, we shall shell them out very handsomely.

Far to the west, troops on both sides were gathering in Missouri for what soon would be the war's second major encounter. It was still a week off when Private **Edwin Martin Whipple (1842–1925)** of the 23rd Illinois Infantry wrote to his mother.

Jefferson City, Missouri
August 4, 1861

I now, for the first time, realize that I am in an enemy's country. We are encamped about two miles from the [state] capitol in a beautiful place called the fairground.

I am glad to hear that you have raised a Union flag at the Center. It reflects great credit on you as well as the young ladies who assisted you in the difficult task. There is but few Union flags here, not any except what we have raised. This place is nearly deserted. All those who profess to be Secessionists have left. There is a few Union people in town. Governor Claiborne Fox Jackson, the leader of the Rebel forces in Missouri, is concentrating all his forces south in this state, preparing for a grand attack which it is hoped will decide the question. The brave General Nathaniel Lyon is on his track.

The "brave Lyon" was indeed on the move. Pro-Southern Missourians (for the state's secessionist faction had not yet officially left the Union) had united with Confederate troops led by General Ben McCulloch in the Ozarks outside Springfield.

Although outnumbered, the aggressive Lyon launched a surprise attack on the combined Southern forces camped along Wilson's Creek shortly after dawn on August 10. In the intense fighting that followed, the Federals were routed, and Lyon was killed, becoming the first Union general to fall in battle. Writing from Massachusetts, **Marietta Comey Stearns's (1838–1891)** brother was in Lyon's army; she relayed his account of the engagement in this letter to a relative.

Framingham, Massachusetts
September 21, 1861

He says the fight commenced, and in less than ½ hour, it became general. Totten's Battery (he was under Totten) was on the extreme right, and the whole of the left wing of McCulloch's army (which we have since learned was 22,000 strong; the other 9,000) charged upon our battery three different times and was driven back each time with great loss. At about this time, the shells from our battery set their tents on fire.

At about 9 o'clock, Lyon was killed, and when it became known, it cast a gloom over the whole of our little army. And if the enemy had charged upon us at that moment, there is no doubt but that there would have been another defeat greater than the Bull Run. But in a few minutes, their feelings changed to hate, rage, and revenge, and they went at them with renewed vigor.

The battle ended shortly after noon when the Federals withdrew. For the second time in three weeks, a Union army had been defeated.

The civilian manpower shortages that had first appeared in the war's early days steadily worsened as more and more men put on the uniform. It also became increasingly difficult for people on one side to correspond with family and friends living on the other. **John W. Hodges (1838–1862)** explained the lengths he went to just to get his letter to his relatives.

Benton, Arkansas
[circa early August 1861]

Crops in Arkansas this year are very abundant. I suppose more abundant than they have ever been. About two-thirds of the voting population of this county are now under arms, which leaves scarcely enough to gather the crops, which are abundant. Our state has about 20,000 volunteers in the field, primarily in Missouri and Virginia, which leaves the force to gather them rather small.

I would like, above all things, to visit Maryland for a few months, but it is impossible to tell when I can do it. I have not received a letter from Maryland for two months, and my anxiety is a fever heat to hear from you all. I will send this letter to the American Letter Express Company in Nashville, Tennessee, to have it forwarded. There is such a company in Louisville, Kentucky, that sends letters South. I suppose they have out advertisements. I hope that peace may again soon smile on our land, and we may be permitted to enjoy a free intercourse with each other.

But even that link was severed days later when the U.S. Post Office suspended all mail delivery to the South (including via private carriers such as Adams Express, American Letter Express, and Whiteside's Express).

That meant people like **Rogena "Genie" Almira Scott (1840–1869)**, a young teacher from New England employed at the Southside Institute, a girls' school in Nashville, were now cut off from corresponding with their loved ones. She dashed off a final letter to her mother while vacationing during summer break with friends.

Hendersonville, Kentucky
August 18, 1861

A Kentucky gentleman visiting here very kindly promised to put this in one of the Federal post offices, so I take this opportunity of sending you a message. My last letter, it may be, until the war is over. You are aware that President Lincoln has very lately stopped all communication between North and South.

46

Even our last ray of light, the American Letter Express Company, has been extinguished. You need not, therefore, take the trouble to reply to this, for I would not receive it. I mailed you a letter by the company over two weeks ago, as it advertised that they would stop all operations in a few days.

Any anxiety about me that you may feel is utterly useless, for if I am in danger in Nashville, I can go into the country. Besides, I do not think the Northern army is so barbaric as to kill women and children while they remain quietly in their houses pursuing their daily avocations. I have no fear of them.

Have just finished a letter to John G. Bailey. If he wants me to come home, he must come for me, for I am afraid to travel alone. If he comes, he must not come before Nov. 1st unless Nashville is attacked before then. If he does not want me to go home, I shall remain in the South.

(Scott and Bailey were married on February 17, 1863, in New Hampshire.)

The military situation remained volatile in Missouri. Following the Southern victory at Wilson's Creek, bitter quarreling over how to proceed erupted between pro-Confederate Missouri State Guard commander General Sterling Price and Confederate General Ben McCulloch. As a result, McCulloch withdrew his troops south to Arkansas while Price advanced deep into Missouri, looking for new recruits and supplies.

He laid siege to the town of Lexington on the Missouri River and captured it on September 20 after an engagement there. An **unidentified Federal soldier** serving in Kentucky mentioned it to his parents.

[Kentucky; location unknown]
September 28, 1861

We got news that we lost a battle in Missouri. The Rebels took 2,000 of our boys prisoner. They said it was hard fighting.

When the struggle was over (having culminated with the Missourians approaching uphill behind a wall of water-soaked hemp bales as a kind of mobile breastworks and giving it the nickname the "Battle of the Hemp Bales"), Colonel James Mulligan and his Irish Brigade surrendered. The news was followed closely in neighboring Iowa, where teenaged **Mary "Mollie" Ellen Teeter (1844–1919)** wrote to her big brother serving in the Union army.

Monroe, Iowa
October 8, 1861

We were very proud of Mulligan and the men at Lexington. I think it is a great pity that he cannot escape from the Secessionists. And those brave men had to take the parole and go home. I believe Mulligan refused the parole thinking "he would soon be rescued by brave Union men."

Our election went off yesterday, and we beat the combined forces of Secession under the name of Democrat and Union Party. We beat it in Vandalia, too. The Union and Democratic tickets are the same. Times are petty warm [emotionally] here. We take the Hawk Eye *now and get the news every day (Mondays excepted.) I guess that some of the volunteers here (perhaps all from town, I don't know) have gone to Newton today to elect their officers. We have written to you the names of the last volunteers. This takes about all the young men from Monroe that are worth anything at all.*

Last night, I attended a social given in honor of the volunteers. Enjoyed myself pretty well part of the time but not half as well as I did sometimes last winter. The volunteers chose their partners to go to the table. W. R. Eyerly took me. I made the acquaintance of a very interesting young gentleman. He is from Missouri. Some think he is a Secessionist. I am not able to say.

Although Price was victorious at Lexington, his strategic situation was precarious. He was 230 miles north of McCulloch's forces with a large Union army approaching from St. Louis. The newly arrived commander there, General John C. Fremont, sat in his headquarters "like a European autocrat," in the words of one observer, complete with imperial airs and a grandiose personal bodyguard dressed in gaudy uniforms. It was widely believed that he tolerated corruption and incompetence.

He set his men marching toward Price at a sluggish pace. However, as an **unidentified Union soldier** described in a letter home, the new recruits had trouble adapting to long marches. And while Fremont (who had been the first Republican presidential candidate in 1856) is remembered today as the "Pathfinder to the West," the soldier used another nickname for his commander.

Georgetown, Missouri
September 30, 1861

I don't know why I didn't see Marcellus Leeds as I saw Fremont's Bodyguard three times while at St. Louis. Still, he might have been with them, as I was much more engaged in looking at the "Wooly Horse" than at those who accompanied him.

We left St. Louis and came as far as within 7 miles of Syracuse, Missouri. The Secesh had burned a railroad bridge. We rested there one night and half a day and then started on toward Lexington. We made a forced march of 20 miles and reached this place at 11 that night, as tired a set of fellows as you ever saw. I don't mind the walk so much, but I had 30 rounds of cartridges by my side, a knapsack with my blanket and all my clothes, besides provisions for two days, a canteen of water, and a gun on my shoulder that weighs 14 lbs. So, you may suppose that the weight and the load proved wearisome. But I do not complain, but am thankful that I am able to bear it.

We keep moving toward Lexington, where we expect a hard fight if Price will stand his ground, which is doubted by many of the citizens here. But he is strongly entrenched, and if he leaves his entrenchments, he will be sure to be in a worse condition than now. We have 8 or 10,000 men here and will not move till we have reinforcements.

Fremont's plodding allowed Price ample time to retreat to the safety of southern Missouri. At the same time, in the Border States, where loyalties were so bitterly divided, a different type of war was emerging. Armed bands of partisan guerillas were starting to carry the conflict to the home front. Nowhere was the problem worse than along the Missouri–Kansas state line, where the so-called Border War was becoming a war within a war. By the fall of 1861, it was growing steadily worse, as **John W. Boyd (unknown)** described to an acquaintance in Bracken County, Kentucky.

St. Joseph, Missouri
October 7, 1861

This section of country is decidedly Southern in their feelings, although we have been kept down by a large Federal army stationed here ranging from 1,500 to 3,000 men. But a very large number of men have gone to Southern

Missouri and are joining General Price's [pro-Confederate] army and are now in the field.

This county and our city have suffered greatly from the [pro-Union] Kansas Jayhawkers—or thieves. They have robbed and stolen at least 500 horses and mules from our citizens and broke open and robbed stores, farmers, and tradesmen of goods and property—openly—just going and taking what they pleased. And there was no help for it. They were here in large numbers with their arms, and our people can do nothing but submit.

Many of our best citizens have been forced to leave their homes and go South to keep from being imprisoned, frequently being arrested without any cause—merely to gratify some drunken Dutchman. We are getting very tired of this sort of thing and hope for a speedy change. Hoping you may be spared the same predicament.

The war suddenly erupted in Kentucky as summer wound down. The Bluegrass State had walked an increasingly tenuous tightrope for nearly four months. In the aftermath of Fort Sumter's bombardment, its legislature had avoided taking sides and proclaimed neutrality. North and South went out of their way to avoid provoking the pivotal state—while also positioning troops in adjacent states just in case.

Everything changed on September 4, when, without consulting his superiors or even informing them in advance, General Leonidas Polk ordered Confederate troops to seize the strategic heights commanding the Mississippi River at Columbus, Kentucky, and immediately set about fortifying them. They even stretched a large chain across the Mississippi to the Missouri side opposite to block river traffic.

With its neutrality now violated, the Union responded on September 6 by sending General Ulysses S. Grant up the Ohio River to occupy Paducah near the confluence of the Tennessee and Cumberland rivers.

Like it or not, the conflict had finally come to the Commonwealth of Kentucky. Its geographic location made controlling it vitally important. As Lincoln wrote that month, "I think to lose Kentucky is nearly the same as to lose the whole game. Kentucky gone, we cannot hold Missouri, nor Maryland. These all against us, and the job on our hands is too large for us."

Yet not all Confederates cheered Polk's move. **Robert Hancock Wood (1826–1901)**, captain of the "Hatchie Hunters" in the 22nd Tennessee Infantry, shared his misgivings with a fellow Southern officer.

Mayfield, Kentucky
September 16, 1861

Your kind favor was received at Columbus just before we took the cars for the Tennessee line. We had a somewhat fatiguing trip from Columbus to this point. We are now 27 miles north of the Tennessee line in Graves County— considerable wealth, large farms hereabouts.

We find the people of this portion of Kentucky very hospitable and well-disposed and anxious for us to overrun the state. But I have felt ever since we came into the state that we were abandoning our principle of self-defense and placing ourselves upon indefensible grounds. The evidence of Kentucky's Union proclivities are too strong and decided to admit of a hope of it coming over to our side except by subjugation. She is not yet ready to take the leap, and we cannot help her decide. I think the whole move on our part will prove to be a military failure, not less marked and pitiable than a similar one made into Missouri. So far as soldiers are concerned, it is a pleasant recreation to move them about from place to place with the hope of giving them work to do. Still, we will not win any laurels in Kentucky this time because the move is premature.

It is understood that President Davis disapproves of the move and did instruct General Polk to send the army back to Tennessee. I do not know how true this is but I believe once the matter is understood by the President, he will order us back at once. I think we will return to the Tennessee line in less than three days from this time.

We are within 25 or 26 miles of Paducah, where it is said the enemy is posted 10 to 12,000 strong. The larger portion are foreigners badly officered and drilled with the exception of one regiment of Zouaves. If we attack the place, we will have to approach from this place on foot as the rolling stock on the road is not sufficient to carry more than 700 men at a time.

As summer gave way to fall, Southern confidence neared the point of cockiness. Writing to a cousin from the now heavily fortified Confederate stronghold at Columbus, young Private **Peter Pryor Perkins (1844–1871)** of the 1st Mississippi Battalion expressed his optimism to a cousin. (He turned 17 exactly one week later.)

Columbus, Kentucky
October 9, 1861

I think our little infant republic will soon be recognized, and then peace will be the result. Probably you would like to know my reasons for thinking thus. A hundred thousand soldiers have crossed the Potomac again, with the same view they had before, viz: of "wiping Virginia and her inhabitants from the face of the earth," there are fifteen thousand soldiers at Paducah, Ky., and they daily are concentrating more. We will "wipe out" these two armies, and this will end the war. Is it not strange what a change can take place in a few months?

On the other end of Kentucky, far to the east, another Confederate offensive was underway. General Felix Zollicoffer's 5,400-man force moved out of Tennessee and seized Cumberland Gap on September 14. After emerging victorious in two very small battles soon afterward, the little band headed up the famous Wilderness Road for a push into the prosperous Bluegrass section in the central part of the state.

Some 7,000 Federals located at Camp Wildcat blocked Zollicoffer's path. A sharp battle (also called the Battle of Wildcat Mountain) ensued on October 21. Minor by the standards of the battles that would soon come (there were only 78 combined casualties on both sides), the Union victory resulted in Zollicoffer's command falling back to the Cumberland Gap area and was widely heralded in the North as a rare reason to cheer. **James Delenbaugh (1843–1862)**, a private in the 38th Ohio Infantry, told about the area's rough terrain. (He died of illness less than 90 days later.)

London, Kentucky
October 29, 1861

It is by the blessing of God that I am spared to answer your letters, for I have been in the enemy's land for some days, and we are expecting a battle every hour to be attacked by old Zollicoffer. He is a Southern commander. His men are as cowardly as they can be. Some of our division shipped him out at Wildcat before we got there a day or two later. The first gun our artillery fired disabled one of their guns, and their firing ceased, and they began to retreat, and we are now following them up. We expect to get him surrounded before long, and if we do, we will give him fits. I saw some of the houses they had robbed as they came along. They tore up everything as they went along. Killed cattle and hogs and took the corn and everything as they went along.

I am now sitting on top of a mountain that is so high that I can see all the town and can see for twenty miles around, and we are well fortified so that it would take a week for the enemy to storm us out of it.

In pro-Confederate sections of Kentucky, Union forces were very much aware that they were now occupiers, as evidenced by this letter from **Henry Lane Markham (1840–1883),** a private in the 2nd Illinois Cavalry, to his cousin.

Paducah, Kentucky
November 27, 1861

I, for the first time in my life, am in a land of slavery, where one race has a right to buy and sell their fellow man. This is a very fine city, but about one-fourth of the inhabitants have left because they were Secessionists and dare not stay. But I do not think that all of the "Secesh" have left, for I heard a girl up in town playing on the piano and singing a secession song. I told her it was a good tune but very poor words.

There is about 8,000 troops here at present, including two batteries of light artillery. This place is at the junction of the Ohio River and the Tennessee River, and there is a 54-pounder stationed in the middle of the Ohio, thereby commanding both rivers. We have no arms yet. I suppose they calculate for us to run over the "Secesh" and tramp on them.

I was very sorry to hear that cousin I. Putnam was killed. I wish you would write and let me know if it was at Lexington, Missouri, or some other Lexington. There may be many more killed before this war is to a close, and if one of them happens to be me, I will willingly make the sacrifice for my country's sake. Yours for the Union—now and forever.

Back in southern Illinois, Grant was never one to remain idle for long. He conceived a daring move in late October. His men understood something important was at hand, as indicated in the letter that **John Downer (unknown),** believed to have been a private in the 7th Iowa Infantry, wrote to a friend at home.

Mound City, Illinois
October 30, 1861

We begin to have stirring times here. Tomorrow, we will launch another
gunboat, and in the course of a day, about three will be in the water. Next
week, we start down the river to meet [Confederate] General Gideon Pillow.

General John McClernand was here to review the troops. The old
general gave us the praise of being the best drilled in service of the Western
Department, which encourages the new recruits greatly. He intends to give
us a chance to show the muscle of our strength soon. He was glad to find a
warlike sentiment in all the soldiers.

We have to guard this place close at present. There is Secessionists all
around us at this time. Night before last, they burnt a bridge below town.
The same night, the rascals made a charge on Fort Holt, Kentucky. One Rebel
captain, and one lieutenant, and four privates were killed. No one on our
side hurt.

The boys have had some fun. The fact of it is some hogs come inside our
lines, and they would not take the oath of allegiance. Consequently, the boys
killed them and made a roast.

On November 6, Grant assembled 3,114 troops on six boats from Cairo,
Illinois, and sent them down the Mississippi River. Escorted by the USS *Tyler*
and USS *Lexington*, they landed the next day at the hamlet of Belmont, Missouri. It consisted of a ferry and three shacks on the lowland directly across
from the fortified heights at Columbus, Kentucky. They surprised and routed
Confederate forces from nearby Camp Johnston. But a prolonged lull after the
attack gave General Leonidas Polk ample time to rush reinforcements across the
river to the Missouri side. Supported by heavy artillery fire from the Columbus
fortifications, they drove back the Federals and sent Grant's men running to
their boats and hurrying back to Cairo.

An **unknown Union soldier** related it to his father.

Camp Lyon near Bird's Point, Missouri
November 8, 1861

As I pen these few lines this evening, we have considerable to think out. We
have to think of yesterday's bloodshed. Oh, how can you or I think of probably
3,000 men being shot to the ground in a few hours?

Yesterday morn about 8, a battle commenced between a part of 6 regiments of ours and 6 of their Secesh 12 miles below. Our men cleared them out and walked into their walls [fortifications], burnt their tents, destroyed their works. Our men had gained the victory and throwed down their arms and gone to pilfering when the Secesh come 10,000 strong. The Secesh at Columbus, Kentucky, got on boats and come up unbeknown to our troops. Had them completely surrounded before they knew it. They then had to fight their way out with a heavy loss. They came back torn apart. The most of the officers were killed and probably half of the privates. All that was wounded in the first [part of the] battle was slain in the second. It seems like we are all to be killed by poor management.

(In most soldiers' letters written immediately after a battle, the numbers they shared were often inflated, sometimes wildly so. They almost invariably reported that the enemy significantly outnumbered them, and casualties were extremely high. That was because they had nothing to go on but camp rumors. The soldier in this case was mistaken about the size of the Federal losses at Belmont. They actually sustained 120 killed and 383 wounded. Confederate losses were almost identical; 105 dead and another 419 wounded.)

Although small compared to later engagements, Belmont was Grant's first Civil War battle. And he began the war with a defeat.

Belmont received extensive national newspaper coverage and reinforced Southern confidence, as **David M. Marsh (1842–1925)**, a private in the 12th Arkansas Infantry, wrote a few weeks later to his aunt and uncle.

Columbus, Kentucky
November 25, 1861

I join you in giving thanks to that omnipotent being for the victory which crowned our men at the Battle of Belmont.

Our camp is in the fort on the hill north of town. Day before yesterday, Lincoln's gunboats came down in sight and fired several times. We were called out in line, expecting to be attacked, but they soon returned. I do not know why they returned so soon or what their object in coming down, without it was to get a view of our gunboat, which arrived here a short time since.

I learned this morning that there had been arrangements made to have us houses [winter quarters] soon. The last two or three days has been very windy and disagreeable, and this morning is quite cold.

Belmont was the first time most of the troops who fought there had "seen the elephant," as soldiers on both sides called combat. As a Federal infantryman in the 7th Iowa Infantry, identified only as **Robert (unknown)**, later wrote to his brother that the battle left them with the understanding that this would not be a quick, easy war.

Camp Benton
St. Louis, Missouri
December 24, 1861

I will tell you something about the war. We was in the Battle of Belmont and got cut up very bad on the 7th of November. There is a great many battles being fought nowadays, and victories won on both sides. I think the war will last for some time. Our regiment is under marching orders just now. Where we are a going, I cannot say. Maybe to have another fight. But I rather think not.

In the east, the North suffered yet another humiliating disaster in late October, one that produced long-term consequences. An erroneous report that Confederates had crossed the upper Potomac River led to the 1st California Volunteer Infantry being sent into Virginia at Ball's Bluff on October 21. Some 520 men crossed the river in six small boats. After a brief firefight, the Confederates fell back as the Federals awaited reinforcements, which did not come. The Southerners soon received additional troops and counterattacked, driving the Northerners into the river. Many were shot from the bluff above them as others frantically climbed into the boats and were shot there; bodies were later recovered as far downriver as Washington and Mount Vernon.
Luther Winship (1841–1861), a wagoner in the 27th Indiana Infantry, was waiting when the survivors returned to Maryland, which he described in a letter home. (Winship died of disease two months later.)

Mud Creek, Maryland
October 27, 1861

You will see before this about the regiment that was murdered here a few days ago, and I will send you the straight of it. It crossed the river by itself and was to be reinforced, but it rained, so it could not be done. It went into the slaughter pen unconscious of this fact against 8,000 men and fought till one third of them bit the dust when they retreated for an island in the river but there was not boats enough for them and some attempted to swim and they fired on them in the water and there was 150 of them that sunk to rise no more, either from lead or drowned. Those that did get through said the most was drowned, so at least one half of the regiment is gone.

Colonel [Edward Baker] is dead. Lieutenant Colonel [Isaac Wistar] had his leg shot off. I seen him myself and a hundred more that was wounded. The floor of the church they were in was slippery with blood. My heart was sick as I passed amongst them, giving them water and them that could eat some of my own scanty store of provisions. I seen any amount of men pass our camp that night naked that had swam the river, and what few of us that was there made coffee the whole four hours we laid there for them. Although I had not slept for the longest time I ever went, I was not sleepy then at all. I must close for we have to march in the morning early and I must sleep.

Baker, the fallen colonel, was also a U.S. senator from Oregon and a close friend of the Lincoln family (whose second son was named Edward Baker Lincoln). He remains the only senator ever killed in combat.

William Line (1843–1862), an 18-year-old private in the 81st Pennsylvania Infantry, was on hand as official Washington said farewell to the fallen legislator turned warrior and wrote about it to his younger brothers. (Line was killed in battle the following year.)

Washington, D.C.
October 25, 1861

I just came from the funeral of General [sic] Baker. There was about four thousand soldiers to his funeral and about one hundred carriages. It was the largest funeral I ever went to in my life. He was shot in the head and in the breast three times. I seen General Scott and General McClellan and President Lincoln to his funeral.

I have been all through Washington. It is a large place. I wish you was here for a week. You would see more than you ever seen in your life. I was down at the Potomac and I seen a man-of-war, steamboats, and schooners going at all times in a day. We can see the batteries on the other side of the Potomac. The Rebels has been about ten miles long. They say it will take one hundred thousand men to take it.

Following on the heels of the rout at Bull Run/Manassas and the defeat at Wilson's Creek (which all occurred within 90 days), Ball's Bluff was one disaster too many for the Federals. Six weeks later, Congress created the Joint Committee on the Conduct of the War. Ostensibly, its mission was to provide civilian oversight of military operations. In reality, the committee was stacked with radical Republicans who injected partisan politics directly into the Union war effort and who made life miserable for generals—especially Democratic ones—who lost on the battlefield.

The uniforms worn by both sides were influenced by Napoleonic tradition some 50 years earlier. Although not as bright and splashy as their forerunners, the Civil War versions were still colorful compared to today's military dress. Yet none were as downright gaudy as those worn by Zouaves, infantry whose clothing was inspired by the loud uniforms worn by French soldiers in North Africa. Some people were impressed by the outfits. Others, such as **Cyril H. Tyler (1841–1913),** a private in the 7th Michigan Infantry, were not. He wrote disapprovingly of them to his wife.

Camp Meridian Hill, Virginia
[circa October 1861]

There is two or three regiments of Zouaves camped near us. I have been to see them. They are the worst-looking persons I ever saw. They are as black [sunburnt] as can be, red cap with a long tassel, red pants with a yellow stripe, red vest all striped off with yellow. The crotch of the pants hangs down halfway from their knees to their ankles, large and loose. Blue sash 12 feet long, 16 inches wide to wind around their body.

As the conflict progressed, the new soldiers were making new discoveries. Many had never traveled farther than 25 miles from home before. Now men on both sides were seeing and experiencing new places and new things. Sometimes, they even experienced new realities that shattered old preconceived beliefs, as **John Hancock Boyd Jenkins (1840–1906),** a private in the 40th New York Infantry, shared to a friend.

Camp Sackett
Alexandria, Virginia
October 28, 1861

It is very cold here now—at least for men exposed to it "25 hours out of 24,"
as Paddy says. It would be only glorious at home, with a warehouse or store
to be in, and only run out occasionally. But when a man is "allers" cold, the
exposure is a constant draft on the natural heat of his body, and he is doubly
sensitive to cold. This may seem queer, but it is true. I believe that the chief
reason for the sensitivity of Nigs to cold is their continual exposure in their
wretched "quarters." I speak of the far [Deep] South, not this region, for the
"cullud pussuns" around here are lodged and fed far better than the majority
of working men in the North. What do you think of three-ply ingrain [car-
pet], Venetian blinds, sofas, rocking chairs, and bureaus in houses occupied by
slaves? There were plenty of such around here when we came, although the
war has made sad inroads on the comforts of life everywhere.

Four months after the Federal defeat at Bull Run/Manassas, its effects were
still being felt. The humiliating loss galvanized the North's resolve. Opponents
of slavery were especially motivated to press for its end.

Despite the war, everyday life also went on as usual. The English poetess
Elizabeth Barrett Browning ("How do I love thee? Let me count the ways")
died on June 29. Both her passing and the changing political atmosphere in
the North were noted by schoolteacher **Emma Graves Shaw (1839–1924)** to a
friend.

Providence, Rhode Island
November 12, 1861

I should like to sit down and talk over with you passing events. How sig-
nificant they are and how surely people seem to be rising to the altitude of
this war, how surely the people are beginning to feel and be glad that slavery
must go. I agree with you most heartily that the defeat at Bull Run was
medicine for our nation. That made more converts to abolitionism than the
abolitionists ever gained.

Old Democrats outrun the Republicans in their cry for liberty. [Long-
time Democrat] General Benjamin Butler has changed his song since he
declared that he would put down all insurrection of the slaves. Times have

altered when they compel [former Secretary of State] Edward Everett to
speak boldly for freedom and even send him abroad in a semi-official capacity
to plead for it.

I am not for the immediate abolition of slavery, but I do want to see
the people beginning to awake to its necessity, its justice; I want to see a
strong public sentiment bearing slavery down and all legislation looking to
its overthrow. A few more disasters would do it all, but I hope we may not
need them. I hope the popular heart will rally for freedom as bravely and
surely as the men of America have rallied for the Union. Union is doubtless
a political and geographical necessity, but I want to hear a nobler battle cry.
Emancipation will surely come sooner or later, with our aid or without, but
how much better if we march with Fate.

Do you read the Atlantic *now? And did you read in it the piece on Mrs.*
Elizabeth Barrett Browning? I am very much interested in it. For Mrs.
Browning's sake, one cannot regret the change, but friends have a double loss
in one like her, and liberty loses a firm advocate. I have read "Aurora Leigh"
again since her death and felt her words all the more because I know that her
voice was silenced forever for earthly ears.

On November 7, as the Battle of Belmont was being fought, the North
launched an amphibious campaign on the South Carolina coast. Warships made
a circular pattern around Port Royal Sound as they bombarded Forts Walker
and Beauregard into submission. That led to the capture of Beaufort and Hilton
Head Island, giving the Union an important base of operations for its Atlantic
Blockading Squadron.

Some 100 miles away in Charleston, **Mary Cross Gayer (1811–1895)**,
widow of a prosperous carriage maker, replied to a friend's offer of shelter in
South Carolina's interior. She also described the anxiety and uncertainty civilians
experienced living in the enemy's potential path and recounted a rumor about
the fate awaiting slaves who fled to the Federals for freedom.

Charleston, South Carolina
November 19, 1861

Thank you very much for your kind invitation to me and my children to share
the hospitalities of your house. We will be glad to accept your generous offer
when we are obliged to leave our homes. At present, there is no immediate
danger, although we do not know at what moment we may be obliged to

leave as the enemy is in possession of Beaufort but have not as yet landed. They visit it in the day and return to their vessels at night. I suppose you have heard they are in possession of Hilton Head, Port Royal, Beaufort, and Pinckney Island, and are now engaged in fortifying them.

By the papers we see that 11,000 troops are expected from New York to reinforce the Federal fleet. If so, they will attempt to land on Beaufort and march to the city—that is, if they can. Our brave boys say they will have to march over a pile of dead bodies and wade in blood before they reach Charleston—that they will meet them with bayonet, knives, and bullets, and they will never be able to return to tell how they fared.

Our city is in great confusion—people moving from the island around to the city for safety. The people in the city are going off in the country. You know when the order from Governor Francis Pickens comes for the women and children to leave the city, they will be obliged to run off without taking a second suit to their backs. When that time comes, you will see us. We were thinking of packing up what things that are valuable and sending them up to you for safekeeping as we will have to leave them for the Yankees take such as silver, etc. If we do, we will send you word.

Our planters have met with heavy losses. Some have burnt up as much as forty thousand dollars worth of cotton [$1.5 million today] before it shall fall in the hands of the enemy. The Yankees have taken off or stolen hundreds of Negroes and had them sent to the fleet. We have understood they have transport vessels that they fill and send to Cuba for sale. Planters that were worth thousands and thousands of dollars are not worth one thousand dollars today. I have heard that one of the richest was obliged to beg for clothing of the societies—his name was Mr. Ephraim Seabrook, the wealthiest planter on Edisto Island. A great many of his Negroes refused to go with him— others took to the woods and threw themselves in the hands of the enemy, thinking to be free, but they will be much disappointed as they will be sold again.

On the banks of the Mississippi River, work was busy on the Union's inland navy. Crews were hurriedly building the city-class gunboats for use on major Western rivers. The first Federal ironclads, they were constructed by James Eads and nicknamed the "Eads Gunboats" and "Pook Turtles" after designer Samuel Pook. They included the USS *Cairo, Carondelet, Cincinnati, Louisville, Mound City, Pittsburgh,* and *St. Louis.* All played a major role in the river campaigns of 1862–1863.

Aaron Brown (1822–1904), then a lieutenant in the 3rd Iowa Infantry, saw the remarkable vessels as they were launched and told his wife about them.

St. Louis, Missouri
November 30, 1861

Nearly all the gunboats are finished and have been sent to Cairo. They are more formidable than you can very well conceive of. The hulls are shaped more like a goose than anything I know of to compare them to. They are constructed of solid oak timber about three feet in thickness that is boarded over with four-inch oak lumber, and then with wrought iron plates 3.5 or 4 inches thick. The form is such that if a ball strikes below the line of the main deck, it will glance under, and if it is above, it will glance over. Some of them will carry 14 heavy guns, and some twenty-four. One of them was taken out into the river a few days ago and fired at several times with a 32-pound rifled gun. The balls glanced off without doing any injury.

The weather is cool but pleasant. We have had no snow yet. There was quite a snowstorm at Cairo, Illinois, a few days ago. Troops continue to flock in here by the thousand.

Fremont was removed as commander of the Western Department on October 23. Because of his large following within the abolitionist faction of the GOP, his dismissal made some Northerners wonder if the war was becoming politicized.

Soon thereafter, a diplomatic crisis emerged that brought the United States dangerously close to war with Great Britain. On November 8, Captain Charles Wilkes of the USS *San Jacinto* stopped the British mailer steamer RMS *Trent* on the open seas and forcibly removed two Confederate emissaries, James Mason and James Slidell, who were bound for Europe. The British were outraged and responded by sending 11,000 troops to Canada.

On the night of December 11, a massive fire raced through Charleston, South Carolina, destroying nearly 600 homes, businesses, and churches. (General Robert E. Lee was visiting and watched the blaze spread from his hotel; he and several other officers narrowly escaped the swift-spreading inferno.)

Stationed 100 miles to the south on the Atlantic coast, **Albert Clark Cooke (1840–1862)**, a private in the 6th Connecticut Infantry, discussed both recent events in a letter to a cousin. (Cooke died of disease on Christmas Day 1862.)

Hilton Head, South Carolina
December 21 1861

I presume you have heard of the burning of the city of Charleston, S.C. The folks here had to hear of it quite a number of times before they would believe it. We were, at last, however, compelled to credit it. A steamer came from there today and confirmed it.

There was quite an excitement here last night when the mail arrived on account of the news relative to the prospect of a war with England. I hope that there is nothing to the reports. Perhaps we shall find out by the next mail. If the foreign powers will only mind their own business, I think we can have the privilege of returning home in 6 or 8 months.

I have not seen anything very enchanting yet in Dixie's Land except "contrabands" [freed slaves]. I think some of taking one home with me if the Putnam, Connecticut girls don't write me a line once in a while.

The Trent Affair was peacefully resolved when Mason and Slidell were eventually released from captivity in Boston's Fort Warren, although Lincoln was widely chastised in the North for caving in to British demands. **Robert P. Bush (1842–1923)**, a 19-year-old private in the 12th New York Infantry, wrote about it to his family.

Upton's Hill, Virginia
December 20, 1861

I do think Captain Charles Wilkes did well as far as he went. It would have been better to have captured the whole party, women and all. Better still to have taken the Trent *or sunk it. I think our government is too cozy with its enemies all around. I think that General John C. Fremont was displaced because someone aspiring to the Presidency feared him as a rival, and I think if McClellan gains the confidence and love of the people to the degree Fremont had it, he will be "shipped" too.*

As the war's first year drew to a close, McClellan was staying very busy. General Winfield Scott was finally eased into retirement in late October, with the "Young Napoleon" named his successor as General in Chief of the Armies on November 1. ("I can do it all," McClellan immodestly bragged when asked about his dual assignments.) He also continued whipping his Army of the Potomac into fighting form. Grand reviews were held to build esprit de corps and establish self-confidence in the ranks. As **Silas Leach (1836–1902),** a private in the 52nd Pennsylvania Infantry and member of its Wyoming Coronet Band, described, something amusing happened during one of them.

Camp Dodge, Maryland
December 16, 1861

About half a mile from here is a large parade ground where most of the reviews on this side of the river take place. A few days ago, I witnessed a review of General Erasmus Keyes' Division. It consisted of four brigades and was reviewed by General McClellan and staff. It was a very favorable day for the purpose, and quite a large number of the beauty and fashion of Washington was there to witness the scene. I stood quite near McClellan and had a good chance to see what he looked like. He is quite robust and appears as if he gets enough to eat. Wears a mustache and quite firm expression of countenance generally. Gov. Edwin Morgan of New York was there. Also, Mrs. Ellen McClellan. Mrs. McClellan is quite young and quite good-looking. She attracted great attention from it being her first appearance in public since her arrival from the West.

The only laughable incident that occurred was when the regiments were passing in review before the general. A drum major of one of the regiments was dressed up very finely and appeared as if he had a due sense of his own importance. When he got in front of McClellan, he gave his staff a pitch into the air, intending to catch it when it came down. But unfortunately, it fell into the mud and caused great laughter. And even McClellan relaxed his countenance enough to smile. The whole affair passed off in very good style.

And so, Americans, North and South alike, hunkered down for the duration. Although the first blood had been shed, many people still viewed the war with an innocence that bordered on naivete. It wouldn't last long.

1862

"Our boys see and experience what they never expected to see."

WITH 1862's ARRIVAL, NORTH AND SOUTH ALIKE WERE GROWING SERIOUS about the war. Both sides were starting to realize that it would be a long, bloody conflict, much longer and far bloodier than they had first imagined.

The new year began with a big shake-up in Washington. On January 11, Lincoln essentially demoted Secretary of War Simon Cameron and sent him as far away as possible by naming him ambassador to Russia. He was replaced with the ruthlessly efficient Edwin Stanton, who had briefly served as attorney general in the previous administration. Although Cameron was notoriously corrupt, the former Pennsylvania senator and 1860 Republican presidential candidate had support within the Republican Party. As Lieutenant **May Humphreys Stacey (1838–1886)** of the 12th United States Infantry wrote to his father, the cabinet change was yet another indication to abolitionists of Lincoln's perceived political weakness.

Fort Hamilton, New York
January 14, 1862

The news from Washington filled us with surprise, and I may add disappointment. The retirement of Simon Cameron, and the appointment of Stanton, one of the cabinet of James Buchanan, argues poorly for the backbone of Uncle Abe and is the death warrant for his administration. Cameron was the only man in the cabinet who appreciated the magnitude of the conflict in which we are now engaged and has the courage to indicate the proper mode of bringing it to a conclusion. Uncle Abe is trying to carry water on both shoulders, and we know from the past what befell the presidents who attempted this.

I see but one road to success now. That is the retirement of General George McClellan from head of the army. It is his damned pro-slavery proclivities which is raising the devil. I pray to God that Congressman Frank Blair's bill may pass providing for the confiscation of all the slaves belonging to Rebels and taking them under the protection of the government. The miserable milk and water policy of the government is fast bringing the country to destruction, and if persisted in, will certainly bring about that result.

In spite of everything, in spite of the votes of more than a million Northern men, we have a President having Southern feelings who, for four hundred thousand Negro owners, is willing, and trying, to sacrifice the interests of the whole country. It would be a very charitable thing to mankind, and Americans in particular, if he would get the colic or some other disorder that would rid the country of a man who is going back on his principles.

Interest in the American Civil War was not limited to America. Across the Atlantic, Europeans were closely following events here. Great Britain was especially divided over it. The English aristocracy supported the Confederacy, while the working class favored the Union. The North's naval blockade of Southern ports imposed the previous year was already being felt on both continents, severely impacting personal travel and commerce. A young Briton identified only as **John M. (unknown),** who had apparently lived in the South before the war, wrote to a friend inside the Confederacy. (His letter likely arrived there on a blockade-runner.) He shared the prevailing opinion there that however the war turned out, America would never be the same.

Liverpool, England
January 18, 1862

This is my wigwam now! When do you intend to open the ports and let me go?! I, perhaps, might give a much better guess myself. In the meanwhile, I must content myself with musing David, "the Confederate!"

A paper from me now and again would have shewn thee how public opinion was blowing and going. And what does the great mind of this nation, and all the nations of Europe, now say? I blush and mourn for very shame at the land of my adoption having given such righteous cause for the pity and contempt which it has brought upon it and which history's pages can only renew and hold up to everlasting time as the disgraced, abased, godforsaken people!

When you recover from your insanity, you will all see it, individually and in body politic. And when the day of exhaustion comes upon you, it will be too late—the door will have been shut upon you and the Confederacy gone out—clean, clear, and free from amongst you—and the late U.S. be known as a fourth rate, or tenth rate power only! So say all the people here and elsewhere this side of the Atlantic always.

In the new year's first days, Union and Confederate forces clashed in the Kentucky mountains. While the Battle of Mill Springs was minor compared to those that would soon come, a little army led by Union General George H. Thomas routed Confederate General Felix Zollicoffer's command on January 19. The Federal victory blunted a Confederate invasion of eastern Kentucky and made national news. Visibility was bad, and the bespectacled Zollicoffer mistakenly rode toward the Union lines—with disastrous results.

Francis Teear (1834–1862), now a sergeant in the 24th New York Infantry serving in Virginia, wrote to his wife that while the battle itself was small, its outcome was a big morale boost to the North. (Teear was killed at the Battle of Second Bull Run/Manassas seven months later.)

Upton's Hill, Virginia
January 23, 1862

Our victory in Kentucky was a glorious victory. It was achieved with little loss on either side in men. True, the Rebels lost their General Zollicoffer and will undoubtedly consider it an almost irreparable loss. But their commissariat [food supply] they will think the greater loss. A victory of that kind is not of much genuine value without we can follow it up with another and more glorious victory, one that will not leave a Rebel in Kentucky.

I fear our generals will not follow an attack while they are in a state of disorder. But every victory will serve to discourage the Rebels while it gives confidence to our boys. We feel as though we could do this job up pretty quick if we could only be allowed to go ahead. We must finish it up by next fall anyhow. More and more I think that the great plan is to surround them at Manassas where the bulk of their army is. We are anxiously looking for General Ambrose Burnside to turn up somewhere. But wherever he turns up, it must be with success. I heard today that the 44th "People's Ellsworth

*Zouaves" are preparing to leave for some unknown region. Some regiments
have already gone and others are soon to follow.*

Mistakes and mishaps, such as the one that cost Zollicoffer his life, were
common in the war's early days. Private **James H. Stewart (1842–1862)**, 39th
Ohio Volunteer Infantry, wrote about one mix-up in this letter to his sweetheart.
(Stewart died of disease four months later.)

*Palmyra, Missouri
January 26, 1862*

*I suppose you have heard of the defeat and death of Zollicoffer. Our forces
gained a glorious victory over old Zollicoffer.*

    *The report came here yesterday morning that the Rebels were burn-
ing North River Bridge on the Quincy Railroad [the Palmyra & Quincy
Railroad], and a while before daylight, the bugle sounded for us to fall in
for a fight, and in about five minutes we were going on double quick for the
Quincy Depot where we found the cars waiting for us. We went to the bridge,
found no fire and no enemy.*

    *We found the cause of the alarm to be this—there was some of our
cavalry guarding the bridge and they had a little fire under the bridge to
keep warm by. The bridge tender, not knowing there was any guards there,
he supposed they were Rebels burning the bridge and fired at them. They
returned the fire and run, thinking that the enemy was upon them. They come
here and went to their quarters without reporting. The bridge tender came
up and reported a strong force of Rebels burning the bridge, so this is what
caused us to get up out of our warm beds and take a car ride and a march
before breakfast. We had to march back a distance of three and a half miles.*

In northern Missouri, occupying Federals had their hands full trying to
keep Confederate recruits from traveling across the state and reaching Southern
ranks.

    Alexander T. Weaver (unknown–1862), a corporal in the 37th Illinois
Infantry, described to his family how captives looked and were treated.

Camp Lamine, Missouri
January 3, 1862

Mary asks if I have been in any skirmishes. No, I have not, although I have guarded a good many prisoners. General John Pope has taken about 13 hundred prisoners, three hundred horses and mules, and a lot of wagons, ammunition, guns, and provisions. He got word that they were on their way to join General Sterling Price at Osceola [in southern Missouri], so we started to cut off all the troops at this place.

There were only four hundred cavalry in the fight. Two of our men were killed, and some 20 of them bit the dust. By this time, the rest had come up, and when they seen our battery directed against them, they dropped their guns (which were double-barrel shotguns). They have no uniforms or blankets, only old quilts. They marched the next day to where we was encamped. We took charge of them and made them get in a square and stationed a guard around. In the night, one of them tried to escape and had his heart blown out for his pains. I tell you, the boys bring them in, and we get them.

The mind-numbing monotony of extended camp life was a challenge for men in blue and gray alike. They were grateful for any diversion that came their way. Nature provided one in early February with a heavy snowfall in Virginia.

George Westfall (1842–1923), a young private in the 17th New York Infantry, excitedly told his future wife about it.

Camp Butterfield
Hall's Hill, Virginia
February 8, 1862

You said the talk was up there that we was a going to have a battle here soon. That is the talk here as well. The sooner we do, the better, for I am a tired of staying here penned up in camp.

We had some snow, and the colonel got the men out on Monday morning, and rolled snowballs, and built a snow fort. They worked all forenoon, and in the afternoon, he had the men divided into two parties and put one party in the fort and the other party outside of the fort. There was 800 in the whole besides the officers, and they had them snowballs and they seen which party would whip. I was in the party outside the fort. We whipped the other party and drew them out of the fort. I got one black eye and was glad to get off with just that. It was the biggest snowball fight I ever saw. It was in the Washington papers the next day.

We have some good times here when the colonel gets the regiment out, and we have a good time playing ball, and I tell you, we have some hard times, too, as well as good times.

On the southern seaboard, an amphibious force led by General Ambrose Burnside captured Roanoke Island in North Carolina, giving the Federals a second important foothold on the Atlantic coast. **John Holt (1837–1902)**, a musician in the 13th Massachusetts Infantry, excitedly passed along the news to an unidentified friend.

[Location unknown]
February 12, 1862

I have just heard some good news by telegraph from Washington. We heard that Burnside's Expedition has captured Roanoke and are in full march upon Elizabeth City. Also, great consternation in Norfolk, Virginia, and vicinity.

That news was likewise cheered by another Federal soldier who was serving in an interesting capacity. Both armies utilized a Pioneer Corps. Much like today's combat engineers (and called sappers in European armies), they moved ahead of the main body of troops, cutting down trees and removing natural obstacles so that soldiers—especially the artillery and support wagons—could pass. Their ranks included **John B. Wilson (1826–1884)**, a private in the 2nd New Jersey Infantry, who mentioned his duties in a letter to his parents. He also expressed his eagerness to go after the enemy.

Camp Kearny
Alexandria, Virginia
February 11, 1862

Great victory from the Burnside Expedition for the Union army to hear. It sounds so good. How it warms the heart of a poor soldier. True as steel is the Jersey Boys—no fear of the Secesh at all. Elizabeth City is taken and in our hands. That is good. Roanoke Island is taken also by that Burnside Expedition. How this news must warm the good old iron wigs to read the news as it will go on the telegraph to the distant North to know of our victory in that glorious cause—to see the Stars and Stripes float over the city and island in the place of the Secesh flag.

Major Brigade General [sic] Philip Kearny has taken me out of the company as a pioneer to go ahead of the army as it goes to march to battle to cut and clear the way so they can go straight to action. We have to make new roads to march in for our army wagons. Our company is twenty men, two from each company in this division here. It will be better for me than to do military duty as I have nothing to do but to be ready to go at five minutes' notice and watch with all my might, which I will do and not turn back till the end of my journey and my work finished and this rebellion trampled to the dust and Jeff Davis hanged to his tree down in Old Virginia which is too good for a traitor in times of war.

It is impossible to move forward to battle, which I do rejoice to have a little sport with them Secesh and give them some of our blue pills. We shall send them all up the Potomac on a rail to lock up Jeff Davis and Beauregard, Slidell and Mason, Polk and Price. For saltpeter can't save them from the hands of the Jersey Boys this time.

A couple of hundred miles to the west, Union General Ulysses S. Grant hatched an audacious plan. Working in cooperation with the Western Gunboat Flotilla stationed at Cairo, Illinois, Grant transported his men up the Tennessee River and attacked Confederate Fort Henry, located on the Tennessee–Kentucky line. After an hour-long bombardment, the Southerners retreated to the much stronger and better-fortified nearby Fort Donelson on the Cumberland River, which safeguarded the approach to Nashville.

Norton W. Campbell (1836–1868), a sergeant in the 12th Illinois Infantry, explained how the fight unfolded in a letter to his sweetheart.

Opposite Fort Henry
On Tennessee River in Kentucky
February 10, 1862

We started from Paducah on 5 February at the Tennessee River. We went within 4 miles of Fort Henry where our troops were camped, about 20,000 of them commanded by General Grant. On the morning of the 6th, we started for the fight. We went up the west side of the river, and the balance on the east side, and the gunboats, seven of them, started for the fort. They went within 600 yards of the fort and opened fire on them. The Rebels returned it. The battle lasted just one hour when the Rebels surrendered the fort. The gunboats had dismounted every gun in the fort, tore the fort all to pieces, and killed a good many.

They got a great deal of stores, a large quantity of ammunition, and all of their artillery. They had 16 large guns in the fort. They had about 10,000 troops, but they took French leave for some of them would get shot, and it was a very good conclusion that we have not much mercy on the Secesh.

The gunboat Essex *was badly damaged in the fight. One ball went into her port hole and bursted both of her boilers and killed seven men. They were completely cooked with the steam. That was the only damage the gunboats got, I believe.*

But we have got a great point here and taking a great deal of Rebel goods. I don't think we will stay here long. I think we will soon be in Nashville. We have got 40,000 troops here now and more coming and you can look for good news soon.

The capture of Fort Henry and Burnside's success in North Carolina were hailed in the North as the Union's first major victories. **Hannibal Augustus Johnson (1841–1913)**, a private in the 3rd Maine Infantry, described to a friend how the double dose of good news was received.

Camp Howard
Alexandria, Virginia
February 14, 1862

Our brigade have been at work for the last six or eight weeks on a building called a theatre. Wednesday was the first night that it had been opened, and of course, the building was full, for the soldiers in the brigade have the privilege of going as long as we have any money. After the performance was through, the manager stepped on the stage and said that Colonel Ward had a few words to say to us, and at once, he read the dispatch, which you know yourself, so there is no need to repeat it.

He said he wanted no demonstration of any kind until after we left the house. But he might as well have talked to the wind as to us. For at once, the voices of more than 2,000 soldiers broke forth, and there was such cheers, clapping of hands, stomping of feet, throwing caps in the air, and in fact, doing most everything that was noisy, for the news was too good to be kept silent about. And as soon as we began to quiet down a little, the bands struck up "Yankee Doodle," and then the men commenced to shout again and did not stop until they were exhausted. I guess you will think us a rough set of men by my explanation, and in fact, we are on such occasions. For every victory of this nature helps kill out treason and brings us nearer home, and this is the way we have to express our joy.

There is a rumor around camp tonight that Fort Donelson is undergoing a siege from our men and also Savannah, Georgia, is being attacked, and if this is so, we may look for some exciting times and news tomorrow. I think these expeditions are the surest and quickest way that secession can be killed out. For myself, I want to be on the move, for this inactive life does not suit me when so many are engaged with the enemy.

Although taking Fort Henry had been a relatively bloodless victory for the North, Fort Donelson was an entirely different matter. Built on a strong position atop a hill commanding the Cumberland River near Dover, Tennessee, it was a powerful bastion. The Federals took it after two days of severe fighting. Its capture triggered another round of celebration in Union ranks. Some Northerners even began thinking the war would soon be over. Private **James H. Stewart (1842–1862)** of the 39th Ohio Volunteer Infantry was one of them.

Benton Barracks
St. Louis, Missouri
February 19, 1862

Well the best news first—Fort Donelson is ours! General Simon Buckner, commander of the Rebel forces at the fort, surrendered his whole force on the morning of the 16th consisting of 15,000 men, 48 pieces of artillery, 2,000 stand of arms, 3,000 horses beside a large lot of commissary stores. Since then, they have captured 1,000 more men.

The greatest excitement prevailed here when we heard of the surrender of Fort Donelson that I ever witnessed. Nearly all the soldiers in camp (3,000) assembled in front of headquarters, and cheer after cheer was given by the happy boys. General William Kerley Strong, commanding here, actually danced to the tune of "Yankee Doodle" played by the brass band. A national salute was fired by the artillery. General Strong made a speech in which he said, "This is the beginning of the end of this hellish rebellion."

General Samuel Curtis has captured all of General Sterling Price's staff officers and is taking about 75 prisoners a day. I send you a paper (St. Louis Evening Democrat) giving the latest news.

Ere 6 months, many of our volunteers will be at home. It may be my luck to be among that number, and it may be that I will have to stay longer. It is not probable that the government will disband all the troops so soon after the Rebels are whipped out, and peace declared, but be it as it may, I am satisfied at present and hope I may continue so. We are going in the morning. Our baggage went to Cairo, Illinois, tonight.

While troops in distant Union armies cheered, for many who fought there, Fort Donelson was their first battle. Seeing the results of combat profoundly affected new recruits such as **George Washington Brown (1845–1902)**, a teenage private in the 68th Ohio Volunteer Infantry, who shared what he had experienced with his family.

Fort Donelson, Tennessee
February 20, 1862

On Thursday evening, 13 boatloads of soldiers and 4 or 6 gunboats ascended the Cumberland River [from Paducah, Kentucky] to Fort Donelson. We landed on Friday morning. There were a great number of our troops here from Fort Henry.

On Friday afternoon, fighting commenced between our forces and the Secesh. On Saturday, our forces attacked them in the rear. There was dreadful hard fighting on Friday and Saturday. On Sunday, it came our turn to fight. I did not like this, for I thought it was not right to fight on the Lord's Day. But all who would not go willingly would be forced to go, so I went. But as the good Lord would have it, when we were ready to pitch in them, they surrendered. Our victory was complete. We took a good many thousand prisoners. The number you will know better than I can tell you.

Three days after the surrender, I traveled over the battleground. They were burying the dead as fast as they could. There were yet over 100 dead Secesh that I saw and quite a number that I did not see that were not buried. I also saw about 30 or 40 dead Union men and lots of horses that were killed. The trees were mowed down like grass. Terrible were the times here. I pray God that by His kind providence, He may induce the whole Confederate Army to surrender so that I may never witness another such a scene.

The consequences for the Confederacy from the back-to-back disasters at Forts Henry and Donelson were swift and serious. On February 23, General Albert Sidney Johnston withdrew from Nashville, making it the first Southern state capital to fall into Union hands and giving the Federals an important base for future campaigns.

Writing in western Tennessee some 150 miles away, **Peter Marchant (1831–1865)**, a second lieutenant in the 47th Tennessee Infantry, saw a silver lining in the setback, which he described in a letter to his wife.

Camp Trenton
Near Trenton, Tennessee
February 26, 1862

The surrender of Nashville produced great excitement, but the Yankees seem to be at a loss to know what to do with it. They had not taken possession of it as of three days ago. They seem to feel that they are on dangerous ground and move very careful. I am not at all discouraged at the misfortune, for I believe it will turn out to our advantage. We are not as well-prepared for a border war as they are, but if they come in our country, I believe we will whip them.

Our loss at Fort Donaldson [sic] was great but not to compare with that of our enemy. Ours is estimated at twelve thousand, but most of them was taken prisoners. I have not seen any account of our loss in killed, but we whipped them four times, killing about four to one. But they are reinforced every day, and our men was at last outdone with fatigue and had to surrender.

When I wrote before, I thought that our regiment would be armed in a short time, but from the best information that I can get, it will be four or five weeks. I expect to come home again before we leave here. But I have learned that a soldier's life is a very uncertain one. Therefore, I make but little calculations on anything. I find myself to be a creature of circumstances.

As the first large-scale battle in the West, Fort Donelson also introduced many soldiers' families to a new reality: the difficulty of recovering their fallen loved one's remains. Consider the case of Charles M. Needham, a 19-year-old private in the 11th Illinois Infantry killed in action there. As **Lucinda Rockwell (1835–1924)** wrote to her sister in Vermont, disinterring their brother's body for reburial was a difficult and gruesome chore made worse because it was performed by a relative.

Hoyleton, Illinois
March 26, 1862

Cornelius came home last night and succeeded in getting the remains of Charles. He sent the coffin by express from Centralia yesterday to Bristol Station, and they probably will arrive there today. But the change was, of course, very great by this time, 6 weeks since his death.

Everything that he could identify corresponded with his recollection of Charles. Capt. George McRee wrote that he buried Charles and three other soldiers, and in the grave that Cornelius opened, he found 4 bodies that were all that were killed in that company. All had dark hair save one, and that he took to be Charles. The soldiers said that the Eleventh Regiment were buried in that place, and the soldiers at the fort remembered seeing them buried on the second day after the battle. Most of them were not buried until after the third day, and guns were fired over the graves, which accords with the captain's letter.

The graves were a little away from the rest. 59 of the 11th Regiment were buried all in a long trench (one grave). One headboard had the names of all on it. He had on a hickory shirt [striped blue and white], gray pants, a soldier's roundabout coat with long sleeves, and a soldier's overcoat. No shoes on his feet. They were probably taken by the Rebels. Had two blankets wrapped around his body. Found nothing in his pockets. Everything was probably taken by the Rebels if he had anything. He says there was no odor at all about the body. It was commencing to mortify in spots, but so was about all the others he examined. That may be from bad habits. Charles was strictly temperate. I am so thankful Cornelius could get it. It cost more than we supposed it would. It will amount to $41 [around $1,500 today].

Four or five others went on the same boat for the same object. One man came from Iowa to get an only son. He had expended $200 [$7,000 now] already. One widow woman and son went to get a church elder and a great many others. In one county south of us, 26 bodies were disinterred and brought home, and all buried together. How many sad hearts this war has caused. I hope it may soon cease. Cornelius has spent the past two weeks to obtain Charles' body. He is all worn down with fatigue and a hard cold, but with care and sufficient rest, he will soon be well again. He did not get a good night's rest in all the time he was gone. Had to wait 3 days on account of the boats not running all the time.

In Arkansas, Union forces under General Samuel Curtis drove the Confederates into the Ozark Mountains. **Alexander T. Weaver (unknown–1862)**, a corporal in the 37th Illinois Infantry, told his sister about it.

Camp Halleck
Benton County, Arkansas
February 27, 1862

We reached within eight miles of Springfield, Missouri, when we encountered Price's pickets and drove them in. We marched two miles further when a short skirmish ensued to see which side should have the water. We got possession of the creek with the loss of one man. They lost five killed and several taken prisoners. When the next morning came, we found Springfield deserted. Not one Secesh left to tell the story. We followed and got possession of all their fodder.

The next day, the cavalry caught up with them again and fired on them but could do nothing on account of the infantry being so far behind. The next night, just at dark, we drove them from their camp, leaving their suppers half-cooked, and so we kept it up every day until the 17th when we crossed the state line and the general took the colors and rode across the line, the band playing "Bully Boys We." After they crossed the line, they played "The Arkansas Traveler." We marched about three miles in Dixie when we ran across Price again with about 20 pieces of cannon, plenty ready for us. The cavalry waited until we, the infantry, came up.

Then General Curtis and General Franz Sigel sent the Pups (a name we gave three small howitzers) up to open the ball. They opened fire on them, and it was returned. By this time the cavalry charged and was met by Price's 3 thousand strong. The Dover 9th Battery got to work on them, so they knew it was time to leave, which they done in a hurry, taking to the bush. We lost 10 killed and 15 wounded. They took their wounded, that is a good many of them, with them. We found 30 dead Secesh. A prisoner we took says that they took 80 away in wagons that was killed by shells thrown from the Pups. We marched to Cross Hollow and drove General Ben McCulloch and Price from there. McCulloch was in winter quarters. He had a very nice place, which is now occupied by part of our troops.

We receive no news here at all. Don't know how the war is progressing in other parts. Have not seen a newspaper in a month. I think if they try half as hard on the Potomac to get a fight as we have, this war would soon be over.

You must not fret about me or think that I am a going to get killed in this war. I have two stripes on my arm and mean to have more if good behavior and soldiering conduct will get them.

Then two significant things happened. Realizing that his line of supply was stretched dangerously thin, Curtis halted his advance. The newly appointed Confederate commander, General Earl Van Dorn, arrived on the scene and seized the initiative. In a daring move, he maneuvered his forces into Curtis's rear, resulting in the highly unusual situation of Southerners attacking from the north and Northerners defending to the south.

Fighting began with a small engagement at Bentonville on March 6, followed by the much larger Battle of Pea Ridge (or Elkhorn Tavern) nearby on March 7–8. An interesting aspect was the participation of Native American soldiers fighting for the Confederacy. That was noted by 22-year-old **Henry Silas Wyman (1839–1897)**, a private in the 8th Indiana Infantry, who described the first day's action to his brother.

Benton County, Arkansas
March 11, 1862

I have written one letter since we came to Arkansas, but suppose it was intercepted by the Rebels as they captured our mail about that time. We had the pleasure of finding our letters scattered over their camp after we routed them from the field of battle.

The Secesh left their [ammunition and wagon] trains off to the south of us and sent their forces around and opened on us from the north. They made an attack on Sigel's forces Thursday, and he fought them all day alone and made a junction with us at night. We spent that day in fortifying ourselves on the hills of Sugar Creek and listening to the roar of cannon in the distance. But the next day, we heard them clearer and deadlier than before.

The battle opened Friday morning with shot and shell and the call of small arms, the Rebels thinking they had our retreat cut off, that they would take no prisoners, or that their Indians and Texas Rangers would have a fine time cutting our throats. But the war-whoop of the Indians nor the utmost science that their gunners possessed—and they had 60 pieces of cannon— were a match for old Sigel, who began to drive the right wing of their army before night. Only the left wing of our regiment was engaged to which my company belongs.

We had been stationed on a certain point to sustain the 1st Indiana Battery. We were ordered out about 4 o'clock to sustain Col. Eugene Carr, whom the enemy were trying to flank, and without any doubt, we were in an awful place. Col. Carr's Iowa boys were on one side of a field and the Secesh on the other, surging backward and forward like waves on the sea. The enemy were moving a large body of Rangers and Indians off to the east with intentions of flanking them.

Our little squad of men were brought in behind the Iowa boys, then right obliqued off through the woods about ¾ of a mile and came to a front and fell on the ground and waited for the charge of the enemy. We gave them the contents of our rifles as soon as they came within shooting distance, then fell back among a shower of bullets thick as hailstones. We got behind the trees, reloaded our guns, and let them have it again. We retreated, and they did not follow us far. By the time we got back to where we started into the woods, it was dark.

Curtis attacked the next day, as **Alexander T. Weaver (unknown–1862)** recounted to his father.

Camp on Sugar Creek
Benton County, Arkansas
March 12, 1862

We slept on the field that night without anything to eat. The next morning, Price told his men that they would not have to fire another gun, that he expected to have us to surrender that morning. But he was very much mistaken. We had followed him too far to give up so easy as that.

At daylight, the 8th, we beat his reveille with a few shells and fought like the devil until noon when we got the order to charge on them. The boys let a yell as if all the devils in Hell was let loose and after them. It would do you good to see them skedaddle. It was a regular stampede. Bulls Run [sic] could not beat it. [German-born] General Franz Sigel said that the fight was over, for the "dampt dogs" would not stop for 25 miles.

I went over the field afterwards, and I counted over 200 dead Secesh, which is not one-half. They sent in five hundred with a flag of truce to bury their dead. Our loss is very heavy, but not as large as theirs. Generals Ben McCulloch and James McIntosh both fell with two other of their generals.

Price was wounded in the arm. This I learned from the prisoners. McCulloch fell under the fire of the 37th [Illinois Infantry, Weaver's regiment].

On the 7th, I received a slight wound to the back of the head, which was very painful all night but not enough to make me leave the field. The doctor cut it out (the ball) for me. I have it in my pocket.

Weaver died one week later. Curtis's victory not only drove Van Dorn out of northwestern Arkansas but also secured Union control of Missouri for the rest of the war.

At that very moment, naval history was being made in the waters of Hampton Roads on the Virginia coast.

All winter, Confederate crews had worked feverishly to transform the captured wooden warship USS *Merrimack* into an ultramodern ironclad. Although officially renamed the CSS *Virginia*, many people still referred to her by her original name.

She steamed out of nearby Norfolk on March 8 and headed straight for the Union vessels blockading the port, wreaking havoc on older ships in hopes of breaking the Union's naval blockade. She sank the USS *Cumberland*, burned the USS *Congress*, and ran the USS *Minnesota* aground before retiring.

When the *Merrimack/Virginia* returned the next day, a new foe was waiting: the USS *Monitor*. Designed by Swedish-born engineer John Ericsson, it featured an innovative revolving turret. After fighting for several hours, the Battle of the Ironclads essentially ended in a draw.

Frank Brown (1836–1894), a private in the 2nd Massachusetts Light Artillery (Nim's Battery), witnessed the action from the shore.

Near Fortress Monroe, Virginia
March 13, 1862

Saturday last, we were all ready to go aboard the steamer DeWitt Clinton *bound for Ship Island, Mississippi, just as the big ball opened when our captain received orders from General John Wool to hold on a bit.*

We had orders for immediate action, and at 8 o'clock, the first section (two artillery pieces) was sent to the above-named place with two hundred infantry expecting an attack by land, and it looked very much like it, too, I assure you.

Sunday morning, the Merrimack *layed off Sewall's Point with two transports loaded with troops which could be seen very plain from our camp the boys say that were left there. But it was a sight worth seeing and very exciting at times.*

Also, the Congress, *when all in flames, was a sight never seen probably by one-third of the troops here, and I assure you it was a melancholy one indeed to see that damned* Merrimack *destroying two of our best frigates, besides the great loss of life. Her powder magazine exploded at half past 12, and such a noise your humble servant never before heard.*

The first night, we were at work throwing up entrenchments by the moonlight. My opinion is that if they had attacked us by land Saturday afternoon or night, they could have easily taken Newport News and the fort with the force that was here at that time. General Wool said that the Monitor *was the only preventive.*

Confederate Congressman **William Nathan Harrel Smith (1812–1889)** was among the many who recognized that warfare on the water had now forever changed. Representing North Carolina in the Confederate Congress, he wrote this letter to a prominent constituent in the Old North State.

Richmond, Virginia
March 14, 1862

The facts reported of the victories and brilliant dash of the Merrimack *among the blockading vessels at Hampton Roads are not over-colored. The Northern accounts agree fully with ours. I send you herein the official reports. She met, however, with a hard-headed opponent in the* Monitor—*or Ericsson's Battery. I understand at close quarters her heavy shot rebounded off the side of the ironclad vessel [the* Monitor] *without making an impression on her. I am afraid she will prove a formidable engine in future operations against Norfolk. The* Merrimack *is not believed to be seriously damaged by the conflict. The wrenching off of her iron prow has caused her to leak some, and repairs have become necessary. This will, for the present, prove a safe-guard to this city [Richmond].*

The news from Arkansas is not encouraging. Our army had to retire from the field after two days of severe fighting with a terrible loss of officers and men.

The great difficulty is the want [lack] of arms and powder. We have the men but have great trouble arming them. We have just had the arrival of both in a Southern port [from European suppliers]. It is said to consist of

30,000 of the first and a large quantity of the latter. Our own powder mills can supply by manufacture all the powder the exigencies of the war may call for, if we had supplies of the only deficient article, niter. The government has an abundance of sulfur and carloads of charcoal.

The army has fallen back from Manassas, and that point, so memorable for early events in the struggle, has passed into the possession of the enemy. We are forced to contract our lines and condense our forces, and yet it is painful to surrender without any effort to hold a spot so dear to us all as the place of our most signal triumph. The Rappahannock River will probably be the line to which we shall retire.

The congressman was correct: after passing the winter near the site of the previous summer's Battle of First Bull Run/Manassas and after having strengthened the position with an extensive line of fortifications bristling with what appeared to be dozens of cannons, Confederate General Joseph E. Johnston abruptly withdrew his army deep into Virginia's interior in early March.

Dexter E. Buell (1842–1923) of the 27th New York Infantry excitedly shared the news with his family.

Fairfax Court House, Virginia
March 12, 1862

Centreville is evacuated, and so is Manassas. Our troops occupy the old battleground where we was before [Bull Run]. We are going to chase them as far as they can go. There is a large body of cavalry and infantry after the flying Rebels. They have blown up their powder magazines and their entrenchments and burnt all the bridges. We will have Richmond in less than a week.

General McClellan has been to Manassas and gone back to Washington. We talk of going back to camp, taking the boat, and going down the river to help General Burnside.

There is 300,000 men on the march after the Rebels. This is the largest army ever had been known, so they say. Just as I am writing, there starts three regiments of cavalry on to Richmond and a large body of infantry and artillery.

However, when Federals troops entered the evacuated Confederate position, they were startled to discover that things didn't turn out to be what they had appeared. As an **unidentified Federal artilleryman** explained that, on closer inspection, a good number of the Southern "cannons" actually turned out to be so-called Quaker guns.

Fairfax Court House, Virginia
March 23, 1862

We got to Bull Run about 8 o'clock that night and camped. We expected to see heavy fortifications there, but we examined and there was nothing but a sort of rifle pit to be seen. It was an embankment thrown up on three sides, so we went back and went to bed.

We were rousted out and started about 6 o'clock. We went 4 miles and stopped, unharnessed, and while the drivers were feeding the horses, we went to the Rebel huts and ransacked them. It was a regular city. There were about 300 log houses that they had lived in and had now deserted, leaving everything behind. One of the boys brought a firkin of butter which had never been opened. We found pails full of sugar, peanuts, etc. There was good flour and articles for cooking, all left as if they had no time to pick them up. Their beds, bed quilts, sabers, bayonets, knives, and everything else they left, and we were thinking all the while that they were suffering for the want of food, and all the while, they had more to eat than we did. We went back and stayed that night and the next day.

The captain had us go out with the horses a foraging. Manassas was about 4 miles from there, so some of the boys and myself thought we would go and see the wonderful fortifications. We at last got there. There was one large fort where there had been about 100 guns, and all around there was about 50 sham forts where there were logs and stove pipe put up to scare somebody [by looking like cannons from afar], and on the forts they had placed a man's suit stuffed with straw and a stick with a bayonet on it so some of our soldiers would be fools enough to shoot at it. But they did not fool us, for we had seen such things before.

As Union soldiers settled into the encampment formerly occupied by their foes, they were surrounded by gruesome reminders of the battle there nearly nine months earlier. **Edwin Matherry (unknown–1863),** a private in the 9th Pennsylvania Reserve Infantry, wrote to his family about the grisly scene. (He would die from wounds received at Fredericksburg at year's end.)

Camp at Manassas Junction, Virginia
April 17, 1862

We are camped in a Rebel camp. The 4th North Carolina regiment was camped here last winter. They had 1,500 men when they came here, and now they have only 800 left.

There are graves all the way from Centerville to Manassas. This is about 5 miles. Our men that was killed at Bulls Run [sic] are buried every way. Some are not a foot underground. Some of them are laying where they fell. I have saw some remains lying beside an old log or fence where they crawled to when they got wounded and died. There was some laying on top of the ground with a little dirt throwed over them. One place, there was a big ditch dug 2 or 3 hundred feet throwed all in together. Some of their feet was sticking out, some their hands, and so on. I write this to give you some idea of how the thing looks. Our fellows are burying the bones of all they see.

We are to march at 3 o'clock. I have got my two days' rations in haversacks. So has all of the rest. It is hard to tell which way we will go.

While Johnston was evacuating Manassas, General Thomas "Stonewall" Jackson was staying busy in Virginia's Shenandoah Valley. Incorrectly informed that a small Federal detachment near Kernstown was vulnerable (in reality, it was an infantry division), he first attacked with cavalry, then ordered a full assault. The larger Union force first stopped a Confederate flanking movement, then counterattacked and drove the Southerners from the field.

This account, written two days later from an **unidentified Union soldier**, summed up the action.

Camp Shields
Near Kernstown, Virginia
March 25, 1862

I finished a letter to you Sunday morning stating that there was a skirmish near Winchester Saturday evening. We supposed it was merely cavalry worrying our pickets and that there was not a large force. We heard firing all Sunday morning, and towards noon, it was much heavier and more frequent. At one o'clock, orders came for the whole brigade to turn out, and we were immediately on the road and reached the battleground about 2:30. When we went out, I do not think much of a battle was expected. When we reached there, a furious artillery fight was going on along a line about 2 miles long. The roar of artillery was almost incessant while shells were bursting in every direction. The fight had been going on since 8 in the morning but conducted for several hours so as to draw out and ascertain each other's forces and strength.

The Rebels had driven our men back about one mile and had themselves secured good positions and were fast "flanking" us when, at about 3:30, Tyler's brigade was ordered to charge on the Rebel battery, which they immediately did.

At 10 minutes before 4, the fire of musketry commenced and was a perfect rattle and roar with no cessation. They advanced steadily, driving the Rebels before them, loading and firing as they went and the Rebels firing and retreating slowly until they reached a strong stone fence near a half mile long, beyond which they got and which afforded them a protection against musketry in front. Here they held our men for about 20 minutes, themselves protected except when they raised to fire while our men were openly exposed or only concealed by trees Indian fashion. Here our men suffered the most until reinforcements were sent them from another direction which dislodged them and laid them open to an awful fire and they [the Confederates] suffered terribly and the run began, our men pressing forward and soon reached the battery. How many guns they took, I do not know. The report is they had 16 guns in the battery and that we captured 6—some say 5—and some only 3. I know that 3 were taken.

The fight was very severe. The guns were taken after sunset, and when the actual charge was made on the battery, it was so dark that the flash of musketry could be seen two miles away. The infantry fight commenced 10 minutes before four and ceased at dark or about 7 o'clock when the Rebels were on a swift retreat. Could we have had an hour or two of daylight, the Rebels' defeat would have been a total rout. Yesterday morning, we had taken about 400 prisoners, including several officers and two of Jackson's staff. Our captain said that he was all the way through the Battle of Manassas or Bulls Run [sic] and that at no time was the fire half so hot as it was here.

Our men bivouacked on the field when the last charge was made, and yesterday morning started in pursuit. The last we heard of them was last night at Cedar Creek, 3 miles this side of Strasburg, without having overtaken the enemy. Some of Banks' troops who had left were recalled and reached here yesterday noon.

Kernstown was significant for several reasons. First, it was one of Stonewall Jackson's very few defeats. It also marked the start of Jackson's famous Valley Campaign. Finally, though a tactical Union victory, the battle produced a strategic advantage for the South. As noted at the conclusion of the excerpt, Banks's orders to reinforce the Army of the Potomac on the Peninsula were countermanded, keeping him in the Shenandoah Valley. As we shall soon see, that planted seeds of suspicion in McClellan's willing mind that Washington was conspiring against him by denying him repeatedly requested reinforcements.

Far to the west, other Federals were likewise moving into their enemy's abandoned fortifications. It was the first phase in a massive, combined army and naval offensive.

After the losses in middle Tennessee, Confederate General Albert Sidney Johnston's entire line stretching 300 miles from the Cumberland Gap to the Mississippi River fell back. On its western end, the Confederates evacuated Columbus, Kentucky, and made nearby Island Number 10 (so named because it was the tenth island below the Mississippi's confluence with the Ohio River) the new key to the upper Mississippi Valley's defenses. Federal troops pursued the Southerners.

Writing from the newly seized Union base towering above the Mississippi, 25-year-old **John Quincy Adams (1836–1866)**, a private in the 60th Illinois Infantry, described to his wife his first view of the place.

Columbus, Kentucky
March 18, 1862

As I am now at leisure and in camp, I will give you a history of our doings since we left Cairo, Illinois. We went down to Island No. 10, and we thought we was a going to have a fight. We saw the gunboats draw up in line of battle and the battery on the shore was throwing shells in the Rebel fortifications. We could see the Rebel forts and tents. We was landed about 2 ½ miles off the island and ate our dinners in a hurry. We was then put on board of our transports ready for to move, we thought, but we was disappointed. We was ordered back to this place to guard it.

The boys was loud in their curses of our colonel for not giving us a chance to try our hand. We was not drilled was the reason for our not taking part in the fight. But we saw the Rebels. That was some satisfaction to us.

Now, as for Columbus, it is such a nice place. We can see so far. We can hear the roar of cannon at No. 10 today. It is one steady roar. There is hot work going on there today. I expect it was well that we did not get to stay for not many would have lived to tell the tale—we was so green.

There were significant problems with Johnston's new precarious position. Chief among them was the vulnerability of New Madrid, Missouri, located in a bend in the Mississippi just above Island No. 10. General John Pope drew his Army of the Mississippi around the town on March 3, forcing its evacuation 10 days later. The following week, an **unknown Union soldier** was telling his wife about approaching the Confederate stronghold from the Missouri shore.

Camp in the field
Below New Madrid, Missouri
March 20, 1862

We have been fighting for the last week. We have to take every advantage we can, for they have 5 gunboats and one revenue cutter. On the morning of the 18th, they attempted to land and take our gun, for we only had one 24-pounder. We disabled one boat, and then they tried to land. But the sharpshooters picked the gentlemen off so fast that they backed out and went down the river. Their loss was some 12 men and one boat disabled, and we did not lose one man after all their throwing shell.

There was a house right back of the battery, and the enemy threw a shell that went through a feather bed and through a partition and then out of the back door and struck a Negro house and bursted and cut things all to pieces.

Yesterday morning, we had moved the battery something about a mile and half down the river and brought in another gun, so we had two guns and our regiment was out as a reserve to save the guns if they attempted to land. They [the Confederates] threw their shells so close that the mud and water went all over the men. They all stood it well, with the exception of one man. I shall not mention the man, for you do not know him anyhow.

We have had a hard time of it lately. We have had nothing much to eat, for we have a long distance to haul our provisions, for we have not got control of the river yet. But I think we will soon.

Capturing New Madrid permitted Flag Officer Andrew Foote to run past Island No. 10's powerful batteries the night of April 4–5, thus enabling Pope to cross the river into the rear of the Confederate garrison. An intense three-day

Union bombardment followed, with the Confederate force of nearly 7,000 surrendering on April 8.

Amos Downing (1840–1880), a private in the 6th Maine Infantry, somehow wound up helping service the powerful gun on Foote's Mortar Boat #11. He excitedly related the news to his father the next day.

No. 10 Island, Missouri
April 9, 1862

Island No. 10 is ours. They surrendered Monday evening. We took four hundred prisoners, three large transports, and all their cannons, one floating battery of fourteen guns. I didn't count the guns, but I would think that there is about 60 heavy pieces ranging from 128 to 32 pounders. They are all good, with the exception of five that they spiked when they had possession of the island. The main land batteries are all tore up by our shells. We would have had the island long ago had it not been for the river rising so high, that's all that kept us back.

The Rebels found out they was cut off by General Pope and a great many made their escape. We heard that he had taken 5,000 prisoners without firing a shot. We have all their tents, wagons, and a great amount of provision. They had plenty to eat with the exception of coffee and tea, that's worth one dollar per pound. Their uniform is rather mean-looking. Their equipment is very bad, some with small rifles and others old muskets with no bayonet on.

The prisoners taken here all say that they were forced in the service and are satisfied to be taken prisoner. They didn't know what to make of matters. They said first there was a big smoke, and next a noise like thunder, and next thing the devil himself would come among them, and that was worse than fighting with sticks. They say the first shell killed 15 men. Their loss is very heavy; our loss is 20 killed and wounded, and that's mostly all from accidents.

Next comes Fort Pillow, which commands Memphis. That will be ours in a few days. Then New Orleans is ours. This is one of the greatest victories won yet. You see, long-range guns saves lives.

Downing was right; while the North was making inroads on the upper Mississippi, the next important move would soon come far below near the mouth of the great river. For the moment, though, Island Number 10 was a consequential victory for Pope. It launched him on a trajectory leading to bigger things that summer.

At the same time, Ulysses Grant was not idle in western Tennessee. He began sending his men down the Tennessee River. The first contingent arrived at the hamlet of Pittsburg Landing in early March, where a brief but sharp skirmish occurred with a handful of Confederates. Grant halted his push and began concentrating his command there, unaware that the place would soon be the scene of far bloodier fighting.

Private **George Benton Aldrich (1828–1908)** of the 48th Ohio Infantry was among the soldiers waiting while Grant's forces steadily grew.

Camp Sullivan, Tennessee River
March 24, 1862

We have got to the enemy's country, but we haven't seen any of the devils yet, and I don't think we will. But still, we may. We had a good time coming here. We have took our camp on the battlefield of Pittsburg. The battle was fought on the 4th of March. It was not a hard fight. The Rebels buried their dead. I said that they had buried their dead, but they just throwed a little dirt over them for we could see their noses sticking out of the ground. Our troops captured 80 bales of cotton and some prisoners yesterday.

I want you to write to me what the general opinion of the war is there.

Unknown to Aldrich, Grant, and others in the Union ranks, General Albert Sidney Johnston was rallying all the Confederate troops he could gather at the rail center of Corinth, Mississippi, some 20 miles away.

Grant—and especially his subordinate General William T. Sherman— repeatedly missed clues that something big was in the works. Less than 24 hours before a massive Confederate surprise attack got underway, Union Captain **Don Carlos Newton (1832–1893)** of the 52nd Illinois Infantry told his wife that he suspected something was stirring.

Pittsburg Landing, Tennessee River
April 5, 1862

The great battle is not far off, and the next news you hear from here may be that it has been fought and victory once more perched on our banner. Last evening, they attacked our pickets and drove them in. But as luck would have it, they waked up a hornet's nest in the shape of a battery of artillery, which was nearby drilling, and were repulsed. Our folks took 50 prisoners—a feast they did not invite themselves to.

You ought to have seen the excitement in camp. The long roll was beaten, and regiments gathered and formed by scores. Men cheered, cheer upon cheer. Sick men all over camp became suddenly well. The boys acted like an old war horse that smells danger from afar—all life and animation, pounce upon prance. Of course, as I always take things cool, I went quietly to work to arrange all things for a forward move if we should be called for. I had the company clean all their guns and see that all their ammunition was in order.

Col. Thomas Sweeny went down to headquarters and came back ordering us to get three days rations in our haversacks. Our cooks were up all night cooking to get ready, and now the orderly is forming the men to give them the rations. I don't think now that there will be any trouble at present, but no telling. White man mighty uncertain. I have no fears, but all will come out right, for the Lord is on our side, and victory is sure to reach us sooner or later.

What followed was the Battle of Shiloh/Pittsburg Landing, one of the war's most savage engagements. **Lawrence B. Worth (1834–1891),** a corporal in the 7th Iowa Infantry, fought in the legendary Hornet's Nest on the first day. He sent his father a concise overview of the battle that is worth sharing at length here. (He also had harsh words for his commanding general.)

Pittsburg Landing, Tennessee
April 11, 1862

The enemy attacked us on Sunday morning at daybreak, and they whipped us badly during the day. Their attack was a complete surprise, and they overpowered us. Our forces were camped on too much ground, and the line of battle was too large for us to defend. They attacked the two outer divisions first and early in the morning, and before the forces could be brought to their assistance from the other 3 divisions, their lines were cut up and broken—the soldiers flying in consternation by our lines, which discouraged many of our men who had yet to come up the work. But our men fought valiantly—stood their ground well for several hours and did not retreat till in the evening when they bore down on the weak and wavering portions of our line, causing them to fall back. And then began a flanking movement on the part of the enemy. We were ordered to retreat, which was done in good order for some distance, but the enemy bore down on them so strong that soon all became confusion and then became a general stampede equal to Bull Run, I suppose.

We retreated back, formed a line running along up and down the Tennessee River near the landing and out for some distance. There was a howitzer (64-pounder) and three or four 24-pound siege pieces placed on the hill near the landing, and with these and one of the gunboats, they rained such torrents of shot and shell into the enemy that they dare not advance. This was kept up for one hour or more when Buell's forces began to come up over the hill from the landing just in time to save us. Had it not been for the reinforcements of Buell, we would have been entirely annihilated, killed or taken prisoners.

During the night, the reinforcements were disposed of in the best manner possible for action in the morning. Our guns kept throwing shells all night, every half hour, into the lines of the enemy till they had to fall back over a mile. How they did it, I do not know, but some prisoners and wounded say that every shell that was thrown landed in their lines.

On Monday morning at daylight, the fight commenced again. This day, the battle turned the other way. The enemy were routed entirely and driven back. All the guns [cannons] they took from us were retaken, and a number of theirs were also taken. The loss on both sides was great. They took a great many prisoners the first day, and we took some of them prisoners the second day. I suppose they took 2,000 of our men on Sunday. On Monday, we took, I think, near 1,000 of them prisoners. The enemy did not destroy any of our camp other than plunder knapsacks and tents, for General Pierre G. T. Beauregard had told them they would capture all.

I was in the fight, tried to do my duty, did not run like some others, but rallied on our colors, obeying the commands of my superior officers. Laid in line Sunday night in a drenching rain and am yet alive and safe, for which I thank God, for I am nearly sick from the exposure of 3 days.

The enemy is about seven miles from our lines, and the supposition is they intend attacking us again soon. Johnston and General Braxton Bragg were killed, and Beauregard is wounded in the arm. The enemy lost some of their best officers and they had the flower of their army here—most of the Manassas troops.

General Grant should be court-martialed for allowing himself to be surprised. He was notified time after time that the enemy was near his lines in strong force and intended to attack him. He hooted at the idea of them attacking him and for two days suffered things to go on in this way and his army to be surprised. I have always disliked the man, and worse now than ever. He is not fit for a military man.

When the battle was over, nearly 3,500 men had been killed and another 16,500 wounded. It was unlike anything that had ever happened before in U.S. history. More Americans died during those two days than had perished in any engagement in the Revolutionary War, the War of 1812, or the Mexican War. The casualties were so horrific that people on both sides of the Mason-Dixon line now whispered, "What have we got ourselves into?"

Among the dead was General Albert Sidney Johnston. (Despite what Worth had heard, General Braxton Bragg was not killed, General Pierre G. T. Beauregard was not wounded, and General Joseph Johnston's troops from Virginia were not present.) Command of the Confederate forces fell to Beauregard, who retreated into nearby Mississippi. Although the army he inherited had been defeated, it remained a potent fighting force, as Lieutenant **Ephraim C. Dawes (1840–1895)** of the 53rd Ohio Volunteer Infantry explained to his sister a few days later.

Near Pittsburg Landing, Tennessee
April 19, 1862

Your questions regarding our forces were sufficiently answered by the events of the 6th, 7th, and 8th. There is a great deal of humbug about the Rebels being poorly provided for. They are, in general, well-armed, well-clothed, and pretty well-supplied. The Arkansas troops are poorest in respect to outfits. The most they complain of is their commissariat [food supply]. One regiment of theirs, the "Crescent Louisiana," was composed of the flower of the young men of New Orleans. They fought well and were badly cut up. Their loss in killed is very much larger than ours. In our camp, 60 dead Rebels and 5 of ours were buried. In front of the 57th and 77th, 98 Rebels. Back of the 77th in one place, 33 Rebels. Three days after the fight, the pickets of our regiment found 14 in a hollow and buried them. A single gunboat shell killed from 50 to 60 Rebel cavalry. Their loss must be near 6 or 7,000 killed and wounded. Some place it much higher.

If anybody has seen fit to enquire about me since the fight, tell them I have lost neither flesh nor stature by over-exertion in running.

I am sorry the Ohio troops fare so poorly in the papers. They deserve some censure, but not half so much as they get. They were all, to a certain extent, raw. They lacked drill and discipline. There is a necessity for these drills and reviews, etc., which cannot be realized until you put troops under fire. It is an absolute necessity that every man must obey his officers. I am also in hopes that the papers will do us justice finally. Individually, I don't care so much, but every man has regimental pride; the "esprit de corps" must be cultivated and sought after. We have division drill daily from 3 p.m. till dark under direct supervision of General Sherman.

I should not be at all surprised if Beauregard should attack us again. I do not fear the results. Buell's veterans are in advance, and a better army than Buell's is hard to find. My reason for thinking that Beauregard may attack is simply this. He must do something. He cannot remain idle long. He is a bold man, a brave man, a good general. His troops have all confidence in him.

The battle's staggering casualties left people everywhere in a state of shock. In Ohio, teenage student **Leanna Compton (1844–1863)** struggled to digest the news when writing to her uncle.

At School
Harveysburg, Ohio
April 17, 1862

The loss at Pittsburg [Shiloh] was enormous. There has been some six or seven columns of the killed and wounded printed in the newspaper in the smallest print. We have a great many soldiers home sick. I think that from appearances that those who do not get killed will die in the hospital.

I heard this morning that they are trying to get volunteers for five years. If they are going to keep up the war for five years, I don't know what the country will come to. News came last night that our forces have taken Corinth, Mississippi, but the loss is reported to be very heavy on both sides and that we have lost several generals. I hope <u>we</u> have not. I don't care for the Rebels. I want old Beauregard killed, though he does not deserve so honorable a death.

We were very agreeably surprised last Saturday evening by the arrival of Father, brother and my stepmother. They are going to repair Uncle RB's house and go to housekeeping. Father declares he is not Secesh nor never has been, but his wife, save her! she is as strong a Secesh as Jeff Davis himself. She says she has never rejoiced at a victory gained by the North, for they are just as much in the wrong as the South. The whole family of White are Secesh, if they dared let it be known.

Although the report of Corinth's capture was premature, the North now turned its attention to that significant rail junction. There was also a major development some 125 miles to the east on one of its important rail lines.

While the Shiloh Campaign was being waged, General Ormsby Mitchel's division left Middle Tennessee, marching over the Cumberland Mountains and heading for the Heart of Dixie. The goal was Huntsville, the eastern control point on the Memphis and Charleston Railroad. The 311-mile railway was one of the Confederacy's main transportation lifelines, running from near Chattanooga, Tennessee, to the Mississippi River.

With all available Southern troops sent to Johnston's army weeks earlier, the city was defenseless, and the Federals easily marched in on April 11. Two days later, **Frank Phelps (1844–1919),** a private in the 10th Wisconsin Infantry, described to friends back home a region drastically different from theirs.

In Camp at Huntsville, Alabama
April 13, 1862

Here I am, "way down south in Dixie" in good earnest. We took our time in going so I had a fine chance to see the country. It is settled all along the road. Some owns very large plantations and 2 or 3 hundred slaves. They were planting when we went by. We could see the Negroes working in the field, and at three or four places, there were Negro women plowing. They say they would rather plow than do any other field labor.

We got to Fayetteville, Tennessee, about 5 o'clock. This town is a regular Secesh place. While here, we got the dispatch telling about the late fight between Pittsburg [Shiloh] and Corinth where we completely whipped them. We don't get the particulars as you do, but we always know as soon as the news can get here when there has been a battle.

Saw nothing new until we crossed the state line into Alabama. We began to see large plantations from 400 to 1,500 acres, and on each, there seemed to be quite a settlement which were the Negro quarters. Each Negro family has a little lot by themselves, which they use as they choose. There was one man that had 1,500 acres and 500 Negroes. He said that he raised 900 acres of cotton last year. There is lots of cotton all ready to ship off.

We thought we would come down here and take possession of the Memphis and Charleston Railroad, the only road that they can run their reinforcements to Corinth. We took or captured here 21 engines and 150 cars or more. The people say they did not expect us so soon, but we told them that they could not send any more troops to Beauregard at Corinth. The day before we got here, 11 trains of cars passed through for there. We stopped 2 trains from going, but the 3rd got away as we could not throw shells far enough. They all fell short, but the Rebels run a heavy train in here loaded with their wounded from Corinth going east. They did not know that we were here.

We don't know how long we will be able to hold this position, for it just cuts the Confederacy in two, just splits them. We expect the Rebels every day. We have got a battery where we can blow up the track four miles ahead if they should try to come from Richmond or any other place east. We ain't afraid of them now. We have marched over 350 miles in two months to catch them. Finally, we have them in a tender spot. We had orders this morning to have our accouterments on all of the time and our guns stacked in front of our tents where we can get them at a moment's notice. We may go on to Decatur, Alabama, so we can reinforce General Don Carlos Buell, but I can't tell. It is all guesswork, you know. Secesh are thicker than hops here. There is a woman that lives just across the road from where we are camped that carries a pistol and says she will shoot the first man that offers to harm any of her folks.

Just received a dispatch from Nashville that there had been another battle at Corinth, and after a hard-fought battle completely routing the enemy. Loss on our side 17,000—Rebels 40,000 killed, wounded, and taken prisoner. The 8th Brigade took Decatur today noon.

(Phelps was mistaken on one point; there was no second battle at Corinth—at least not yet.)

On the Atlantic coast, the Union made a big step in curtailing Confederate trade with Europe. Fort Pulaski guarded the waterway leading to Savannah, Georgia. Its 48 powerful guns protected blockade-runners slipping in and out of that important seaport.

Federal forces had landed on Tybee Island across the Savannah River from the fortification late the previous year and built up their presence there. In mid-March, General **Quincy Adams Gillmore (1825–1888)** began assembling 35 cannons to bombard the fort. They included 10 relatively new rifled guns. Although his superiors were skeptical, Gillmore believed that their more accurate firepower would be devastatingly effective against the fortress's masonry walls. Working under cover of darkness, the artillery was painstakingly hauled into 11 battery positions and concealed with camouflage.

Gillmore's guns opened fire on the morning of April 10. He reported what happened the next day in this letter to his commanding general.

Fort Pulaski, Georgia
April 11, 1862

I have the honor to transmit the terms of the capitulation for the surrender to the United States of Fort Pulaski, Georgia, signed by me on this day.

The fort hoisted the white flag at a quarter before 2 o'clock this afternoon after a resistance since eight o'clock yesterday morning to the continuous fire of our batteries. A breach in the walls was made in eighteen and a half hours of firing by daylight.

Gillmore's successful shelling established the offensive capabilities of rifled artillery, spelling doom for traditional brick and stone fortifications that had until then been almost impregnable for centuries.

As fighting raged on the battlefield, slavery went on as usual in the places where it existed. Some slaves ran away whenever an opportunity arose. In one such case, a man who had leased a slave had to notify the owner of his disappearance. **Eleanor Beanes Mullikin Hilleary (1806–1886),** a modestly well-to-do slave owner in Prince George's County, Maryland, then informed a local judge of the situation.

Washington, D.C.
April 17, 1862

Spencer left here on Monday morning. Where he has gone, I know not, but considered it my duty to inform you of the fact. Very Respectfully
—J. D. Gilman

Judge Tuck:
Dear Sir: I felt it my duty to forward this letter to you. Yours respectfully
—Eleanor B. M. Hilleary

In a subsequent letter, Tuck replied that he had heard that Spencer Snowden had gone off with Union troops, though it is unclear in what capacity (such as a personal servant to an officer or working for a sutler, as blacks were not yet allowed to enlist). Either way, Spencer's timing was significant. The day after he ran away, Lincoln signed into law the District of Columbia Compensated Emancipation Act on April 16.

Hilleary later petitioned for—and eventually received—compensation for Spencer and three other slaves. Because she had leased them to work inside the District, they were thus freed. One of the trio, an approximately 23-year-old named **Isaac Hamilton (unknown)**, wrote to her within weeks requesting his emancipation papers. (It was against the law in most Southern states to teach slaves to read and write, meaning that letters written by them are exceedingly rare. Hamilton wrote in an almost childish scrawl and had difficulty spelling. The version below is corrected for easier reading.)

Washington, D.C.
June [actually July] 8, 1862

Miss E. Hilleary, Ma'am
I am just a going to leave Washington and would like to have my papers, if you please. I expect to leave in about five days for New York and would be very glad if you would secure them for me.

Your obedient servant,
Isaac Hamilton

It appears that Hamilton got the month wrong in his letter because when Hilleary received it a few days later, she wasted no time in immediately forwarding it to Judge Tuck.

Mount Retreat, Maryland
July 12, 1862

Enclosed I send you a note I have just received from my servant Isaac Hamilton, who was hired to Robinson, asking me to send him his free papers. I have no intention to comply with his desire. From his note, you will see that he intends to remove to New York in a few days. I write this so that you may act in the matter as your better judgment may think proper. I earnestly request your earliest attention to this matter.

The day before Hilleary wrote her second letter, Judge Tuck had filed a petition on Hilleary's behalf with the District of Columbia's three-member Emancipation Commission proclaiming her loyalty, establishing that she was the lawful owner of four slaves, and stating their combined value was $4,600 (about $165,000 today), nearly four times more than the $1,200 total authorized by the Compensated Emancipation Act.

As slavery was coming to an end inside the District of Columbia, the Union's largest army was finally departing Washington. For months, Lincoln had prodded General George McClellan to act. In March, he was relieved as general-in-chief of all Federal armies so that he could focus on his upcoming campaign to capture Richmond. (The position's duties would remain under Secretary of War Edwin Stanton's nominal control until late July.)

At long last, the Army of the Potomac was set in motion on March 17.

That was when the "Young Napoleon" began transferring his massive force—121,500 men, more than 200 cannons, nearly 15,000 horses and mules, and almost 1,200 wagons and ambulances plus tons of food, fodder, ammunition, and other supplies—on an end run around Johnston's new defensive line. Rather than marching across Virginia from the north and slugging it out in bloody fighting, McClellan sent his army by water down the Potomac River to Fortress Monroe. From there, it would advance up the sliver of land between the James and York rivers in what came to be known as the Peninsula Campaign.

The Confederates were entrenched in a line stretching between the two rivers as McClellan's men headed for the Revolutionary War landmark of Yorktown, where Lord Cornwallis had surrendered to George Washington 80 years earlier.

Private **Albert Henry Bancroft (1840–1864)** of the 85th New York Infantry was part of the Northern offensive. He penned this letter to his sister. (Bancroft died at Andersonville Prison two years later.)

Camp Casey, Virginia
April 8, 1862

In accordance with your wishes for me to write when we crossed the Potomac River, I will take this opportunity to let you know that I am well and in camp about several miles beyond Fortress Monroe in the pine woods. We started for here last Monday on board the Elm City steamer. We were about 24 hours in coming at about the rate of 7 miles per hour and arrived on the same waters that were the scene of the Merrimack's *exploits and saw the steamer that she sank and the one that was burned to the water's edge. And the little* Monitor *was puffing about as large as a Broadway dandy and looked rakish as could be and ready for anything. And the harbor was full of all sorts of vessels loaded with munitions of war. And over all looked the old fortress—the largest in the United States—the Lord of the Chesapeake, or Hampton Roads.*

Tuesday in the afternoon, we disembarked and marched over here. On our way we went through Hampton, the town that the Rebels burned down some time ago. You have heard of it in the papers. The place covered about one square mile and was a very nice place but built in the old style. But it is well burned, and there is but two or three houses left standing, and these not worth burning.

The Army of the Potomac had expected to advance with little resistance. However, the Confederates used military sleight of hand to appear substantially larger than their actual numbers. That rattled McClellan, who was deeply cautious by nature. Instead of risking a big battle, he ordered his men to dig in and prepare for a prolonged siege. He also employed the latest technology by conducting aerial reconnaissance—using hot-air balloons—though the information they provided wasn't always accurate.

Sergeant **Thomas Zahniser (1835–1862)** of the 57th Pennsylvania Infantry updated his brother on the siege. (A schoolteacher before the war, he was hospitalized with a fever a few weeks after writing this letter. The facility was captured by the Confederates, and it is believed that Zahniser died soon afterward.)

Camp Winfield Scott Virginia
April 29, 1862

A balloon reconnaissance is made every day viewing the Rebel batteries. They have three tiers of batteries that mount 800 guns. They are strongly entrenched. Language fails me to tell you the amount of work our army has done within the last two weeks in making roads, breastworks, rifle pits, batteries, bridges, etc.

The rifle pits are nearly completed. They extend from one end of the lines to the other—a distance of seven miles. They are five feet deep and 12 feet wide. Roads are being made along hillsides and through the woods in every direction towards the enemy and graded as level as a floor. Many cannon balls have been dug up which no doubt was shot at the Battle of Yorktown [during the Revolutionary War]. It matters not what kind of weather we have—fair to foul, rain or shine, night or day—thousands are at work all the time. There is a fine steam sawmill in this vicinity, which is kept running all the time. Logs are cut and hauled with Secesh property.

We scarcely get a night's sleep. Night before last, we were placed in rifle pits. Last night, we stood under arms from three o'clock till morning. Tonight we go on picket. Ours is a soldier's life—"days of danger, nights of wakin'." But we do it cheerfully, at least the most of us. There are some old grannies among us who had better be at home. Last night, there was heavy cannonading, but I have learned nothing in regard to it.

I would not be surprised if this battle was not fought for three weeks yet. McClellan is busy viewing the roads and breastworks. He is a nice-looking man—wears a private's coat. He feels confident of success and will do it with as little loss of life as possible. I hope it will be so. But there surely will be a big fight.

Oh! the desolation! the desolation! of this country. No one can form an idea till they see it.

In regard to the war news, you know as much about them as I do. The Battle of Pittsburg Landing [Shiloh] was bloody, and nothing gained by either side. It was nothing but the hand of Providence that saved Grant's army. At Corinth will be another desperate battle. Halleck will command in person. Has not his department of the army done much to quell this mighty rebellion? McClellan laid the plans, and he [Halleck] executed them. Such skill, engineering, bravery, and energy, as exhibited at Island No. 10, Fort Pulaski, Fort Donelson, never was known in the annals of history. There are Henry Halleck and Andrew Foote, Ambrose Burnside, Don Carlos Buell, Ulysses Grant, and John Pope have covered themselves with immortal fame in quelling this cursed rebellion. It is reported that McClellan received a telegram that New Orleans was taken. If we are successful here and at Corinth, then Jeff Davis may hang his bacon.

The news that Zahniser heard was correct. New Orleans, the largest city in the Confederacy, fell in late April. Guarded to the south by Forts Jackson and St. Philip on opposite sides of the Mississippi River, they were supplemented by a ragtag collection of homemade gunboats of dubious value.

The Federals assembled a combined land–water force and moved in mid-April. For five days, the forts were bombarded by 21 mortar schooners led by Commander David Dixon Porter. When that didn't produce the desired results,

Porter's adoptive brother, Flag Officer David Farragut, sent his seven more powerful warships into action. **Albert Phillips (unknown–1864)** was aboard one of them, the USS *Oneida*, and described what happened next to his brother. (Phillips was killed in the 1864 Battle of Mobile Bay.)

New Orleans, Louisiana
May 1, 1862

We hauled up to the Flag Officer's [Farragut's] ship the 18th of April when the mortar boats drew up in line of battle to fire at these forts (Jackson and St. Phillips). They commenced bombarding the next day, the 19th, and continued until the afternoon of the 24th without intermission, having fired 9,000 shells. They are damageable when they fall, clearing the ground for 200 or 300 yards and falling to the enormous might of 9 tons.

On the morning of the 24th, we beat to quarters at 3 o'clock a.m. We, being the fifth ship in line of battle, attacked the forts, one on each side of us (mounting altogether 230 guns), and opened fire on them. Finding they were too much for us, we ran by them after having stood their fire for 32 minutes, the Commodore's main object being to capture New Orleans, and then the forts would give in themselves. After having got by the forts, there were 12 Rebel gunboats and 2 battery rams (vessels coated over with iron and mounting 18 guns apiece). We succeeded in sinking one of the batteries and 9 gunboats, but the rest ran away upriver.

We then went on up to New Orleans. Such sights of destruction as met us on all sides never was before seen, the Rebels having burned everything they thought we could get hold of. When we arrived at the city, the Commodore sent his flag of truce ashore, accompanied by his proclamation stating that if the city was not given up in 24 hours, we would lay it in ashes. The mayor then came on board and gave the city up.

The Commodore then started up the river and took a Rebel battery of 40 guns without their firing a shot. This ship then hauled down the river to cut off all supplies to the forts, and last Monday, the forts surrendered after having blown up their battery ram [CSS Manassas] and giving us 2,000 Rebel prisoners.

So, the American flag now flies over Forts Jackson and St. Phillip and the city of New Orleans. So ends another page to be recorded in American history. We received orders yesterday to coal up, take in provisions and ordinance stores to go up the river as far as Memphis, Tennessee. I expect soon to be able to tell you of another victory accomplished by this gallant little fleet.

In early May, the Federals were preparing to move on Norfolk, Virginia. Its residents were among the first to experience what people in other Southern cities and towns went through as the enemy approached, forcing them to face new realities.

An **unknown attorney** dashed off this letter seeking assistance from William Thomas Sutherlin, a wealthy tobacco merchant and former mayor of Danville, Virginia.

Norfolk, Virginia
May 3, 1862

Thank you kindly for your offer to serve us, for we think we shall stand in need of a friend to look after our interests in Danville and Yanceyville, Virginia, ere long. The Yankees are pressing heavily, and General John B. Magruder will no doubt be forced to fall back towards Richmond out of reach of the gunboats. We here in Norfolk are pretty much in the same condition. We should not be surprised at the fall of our city at any moment. We must therefore beg of you in such an event that you will take charge of our interests there and do as if the property were your own, and we shall be under many obligations to you.

At the same time, the USS *Monitor* and several other Federal warships bombarded Confederate batteries at nearby Sewall's Point, Virginia. (The attack was witnessed by President Lincoln, who was visiting the front.) That drew out her old rival, the CSS *Virginia/Merrimack*, in response. For a moment, it seemed that a rematch of the Battle of the Ironclads might happen. An **unidentified Union officer** related the news to a friend.

[Virginia; location unknown]
May 9, 1862

Had everything packed up in boxes. Our baggage was reduced to what we could carry in our hands. While we were packing up, the Monitor *and 3 and 4 or more large war vessels were shelling Sewall's Point, firing very rapidly, the Rebels replying slowly. Our guns, or rather shells, set something on fire judging from the black smoke that arose after a half-hour of shelling. The reply of the Rebels slackened gradually until it entirely ceased, when from Norfolk came the* Merrimack, *or a vessel like her. While this last part of the drama was enacted, we were on our way to the transports. Our boats retreated without firing a shot, being part of their plan, which was to draw the* Merrimack *near Fortress Monroe, where the water is deeper and they can get at her better.*

The Monitor *has been exchanging a few shots with Sewall's Point and now lies abreast of it, trying to tempt the* Merrimack *to chase her. The* Merrimack *was in sight this morning but we have not seen her since. The firing yesterday was very heavy and rapid. The* Galena *and two other gunboats went up the James River yesterday. Have not heard any reliable news yet from them except firing.*

We are getting very indifferent here now. Don't seem to care what is done. Heard firing; at least, I was told it was the Monitor. *Didn't take trouble to see. I have arrived at the state of mind that it is indifferent to what turns up.*

After staying on board the boat all night, we were ordered back to camp, and I am now writing this in my new house. I suppose you know the regiments have passed in review before General Lincoln, I mean President, the other day. He is yet here.

As it turned out, the action at Sewall's Point was the last time the *Merrimack/Virginia* sailed out to face the enemy. Union troops seized her port on May 10, forcing her to retreat up the shallow James River. She was destroyed early on the morning of May 11 to keep her from falling into Federal hands.

That same evening, **Andrew Lane (1841–1925),** a private in the 32nd Massachusetts Infantry, shared the news with his brother. Writing from a fort used as a prison for Confederate officers, he also mentioned the commanders captured at Forts Henry and Donelson in Tennessee 90 days earlier.

Fort Warren
Boston, Massachusetts
May 11, 1862

Good news tonight. Norfolk, Virginia, and the Portsmouth Navy Yard taken, the gunboat Merrimack *blown up, the* Yorktown *sunk, Jamestown also taken. They are giving it to them good.*

General John Dix was here the other day. He gave all prisoners but Generals Simon Bolivar Buckner and Lloyd Tilghman parole of the fort, so they can go anywhere they please until retreat [sounded at 5:00 p.m., when the colors were secured].

(Lane was mistaken about one thing: the steamer *Yorktown*, which the Confederates renamed the CSS *Patrick Henry*, was not sunk. It remained in use until it was destroyed when Richmond fell in 1865.)

The Union Navy was strengthening its blockade of Southern ports almost daily. As the Federal fleet grew, its stranglehold tightened on the incoming flow of European materiel imports the Confederates desperately needed to continue waging war.

Federal officers and sailors loved capturing blockade-runners because the steamer and its contents were later auctioned in naval prize courts, and the proceeds were divided among the crew. But sometimes, misunderstandings happened among the South Atlantic Blockading Squadron's ships. **Dr. Joseph Rodney Layton (1820–unknown),** an assistant surgeon, experienced one of them, as he told his father.

U.S.S. Steamer Flambeau
Off Charleston, South Carolina
May 11, 1862

We are now in full chase after a sidewheel steamer about 20 miles offshore, standing southeast. She looks very suspicious. I hope she may prove a prize. We are sure to catch her. (Nothing can outrun us in these waters—we are said to be the fastest ship in the Navy.) If she should prove a prize, it will be all our own as there are no other vessels in sight.

We are playing the deuce with the Rebel vessels trying to run the blockade. This appears to be the principal place for them now. Hardly a night or day passes without someone from the fleet taking or destroying one of them. We have taken or destroyed about 30 within the last five weeks. If they [blockade-runner captains] have the chance, they run them ashore. We then send in, burn, and sink them. So the loss is the same to the Rebels in either case, but different to us.

The latest news up to the 6th would tend one to believe that the rebellion is pretty well played out and that the war will soon be ended. I hope so. I, for one, am tired of it and being away from home. I begin to want to get home again badly and see my relations and friends again.

I suppose McClellan is in Richmond by this time. Our turn for the fun must come soon. The sooner, the better. We have 16 vessels in the fleet off here—13 of them steamers. The chance of a vessel getting in or out of the harbor is rather slim, though they occasionally slip in and out.

We exchanged a few shots yesterday morning with one of the Rebel gunboats. They did us no damage. We hit her three times and sent her back to Charleston with a flea in her ear. (We are not allowed to make public any movements or transactions down here by a late order from the Navy Department.) The ship trembles so from the press of steam in running fast, I can hardly write. My love to all.

P.S. We have just overhauled the steamer we have been in chase of for several hours. She proves to be one of our own vessels and said to be one of the fastest we have, but we were too much for her and almost ran her down. We are all disappointed, for we had been looking upon her for the last two hours as a prize. We were in chase of her for five hours. She acted very queer—it made our captain quite nasty. We ran nearly seventy miles after her and only had the excitement and pleasure of the chase for our trouble.

Back in Tennessee, the shockingly high casualties and near defeat at Shiloh for the Federals led to blistering press attacks on Grant. General Henry W. Halleck, commander of Union forces in the West, arrived and personally took command of the large Federal army assembled there. He essentially demoted Grant, then led his force on a painfully slow approach to the strategic rail center of Corinth, Mississippi.

There was much skirmishing, and on May 9, the Confederates attacked at nearby Farmington. Although on the field of battle for the first time, the 14th Texas Cavalry (Dismounted) was not directly engaged in the fighting that day. (Its baptism of fire would come two weeks later). Still, **J. H. Briscoe (unknown)**, a captain in the regiment, told his aunt how even coming close to combat was thrilling.

Camp Ashley
Near Corinth, Mississippi
May 15, 1862

We were marched to the battlefield and had a little round, each party 20 or 30 thousand strong. They posted in the brush, and we had to march through an open field to them, our artillery giving them gas all the time. But when our boys got close enough to open on them with double-barreled shotguns, they could not stand it for longer than an hour and all the running they did, making two forty time. Our regiment did not get a single fire but was close enough for the Yankee bullets to whistle around us. The boys were all keen for the dance as they called it. The Feds left large quantities of clothing on the ground, the best of their blankets and coats, and after the boys had helped themselves, they were burned.

I saw several of them that had been killed myself. The most of them had been killed by cannon shot. Lord Aunt, but the cannon did sing so prettily. You have no idea how it animates a fellow. He feels fight all over and don't care for the bullets. We are ready for the enemy all the time but do not know how soon the fight will become general. It may commence any hour. We keep three days rations cooked ahead all the time. I saw Dr. [and future General Richard] Gano the morning of the 9th. He was ordered to central Kentucky.

Halleck's army then dug in for a prolonged siege of Corinth. At month's end, Beauregard secretly slipped away overnight without a major battle. Captain **Don Carlos Newton (1832–1893)** of the 52nd Illinois Infantry dashed off the news to his wife.

Camp Near Corinth, Mississippi
May 30, 1862

The Rebs skedaddled from Corinth last night. We had been gradually surrounding them until they felt the cords draw too tight, and they left on the double quick. This morning at sunrise, they blowed up their works. We were laying on our arms in the woods, only two miles from the town and half a mile from their outer breastworks. Our pickets advanced into their breastworks, and in one-half hour, we had cavalry in Corinth. The report is that their works are very strong and would have bothered us a great deal had they obstinately defended it, but we should have killed hosts of them.

We march to Farmington today. I suppose General John Pope is hot after them. I have not much time to write. I have had no letter from you for six days.

After Corinth's capture, Grant was restored to command, and Halleck, known without affection as "Old Brains," was summoned to Washington to become the North's general-in-chief.

Just a week after Union troops entered Corinth, a brief but intense naval battle on the Mississippi enabled Federal forces to capture the river town of Memphis, Tennessee, giving them yet another important new base of operations.

Confederate forces fell back and regrouped in northern Mississippi. Conditions there were extremely bad, as 22-year-old Private **John Clayton (1840–unknown)** of the 39th Alabama Infantry described in a letter to his sister. Still, despite their desperate circumstances, the soldiers—many of whom were young—were often preoccupied by romantic and sometimes even sexual entanglements.

Itawamba County, Mississippi
June 16, 1862

We have had trials to encounter with here, sure. We have had nothing to eat this morning at all. Sis, I tell you, you live in a happy land to what this is sure. Sis, when I get home, I will tell you the destruction of this country. I can't write anything about it. We are needing rain very much at this time. The water that we have to drink here is very bad, sure. There is no crop here hardly at all. The soldiers tear things up. They kill the stock, steal the chickens and geese, sheep, goats, and everything else. Sis, I have always heard of hard times, but I never saw hard times before.

Sis, you said something about Sampson Renfro being called Pap. I told him about it. He laughed very hearty about his boy but did not deny it at all. Sis, must tell those girls back there to prepare themselves, for I am going to have some of them when I get home. Tell that bitch Sally Hildenhunt not to fret. Daggone fool, I wouldn't write to her again to save her life. She thinks she has now got me safe as a suitor [boyfriend]. She thinks that Jordan Davis is a good hard boy now, dang bitch. Sis, you must make her think that I love her and can't rest.

As the fighting raged, the U.S. Congress passed some of the most important legislation of the war years. In May, it approved the construction of a transcontinental railroad. That same month, it sent the Homestead Act to President Lincoln for his signature. That got 17-year-old farmer and shoemaker **James W. Griffith (1844–1934)** thinking about becoming a settler, as he suggested to his aunt and uncle. (Four months later, after turning 18, he was a private in the 117th Ohio Infantry.)

Youngsville, Ohio
June 1, 1862

My Western fever is somewhat increased. I was reading last night where the President signed the Homestead Bill that gives every man 160 acres of land if they will go and live on it for five years. So I would like to go and verify mine. Will you go along? I think we would stay now if we were in the West; as you say it takes two trips to satisfy some folks. Now don't write back to our friends that we are going West again. If you do, I will not tell you any more of my secrets.

The Army of the Potomac was finally in the field on the tip of Virginia's Peninsula, but it was moving at a snail's pace—when it moved at all. Although he commanded the largest American army ever assembled up to that time, McClellan believed that he faced a numerically superior foe. He spent April hauling heavy siege artillery into position at Yorktown in preparation for a massive bombardment on May 5. The Confederates received word that the assault was imminent and withdrew on May 3. On May 4, Union balloon reconnaissance found the Southern fortifications deserted.

A sharp but inconclusive battle the next day at Williamsburg, the campaign's first, saw the Southerners withdraw toward Richmond.

The Civil War was a transitional period in warfare. Often called the last of the old wars and the first of the modern, its many innovations included the use of reconnaissance balloon flights and what we know today as land and naval mines. Called "infernal devices" and "torpedoes," they were nothing like modern torpedoes fired from submarines. Their basic principle was the same as today's landmines. First appearing in the Peninsula Campaign, their use was controversial at the time.

Samuel Durant (1819–1862), a private in the 81st New York Infantry and an immigrant from England, recounted both to his adult daughter.

Virginia; location unknown
May 11, 1862

Sunday morning we started for the forts [at Yorktown]. The Rebels had all left. As we were going along, I heard a report [blast] like a cannon. I thought they was not gone. When I got a little farther, I saw a man lying there badly wounded. There was one killed and seven badly wounded. They had buried bomb shells in the road and all along where they thought we would go. As soon as you touch one of them, off they go. I said, "G. Van Patten, what's the matter?" He said, "See them shells buried? Mind you don't step on them." We had to be very careful.

We traveled all day through forts and rifle pits until night and then laid down in the rain. It rained all day and about all night. I was wet to the skin. My coat was so wet that I could barely carry it.

There was firing all day just ahead of us. In the morning, we marched around to get on the east side of them, but they was just one day too fast. They had to fight like the devil. They did fight too, I tell you. [Battle of Williamsburg] General McClellan was up in the balloon. He seen the Louisiana Tigers come out of the woods and put down the balloon. When he got there, they had cut them all to pieces. The officer gave up his sword and said "You have whipped the best regiment in the Confederate Army." It is a very large field, I should think 1,000 acres, with five forts and ditches, around 15 feet deep, they got in there. Our boys got on one shoulder and the gun in the other hand and away they run, throwed [wooden] rails across the ditch and over they went, driving them out.

They took some prisoners, but how many I don't know. I saw 150 wounded Rebels in one barn. That was on Wednesday night. The doctors cutting off legs and arms, some screaming all night. I couldn't sleep.

(Durant was wrong; though McClellan did ascend in a balloon once, the year before, to assess the value of early aerial reconnaissance, he never went up again. Durant died of chronic diarrhea four months later.)

McClellan followed the Confederates with glacial slowness. Still, the much-anticipated Federal advance was finally underway at last—a fact not lost on Corporal **Henry Scott Murray (1836–1905)** of the 8th New York Independent Light Artillery, who excitedly shared the news with his brother.

May 11, 1862
In camp near West Point, Virginia

On the way to Richmond

I now sit down to write you a few lines to let you know how we are all getting along on our way to Richmond. In my last letter, I told you we were then encamped on the battleground [Williamsburg] of last Monday. We remained there until Friday morning when we again started on the march, and this time it is "On to Richmond" in reality. It is no longer the feeble cry of a few aspiring politicians and newspaper editors, but it is now the order of the Commander in Chief of the great Army of the Potomac and, with him at its head, we are now moving slowly but surely to the city of Richmond—and, in a few days, we will be in possession of that great capital of the Southern Confederacy which so long has been the boasted stronghold of the Rebels, but which must soon fall before the onward march of this great army. And then, when the old Stars and Stripes are again floating in triumph over that rebellious city, we may consider this rebellion as nearly at an end. For with Yorktown and Richmond in the hands of the government, it will be impossible for them to make a stand anywhere in Virginia.

It is said that the Rebels are going to make a stand some 12 miles from Richmond and that they are now throwing up fortifications and making every preparation for a desperate battle. But very likely it will turn out like Yorktown; when our forces are ready to make an attack, they will evacuate for I think from the appearance of their forts in front of Yorktown that if they could not make a stand in such forts, it will be impossible for them to build stronger forts before this army reaches there.

We passed through Williamsburg on our way here. It is a small village, and everything in it gave evidence of a hasty retreat. In the streets were to be seen wagons, forges, and ammunition chests having stuck in the mud and were set on fire or cut to pieces to prevent them from falling into our hands. Horses and mules were lying on the road dead this side of Williamsburg, and as we came along, we met several who had deserted from them, and they say that Rebel soldiers are getting disheartened and are almost in a state of mutiny.

I have seen hundreds of acres of wheat, and we can't find room enough to encamp unless we go into a wheat field. It looks rather bad to see so much fine grain destroyed, but it belongs to Secesh, so of course, it must go. Every house we come to, there is a white rag stuck out as a protection, and no one is allowed to take anything that belongs to them. But our boys will not pass by corn without helping themselves for they must have feed for the horses.

The roads are getting very dusty. McClellan is here, and he will not let his army march on Sunday as he does not consider it necessary.

McClellan's army crept up the Peninsula amid increasingly heavy fighting as Johnston grudgingly fell back.

Meanwhile, Stonewall Jackson was staying remarkably busy in the Shenandoah Valley. Over the course of 48 days, his little 17,000-man army marched some 650 miles, fought several pitched battles, and defeated three separate Federal armies totaling nearly 55,000 men.

On May 23, Jackson captured the garrison at Front Royal, forcing Union General Nathaniel Banks to retire. Banks was then defeated in the First Battle of Winchester on May 25, with Jackson pursuing the retreating Federals until they crossed the Potomac.

The news caused much distress when it reached McClellan's army, even as it sat poised on the outskirts of its objective. As **John Boultwood Edson (1839–1863),** a private in the 27th New York Infantry, told his father, the Confederate capital was now literally within sight.

Mechanicsville, Virginia
May 28, 1862

It will not be many days before we'll be in Richmond, being only five miles from there. The steeples of the different churches can be seen by getting on a high piece of ground or on the top of a house. You will soon hear of a big battle near Richmond.

Last evening, we heard for the first time of General Banks' retreat back across the Potomac. It had a tendency to depress to some degree the minds of the boys, but I have full confidence in the strong arm of the North. This affair of Banks will no doubt prolong the war for a few weeks longer than it would have lasted had this misfortune not happened. Some here think it a plan to draw Stonewall Jackson away from these parts and keep him from reinforcing the Rebels in our front.

We have a very powerful army directly in front of us, and we have to be on the watch constantly. We have to arise an hour before sunrise and remain under arms until daylight to prevent a surprise. Our regiment expects to go out on picket tonight, where we will be within 60 rods of them. Our regiment is in the advance now. I shall not probably write again until we are in Richmond.

Denied the reinforcements that he had been promised (and that he had counted on to overcome the phantom Confederate superiority that existed only in his mind), McClellan now believed that Washington was conspiring to ensure his defeat. But he suddenly faced a much bigger problem than that, one he had not foreseen. Just as the Army of the Potomac inched its way to Richmond's very outskirts, the campaign took a dramatic turn.

On the last day of May and the first day of June, Johnston attacked. The Battle of Seven Pines (or Fair Oaks) was brutally contested and was the war's second-bloodiest engagement up to that time. Young **George W. Fernald (1840–1918),** a private in the 82nd New York Infantry, told his cousin in New York City about it. He also detailed the ugly reality of a battle's aftermath.

Seven Pines, Virginia
June 2, 1862

We have just had another bloody battle within seven miles of Richmond. The enemy attacked our advance on Friday and were driven back. On Saturday, they got reinforcements and drove our advance in. So we were ordered to the front and marched about four miles at the double quick step, and we had about one hour's hard fighting. We drove the enemy back but had to sleep on the battlefield with the dead and wounded, which you know was not very pleasant.

Yesterday, we were ordered down to support the Irish Brigade. We have not had anything to eat but a few crackers since we left camp on Saturday. It makes me sick to see the battlefield, for it is covered with the dead and wounded. The dead are beginning to bloat and smell bad, but I hope they will soon be buried and the wounded cared for. The enemy retreated last night to Richmond. We have not heard what our loss is yet, but it is heavy, while that of the enemy is still heavier. I think the loss in our regiment is about fifty.

Please excuse this as I wrote it on my cartridge box and am very tired.

Even while troops were on the move in the field, the amount of military paperwork produced daily was staggering. Consider what confronted **John Hancock Boyd Jenkins (1840–1906),** a private in the 40th New York Infantry, in the aftermath of Seven Pines. As he explained to his girlfriend, all that work put him behind on his personal writing.

On picket before Kearny's Division
Near Richmond, Virginia
June 19, 1862

I was prevented from writing sooner through a press of work, owing to my being the only thoroughly trained clerk in the regiment. The work of prepar-

ing the list of killed and wounded, the reports of the commanding officers of the regiment and brigade, with duplicates for Gov. Edwin Morgan of New York and triplicates and quadruplicates for Tom, Dick, and Harry fell upon me, and besides that, there was a voluminous correspondence of Col. Thomas Egan's which had to be copied in quadruple, so that seven days or more were occupied, three in getting settled in camp after the fight, and four in doing up all the writing.

While the Battle of Seven Pines was a tactical draw, with both sides claiming victory, it brought McClellan's offense to a grinding halt. More important, a single rifle shot during the fighting changed the entire direction of the war.

Confederate commander Joseph E. Johnston was severely wounded on May 31. His replacement, General Robert E. Lee, was Johnston's exact opposite. Bold, daring, and aggressive, Lee was not afraid to take a chance and attack against long odds. He took command on June 1, promptly renaming his force the Army of Northern Virginia and plunging into plans to drive McClellan all the way back to Fortress Monroe.

Combat was transforming soldiers from raw recruits into hardened veterans. But as this letter, written to his father by an **unidentified soldier** in the 85th New York Infantry, reveals, the men were also growing accustomed to the little daily occurrences of life in the field.

Gaines Mill, Virginia
June 10, 1862

Nothing of any account is going on just now. Our troops are building bridges across the Chickahominy River, some of them under fire of the Rebels. I would not be surprised if we were not ordered to march inside of a month yet. I think that McClellan is going to give them another Yorktown full [siege]. We had a grand review yesterday before those foreign officers, etc. that go around with General McClellan. It was a splendid sight.

    This is the prettiest and best farm that I have ever seen. About 8,000 acres of land. The owner was caught trying to signal the Rebels the other day. (The chance is for a shooting match.) He said, "You can bury all of the Rebel soldiers you like on my farm but no damned Yankees can be buried on it. If you do bury any of them, I will dig them up and throw them in the street." He is under strong guard, not allowed to go out of his house. His barns, etc. are used for hospitals.

Albert Turner's being drummed out of the regiment is all a hoax. Our Parrot guns are playing on the Rebels now.

Throughout the war, the tales of battle that officers and men related in their letters home frequently made their way into the local newspaper. For example, the colonel of the 11th Maine Infantry reported how "men were being shot on all sides of me" in the Battle of Seven Pines. But that didn't ring true with **Albert Greenleaf Mudgett (1826–1903),** a first lieutenant in the same regiment, who recounted a much different version of the fighting to his family.

Camp near Seven Pines, Virginia
June 25, 1862

I suppose that you saw Col. Harris Plaisted's report of that immortal ninety men who went out to fight and was half killed and wounded. But as near as I can learn, they were nearly all wounded in the back. The colonel was behind a large pine stump, so you see he was safe. He ordered the major down the line to make them fire low, so the major walked up and down the line and gave the command, "Fire low! Fire low!" The line of ninety in two ranks would be near 75 feet. The poor man's lungs must have been weak in order to make them hear. Every man that he puffed so high in his report are the fastest runners we have got in the regiment. I was not there, but Mel says that when they run, the colonel started ahead and that the bravest men overtook him—or the best runners.

Our regiment don't amount to much anyway. There is not over 150 effective men in it. They worked them to death before we got here. Our regiment had to go ahead and take all the hard knocks and it used the men up.

In the Shenandoah Valley, Jackson's Valley Campaign came to a spectacular conclusion with Union defeats at Cross Keys and Port Republic, clearing the last of the combined 55,000 Federals from Virginia's vital breadbasket. Not only had those forces been diverted from helping McClellan's move on Richmond as originally planned, but their defeat convinced Lincoln to keep other Union troops stationed in Washington—troops that had also been promised to McClellan—to defend the capital.

Writing from the Union base at Manassas following the campaign's conclusion, **Jesse Hughes (1839–1864),** a corporal in the 1st Pennsylvania Cavalry, described its closing chapters to a friend, though he didn't seem to realize that his side had lost.

Camp of the Regiment
Near Manassas, Virginia
June 24, 1862

Well, Billy, we have been having some fun since I last wrote you and pretty hard fun. We had a hard chase after Old Jackson but couldn't catch him. He could run too fast for us but General George Bayard's Flying Brigade made him git up the valley on double quick time. It was the hardest trip that we ever had. We had three or four fights with him.

Our brigade led the advance up the valley. There was 123 of the Bucktails [13th Regiment, Pennsylvania Reserve Infantry] fought three regiment of Rebels. The Bucktails had 7 killed and 42 wounded. The Rebels left 56 dead on the field, and we could not tell how many they wounded, for they took them away with them. The Bucktails fought till they was surrounded and cut their way out.

Col. Thomas Kane was taken prisoner and Capt. Taylor, too. That fight was on Friday [Harrisonburg], and the big fight was on Sunday [Cross Keys]. Our brigade was not in the battle. The woods was so thick that we could not do anything but we was close to it. The shells and cannon balls make very nice music flying around a feller's head. The Bucktails was in again. They made Rebels fall. It was a hard sight to go over the field after the battle was over. We had 125 killed and about 400 wounded. The Rebels had 275 killed. That is, they left that many on the field. They took all their wounded, and we could not tell how many they had, but they had a good many more than we had. It was a pretty hard battle. We drove them on the right, and they drove our men back on the left.

The battle commenced at 11 o'clock and lasted till dark. It was just one roar of cannons all the time. We marched over the field the next day. It was the hardest sight that I ever seen to see some men dead and some dying. Some had one of their legs shot off, and some had both of their legs off. I seen one man that had his head all shot off with a cannon ball. It is hard to see the way that they buried them, but it can't be helped where there is so many killed.

During the night Old Jackson left and as soon as it got light we took after him again and run him to Port Republic where he crossed the river and burnt the bridge and there he met a part of General James Shields' force and drove them back and got out but if Col. Samuel Carrol had a burnt the bridge before Jackson crossed, General John C. Fremont would have of took his [Jackson's] whole army. But he wanted to get a big name and so he tried to hold it and got his men all cut to pieces and let Jackson get out. Some of Carrol's men had to swim the river to get away. Fremont could not get across the river, and so we had to turn back again after running him 90 miles. We took 600 prisoners.

We are laying at Manassas now for a few days to rest. Our horses was all run down. There was a good many of our horses that was run to death.

We expect to march soon again but I can't tell where we will go to. I heard that they have you to Richmond. I think that the battle there will end the war. I guess that we will go there the next trip.

Jackson and his troops were summoned from the Shenandoah Valley, and then Lee went on the attack. In a series of engagements from June 25 to July 1 known as the Seven Days Battles, he forced McClellan to retrace his steps. Suddenly finding themselves fighting defense, many Union soldiers were perplexed by the abrupt turn of events, as an **unknown soldier** explained to his wife.

Camp near City Point, Virginia
July 5, 1862

You have heard more about what has transpired in the army this last week than I can begin to tell you. All I know about it is there has been some very queer movements made—and some very hard battles fought—and instead of us taking Richmond, we have marched away from it. Our generals pretend to say that it is strategy, but for my part I can't see the point.

On last Saturday afternoon [June 28], one of Stackhouse's boys come into our camp and told us some of the awfullest stories about General McClellan getting defeated on the right [Gaines Mill]. He belongs to the Pennsylvania Reserves. He said that they had an awful battle and that Jackson came in and cut off our supplies and that we had been outflanked and badly whipped. Our colonel heard him tell his story and then cleared him out of the camp. His story created a regular panic among us, and the men were almost crazy. Well, we got orders to march at 3 in the morning [June 29] and everything that we could not carry we were to destroy, which made things look very strange indeed. The officers cut their tents all up, broke their trunks all to pieces, and many a good uniform was destroyed. And the worst of all, we had to burn all of our provisions that we could not carry. We had piles of it as high as a house. I suppose we had $100,000 [$3.6 million today] worth of it.

Well, we left our camp and fortification and marched about a mile when the enemy nearly surrounded us and we had to halt and fight him [Savage's Station]. We whipped them badly, and we run clear out of sight, and then we started on our march again which was about 3 o'clock in the afternoon and we were not disturbed again that day. The next morning [June 30], we started about daylight and marched about one mile, and then we halted to cover the retreat so as to fetch off our baggage wagons and artillery. The enemy made his appearance again in large force about 2 in the afternoon, and we had a hard fight [Glendale/Frayser's Farm] until 9 at night when we whipped them again and then retreated again. The enemy came after us hotfoot, and we had to stand and fight again. We were exposed to a very hot fire all day but whipped them again and took 2 batteries and a whole brigade prisoners.

The next morning, we started again and marched all day without any disturbance and encamped within a half mile of the James River and near City Point. The enemy attacked us [Malvern Hill], and we whipped him again and took 2 guns and 800 prisoners. And now they are not to be seen. I think we will cross the James River and wait and get reinforcements and then take Richmond.

The sense of confusion within Union ranks was echoed in a letter written the same day by a Federal soldier named **C. F. Bennett (unknown; regiment unknown)** to his mother.

Camp of the First Brigade, Hooker's Division
Near James River, Virginia
July 5, 1862

We have been making some great movements since I wrote you. We left Fair Oaks a week ago and have been marching or fighting ever since. We have been in three fights within 10 days. Our colonel was killed in the last fight and the lieutenant and adjutant wounded. I am all right; have not been hit so far.

We had to march 15 or 20 miles to get here, through one of the worst roads you can imagine. It rained all one day and night, and that made it ten times worse and the Rebels close at our heels, everything in confusion, wagons stuck in the road, men hollering and shouting, yelling, and mules braying. If a wagon got stuck and they could not get it out, they would smash up the wagon and the stuff that was in it, no matter what it was, to make room for the others.

We stopped one night in a big cornfield, a hundred acres I should think. The corn was about two foot high, and it was raining then. After we had been there an hour, it was just like hasty pudding, a foot deep and not a blade of corn to be seen. The wheat is all cut here and stacked up in the fields. Wherever we stop, the men take to themselves as much as they want. I have got four or five bundles under me now. It seems too bad to waste it so, but the owners have left and there is no one to look after it.

They say we are going to have a rest now. I hope we will, we need it bad enough. The whole army is pretty well played out. Our division covered the retreat most all of the way here. I hope this may be a good move, but there is an awful lot of stuff destroyed. Stores of all kinds, clothing, arms, ammunition, and everything we could not bring with us. There is not five men in our brigade that has got a second shirt. The last fight we were in lasted till dark, and we took off our knapsacks before we went in, and when we came out, we came another way and there was no time to go back for them. General Ambrose Burnside's troops are coming [from North Carolina], I believe. I hope this will be a good move of McClellan's, but I don't know.

Malvern Hill was the final battle of the Peninsula Campaign and marked the conclusion of the Seven Days fighting. The Army of the Potomac amassed most of its 171 cannons, supported by those of three gunboats on the nearby James River, on the hilltop to beat back poorly coordinated attacks.

Charles S. Cockett (1835–1888), a sergeant in the 70th New York Infantry, detailed the powerful superiority of Federal artillery to a friend.

Camp Near Harrison's Landing, Virginia
July 31, 1862

The Battle of Malvern Hill was the most magnificent (though terrible) sight that I ever witnessed. The fight was continued until between 9 and 10 o'clock in the evening. We had over 100 pieces of cannon playing upon the enemy in addition to the gunboats. After it became dark, we had the grandest exhibition of fireworks ever I saw. The country all around was lit up by the shells streaking and bursting through the air. The groaning of canister, the groans of the wounded, the yells of the graybacks (as we call them) made such a scene and sight as I never wish to see again.

We were thrown forward under cover of our guns to form a picket line. I would gladly have quit were it possible. I cannot tell you how we felt marching slowly along while a perfect shower of shells was being thrown over us to drive them back until we had established the line. We could not hear an order, there was such a deafening roar all the time. After we had established the line, the artillery ceased, and then came the groans of the wounded and dying, which were scattered through the woods in heaps. Some calling for water, some cursing and swearing because they were not taken in. But it was an absolute impossibility to do anything for them, and there we had to leave them to get along as best they might.

Oh John, that was an awful night. The men were so tired and exhausted that they could not be kept awake hardly and what few officers and non-commissioned officers there were kept busy walking up and down the lines, punching and kicking to keep them awake. Nothing but the firmest determination of both men and officers could have saved us through those terrible 7 days of hard fighting.

McClellan's campaign loss was a stinging rebuke to the Federals in general and himself personally. Far to the south, Private **Frederick Gallup (1841–1922)**, 8th Connecticut Infantry, was among the forces in Burnside's command that were quickly summoned from the North Carolina coast by sea to reinforce the Army of the Potomac. Writing to a friend, he didn't hesitate to place blame for the defeat.

On Board the Steamer Admiral
Nearing Fortress Monroe
July 7, 1862

The reverses of McClellan undoubtedly is the cause of this sudden movement of ours. On July 3 we were marched down to the depot expecting to go on board. While we were waiting for the steamer to get in readiness, an engine alone came helter-skelter down from Newbern, North Carolina, bringing the important and highly interesting news that the left wing of Mac's army were resting in Richmond and countermanding our orders. Then, we were detained in Morehead for further orders. We reckoned there was something up, that all was not right at Richmond.

Since coming on the boat, I have learned that the left wing of our army was only engaged and that it was compelled to fall as far back as the James

River. We are going to help McClellan, help him to retrieve his immense loss. It seems that there was treachery somewhere. McClellan must soon retrieve his loss or his reputation—his name which he has gained—will be gone.

Still, I have confidence in him. He has been badly whipped—awfully whipped—and this whipping which we have had to take will put the war back a full six months. You need not expect me at home as soon by six months as you did before the Rebels whipped us. I blame McClellan in that he has not moved sooner but waited until they had completely impregnably entrenched themselves. Where we will be a month from now is uncertain.

Likewise, folks on the Northern home front were also trying to understand what had gone wrong. This letter, written by an **unknown civilian** to a friend, was typical of many who were perplexed.

Columbus, Ohio
July 24, 1862

What a terrible series of battles those were the last week in June on the Peninsula. And what did they result in? It appears to me that it was a defeat for us, however much the movement of the right wing may be lauded by McClellan's particular friends. It was a hazardous undertaking, and had he not been sorely pressed, he never would have resorted to so perilous an expedient. It may have been a great bargain for the U.S., but it was rather costly. 15,000 men were slain, wounded, or captured and when we had done fighting were 35 miles farther from Richmond than before. I confess that my confidence in the general commanding is not so strong as before, and I think that the facts in the case warrant such lack or loss of opinion.

I do not know who we can look to among men in our country to lead us in the contest if McClellan is not the man. He promised that he would not hesitate till he "drove the enemy to the wall," but has he not done the first and consequently failed in the second? I hope most sincerely that he will be successful, but fear that he will not.

There seems to be a great want [lack] of dash, snap, vim, or any other term you choose to apply to the characteristic that you as well I can see that he is deficient in. Beauregard or Stonewall have that quality if they have no other. John Pope has more of it, I think, than any other of our commanders, and it has done more to give him success than anything else, I believe. How is recruiting progressing in your township?

Far away from the field of battle, soldiers who were stationed on garrison duty confronted a different enemy: boredom. The daily routine rarely varied, and monotony ruled. Some soldiers who were posted at a fortification in Baltimore found a unique—and communal—way to relax, according to this letter from an **unknown Federal officer** to his sisters.

Fort Federal Hill
Baltimore, Maryland
June 10, 1862

The fort is on a high hill, overlooking and commanding the whole of Baltimore, so if the Secesh happen to kick up a row, this fort should soon burn the city. The boys found this place in the most filthy condition, the barracks even like pig sties, and it was necessary to first hoe and shovel out the dirt, and then go back to work and clean house. The place is now pretty clean.

One of the greatest institutions in the place is the Company Pipe. On the center of the parade is a tree which has had a branch cut off about four feet from the ground; the end has rotted in a little ways in the center, which the company cleaned out and then bored through the side of the butt, and inserted seven flexible pipe stems, and seven men squat around and all smoke the same pipe. It excites a great deal of interest. I have tried it and pronounced it good.

As usual, the staff are very comfortable. We have a room in the officers' quarters and are very comfortably situated. The rest of the staff all laugh at me because I will bunk on the floor with nothing but my blanket. I thought it might be just as well to get used to it before they sent us where we could not get mattresses.

Other soldiers used humor to offset their boredom. Private **Lewis Capet Shephard (1841–1919)** of the 11th New York Infantry (who went on to receive the Medal of Honor for valor at Fort Fisher, North Carolina, three years later) was on hand when Lincoln, Secretary of State William Seward, and General Samuel Sturgis inspected forts and encampments around the federal capital. Starting off with a serious account in his letter to some friends, he slipped into satire and exaggeration to get a laugh (including mentioning a daughter Lincoln didn't have; the recipients would have got the joke).

Camp Sturgis
Outside Washington, D.C.
August 5, 1862

We had a great review here by the President. Here where we are encamped, there is as much as 2,000 acres of smooth pastureland, so you see it is a beautiful place for a review. At 3:00 o'clock, the old Rail Splitter made his appearance. Then, Fort Ward fired a salute of 31 guns, and the troops began to shout and such a racket you never heard. It made the chills run down my back and my hair stand up on end. Stub says it was the same with him.

Now, I will proceed to give you a description of Old Abe. He was dressed like some old tablecloth peddler, an old alpaca loose coat, a two-story stove pipe, black pants that reached just below the knees, and he rode an old skeleton of a horse without any stirrups to the saddle, and when he rode, he locked his toes under the horse. When he wanted to dismount, he stretched his legs down and drove the horse from under him. When he got in front of the battalion and the boys were shouting so he jerked off his old tarpaulin in front like some little urchin going into the school room. It was so warm and he sweat so that the starch was taken out of his shirt collar on one side, and it lopped down over his shoulder, and the other one stood up to his ear so sharp that in consequence thereof he rode sideways. His daughter and wife was here likewise. I went and shook hands with his daughter and asked her how she did. She said she did very well, only she was pining away because I did not come over and see her oftener. I told her how the captain would not sign my pass. Well, I will stop until we come in from drill.

It is now 10:00 o'clock, and it is hot enough to roast oil out of a stone. There is not a tree to get under here. We either have to sit in the tents and roast and be eaten by the flies or go outdoors and bake until our hair falls off. Excuse this language, but the fact of it is I have been so long from society that I don't know how to speak, act, or write fact, by gracious. Well, I must stop for dinner, which consists of the following articles to wit: fried steak, potatoes, onions, tomatoes, bread, and water. You see we fare hard as ever. O yes, applesauce sweetened with molasses and boiled beets in vinegar.

Conflicts weren't limited to the battlefield. Or even to land. Consider what happened when businessman Clement Dennington took his wife and teenage daughter to Europe. The elegant British steamer SS *Great Eastern*'s large passenger manifest included Northerners and some Confederates.

1862

Clementine Dennington (1846–1924) told her younger brother back in Brooklyn about high tension on the high seas.

London, England
August 12, 1862

On Friday evening, we had a ball which was given by the captain in the second dining saloon. The tables were all removed, and the band was stationed in the corner. It commenced at nine, had supper at eleven, and broke up a little before two. The room was decorated with American flags. There was a great uproar made by some of the secessionists who would not go into the room but stayed in the grand saloon. They wanted the Federal flag taken down and the Confederate flag put up in its place. They drank and shouted like wild Indians, and the captain came in three times and spoke to them. Some of the passengers were frightened and were afraid there would be trouble with them before morning.

Frustrated by McClellan's failure to capture Richmond, Lincoln ordered General John Pope, the victor at Island Number 10, to Virginia. He took command of a new force called the Army of Virginia. Confident to the point of arrogance, he issued a condescending general order to his men that proclaimed, "Let us understand each other; I have come to you from the West, where we have always seen the backs of our enemies." It was datelined "Headquarters in the Saddle," prompting the joke that Pope's "headquarters are where his hindquarters should be." Supposedly, even Lincoln and Robert E. Lee ridiculed the phrase. Needless to say, Pope's braggadocio did not instill confidence.

On August 4, McClellan was ordered to move the Army of the Potomac to Aquia Creek Landing in central Virginia, where it could both defend Washington and be positioned to assist Pope. However, in the appalling slowness that had become McClellan's trademark, the bulk of the army was still on the Peninsula two weeks later.

McClellan would have to rely on the same fleet of private watercraft to return him to the Virginia mainland that had conveyed his enormous army to the Peninsula five months earlier. The War Department had under contract the services of 113 steamboats, 188 schooners, and 88 barges to transport and supply the Army of the Potomac.

That included the steamboat *Swan*, whose captain, **Samuel Prior Jr. (unknown)**, wondered what the future held with the campaign winding down. He also shared with his son his low opinion of the army's commander.

York River
Opposite Yorktown, Virginia
August 18, 1862

We are now drifting about at Yorktown. Last night at 10 o'clock we were ordered to proceed immediately to this place. We took a schooner in tow and, with a government pilot on board, left Hampton Roads at 12 midnight. Arrived at Yorktown at 8:30 and here we are waiting for General McClellan and staff. We waited until 12 o'clock when the steamship Pensacola *arrived especially for him. The* Swan *soon became small potatoes. So here we are. I went in the* Seth Low *with McClellan and his staff to the* Pensacola, *and that was as much of his company as I desire until he proves he can do something in the way of breaking down this rebellion.*

Hooker and Sumner's Divisions have been arriving all afternoon from Harrison's Landing. The distance, I should think, was about 50 miles. It was said 35,000 of McClellan's forces had gone to Fortress Monroe. I think fully 50,000 have arrived here since we anchored. The presumption is they will be sent to Aquia Creek Landing on the Potomac to join Burnside and that boats and vessels will take them from here in a day or two.

After the army gets up the Potomac, I should think two or three hundred steamboats would be discharged. If so, we may be among the number. Or it may be we shall be used here until the latter part of September and then sent down the coast to South Carolina. All is uncertainty, all is inexplicable.

Wednesday morning, Aug. 20th. We still lay at anchor in York River.

A vague uneasiness began passing through Union ranks. Private **Robert Alexander Hubbel (1833–1868),** 14th New York Infantry, revealed to his parents a belief shared by his comrades that something wasn't quite right.

On the Rappahannock River
Camp near Falmouth Station, Virginia
August 21, 1862

Burnside's forces are here. Have been here five or six days. Pope is somewhere around here, but cannot tell where, nor any but those high in authority know what is up. Certain it is, however, that action is at hand and in my opinion, we lack something. Let that something be troops or generals.

Our men are a worn-out lot of troops, you may guess, after such fatiguing marches through the hot sun and burning sands of this land. Stragglers are continually coming in, almost gone in. Several are fallen back from our company but will be picked up by the rear guard and shoved forward.

We were led to Newport News, from where we were shipped on board the steamer John Warner *and sleeping aboard that night, arrived at Aquia Creek where we were crowded aboard the [railroad] cars coming 12 miles to Falmouth Station the night before last where we are camped. For how long a time is more than I can tell.*

As Federal soldiers tried to discern what was missing, Lee sensed a strategic opportunity. The bulk of McClellan's army remained encamped on the Peninsula, licking its wounds while Pope and other Federal commands were scattered around northern Virginia. If Lee's army could reach them before McClellan could reinforce them, a Confederate victory might be within reach.

So he sent Stonewall Jackson's troops rapidly marching northward. The Yankees were in hot pursuit, as **Andrew Lane (1841–1925),** a private in the 32nd Massachusetts Infantry, reported in a letter to his father.

Near Manassas Gap, Virginia
August 28, 1862

We have been on the march for a fortnight tonight. We have been all over Virginia, and now we are getting to where we started from in the first place. We are following up Stonewall Jackson. He is close ahead of us. We are stopped tonight, where they had a fight yesterday [Kettle Run]. Sigel fought him. There was one hundred of men killed and wounded, there are about seventy dead Rebels lying about the field, not buried yet, and there are four houses full of wounded Rebels. The Rebels retreated to Manassas.

Here is the army, and Banks and Burnside's here; Pope is somewhere. They think that they've got Jackson penned in. The Rebels burned a railroad bridge and lots of cars and two engines [Catlett's Station] after they crossed. I expect we should have a fight before long now, but there is any quantity of troops ahead of us. I can hear cannonading now, eight or ten miles off. Our brigade is pretty well jacked out, for they have marched night and day.

The cannon fire that Lane heard was the opening action that led to the Battle of Second Bull Run/Manassas, as explained in this dramatic letter written by a highly placed but **unidentified Union staff officer** to his mother.

Washington, D.C.
August 30, 1862

Three or four days ago, the Rebel army got in Pope's rear, burnt all the bridges to within eight miles of Alexandria, and severely frightened the few who knew the real facts of the case, the public supposing it was a mere raid.

Fighting has been in progress for nearly a week, and yesterday, an immense battle was fought. Up to 4:00 p.m., neither party had gained any advantage, our forces being 80,000 and the Confeds 50,000. It is probable the fight will, or rather has been, renewed today. Uncle George is there. If you do not receive a telegraph from me, you may be sure he is alright.

The battle is being fought almost on the same ground of the Battle of Bull Run.

We (Col. Rucker and I) worked until after 2:00 this morning, so you will please excuse my shaky hand—I have for three nights been called up from two to four times each night.

Don't believe Pope's official dispatches—when he tells the truth, he does so accidentally.

Do not credit a word you see in the newspapers as correspondents are excluded from the army and write as facts the street rumors current in this city.

That officer's low opinion of newspaper reporters was widely shared in the ranks. In his letter from June mentioned earlier, **John Hancock Boyd Jenkins (1840–1906)**, a clerk in the 40th New York Infantry, didn't hold back how he felt about journalists.

I suppose that Birney's Brigade will "ketch it again" in the newspapers. A general who presumes to clip the wings of "our special correspondent" and kicks him out of camp for impertinence rarely gets a "first-rate notice," and they whip him at a distance accordingly, caring nothing for the injustice done to the brave boys who fight and die under him. These correspondents brag up their bravery in procuring news, and to believe them, they are always ahead of the troops, bearing down on the enemy with rampant quills. But the truth is just about what Joe says in the letter I received from him today. He says, "These newspaper correspondents hang around the tail end of the army and collect news from the 'cut to pieces' crowd, and then send home a flowery report of the whole engagement."

He just about hits it. Those artists and correspondents care just as much for their bacon as anybody, and it is only when political reports come in that the regiments and other bodies who do the real fighting come in for their share of the credit. But this only makes us despise the papers more and more, and care more in exact proportion for the approval of our commanders. Anyone of us would give more for one good word from General McClellan than for a whole armload of newspaper puffs.

Don't place any reliance on newspaper stories of misbehavior by General David Birney or his troops. Wait for the official reports, and you will then see.

When the Battle of Second Bull Run/Manassas was over, Pope had been soundly defeated. As night fell, his troops limped off to the north—though in a far more orderly manner than the Union withdrawal from the same field 13 months earlier (the utter rout following First Bull Run/Manassas).

Days later, Stonewall Jackson attacked at Chantilly, Virginia, hoping to cut off the Union line of retreat. Although he did not stop the withdrawal, the Federals sustained heavy casualties and lost two division commanders in the fighting. One of them, the one-armed warrior Major General Philip Kearny, was described in the same letter from **John Hancock Boyd Jenkins**.

General Kearny claims to have the fighting division and calls us the "fighting brigade," and I do not think he would compliment a parcel of cowards or slow coaches. You ought to see him in a great battle some day. I really believe he loves it, for he goes galloping around through the thickest of the fire, his eyes shining and his face lighted up as if it was a first-rate thing.

As his armies' fortunes lagged, Lincoln came to realize that more Union troops were needed. On July 1, he had urgently called for another 300,000 volunteers to fill Federal ranks. Each state was given a quota of men to supply; those that did not meet it were authorized to make up the difference by drafting. That call led to Stephen Foster penning a highly popular song, "We Are Coming Father Abra'am (300,000 More)." That, plus the recent reversals on the battlefield, motivated thousands of Northern men to respond.

Twenty-four-year-old **Lewis Morris Cleaver (1837–1925)** of Centerville, Pennsylvania, wrote to a cousin about his upcoming enlistment as a private in the 140th Pennsylvania Infantry.

East Bethlehem, Pennsylvania
August 6, 1862

In the call for 300,000 more soldiers, I am one of the number. An officer from Harrisburg will be here in a few days and locate a camp in Washington County. Walter Cleaver and Jefferson Cleaver go with me. Also, Charles and Eli Linton, Austin Richards, David Ruble, William Horton, and others. I think we can raise our quota in our county without drafting, but it will only be by shouldering the musket and marching at once. I know what camp life is, and I am ready for whatever comes.

By the summer of 1862, the Confederacy had begun drafting men for military service. In the North, states that failed to meet their troop quotas began doing likewise. Much as happened during the Vietnam War a century later, some men avoided compulsory service by fleeing to Canada. An **unknown Southern-born New Yorker** replied to his aunt in Canada, who had offered to shelter the man's son.

New York City
August 30, 1862

Your truly kind and affectionate letter reached me, and one and all return our sincere thanks for your kindness in inviting my son James to your house. But we find that companies, in all likelihood, in Jersey City, New Jersey, will be made up without drafting. In fact, the bounty that had been offered, $150 [$5,500 now] with a pension also for the family of the volunteer, has induced many an unfortunate white to come forth. Besides, James has a situation [job] in a highly respectable [banking] house that promises well for his future welfare, and if he were to leave the city, he would have to give up his situation. I have also understood that armed soldiers are stationed along the line to prevent anyone from going into Canada from the States. So you see, if we had sent James to you, they would have sent him back. I trust in God all will go well with him, for as I have said before, they can drag him to prison, but they can never make him take up a gun against the South.

Let me thank you again, my dear Aunt, for your goodness, and may God bless you and help you in this World and in the World to come.

You ask me if any of our relatives have been killed or wounded in the recent battles. None that I know of. You remember Hodge Pinkney. He had two grandsons killed in the last battle, young men of 19 and 21. I will try and send you the Charleston paper that I saw, and you will see some old family names that will be familiar to you. It is refreshing to find that your heart is with the South and that you are against this Black Republican Abolition War.

With certain Northern states now drafting, people who traveled extensively sometimes carried papers with them as a precaution, as this letter shows.

Cleveland, Ohio
August 12, 1862

This is to certify that Sherburn. P. Blake of the age of 37 years, complexion light, height 5 feet 5 inches, and now desiring to leave this district for the purpose of proceeding to Toledo, Ohio, is known to me, and I am satisfied from due proofs that he is a loyal citizen and that his said intended journey is legitimate and necessary and with no purpose to avoid being drafted into the military service of the United States.

> *Edward Bell*
> *United States Marshal*
> *Northern District of Ohio*

To meet their enlistment quotas and avoid imposing a draft in their state, many Northern cities began offering large cash bounties to recruits. This, in turn, enticed the unscrupulous to take advantage of it. After barely 90 days in uniform, **George Granville Nichols (1836–1899)**, a sergeant in the 42nd Massachusetts Infantry, had witnessed the shady side of recruiting and explained to his father how it worked.

Boston, Massachusetts
September 24, 1862

I have a chance to see the corruption carried on in the business, and as we advance on, more will come to light. Some towns pay $200 bounty. They *have agents around Boston who pick up aliens [foreign immigrants] and enlist them. They give them $100 and keep the other half. Sometimes, they pay $125. The police make a good thing of it by getting a man drunk and threaten to send him to jail, or he must enlist. Then they take him to some office, pass him [enlist him], get $25 for the man, and send him off to camp.*

While the home fronts, Northern and Southern alike, were busily engaged in supporting the war effort, it was a totally different story in the Border States. Loyalties there were still bitterly divided. Railroad contractor **Elisha Q. Harding (1818–1863)** witnessed the transformation himself as he rode the rails from the North to the Border territory and told his wife about it.

St. Louis, Missouri
August 31, 1862

I arrived here last evening. In traveling along my journey, I noticed at almost every town and hamlet crowds of men not infrequently interspersed with women moving rapidly to and fro, drums beating, fifes whistling, everywhere evidencing the busy preparation of war. I saw little else—heard little else. It is the all-absorbing question of the day. War, war—you see it in the measured tread of men, hear it in the martial strains borne upon the breeze, in the conversations of men and in the blab of drunken loafers, feel it in the jostle of the throng and in the crowded cars. Crowd? That's no name for it!! We were jammed. But as it is for the good of our country and I believe in the cause, I do not murmur but rather rejoice that our country has not companies, but crowds of men to defend her. Would to God that these crowds had competent leaders to direct them. Then should we see rebellion not only crushed but annihilated. All through the free states was noise, bustle, and confusion.

    How changed the scene here [Missouri]. All is quiet—little talk of war. It appears to be an unwelcome subject. Men speak in whispers, look doubtful, and shake their heads. Union men are not confident, and Secesh doubtful, if not despondent, so we have little excitement here. At present, stores and shops close at 4:00 p.m., and clerks drill two hours when they return and open shop, and business goes on again. I believe all who are subject to military duty have to drill the aforesaid two hours. There is but little apprehension of an attack on this city at present. All is quiet—too quiet. One feels lost for excitement.

Behind the lines, things grew increasingly difficult for people who supported the opposing side. In the North, Southern supporters were required to take an Oath of Allegiance to the Union to prove their loyalty.

George W. Saner (unknown), a private in the 45th Illinois Infantry, told a friend how secessionists were treated in a little town in northern Illinois.

Cambridge, Illinois
August 29, 1862

I will tell you that we have great times here in town rail riding the damn Disunionists. Last Monday, we had one on a wooden rail from one o'clock until almost sundown. We then took him off the rail and asked him to take the oath. He refused it. He was put in jail in this town and is there yet, and by God, he must take the oath, or we will put him through another course of sprouts. We have made and will make more take the oath before we leave.

Military action was not limited to the major theaters of operation. With thousands of Union troops recalled from the Western frontier to fight the Confederates, settlers in rural Minnesota were left unprotected. In August and September 1862, Native Americans struck back in what was called the Sioux Uprising or the Dakota War. Some 360 settlers, 110 soldiers, and an estimated 150 braves were killed in vicious fighting. Dozens of native leaders were captured, and 38 were hanged on December 26 in what remains the largest mass execution in American history.

An **unknown Minnesota resident** tried to reassure his brother and relatives back in upstate New York that there was no reason to fear for his safety.

Warsaw, Minnesota
August 26, 1862

We are in a great state of excitement in Minnesota at present. You have doubtless ere this heard about our Indian troubles here and probably heard them worse than they really are. But the truth is horrid enough to make one's blood run cold to think of the outrages they have committed already. It is hard to ascertain the correct account of the amount of whites massacred, for it is estimated at from 100 to 1,000.

They first commenced at their agency near Fort Ridgely (the fort I was at one year ago last spring). They came to the fort and tried to take it, but the

soldiers brought the artillery to bear on them and throwed shells among them,
which drove them away. They then attacked a town a little below the fort
called New Ulm and burned some buildings, and killed a number of whites.
But they were driven away with the loss of their chief. They are now led, in
fact, by their 2nd chief Chakopee, an Indian that I have often fed and been
acquainted with ever since I have been in Minnesota. He always appeared
to be very friendly. I know it is said of the Indians that if you do them a
kindness, they never forget it.

Well, this is one link of the great Rebellion. Southern gold has set them
at work, and they are led on by Southern Rebels disguised as Negroes.

The whole country here is aroused, and nearly every little town keeps a
heavy guard posted nights to prevent being surprised by them. And we have
formed a company here of Minute Men. The way the signal is given is by
blowing horns in case of a surprise. I was elected captain of the company. It
numbers some 50 members. Night before last, I had a pretty good houseful of
people. Some was families that came out of the Big Woods, and some were the
guard. I made it the headquarters for the guard that night. All left Faribault
on horse last week for St. Peter, all that could get horses here, men with them.

Tell mother not to worry or be uneasy about us here, for there is not
much chance for their getting here, for they have got to come through heavy
settlements to get as far into the interior of the state as this. I thought I would
write and let you know that we are all right here, for I am afraid you will
borrow trouble about us unnecessarily. Give yourselves no uneasiness about us.

As summer headed into its closing weeks, Confederate forces everywhere were going on the offensive. A push to retake Louisiana's capital, which had fallen into Union hands shortly after New Orleans was captured that spring, was set in motion. General Robert E. Lee wasted no time after his victory at Second Bull Run/Manassas preparing to invade the North for the first time. Southern troops in eastern Tennessee under the command of General Edmund Kirby Smith were preparing to push into Kentucky as General Braxton Bragg's Army of Tennessee made ready to enter it from the center. And in Mississippi, the Confederate Army of the West was gearing up for action there. Captain **John M. Weidemeyer (1834–1911)** of the 6th Missouri Infantry (Confederate) related to his wife how he eagerly anticipated taking the war to the North's doorstep. (He wrongly believed that General Samuel Curtis commanded nearby Federal troops.)

Camp at Guntown, Mississippi
August 5, 1862

I have not received a line in reply to any of my letters, and although I am naturally of buoyant spirits I cannot help but feel displeased and low-spirited at times, situated as I am in a strange land with only one true friend beside me. But I do not allow such feelings to maintain the mastery over me. I cast them aside and look habitually to the bright side of the future, trusting that the vile invader of our sacred rights will soon meet with the just retribution for his tyrannical oppression. Then and not till then will the dark cloud that now obscures the horizon of our country be dispelled, and peace and prosperity smile on our land.

General Sterling Price is now in command (temporarily) of the District of Tennessee which comprises all the troops this side of the Mississippi River, not including the Department of Mississippi and the Department of the Gulf. He has issued orders to prepare immediately for active operations in the field in emulation of the deeds of our gallant soldiers in the East and to carry the war into the boundaries of Ohio. Everything indicates that we will soon unfurl our banners to the breeze and march to meet the enemy.

I believe it is a general advance along the whole line. Already, (reports say), the battle has commenced at Chattanooga. Our men have been eager for the fray and wait impatiently for the command "Forward" to be given. Curtis is in our front, and the [Confederate] Missourians have not forgotten the retreat from Elk Horn [Pea Ridge, Arkansas] and burn to wipe out its disgrace in the blood of the invaders. Let General Price but pronounce the manic words, "Onward, your foes are before you," and every heart will respond with a shout of joy, and long, weary marches and all the attendant hardships would be undertaken with cheerfulness and alacrity.

There is some Northern papers in camp. They do not talk in their usual braggard style. Their tone is subdued, their spirits cowed. The star of the North is waning. King Abe's throne is tottering and shaken to the base by the late disastrous overthrow of his minions. Now, let us strike for liberty, honor, home, and friends and complete the work so nobly begun, make them feel the might of the uplifted arm of an outraged people struggling to free themselves and posterity from the merciless rule of a fanatical despot. By following up our advantages energetically, we will be able to drive the vandals from our shores and dictate to them terms of peace of our own making.

I have just returned from dress parade, and orders were read for all the sick that were not able to travel to the sent to the hospital, a sure sign that we will move soon.

As Price's Confederates got ready to advance in Mississippi, another Confederate offensive was underway farther south. A small force led by former U.S. Vice President turned Confederate General John C. Breckinridge tried to recapture Baton Rouge, Louisiana. It began with a predawn attack, as **Francis G. Brown (1836–1894),** a private in the 2nd Massachusetts Light Artillery (Nim's Battery), related to a friend.

New Orleans, Louisiana
September 9, 1862

Our small force was attacked on the morning of the 5th of August at 4 o'clock. The heaviest of the fighting was on the right and left, but being repulsed there, they tried to make a break in the center where we were stationed. Had orders to fire, and we did so. We used between two and three hundred shells, and they made many a Rebel turn up their toes. I saw 63 buried in one trench, besides many others lying on the battlefield. It was a most horrid sight to look upon, I assure you.

The reason we lost so few in comparison to them was because they fired so high, the bullets flew over our precious heads like rain. And I am happy to say none of our boys were killed. Two wounded, but not seriously.

The original plan called for Breckinridge to be supported by water from the ironclad CSS *Arkansas.* Completed at Yazoo City, Mississippi, she ran past Union warships and made it to Vicksburg, then headed downriver to support Breckinridge's attack. Disabled by mechanical trouble, the *Arkansas* was destroyed by her crew the day after the battle. It was described in this letter from **an unidentified Federal sailor** to his brother written a few weeks later.

USS Cayuga
Off Mobile, Alabama
September 6, 1862

You have probably heard of the ram Arkansas. *She came down to Baton Rouge to assist in the attack on that place, but she did not come down far enough to render any service. We could see the black smoke from her smoke-stack over a point of land, but she was afraid to come down around the bend, and we were afraid to go up. We stayed in this interesting position two days, when Capt. William Porter of the* Essex *started up the river to have a look at her and give us orders to support him. He steamed up towards the bend. We followed at a respectful distance every time the man in the masthead cried. It was soon discovered from the masthead that the ram was on fire, whereupon we turned back and followed the* Essex *at a very respectful distance to take a look at her.*

I went ashore at Baton Rouge and made a visit to the battlefield where I had a good opportunity of witnessing the horrors of war. It was a disgusting sight, and I do not wish to see another like it. There was five hundred men killed in the engagement, the number of wounded I could not ascertain.

We had no trouble with our engines this voyage of any account. The forward cylinder is cut a little, caused by the boilers foaming when leaving the Mississippi River. Pumping sea water into the muddy river water causes the boilers to foam; it stirs up all the mud that has settled in the water bottoms.

In the Bluegrass State, Union troops were retreating into Kentucky as the Confederates approached on two fronts. Kirby Smith's Army of Kentucky met an equal force of mostly raw Union troops at Richmond, Kentucky, on August 30 and utterly destroyed them in what some historians consider the most complete Confederate victory of the war. It was described in detail in this letter from an **unidentified Southern officer** to his aunt in Texas.

In Camp
Near Lexington, Kentucky
September 2, 1862

We took up the line of march about sunup or before march common time when we heard the artillery some 3 miles in advance. We were halted, ordered to load, and commenced marching at a quick but was soon put out to a double quick, which we kept up for about 4 miles when we came up to the Yanks. We never halted, the order having been given by the right flank charge, which was done with a right good will in full-blooded Texas style. In the first charge, our color sergeant was shot in the head and fell dead speaking only the following words, "They have killed me, but take out the colors and rally them," which was done instantly by a private of Capt. Merchant's company with the remark, "Let them try me."

They [the Federals] were the worst whipped set of men that ever went on the battlefield. After the first charge, they outrun us. We could not catch them. They went a couple of miles and formed in a cornfield. We were halted before we got in range of their small arms but not out of reach of shell and grapeshot. Then we were ordered to advance to a small ditch some 60 yards in advance. The ditch was not more than 18 inches deep at the deepest part, it being concave and not more than 4 feet wide, so you can imagine what kind of shelter we had and to make the matter worse on my part, I had to hold my horse, and he was rearing and prancing all the time and half the time had me on top of the ditch. You had better believe that was one of the times I wanted to crawl in the earth, but 'twas no go. The way the balls whistled over us was not slow. Bombs, balls, minie balls, and everything killable and hurtable so that it seemed it was an utter impossibility for a large number of us not to be killed. But only two men were wounded. One, while lying with his face to the ground with his prominent part projecting, was shot about ball deep through both cheeks of the unmentionable.

We marched by the left flank to a woodland position where the Feds were trying to flank us. There was done the hardest fighting of the war. About 1,000 of us, completely exhausted, nearly dead for water, melting with heat, charged and defeated at least 3,500. They all seemed willing to go home and stay there. William Penn was wounded in the arm pretty badly; a better and braver boy never fought for the rights of a bleeding country, and his parents need not be ashamed to have him as their own.

Nearly everybody in this area, as well as all the sensible parts of the country, are Secesh. Union fools only found in the poorest hills. The prisoners we took counted between 5 and 6 thousand, about 1,000 more than the lying whelps said they had. We are now in camp near Cynthiana, Kentucky. We are closing on the Yanks and will give them fits more. Morgan is not far off.

Indeed, cavalry, led by General John Hunt Morgan, the "Thunderbolt of the Confederacy," was raiding in the Federals' rear. An exasperated **William T. Clark (1836–1911),** a private in the 79th Pennsylvania Infantry, tried to put the best face on the situation to his cousin. (He would be wounded in the Battle of Perryville four weeks later.)

Bowling Green, Kentucky
September 10, 1862

You will no doubt be surprised to hear from me at this point, but we have become so used to moving that we are not surprised at anything concerning where we find ourselves at the end of a march. Very likely, there is a great deal of excitement throughout our country concerning the falling back of our army in the past two weeks. But never fear. Although the picture looks dark at present, it will learn many of the leading officers of our army a lesson to desist from treating these Rebels as friends.

General John Hunt Morgan is still committing his depredations throughout the country, and a few days ago, his band burned a bridge across Salt River 20 miles this side of Louisville. He had better keep a sharp lookout, or we will give him a free passage up that noted river.

The Rebels have become desperate by their condition regarding forage and rations for their army. They are starving, and necessity has drove them to this bold strike while their rear is carrying off all the grain and forage from Virginia and eastern Kentucky. But some fine morning they will wake up and find themselves caged fast and tight by the army of the Union.

We left Nashville on the night of September 4th and marched to this place. There is quite an amount of troops at Nashville yet; two divisions arrived there this evening. About the first of this month, our mail communications between Louisville and Nashville was restored. The weather here is quite dry and water scarce, but we have plenty to eat and get along very well.

Bragg's Confederates advanced through middle Tennessee, bypassed heavily fortified Nashville, and drove into the heart of Kentucky. Private **Leonard Lusted (1844–1923)** of the 3rd Independent Battery, Wisconsin Light Artillery, helped resist the Confederate invasion, as he described in this letter to his parents.

Mount Vernon, Kentucky
September 16, 1862

We have been marching ever since I wrote before and have almost been within a good shot of them. Our cavalry went by them before they knew it, and the Rebels fired into them, cutting them up pretty bad. We have had two or three skirmishes with them. They will run a little ways and then turn around and fire upon us. Their shells hummed over our heads, and some of them bursted about twenty feet behind us. It made the boys start, you had better believe. We fired into them and dismounted one of their guns and smashed their wagons. We followed them until dark and then camped, and before we could get the horses unharnessed, their cavalry came down the road to charge on us. Our pickets were going out, and they fired into them, and they turned and went back.

We shelled them out of Mount Washington and drove them out of Bardstown, Perryville, and Danville, and they have come around into Bardstown, but they won't do it long. We have fought them for the last eight or nine days and have marched about fifty miles and are going all the time as fast as we can. There is dead horses all along the road and broken wagons, plenty of them. We have taken some prisoners, how many don't know, and some have deserted and came to us and a good many more would if they could. They are the raggedest looking things you ever saw. They say that they have not had half enough to eat, and they want to be taken prisoner and released and go home.

With Unionists in the Ohio River valley in a panic, one of the war's most high-profile crimes occurred. As two Confederate armies advanced deep into central Kentucky, the atmosphere was extremely tense inside Louisville's Galt House hotel, the Federal headquarters. A heated argument erupted between General William "Bull" Nelson, the city's commander, and General Jefferson C. Davis. Tempers flared. Nelson called Davis an "insolent puppy" and slapped him. Davis fired a pistol point blank into Nelson's chest, mortally wounding him.

Cornelius J. Madden (1842–1903), a private in the 102nd Ohio Volunteer Infantry, had enlisted just six weeks earlier. His regiment had rushed to Louisville, the rendezvous point for new troops being raised to thwart an anticipated Confederate invasion of Ohio. In a letter to his mother, he mentioned the murder, the obsolete Belgian or Austrian muskets the new recruits had been hastily issued, and the difficulties confronting his 49-year-old father serving as a private in a different Ohio regiment.

In Camp near Louisville, Kentucky
September 29, 1862

General Jeff Davis shot General Nelson today, the darned old tyrant. I am glad of it. The provost guard shoots two or three soldiers a day up in the city.

They killed two of the 26th Ohio Infantry yesterday, and the 26th boys tied the guards and mauled them like blazes.

I saw George Marvin today. He said that when they came through Nashville, father had a pass from the commander there and was out of the city. They did not know where he was. He might have done it to avoid the regiment. I don't blame him if he did, for this long march of 370 miles in 31 days would have been too much for him. If he would try, I know he could get discharged, for they can't hold one overage if they don't want to stay and I want him out of this damn army, although I am perfectly contented and satisfied. I like home as well as anyone, but I would rather be here. And although the danger is pretty great, I am coming back all right, you may rest easy on that.

The other day, we marched up to our brigade general headquarters and corded up our guns, and now we are going to have new ones. The ones we drew wasn't worth anything. We have been transferred to General Thomas Crittenden's Division. They are mixing the old and new troops all up together.

Simultaneously, yet another push northward was getting underway in Virginia. On September 4, just four days after Second Bull Run/Manassas, Lee's 55,000-man Army of Northern Virginia crossed the Potomac River and entered Maryland. McClellan marched the Army of the Potomac there to challenge him, absorbing much of Pope's defeated command and shielding Washington in the process. People in the Union and the Confederacy alike, military and civilian, understood that a major battle was in the offing.

In the North, regiments were urgently recruited and rushed into service in response to the crisis. They included the 138th New York Infantry. On September 1, 16-year-old **Lewis M. Foster (1846–1912)** lied about his age and enlisted in the regiment, mustering in one week later. Five days after that, his aunt wrote to the boy's frantic mother.

Butler, New York
September 12, 1862

As I know you feel anxious to know about Lewis, I thought I would let you know what I have learned about it. I went out last Sunday night to see him. He (Lewis) said he had no fuss with Mr. Mack but that he wanted to enlist, and he knew that if he said anything about it, you wouldn't let him go. He intended to get a furlough and come home to see you. But he said he did not have time to go and see you, for he had got to enlist that day if he was to get his bounty. When I bade him goodbye, he looked sorry enough, I can tell you.

He chose for his guardian his lieutenant, who you will be pleased to learn is Harvey Follet. I saw and talked with him and asked if he could get Lewis clear. He asked how old he was and I told him you said he was 16, and he said if that was the case, you had better keep still unless you wanted Lewis to get in worse trouble than he was now, for he said he did not know Lewis when he came there but that he questioned him, and Lewis told him that he was an orphan and that he swore that he was 18 years old, and that false swearing would put him in state prison. He said the less said about it, the better. Get John or Pa to take you out here and come this way and see me. I can tell you more in ten minutes than I can write in an hour.

Do not worry yourself to death about Lewis, for you cannot make it any different, and it may be all for the best. If he should live to come back, he will be worth more [financially] when the war is over than he could possibly be in a long time at home. The best you can do is give him good advice and pray that he may be kept from the evils and temptations of camp life, and I will do the same. I sympathize with you fully, my dear sister, in this, your latest affliction, but remember that whom the Lord loveth He chasteneth. Above all, charge Lewis to keep his clothes and person as free from lice as he possibly can. Write to me or come to see me as soon as you possibly can. Yours in affliction, Lucy

Sunday: I have since learned that the regiment has left Auburn. No one knows where they went or where they were going.

Likewise, another young recruit was rushing to Maryland. Private **Charles Howe (1845–1864)** of the 36th Massachusetts Infantry had been a troubled teen in his hometown of Lancaster who fell in with the wrong crowd, shirked work, and got a reputation for laziness. Charley begged his parents to let him enlist at age 17, which he did on August 15. This letter penned to them is filled with a mixture of both ominous foreboding and youthful overconfidence. (Howe died at Andersonville Prison two years later.)

Camp Forbes
Brookville, Maryland
September 14, 1862

This is my fourth and perhaps my last letter. A messenger came to Col. Henry Bowman today in great haste, and the order has now been given out to cook three days' rations and to be ready tomorrow morning in light marching order—that is, we are to take our blankets, overcoats, an extra pair of socks, an extra shirt with us, and to leave behind our knapsacks and extra baggage.

Thirty rounds of ammunition have been given us and the whole amounts to just this: That we have a long march before us and a fight not long afterward.

Some of the men wear a long, sober face. They think they realize what they have to go through. I don't suppose I do. Neither do I wish to, for I don't want to be dreading events to come. I think I am as capable of enduring the hardships and dangers of a campaign as the best of them, and if I am alive, I am confident that I shall see home at least by next July. This war cannot last six months longer. There are troops enough in and around Washington to wipe out all the Rebels in Virginia. All are confident of success. Have no fears of the Rebels ever getting Washington, for it is too well fortified. The Rebel General Stonewall Jackson has won his last battle. He will be in Fort Warren 'ere many days—depend upon it.

But Stonewall Jackson was far from captured. He swung his men down from Maryland and seized the heights surrounding the river junction and arsenal at Harpers Ferry (now in West Virginia). After an intense artillery barrage, the Federals surrendered, as **Constantine Hege (1843–1914),** a private in the 48th North Carolina Infantry, told his parents.

Near Martinsburg, Virginia
Sunday, September 21, 1862

We have been marching for about 20 days, and sometimes, we have to march all night. We crossed the Potomac River four times and went over into Maryland. The first time that we went over, we stayed 2 or 3 days and came back safe. And then we went to Harpers Ferry, and there we had a very hard bombing last Monday, but we whipped the Yankees without any musket firing except from the pickets. We captured a great many wagons and cannons and taken about 800 prisoners.

Hege was mistaken; Jackson captured far more prisoners. He seized 73 pieces of artillery, 12,000 stands of arms, 200 wagons, and 12,419 prisoners—the largest number of U.S. troops surrendered until Bataan fell in World War II.

While that was going on, there was fighting not far away at South Mountain in Maryland at key passes as the two armies headed toward their showdown.

Corporal **T. John Bell (unknown)** of the 69th Pennsylvania Infantry mentioned them while writing home the day before the big battle.

> *[Maryland; location unknown]*
> *September 16, 1862*
>
> *You must forgive me for not writing, for we have been marching for 12 days and chasing the enemy before us. Sunday night, we laid on the battlefield [South Mountain].*
> *Today, we are a going to the Potomac. They have Jackson hemmed in, and we will give him what he wants. We have the news that we got 9,000 prisoners last night.*

The Battle of Antietam/Sharpsburg was fought on September 17. Jackson had rushed his troops from Harpers Ferry to join Lee, as **Constantine Hege** continued in his letter to his family.

> *We then marched over into Maryland again on last Tuesday evening, and on Wednesday morning, about nine or ten o'clock, we were marched to the battlefield, and we made a charge on one of the enemy's batteries. But when we got within about 75 or 100 yards of them, we were bound to retreat because they were too strong for us. A great many of our men were killed and wounded. There were about twenty wounded in our company. I cannot write the hundreth part of the horrors of the battlefield.*

September 17 remains the single bloodiest day in American history. More than 3,600 men were killed. Another 17,000 were wounded, a significant number of whom would go on to die from their injuries and infection. People everywhere struggled to grasp the battle's enormity.

Captain **Daniel Marston (1813–1891)** of the 16th Maine Infantry arrived shortly after the fighting had ended. While this letter to his wife included the typical misinformation soldiers often hear after a major engagement, it did capture the feeling of the moment.

> *Blue Ridge, Maryland*
> *September 18, 1862*
>
> *We are now some 4 miles from Middleton and 12 from Frederick in this state. This is one of the finest sections of country I ever passed through, although the*

presence of so many soldiers in passing through it has made a ruinous look on the road. Tonight we camp on the ground where the first battle [South Mountain] was fought and where the Rebels camped and are now but about 5 or 6 miles from the present armies. Tomorrow will bring us with them.

The results of the battle [Antietam] no doubt you will hear as soon by papers as you will by this note. Suffice it to say it has been hard-fought, and the Rebels have had the worst of it.

Some 2,100 prisoners we met today, and we think the battle is very much in our favor. It is said Stonewall Jackson and Lee are taken, and many others of the Rebel generals wounded. We also have lost some good men and many brave soldiers.

Let that be as it may, very many of our men are badly wounded, and I have met them all day coming into Middleton and Frederick and also went into the four meeting houses [churches], and they were all full of the wounded. The injured soldiers all seem to be cheery and bear their legs and arms to be amputated or suffer any hardships with the greatest patience. I am glad my own dear ones at home will never see such sights as must us here. What is ahead for us, no one can tell. Yesterday, we hauled about 16 miles. Today, 12 miles. Tomorrow, we expect to go 12 or 15 miles. No battles this day, and we cannot tell how soon we will have another.

A short while later, Marston's regiment reached the battlefield. In a second letter to his wife, he was clearly traumatized by what he had seen.

Potomac River below and near Sharpsburg, Maryland
and between the battlefield & River Potomac in the oak woods
[circa September 20–22, 1862]

Without tent or shelter arrived here this day at noon and expect to do picket duty for one day. We camped on the battlefield last night. This morning, we crossed a part of it, and such a sight you never saw in your life. All the wounded had been taken into houses, barns, churches, and schoolhouses, and finally everywhere and anywhere from here to Washington, and there is also any amount of dead men now lying on the field, still unburied. Such looking objects as you never saw nor do I wish you to ever see. It would shock you so that you would not get over it. You will see them in any amount. It is said there is still 1,200 Rebels now lying on the ground, having laid there 3 or 4 days. I will not write more now as I am to go on duty at once. Our boys see and experience what they never expected to see.

Although the battle was tactically a draw, Lee was compelled to return to Virginia, making it a strategic victory for the North. On September 22, Lincoln seized the recent engagement as an opportunity to announce his Preliminary Emancipation Proclamation. On January 1, 1863, all slaves held inside the Confederacy would be free. Those in Northern states would remain enslaved.

Private **Joseph Edward Kimball (1839–1896)**, 1st Massachusetts Infantry, came from an antislavery New England family. But a few days after Lincoln's announcement, he shared his concerns with his older brother, Reverend John Calvin Kimball, a virulent abolitionist.

Hampton Hospital
Near Fortress Monroe, Virginia
September 30, 1862

President Lincoln has issued his Emancipation Proclamation. It is hard to say whether its results will be good or evil. At any rate, the people should be a unit in supporting him. Those who have the good of the Union at heart must feel that as the proclamation has gone forth, they have no other course open but to use every means to strengthen the government in order that it may be effective. Much of its result will depend upon the progress of our armies between this and the first of January. Of course, it will greatly intensify the struggle.

I am not opposed to abolition. I speak of the "Ultra Abolitionists" because they are the Rule or Ruin Party. Do you not see the great importance of the people being a unit in order to crush out this rebellion? Are there not tens and hundreds of thousands of good loyal people in the North who are opposed from purist principles to prevent Negro emancipation? Having arrived at this conclusion, how can they cordially aid you in carrying out your Ultra ideas any more than you could relinquish yours to aid the opposite Ultras in carrying out theirs? But there is a ground on which all can meet. It is aiding—not embarrassing—the government in carrying out its own measure.

The present government is of your own choice, and you ought to trust its ability and resolution of purpose. If President Lincoln says emancipation, let the people be a unit in supporting him. I think President Lincoln desires to execute the will of the people. I think he has striven to act so as to keep them united. In his delay in issuing the late proclamation, I think he has adopted its policy and the approval of the majority of the people. It is all twiddle about our inability to crush the rebellion without interfering with slavery. Let us have united will and action, and we must either crush it or acknowledge ourselves cowards and imbeciles. It is the fault of this faction who have left no means untried to thrust this one idea of slave emancipation upon the President, thereby embarrassing the government that has so long prolonged the struggle. They would displace the greatest chief of our armies today solely on account of party.

I received your anti-slavery sermon—it is very fine.

With the important midterm congressional elections—the first since fighting began—now just weeks away, Lincoln and his supporters nervously waited to see how Northern voters would react to both the war and the impending Emancipation Proclamation.

In Washington, 16-year-old new recruit **Lewis M. Foster (1846–1912)** found army life to his liking, as he explained to his aunt.

Camp Welling
Outside Washington, D.C.
September 27, 1862

I now sit down to write you to let you know how we are getting along. We had a good train ride from Auburn, New York, to New York City and from there to Washington. We are encamped near Fort Bunker Hill. They have been firing cannons every half hour all day, for General Joseph Mansfield is dead. We haven't drilled any since we came here. We have been building military roads all the time. We are in good spirits here and anxious for a fight.

We sleep in tents on the ground. We marched from Washington to Arlington Heights, Virginia, slept on the ground all night, and started the next afternoon for Washington again. Many of the boys could not stand the march and fell down and had to be carried, but I stood it as well as any of them. I had to carry a knapsack that weighed about thirty pounds and my gun, cartridge box, cap box, and all those things.

Some of the boys have got letters from home, and they heard that we had had a awful battle between Baltimore and Washington, but I have not heard anything about it. There is no prospect of our moving soon.

Harvey Follett and the officers have got away from home, and they play cards and such things.

Our lieutenant colonel is the son of Secretary of State William H. Seward. William Seward has visited this regiment several times and says it is the finest regiment he has seen during the war.

We saw some grand sights while we was coming here. There was lot of black boys and black hogs in the roads. We seen black boys in the road that had nothing on but half a pair of trousers and nothing else. We passed through one tunnel while we was coming here. It was dug through solid rock. We rode the toughest country that I ever thought of. The road in some places was cut through solid rock. Nothing but rock for forty feet up on both sides.

When we got to New York City, we heard the greatest noise. The barracks were on Broadway and then the street railroad and them carts kept up a continual clatter all day long Sunday. And there was a fountain in the park where we was that gushed up four or five feet. But I must close, for I want to write to Grandpa today.

From a True Soldier, Lewis M. Foster

Throughout the summer, Confederate forces had scoured western Missouri far behind Union lines, rounding up recruits and horses. Guerrilla raiders were also active in the area. As fall approached, Federal commanders finally had enough of the threat in their rear and began cracking down.

At the same time in their front, a new Confederate army was taking shape in neighboring northwest Arkansas. A scouting force of 5,500 men was sent across the state line to the hamlet of Newtonia, Missouri. A see-saw battle there on September 30 ended in a Federal rout. When the Confederates withdrew a few days later, the reinforced Northerners attacked the Southerners' rearguard. When the fighting was over, the little village of 100 people was put to the torch, a foretaste of even worse destruction to come.

As **John Danforth Wilkinson (1840–1918)**, a private in the 1st Missouri Light Artillery (Federal), told relatives in New York, the Civil War was more than just brother against brother. For Native American soldiers from nearby Indian Territory (modern Oklahoma), it was also tribe against tribe.

Camp near Newtonia, Missouri
October 6, 1862

We advanced on this place, which was occupied by the enemy day before yesterday. The enemy were aware of our approach and had most of their army under retreat. We threw 24 shells at the force which covered the retreat, and with Gen. James Blunt's command coming up, started in pursuit. But the Rebels succeeded in getting away. The charge of Blunt's Indians on the Rebels was a sight. The painted devils went yelling across the prairie like so many wolves. They are of the Delaware and Cherokee tribes. The enemy also had Choctaws and a few disloyal Cherokees.

Last night, one or two of our guards were killed in town, and now at two o'clock in the afternoon, Newtonia is in ashes. This is doing things up right, and it is my prayer that the homes of all Rebels are served the same way. We are near the Arkansas line, four miles from the celebrated Granby lead mines, 25 miles from Pea Ridge, and 40 miles from Cross Hollows, Arkansas, where the enemy is now supposed to be. Excuse this scribbling, for I have nothing to lay my paper on except my knee.

Things grew relatively quiet in that part of the Trans-Mississippi. But they wouldn't remain that way very long. Events were soon set in motion that led to a bloody battle there at year's end.

Confederate forces far to the south were also staying busy. In mid-September, General Sterling Price's Army of the West moved to keep Union Generals Grant and William Rosecrans from reinforcing the Federals in Kentucky. He halted in the small town of Iuka, Mississippi, and waited for General Earl Van Dorn's Army of West Tennessee to arrive.

Grant devised a two-phase strategy to ensnare Price. He would swing a large force northwest of the town. Rosecrans would attack from the southwest; when Grant heard the sounds of battle, he would join in and thus encircle Price's command.

But it didn't turn out that way. **Calvin R. Johnson (1822–1897),** a captain in the 14th Wisconsin Infantry, told his wife how Federal troops were put into position. (He also told how answering an unfortunately timed call of nature ended the war for one soldier.)

Near Corinth, Mississippi
September 23, 1862

At 2 o'clock a.m., our regiment was marching south. I learned that we formed part of an army of 12 or 15,000 strong with 60 pieces of artillery and that our destination was Iuka on the Mobile and Ohio Railroad, some 25 miles from here where General Price was. Iuka has been in our possession all summer until quite lately, when it was evacuated in a most cowardly manner by

Col. Robert C. Murphy of the 8th Wisconsin, who had 1,500 men under his command. He is now under arrest, at all events.

We arrived within 10 miles of Iuka under the guidance of a native and were ordered to make a detour around to the left of our army and Iuka. We were supposed to halt 6 miles from there where, I supposed, our advance would commence against the enemy from right to left. A line of battle generally is an army of men facing the supposed position of the enemy and is two ranks deep (that is, one man behind another); our line was almost 3 miles long. But instead of halting at 6 miles, the guide took us within 2 miles of the enemy.

Traveling along a road lined on either side with timber, the dozen cavalry we had with us came upon a Rebel picket who had dismounted and was doing his business beside a tree. He was captured without any trouble. He told us that Price had 50,000 men within 2 miles of us. We told him we believed he lied and went on.

Rosecrans attacked on September 19. Due to an acoustical anomaly, the sound never reached Grant, who remained inactive. Still, Rosecrans was able to drive off Price after stiff fighting as **G. L. Haywood (unknown)**, a commissary sergeant in the 1st Minnesota Artillery, reported to his brother.

Corinth, Mississippi
September 28, 1862

We have been out in the state of Alabama after Price. But he is too sharp to be caught in any trap that General Grant could set for him. He [Grant] thought that he had the old Rebel surrounded so that escape was impossible. He held the town of Iuka with twenty thousand men. General Rosecrans was there with his forces. The [Union] troops in Corinth went out to the number of fifteen thousand under General Edward Ord. This division was stationed on the road leading toward Corinth. The artillery of the division, twenty pieces, were posted so as to command the road. It is a hilly country about Iuka, and we had excellent positions. The hills were fairly bristling with Federal artillery and bayonets. To pass us would have been an impossibility. But Price knew the country better than our generals and consequently had the advantage of us.

On the 19th, General Rosecrans attacked the enemy, and a most des-
perate struggle ensued, lasting about two hours, when darkness separated the
combatants. We were seven miles distant when we heard the cannonade and
made all possible haste to reach the battlefield in season to take a hand in the
game. But there were steep hills to climb, and the roads were muddy, and we
were too late to render any assistance except in burying the dead and taking
care of the wounded, of which there were plenty, for Price, in his hurry to
get out of the reach of our men, left his killed and wounded to the care of his
enemies.

Most of the inhabitants left the town when the Rebels did. Deserted
houses were quickly converted into hospitals, and the wounded moved into
them. We found plenty of provisions in the houses, and we made a better
breakfast than we have eaten for a long time. We lived on the Secesh while
they were absent. We managed to encamp every night near some cornfield
where we could gather the ears of corn for our horses, and woe to the luckless
pig or sheep or chicken that came in our sight, for it was sure to be confiscated.
Every night, some of the boys would bring in calves, sheep, or pigs, and one
night, we killed an ox. Each man takes just such a piece of meat as suits him
best and roasts it by holding it to the fire on the point of a sharp stick. This,
with a cup of hot coffee and a hard cracker or two, makes a supper which is
very palatable to a hungry man.

During the night, the Rebels stole away by a route that our officers
were ignorant of. When Price was moving from the east, General John C.
Breckinridge [actually Van Dorn] with another army was approaching from
the west with the probable intention of uniting their forces for an attack
on Corinth. But that piece of strategy is foiled. Price has been defeated and
driven back, while Breckinridge, of his own accord, has fallen back in the
opposite direction.

In the previously cited letter, Calvin R. Johnson reported that Corinth was
ready for whatever may come next.

It is thought we shall be attacked. But whichever Rebel general thinks he can
oust us out of here now will find himself laboring under a horrible delusion,
for we have been reinforced and feel strong enough to not only keep Corinth
but to cut up the enemy whenever he shows himself in our neighborhood.

Price and Van Dorn linked up five days later. The two had fought together at Pea Ridge, Arkansas, six months earlier. Against Price's advice, Van Dorn attacked Corinth on October 3-4 and was repulsed in a bloody battle.

Seventeen-year-old **David C. Jones (1845–1863)**, a private in the 26th Missouri Infantry (Federal), was in the engagement. Writing to his family a week later, he mentioned his teenage cousin Andrew Jackson Jones, who had fallen in the previous fight. (David Jones died of disease the following year.)

Corinth, Mississippi
October 12, 1862

I suppose you have heard about the fight at Iuka, for I wrote a letter not long ago. Poor cousin Jackson. I hope he is happy.

We have had another fight at Corinth, and it was a hard one. You will hear about it soon. We was on the right wing, but we drove them back without firing a gun—only cannon. They was firing at us but they didn't hurt many. There was a shell exploded in my face and killed John Maxwell beside me. It cut his head pertnear off and throwed blood and flesh on me, but it didn't hurt me any—only burnt a little. Robey Dyson is wounded, as are several other Franklin County boys.

You must excuse my short letter, for we have been a marching for more than a week after Price. We just got here last night and I expect to march tomorrow. We hain't been in camp more than one day at a time since the 17th of September.

The fighting now shifted to Kentucky. A few days later, Bragg's army clashed with Federals under the command of General Don Carlos Buell at Perryville on October 8. It was the largest battle fought in that state. As **E. W. Curtis (1837–1917),** a private in the 88th Illinois Infantry, wrote to his aunt, the struggle was severe.

Battlefield near Perryville, Kentucky
October 10, 1862

I hasten to drop you a line to let you know that I still survive after the battle of the day before yesterday (8th) when we met the enemy under Generals Braxton Bragg, Simon Buckner, and Edmund Kirby Smith and had a hotly contested fight lasting all day. During the night, the Secesh skedaddled northward to Harrodsburg, leaving from 3 to 5 thousand stand of arms and one battery in their haste, and we have taken about 3,000 prisoners. Our regiment lost 4 killed and 36 wounded. The Rebels left theirs behind, their dead being scattered around in heaps.

The hardest part of the battle was on the left, some regiments losing one half. Our regiment was under fire from 4:00 to 5:00 p.m. when the Mississippi Tigers made a charge through a cornfield to get possession of the 2nd Illinois Battery. For that time, we lay on the ground firing, thus with the battery playing over our heads. We retired to the rear of the battery once to give them a chance to pour grape and canister. I do not know that I felt at all or much excited before or after the engagement. We had 100,000 to 150,000 men, but not all engaged.

Similarly, **James Sifleet (1841–1863),** a private in the 36th Illinois Infantry, told his parents that he couldn't understand why the entire Union force hadn't been engaged in the battle. (He was killed in action at Stones River/Murfreesboro less than 90 days later.)

Camp near Crab Orchard, Kentucky
October 18, 1862

I suppose before this time you have been quite uneasy, but I am alright, although it seems a wonder how any could escape the way the bullets flew. But it was not my lot to be killed in that battle. The Lord seen fit to save my life. The man standing next to me only shot his gun once when he fell and bled to death. You well know what a faint-hearted thing I have always been, but during the fighting, I could do almost anything with the wounded. Blood would not make me faint. I was around men that was cut most all to pieces and was handling them, but when I laid down that night, I offered my sincere thanks to God for bringing me safe through the battle.

I thought that the fight had not fairly commenced, for I knew that our men had not scarcely arrived there. There was only about 15,000 in the fight on our side. But the enemy skedaddled through the night. It seems as though something was wrong someplace. We had about 100,000 lazing near there and only 15,000 of us fighting the enemy and being cut to pieces. It seems as though if all had been in it, we could have bagged them on the spot. The enemy that fought us are said to be 60 or 70,000, and if 15,000 could whip them, it seems as though 100,000 had ought to have taken them.

We have been here now three days. I believe part of the force is pursuing the enemy toward Cumberland Gap. I do not know how soon we shall leave here. We may start tonight, and we may stay here a week. It is very uncertain.

Much like Antietam/Sharpsburg, the battle itself could be considered another draw. But it convinced Bragg that he could not sustain his army so far from his base of supplies, and so, that night, he began a long, fighting withdrawal back to Tennessee.

Once again, Private **Leonard Lusted (1844–1923)** described the southerly movement in a letter home to his parents.

[Kentucky; location unknown]
October 17, 1862

Well, we started out this morning and went about four miles and had to come back. We couldn't go any farther. General Bragg has got where he can whip us, and we cannot touch him without cannon. But we have got some cavalry and infantry after him. Our cavalry ran into his this morning, and one of our colonels was killed.

The land is very hilly here and very thick with woods such as beech, maple, walnut, butternut, chestnut, hog oak, hickory, birch, and elm. The roads are awful. It is just like driving over a pile of big hard heads—all rocks and nothing else.

I would write oftener and let you know about affairs, but I can't get any postage stamps. They are a hard thing to get hold of. I would like to see you first-rate and the rest of the folks. I have not heard from home since I left. I am getting fat as a hog and ain't homesick a bit. I like this first-rate.

Dozens of newly formed Federal regiments hurriedly marched to Kentucky and Tennessee during Bragg's invasion. It was the first time many raw recruits had been farther than 25 miles from home. They savored sights they had never seen before and wrote letters about them that sounded as much like travelogues as reports from the front (a common practice on both sides). **Charles Henthorn (1841–1910),** a private in the 77th Illinois Infantry, described Kentucky's capital to his sister.

Frankfort, Kentucky
November 14, 1862

At noon came inside of the city. Approaching as we did by the turnpike, it cannot be seen until one is almost upon it. It is set down in the valley among the hills and on both sides of the Kentucky River. Expected the capital city of the state to be a larger place. It is not near as large as Peoria, Illinois. The Kentucky penitentiary, arsenal, and State House are among the most notable buildings of the place. The latter is a good large building with nothing very striking in its external appearance, being built of limestone rock probably taken from quarries in the vicinity. The bridge across the river is a good structure, and I should judge 700 or 800 feet long. The country along our route is very fine and under good cultivation. I saw a great many fields of hemp, either in stacks or spread upon the ground. Another thing which you don't see in Illinois is the stone fences. There are a great many along the road we have traveled. The turnpikes are generally lined on both sides with them. Just across the river from our camp, on top of an almost perpendicular bluff, the Frankfort Cemetery is situated. Here are the remains of Daniel Boone deposited and a splendid monument erected to his memory. I should like to go over and see it, but the river is in the way, and only a stone's throw across at that. But I must stop writing. It is getting late, and the bugle has just given the signal for lights to be extinguished. Tomorrow, we march again. It is said toward Louisville.

Both sides struggled over what to do with captured combatants. They were frequently exchanged during the first half of the war, as **Charles Darwin Carpenter (1839–1925),** a sergeant in the 20th Ohio Volunteer Infantry, noted to his parents.

Bolivar, Tennessee
October 13, 1862

I have just been up town on some little business. Saw them start off with the prisoners that were taken out at Matamoras [or Hatchie's Bridge, Tennessee, the previous week]. There was about three hundred of them. They have gone to Holly Springs, Mississippi, for exchange. There was some from most every state in the South. Pretty hard-looking fellows, too. They say they are coming back here in a few days with guns in their hands. We told them to come along, we'll give them the best we had in the shop. The ladies, too, made a great fuss over them. Told them to hurry back, for they didn't want the Union flag hoisted over their houses. I believe they beat the Northern ladies for patriotism.

Oh yes, you wanted to know something about Bolivar. Well, it is a very pretty town—a county seat, three churches, a good courthouse, five or six stores, some splendid dwellings, and a few good-looking ladies, but they are about as severe as hen's teeth. The majority of the inhabitants are niggers.

Getting exchanged prisoners back to their own side was often difficult. For example, take the challenges that **Samuel Swats (1833–1908)**, a private in the 11th Virginia Cavalry, encountered. After being captured in Virginia in September, he was initially sent to Camp Chase in Ohio and then to Camp Douglas in Illinois. In a letter to a prisoner still held at Camp Chase, he wrote that the journey to rejoin Confederate ranks at the western designated exchange point in Mississippi was long, hard, and uncertain.

Cairo, Illinois
October 17, 1862

I embrace the present opportunity to let you know how we are progressing on our trip south. We got here on Monday and have been in occupation of a horse stable ever since. Our prison is nothing like so pleasant as it was at Camp Chase. Our provision is not so plenty or so good, nor is the water. We use the water from the Ohio River. There is a good many of our boys sick, and nearly all of them complaining.

Our progress is very slow. We found 140 prisoners here from Camp Douglas, and the last squad from Camp Chase got in here two days ago. We know nothing about why we are detained here. Some of the officers say it is for want of transportation. Others say we are waiting for other prisoners to come in.

There have been some 8 or 10 taken the oath (of loyalty to the Union) here.

I will write again before crossing the lines if it is possible. We may start from here in a day or two, but it is uncertain. It may be a week or two.

As with any conflict, there were many cases of prisoners on both sides escaping their captivity. In his letter of April 11, cited previously, **Lawrence B. Worth (1834–1891)** of the 7th Iowa Infantry wrote to his father about one daring escape.

Two of our men taken prisoners [in the Battle of Belmont, Missouri, the previous November] came to us yesterday—one of our company by the name of John W. Pierson. He is a man of iron will and determination. He escaped from them for the second time. He left them the first time at Memphis but was retaken at Jackson, Tennessee, and was on the way to Tuscaloosa, Alabama. When they arrived at Corinth, Mississippi, in company with other prisoners, they had him in a house where they were to remain for the night. He slipped upstairs unnoticed by the guard, made a rope of carpet, fastening it to a bed rail which reached from one house to the other. Letting themselves down, he and his comrade made their escape through the guard lines, passed on their way the retreating portion of the Secesh army, shunned their camp, and came into our lines safe.

As the fighting dragged on, confusion on the battlefield often led to misery for soldiers' loved ones at home. Chaotic conditions and imperfect communication sometimes resulted in families receiving contradictory information. Consider E. B. Taylor. The 23-year-old carpenter was a private in the 2nd Massachusetts Infantry. Fighting in the rearguard at the Battle of First Winchester, Virginia, on May 25, he was wounded and captured. His mother was first told that he had died in captivity. Months later, she was informed that he was wounded and paroled. Like any parent hoping for the best, she wrote to her son's chaplain, seeking his assistance in ascertaining just what had happened. **J. N. Alvord (1807–1880),** the chaplain of the 2nd Massachusetts, forwarded her letter to Washington. (Taylor had indeed been injured, captured, and died while a prisoner in Richmond on August 16, as originally reported.)

Wilmington, Massachusetts
November 12, 1862

Kind sir, can you give me any information about my son, Elbridge B. Taylor, 2nd Mass. Vol. Co. I. He has been missing since last May. We received a letter from Henry C. Ames stating that he died in Richmond on Aug. 16 last, and Nov. 7, we received a letter from the Adjutant General at Washington stating that my son was a paroled wounded prisoner of war, that he was not reported Aug. 31/62. Any information will be gratefully received, or can you tell me where I can learn anything about him? Yours with Respect —Abby L. Taylor (Mother)

Washington
November 17, 1862

Dear Brother Quint,

I enclose a letter received and have ascertained at the Adjutant General's office that Taylor was wounded and taken last May at Winchester. Can find nothing further; do you know any more about him? Where he is now, etc.? Fraternally —J. N. Alvord

In the midterm elections on November 4, Lincoln's Republicans held both houses of Congress, though with a reduced majority. Still, the results were encouraging to Democrats, as Indiana farmer **Freeman E. Aldrich (1833–1888)** noted in a postelection letter to relatives.

[Indiana; location unknown]
November 24, 1862

The Democrats have played thunder with abolitionists, ain't they? Amen to it. The woolly heads are beat forever. I am very glad of it.

We are well at present, except I have got a very sore finger. It is as big as a whiskey barrel.

John, we have not been drafted yet, thank God, but we had to muster like the Devil. We had to stand guard for a long time along the Ohio River, and we had to go to Vevay, Indiana, two nights, and we would of had a big fight if General Bragg had not sent for reinforcements. It saved our bacon.

Excuse my bad writing and spelling for my finger pains me very bad.

Hurray for the Democrats!

The election results allowed Lincoln to do something he had wanted to do for months. General George McClellan had finally exhausted the commander in chief's patience. But because McClellan was a prominent Democrat, Republican Lincoln was unwilling to fire him before Election Day. Once the votes were counted, Lincoln removed McClellan from command on November 5, replacing him with General Ambrose Burnside.

The change set off a firestorm of outrage among rank-and-file Union soldiers, as **Phillip J. Crewell (1840–1917),** a corporal in the 34th New York Infantry, wrote to his brother.

Camp Warrenton, Virginia
November 10, 1862

McClellan left for Washington this morning. He is relieved of his command, and Burnside takes his place as commander of the Potomac troops. McClellan takes Halleck's place as general-in-chief. Now we will see who the blame will be laid to, but as sure as there is a God in Heaven, if McClellan leaves the army, the day is lost with us, for we don't have the same confidence in Burnside that we do in McClellan. The Rebels will fight more desperate, for they all fear McClellan. But time will tell, and that won't be long, and this war won't be settled in 10 years as long as we have them damn speculators at Washington, for they are all that keeps this war up, and as long as they don't have to pay anything they will try to keep it up. But I ain't got but seven months longer if we have to stay till the 15 of June, so let them work.

(Crewell has misinformed; McClellan did not replace Halleck as general-in-chief.)

The reaction was overwhelmingly negative in the army that McClellan had created and molded into his image. **August Josiah Robbins (1839–1909),** a second lieutenant in the 2nd Vermont Infantry, expressed the prevailing sentiment to his fiancée. (Eighteen months later, Robbins would be severely wounded in the Battle of Spotsylvania Courthouse while displaying heroism, for which he would receive the Medal of Honor in 1894.)

Camp near New Baltimore, Virginia
November 13, 1862

I have not much news to write except great dissatisfaction in the old Army of the Potomac in the removal of General McClellan from command of the army. It is rumored in camp tonight that 2nd Corps have laid down their arms and refuse to fight under any other commander. I do not think this is true, but if it could restore Little Mac to us, I would be glad, but I do think it would. I believe the President made a sad mistake in removing Little Mac just at this time. I believe our troops will not fight as well under Burnside as Little Mac. Mac has made this army, and he is the man to lead it in the coming battles for the right of the constitution and laws. Yet we must, as loyal men in the army, put our confidence in our new leader, Burnside. I would tell you, dear, many things if I could see you which I dare not write at present.

McClellan was a divisive figure in the North. Opinions of him were largely split along partisan lines. Although unsuccessful on the battlefield, he retained the army's love and admiration long after he had left it. **Dexter E. Buell (1842–1923),** a young private in the 27th New York Infantry, was among the thousands of soldiers who were disgusted at seeing their beloved commander (and, in Buell's case, fellow Democrat) cashiered.

Camp in the Woods
5 miles from Aquia Creek Landing, Virginia
November 19, 1862

Them damn abolitionists are a blowing their horn, "Why don't the army move? Why don't they move?" I would like to have some of them down here with a knapsack on that weighs about 200 lbs. I would run them on a double quick all day long, and if they did not go, I would run a bayonet through them. I will tell you one thing. There is no other general in the world that will do as well as General McClellan. The whole army will soon be fighting amongst themselves. There are officers resigning every day just because General McClellan was turned out of his position, and I don't blame them for doing it. I must close, for there is no use talking about it.

Hurrah for [Democratic New York Governor-elect Horatio] Seymour!

At the same time, McClellan's overly cautious approach to leading the army made many Republicans and abolitionists highly suspicious of his loyalty, as **George A. Brown (unknown)** wrote to his son serving in the Union ranks in New Bern, North Carolina.

Manchester, New Hampshire
November 24, 1862

The change in the commanders of the Army of the Potomac gives me great satisfaction, for I think that McClellan is a traitor and has been sacrificing our men to no purpose but for the benefit of the South.

I suppose you have before seen many of the Manchester, New Hampshire, men that have arrived at New Bern, and they will tell you all that there is of consequence here.

Heavy rain delayed Burnside in setting the army in motion. Once again, the White House applied intense pressure on him to move. However, many soldiers in the Army of the Potomac were skeptical of both the strategic situation and their new commander.

In the same letter to his parents of November 19 cited above, where he expressed his contempt for McClellan's departure, **Dexter E. Buell** shared a sense of foreboding about the coming campaign. His words proved eerily prescient.

We are lying still for a few days because the roads are too muddy to travel. I think we will see worse roads than we see now before the winter is over with. They all seem to think they are going to carry on a winter campaign. If they do, they will have to make a new call for troops in the spring, I tell you. We never can stand it, and it will take many a poor soldier to his grave.

Burnside planned to rapidly push south, cross the Rappahannock River at Fredericksburg, and then make a dash for Richmond. But that required a large contingent of pontoon bridges. The first soldiers arrived at nearby Falmouth on November 17, but the bridges did not. An administrative snafu kept them in Washington while the Federal troops impatiently waited. The delay gave Lee ample time to shift his army to the hills outside Fredericksburg and prepare for the onslaught that was coming. All the Yankees could do was hope the pontoons would arrive soon.

Yet, as the days turned into weeks, the Northerners began growing uneasy. Captain **William Washburn (1840–1922)** of the 35th Massachusetts Infantry told his sweetheart that the bridges weren't the only thing being delayed by bureaucratic bungling.

Near Falmouth, Virginia
November 22, 1862

I've been sitting for the last half hour at the door of my tent, scanning the hills on the opposite bank of the river, trying to arrive at some conclusion concerning the numerical force of the enemy in this vicinity. After thirty minutes cogitations, I've almost made up my mind that there is a small million of Rebels over there, for nearly every piece of woods is overhung by a dense cloud of smoke arising from the campfires. The distance from here is hardly a mile and a half, and although between twenty and thirty batteries from our side are bearing directly upon them, and doubtless the same number—and perhaps more—on their side aiming at us, the camp is as quiet as Boston on the Sabbath day. Both sides are evidently preparing for a tremendous struggle, and this is the "calm before the storm."

Fredericksburg, which is in plain view from the place I write from, is a much smaller city than I expected to find it. It looks very prettily from a distance, situated as it is in a hollow on the banks of a fine river, with very high hills on nearly every side. If its streets present no better appearance upon close inspection than did those of Falmouth, Virginia, I can't speak much in its favor as a cleanly city. However, I may not have an opportunity to form an opinion in that respect, for there's every prospect now of being obliged to shell the place before the Rebels will surrender it. In that event, it will probably be entirely destroyed or so disfigured as to make it impossible to gain an idea of its previous appearance. We have now been here for three days, and during that time, the cars have been running constantly to and from Fredericksburg, either bringing reinforcements to or carrying supplies from there.

Another great drawback to the advance is the want of shoes. Perhaps you will be loathe to believe it, but it is a fact nevertheless that a great many of our soldiers—even in this new regiment—are entirely destitute of shoes or boots. Some are actually barefooted, and out of my company alone, numbering now but sixteen, twelve are unable to march any great distance because of the worn-out condition of their shoes. Requisition after requisition has been sent in to headquarters, and always with the same result. "You will get them as soon as they come," is the invariable answer. In the meanwhile, the soldier is obliged to go around in his bare feet or wear shoes so full of holes as to render his going any distance without wetting his feet an impossibility.

Whose fault is it? If the government is unable to better provide for its soldiers than this, at this season of the year, it had much better send the men home, for they cannot stand it a great while longer. I've sent in a new requisition for shoes for my men this morning, and the only comfort I got was that they were probably on their way from Washington.

Fredericksburg was eventually shelled by about 150 cannons, as predicted. The pontoons at long last arrived, and on December 11, Burnside's men finally crossed the river and entered the battered city. That was encouraging news to Northerners watching from afar, such as **Robert Hill (unknown),** who wrote to his sisters from the fortifications that ringed Washington.

Camp Jersey
[Near Washington, D.C.]
December 13, 1862

The news that Fredericksburg was taken came in last night, and there was some good hearty cheering. We are expecting to hear of Richmond being taken every day. We are in hopes that Burnside will do something while it is good weather. There never was a better time to move an army than there is at the present time, for the ground is dry. There has been troops leaving this place every day for over a week.

In fact, Burnside moved while those words were being written. On December 13, he attacked uphill across open fields in the face of withering Confederate fire. Lincoln called it "butchery," and the losses bore him out. The Union reported 12,653 casualties to 5,377 for the Confederates. As he watched the fighting, Lee observed, "It is well war is so terrible, or we should grow too fond of it."

John Boulton Edson (1839–1863), a private in the 27th New York Infantry, wrote about it to his father that very night.

On the Battlefield
Fredericksburg, Virginia
December 13, 1862

The enemy is in a strong position before us. We crossed the Rappahannock in force yesterday morning after our forces had finished shelling the city the night before. Our regiment was ordered over and deployed as skirmishers and scoured the country a short distance in front, after which we returned across the river. The next morning—yesterday, I mean—the whole left Grand Division crossed. Our position is near the center. Our lines is about 10 miles long, so you may judge of the quantity of ground we cover and have to fight over. Our brigade lay under the fire of the Rebel batteries all day. It is a hard-contested field. It is nip and tuck with both sides so far, although I believe the advantage, if any, is with Stonewall Jackson, who I hear commands the Rebels.

We attacked them on the left this forenoon with a view of flanking them but did not make much headway. They have a very strong position. The troops have to spend the night in the open air, and tonight are not allowed to unpack their knapsacks. This order is that we may be ready to support the

skirmishers in case they are being driven in. If we should beat the Rebs here,
I think it would be a final one for them.

But the Rebels were not beaten. Far from it. Writing exactly one week after
the battle, Captain **William Washburn** captured the spirit of profound dejection
that had now settled over the Union army.

Camp Opposite Fredericksburg, Virginia
December 20, 1862

Little did I think last Saturday, just one week ago today, that I should be
in this place a week hence. But you know that we can't look forward to the
future with any degree of certainty. "Man proposes, and God disposes" is as
true today as ever, and when I said a week ago, "In a fortnight, I shall be in
Richmond," I should have put in the proviso, "God willing." But never mind.
There is no use in crying over spilt milk.

We are still at Falmouth, without the remotest idea of crossing over
to Fredericksburg again this winter. We visited the city last Monday and
have no desire to repeat the journey at present. Nearly everybody, as far as
I've been able to ascertain, are perfectly satisfied to allow the Rebels to hold
possession of Fredericksburg during cold weather. They complain of finding
the houses too well-ventilated and infinitely prefer shelter tents to mansions
perforated in dozens of places by 20 lb. shells.

The papers have undoubtedly given you full and authentic accounts of
the downfall of Fredericksburg, the battle of the 13th, and the subsequent
evacuation by our troops. Nothing is left me to tell but some minor details
that wouldn't be likely to find their way into the papers.

Saturday morning before the fight, the Massachusetts 1st was on picket,
and the most friendly relations existed for the time being between them and
the enemy's outposts. They intermingled freely with each other, exchanging
sugar and coffee for tobacco. Two even went so far as to indulge in a game
of euchre to determine the fate of the Southern Confederacy. Before the game
was finished, however, the two lines of pickets had to separate and "go to
work," as a Rebel expressed it. The Federal had the best of the game, though.
In a few moments, both sides were doing their best to kill each other.

The day after the evacuation of Fredericksburg, Capt. Joseph Hubbard
of the 2nd New Hampshire went over the river with a flag of truce. A Rebel
colonel, who was wearing one of our blue overcoats, remarked to Capt. H.

that he found our coats very comfortable during this weather. "Oh yes," said Capt. H., "it's a part of our mission to clothe the naked and feed the hungry."

I've seen several papers from Boston and New York, representing the spirits of the troops as excellent and the men as eager for another fight "as ever." It is not so. We are not chafing for another battle, and the man must be a perfect ignoramus to write such articles. They do more towards the demoralization of the army than any other thing. The soldiers know better and consequently lose all faith in those officers who sanction such fabrications. If you could but go through this army now and talk with the men, you would readily see why they do not wish another fight. They have lost confidence in their generals and do not wish to be forced into an engagement under them. Even General Joseph Hooker is below par, for they believe him to be one of the prime movers of this last blunder. Some, pretty high in authority, charge him with being the originator of the plan of attack. Whoever is to blame for our failure, there is not that feeling of confidence amongst the troops that formerly existed, and I'm sorry to say that there is a sentiment growing in the army which looks to an acknowledgment of the Southern Confederacy. You may rest assured that our soldiers will never fight so well again. They know that we have been whipped severely, with a loss larger than that at Antietam. Will any editorial in The New York Herald *make them believe otherwise?*

The North sank into a deep depression following the debacle. The year's seemingly never-ending string of deaths sparked a fascination with Spiritualism. It taught that departed loved ones could be reached via mediums who relayed messages between the living and the dead. Even First Lady Mary Lincoln is believed to have hosted séances in the White House to contact her dead children. **Louise M. Howe (unknown)** was a war widow who wrote to a friend in Massachusetts about her interest in the subject.

Guilford, Vermont
December 21, 1862

You ask when will this dreadful war end? I wish I could answer, but I fear not till all are slain. Look at our last defeat [Fredericksburg]. How many precious lives were lost. It seems to me that we are out-generaled. Have we no competent men at the North? Give me the Union as it was rather than what it will be.

*Addie, are you a believer in Spiritualism? I have always thought a
great deal on the subject, but more of late [recently]. 'Tis pleasant indeed to
commune with our departed friends and feel they are watching over us from
the spirit land. It may all be humbug, but I don't see it in that light. I hope,
at last, when I "depart and go hence," I may be permitted to watch over and
communicate with my friends. To me, it takes away the sting of death. I
wish I could see a spirit picture. I would almost be willing to make the trip
to Boston if I could be assured of having a picture of my dear husband. I am
not a true believer—neither am I a skeptic. I think it is something that will
be more fully developed at some future time.*

*You remember our Thanksgiving was not until a week after yours. I
spent that day and the ten following at my dear husband's father's. 'Tis a sad
day to me; it reminds me so strongly of him who is "bygone," yet I never like
to absent myself from the home circle. Think you not there were many a lonely
fireside and vacant seat on our last Thanksgiving?*

In the Trans-Mississippi Theater, Union forces opposing Confederates in
northwest Arkansas were scattered throughout the Ozarks. Confederate General
Thomas Hindman tried to exploit the situation before they could unite. But
when the Federals were reinforced, Hindman was forced to take a defensive
position on high ground near Prairie Grove. The battle that followed on December
7 saw a series of ferocious attacks and counterattacks until the Southerners
were compelled to retire.

John Danforth Wilkinson (1840–1918), a private in the 1st Missouri
Light Artillery (Federal), chronicled the killing to his brother.

*Camp at Prairie Grove, Arkansas
December 21, 1862*

*You have probably heard of the battle here. We were in the advance and were
in such close quarters as to use our short-range canister shot, which we threw
with great effect. One of our caissons was lost and retaken, the horses being
killed. Our extra horses were not brought up when most needed. I put my saddle
horse in place of one killed in a team, and now ride an iron gray captured
from the enemy. Two more of our brave boys have gone up [killed], and several
are suffering from severe wounds in the hospitals of Fayetteville, Arkansas.*

*The force we engaged was under Gen. Thomas Hindman and was supposed
to be 30,000 strong. We had marched from Springfield, Missouri [160*

miles away], and were tired and worn out. But we met and whipped that army of more than double our numbers, and the best of Texan, Mississippi, and Arkansas troops, and they in their own chosen position. We threw over 1,000 shot and shell. The loss of the 20th Wisconsin Infantry was very great, being due to the mismanagement of their commanding officer, thrown alone against a whole brigade of the enemy.

I thought our loss was heavy, but when I went over the ground where our shells fell, the sight was sickening in the extreme. The Rebels lay in heaps. I counted 43 in one of the many piles that lay around, and for miles on the line of their retreat, the houses and yards were filled with the dead and dying.

With their victory, the Federals were firmly in control of northwest Arkansas. Although 1862 was rapidly drawing to a close, there was no letup in military activity. Grant's attention was now focused on capturing the Confederate stronghold of Vicksburg, Mississippi. He dispatched General William Sherman to attack it from the north. And just before Christmas, General Earl Van Dorn found redemption in the field. Bounced from commanding an army after his defeats earlier in the year at Pea Ridge/Elkhorn Tavern and Corinth, he returned to doing what he did best: leading cavalry. He directed 3,500 Confederate horsemen in one of the war's most successful cavalry raids. Van Dorn rode into Grant's rear and stuck where it hurt most: the large Federal supply base at Holly Springs, Mississippi.

Francis J. McKee (1836–unknown), a private in the 16th Ohio Volunteer Infantry, told friends at home about both matters in this letter to them.

Camp Oliver, Tennessee
December 21, 1862

Well, we are on our way down the Mississippi River. We got on the boat yesterday morning. We traveled all night. We went about 90 miles, and this is Sunday morning, and we are landed here where there is fifty or sixty thousand of our troops.

While we are stopped here, there is a large gunboat that passed us going down the river. It had 14 large guns on it. If you was here, you would see some big sights. I am on the hurricane deck writing this letter, where I can see every boat that passes by. There is another boatload went past. They had a brass band. They played "Yankee Doodle" as they passed us.

A.J., there is more boats here than you ever seen just in a little bend of the river. You see as much as 40 boats. We are on our way to Vicksburg. There is where we will make the Rebels skedaddle.

I heard this morning that the Rebels captured 3,000 of our men yesterday at Holly Springs. They took them by surprise. I can't say whether it is true or not. That is the report.

P.S. Christmas Day. We are, at this time, 8 miles from Vicksburg.

Edwin Imes (1836–1915), a private in the 83rd Ohio Volunteer Infantry, was part of Sherman's assault force. He later wrote to his wife about what happened next at Chickasaw Bayou.

On the Mississippi River
[Mississippi; location unknown]
January 6, 1863

We spent our Christmas on board the boat with nothing going on more than any other day.

We got to our destination between Christmas and New Years, which was about 10 miles up the Yazoo River, where the whole fleet disembarked and which consisted of about 100 steamboats, which made a good long string.

We proceeded by land in the direction of Vicksburg, but we did not get very far before we came upon the Rebels' outposts, which was a very strongly fortified hill, and we had to cross a large swamp to get there. But we went through while our troops were building a bridge across a bayou that lay at the edge of the swamp on our side and the foot of the hill on the Rebs' side. They were attacked by a large force of Rebels, and after about 4 hours of hard fighting, they were repulsed.

We were not in this engagement but close by, ready if they should need any reinforcements. But while this was going on, we was placed in the rear of 4 of our batteries, which kept shelling the Rebels' batteries all day steady, and they shelled ours in return. A good many of their shells were aimed too high and came crashing through the woods right in among us, one of which did not go over my head more than 8 feet and struck the ground about 20 feet behind me. At first, they made me feel a little squeamish, but I soon got used to them and did not mind them much.

Well, after laying there in the swamp four days, one night after we were all asleep, we were waked up and ordered to fall in line with as little noise as possible and was marched back to the boats, and we came to find out what was the matter. It was just this: we were to take there only 40,000 men, all told, to whip 200,000 and them well fortified. If we had stayed in the swamp another day, we would have been all cut to pieces, for the Rebels had us nearly surrounded before we knew it. We got everything on board and started back up the river again. We lost about 500 men in killed, and I do not know how many wounded. Where we will go to next, I cannot tell. We are stayed [anchored] today taking on wood. We are now about halfway from Vicksburg to Memphis.

The defeat at Chickasaw Bayou has been called "Sherman's failure." That, coupled with the Holly Springs Raid, forced Grant to abandon his plans to attack Vicksburg from the north. **Solon Langworthy (1814–1886)**, quartermaster of the 27th Iowa Infantry, was among the Federals captured in the daring Confederate raid. Writing to Iowa's adjutant general three weeks later, he didn't bother hiding his contempt for the colonel who had been in charge of the massive supply depot.

Dubuque, Iowa
January 12, 1863

I am now a paroled prisoner taken by Van Dorn's cavalry at Holly Springs, Mississippi, in the raid of 20 December last. 1,333 prisoners were taken there, and some $1 or $2 million government stores and munitions were destroyed [almost $72 million today]. Had Colonel Robert Murphy, who was in command of the post and who had timely notice by telegraph from headquarters, used the cotton for barricading and other resources within his control, the disaster could've been avoided. He is the same Murphy who surrendered Iuka so gloriously. My horse, saddle, papers, and sidearms were all taken by the Secesh. But I intend to have a full equivalent for them sooner or later if possible.

December concluded on a serious down note for the North. In Virginia, Burnside's badly battered Army of the Potomac was licking its wounds along the Rappahannock. And in middle Tennessee, Union and Confederate armies clashed in a brutal battle along the banks of little Stones River outside Murfreesboro on the very last day of the year. Its outcome wouldn't be decided until the second day of 1863.

1863

"Three hundred dollars don't pay for one battle."

By the time 1863 began, hopes for a short war had long vanished. People North and South, military and civilian alike, now understood they were locked in a death struggle. However, as January began, no one could fully appreciate just how bloody this new year would be.

For men in the field, including this **unidentified Federal soldier** serving in what is now West Virginia, 1863 started with the same military routine as always. He also tried to reassure his sister about his personal morals.

Romney, Virginia
January 6, 1863

On New Year's Eve night, I was on picket duty. I walked the old year out and the new year in and looked for the Secesh in, too, but they did not come that night. I never liked anything better in my life than soldiering, but I don't like this thing of running like we had to do on Christmas Day.

I am very sorry that you have such a bad opinion of me since I came in the army to think that I would play cards. You can tell mother that I have never drank one drop of liquor since I came here, and I don't calculate [gamble], too. But I have played a few games of cards since I came here, but I quit it some time ago. Don't intend to play anymore. I think you will find when I come home that I am a better boy than when I started.

The first week of January brought word of a tragedy at sea. As the revolutionary USS *Monitor* was being towed along the Atlantic coast, she sank in a strong storm off Cape Hatteras, North Carolina, on the night of December 31.

Northerners had been especially fond of the plucky little warship since its historic battle with the CSS *Virginia/Merrimack* nine months earlier. **Winfield Scott Hills (1846–1916),** a teenage landsman aboard the USS *New Ironsides,* related the news to his father.

Near Portsmouth, Virginia
January 5, 1863

We have met with a great loss. The best boat we had got sunk. The bad news came here that the Monitor *lost 38 men and all of her officers. It is as great a loss as we have had during the war. I was on the* Monitor *the Sunday before she left here. I thought that I would like to trade places, but this is as good a ship as I can get on.*

(Hills was misinformed; 16 men went down with the *Monitor.* Another 47 were rescued by the USS *Rhode Island.*)

The first indication of 1863's deadliness came on the new year's second day. Confederates under General Braxton Bragg fought with General William Rosecrans's Federals in the cedar woods and farmlands along the banks of Stones River outside Murfreesboro, Tennessee. The action began early on December 31, essentially paused on New Year's Day, and then concluded on January 2.

Amos Gorrell (1837–1928), a private in the 18th Ohio Infantry, described the fierce fighting to friends at home.

Murfreesboro, Tennessee
January 12, 1863

Our division was up early [on December 31] and ready for the fight which soon commenced on our right by very heavy firing of both musketry and artillery. It was soon discovered our right wing was falling back. And we seen the Rebels in heavy columns.

We moved forward a little and opened a heavy fire on them with muskets and artillery, which checked them for a while. And there we stood, both sides pouring forth tremendous volleys of musketry, shot, and shell. There we fought until our artillery run out of ammunition and had to leave the field. The Rebel artillery then advanced within 1,000 yards of us and threw solid shot and shell amongst us which cut down trees over our heads. Some fell in the ranks killing and wounding our men. I was brushed with the top of a tree

*which fell among us. My rear rank man was killed, but I was not touched
by a ball. We soon found that the Rebels was flanking us and trying to get in
our rear and we had to fall back a short distance.*

*We made another stand, which we held until we run out of ammuni-
tion. We then fell back under cover of some artillery, which got in a good position in our rear, the men on our right having a fell back sometime previous.
General Lovell Rosseau came to our lieutenant colonel, telling him he wanted
a regiment to make a charge to check the enemy. Our regiment, though pretty
badly cut up already, was ready and we turned on the enemy and made a
charge led by Rosseau, as brave a man as ever appeared on a battlefield. We
charged with a fierce yell. Checked the Rebels and started them back with the
assistance of artillery, which then opened on the Rebels and slew them with
tremendous slaughter. The ground was strewn with dead and wounded.*

*Our division then fell back for ammunition, and other troops took our
place. The fight was kept up all day. Our men drove the Rebels back a considerable distance. At night, our men held about half of the field and the Rebels
the other. The officers and men of our division behaved nobly. The loss was
heavy on both sides. The reason of our right being drove back in the morning
was the negligence of General Richard W. Johnson. He made no preparations
but allowed his men to be surprised. His artillerymen was away watering
their horses, his men having breakfast, all entirely unprepared for an attack,
and the Rebels rushed on them in heavy columns, took part of their artillery,
and routed their men.*

*On January 2 our left wing was attacked by the forces of General John
C. Breckinridge. Our first line gave way once. Our brigade rushed forward
and filled the vacancy. We succeeded in driving the Rebels from the field.*

Bragg fell back about 25 miles. A few days later, when Rosecrans halted his
pursuit and both armies went into winter quarters, an **unidentified Confederate
soldier** dashed off a quick report to his father.

Camp near Shelbyville, Tennessee
January 18, 1863

*It is cold and snowy up here, and times is hard, and you have already heard
of the fight at Murfreesboro. I was in the fight but did not get hurt any. But
there was a great many of the boys hurt. A. C. Ball was killed dead and four
wounded, but all the boys from about Betah came through, and you can tell*

folks that it was worse than Shiloh to the number that was engaged, and I expect that there will be another fight in time before we leave.

(His observation that the battle was "worse than Shiloh to the number that was engaged" is accurate. The Federals suffered 16.2 percent casualties at Shiloh and 21.1 percent at Stones River; Confederate losses were 24.1 and 26.9 percent, respectively.)

The many recent Confederate reversals in the theater had prompted President Jefferson Davis to appoint General Joseph Johnston, who was still recovering from his wound received the year before at Seven Pines, to lead the Department of the West the previous November. Following the loss at Stones River/Murfreesboro, Davis ordered him to visit Bragg, personally inspect conditions within the Army of Tennessee, and report his findings to Richmond.

James B. Cox (1834–1889), a sergeant in the 29th Mississippi Infantry, told his wife that it was obvious that his commander was still suffering.

Camp Autry near Shelbyville, Tennessee
February 13, 1863

General Joseph E. Johnston reviewed us a few days ago and expressed great satisfaction with our appearance and discipline. I was under him in Virginia. I think he has changed in appearance very much. He looks careworn. He is a fighter. He has received no less than 13 wounds during this war. He is none of your Hotel Generals.

There is some talk of us moving from here shortly, and I heard today that Tullahoma was being fortified, and we may probably fall back there and fight. But it is very uncertain. We hear so many reports it is hard to tell what we are going to do. But I am of the opinion that it will not be long before we do something, for from the stir, preparation is evidently being made for a move of some sort.

Cox was mistaken; Johnston had not been wounded 13 times in the war; just once. Cox went on to discuss something soldiers and their loved ones at home frequently faced: premotions of misfortune.

I send you, according to your wish, the address of my father and that of my grandfather. It looks to me like you must have some foreboding of evil going to happen to me. If you have, I want you to let me know. I am aware life is uncertain, and even more so in an army actively engaged in the face of the enemy. But if I should fall, you will have the consolation of knowing I fell defending all I hold dear on earth: you, my dear, and [daughter] Mamie. God help you, but I have no fears or foreboding myself or anything of the kind.

The many changes in everyday life caused by the war included the first widespread use of a national paper currency since the Revolutionary War. Both sides issued paper money. Bills released by the Lincoln administration were nicknamed Greenbacks because they were printed in that color. The paper money was not backed by specie and could not be redeemed for gold or silver, causing public skepticism of it.

It was also the subject of a riddle that young **Warren B. Hill (unknown),** a civilian clerk at an insurance agency, shared with his little sister. Although considered offensive to some by today's standards, it reflects mid-Victorian humor.

Des Moines, Iowa
January 24, 1863

I know a conundrum got up at the expense of the Greenbacks by Mrs. Abbott, wife of a clerk in our office. It is as follows: "Why are the Greenbacks like the Jews?" Now, guess and guess again, but I don't believe you will find it out, so I will tell you the answer. "Because they are the issue of Abraham and know not their redeemer." You know that they [Greenbacks] are issued by Abe Lincoln and that they do not know who will redeem them. I think it is capital.

The American Civil War was not limited to the United States. Naval operations took place around the world. The most celebrated warship on the high seas was the CSS *Alabama.* She quickly charged into action on being launched in Liverpool, England, in August 1862. In a career lasting 22 months, the daring commerce raider never docked in a Southern port, yet she severely crippled Northern shipping by capturing 65 vessels valued at $6 million (more than $210 million today).

L. A. Woodcock (unknown), a missionary from New England living in the Caribbean, excitedly told her sister about seeing the famous—and feared—commerce raider.

Sea View
Jamaica, West Indies
January 27, 1863

There is a little exciting war news. In Kingston, the Rebel war steamer Alabama *is at Port Royal, the entrance to Kingston Harbor. She came in without liberty. She put in distress as she had a skirmish with the USS* Hatteras *off Galveston, Texas. The* Alabama *had on board 118 prisoners off the* Hatteras. *Mr. Camp, the American Consul, has succeeded and has gotten them all liberated. The Rebel steamer has to leave, and the British government has forbid it to have any wood, coal, water, or provisions of any kind. There are two U.S. steamers off way out of the harbor in waiting for her, and she is commanded to leave immediately. Some of the men of the* Alabama *have deserted her, and more of them would if they could. The captain [Raphael Semmes] says he and all his men will go down first before he will allow himself to be taken by those two steamers that are waiting for him soon as he puts out to sea.*

The Rebel steamer has been giving trouble on the seas by boarding vessels from Jamaica that are freighted with provisions for this island. She boarded one that was to enter one of the ports nearby to me and took off all the provisions that were consigned from America to any part of this island. I saw the steamer as she came along the north side of the island. It was the last day of December.

I am in hopes to hear soon that there will be measures taken to put an end to this war and save the lives of thousands. I open every letter with a trembling hand, for I do know what sad news it may convey to me.

With the war nearing its midpoint, men in the ranks were accepting a sobering reality: camps and hospitals were more lethal than the battlefield. In fact, for every three soldiers killed in combat, five died of disease.

George T. Woodard (1835–1864), a sergeant in the 8th Wisconsin Infantry, shared his concerns with a friend who was serving in the 29th Wisconsin Infantry. (The postscript was male banter between chums and not an actual threat.)

Germantown, Tennessee
January 30, 1863

I am sorry to hear of the severe loss that your company has sustained by death. It only corroborates the truth—that camp diseases are more fatal to soldiers than the bullets of the enemy. Our company has lost by disease 15 men; but the bullets of the enemy only 4 killed and 13 wounded. And there has been 17 discharged for disability while 4 have been transferred, thus making a total loss to the company of 40 men. And as our term of service is about half out, we can safely calculate on having a remainder of 20 men of the original 100 at the expiration of the three years service. I wonder if I am one of that lucky 20? That's the question that is of more importance to me than anything else.

The duty on which our regiment is now engaged is guarding the Memphis and Charleston Railroad at this point, fourteen miles from Memphis. We are having quite a vacation after five or six months of the most active campaigning. Till we camped here, our regiment has not remained in one camp over five days at a time since the 18th of August. We have marched 1,237 miles since we entered the service, participated in three regular battles, and a half dozen skirmishes. Our severest loss was at the Battle of Corinth, where we lost 132 men in killed and wounded in less than 25 minutes. I presume there are other regiments that have done more than we have, yet we have done enough to satisfy me with soldiering.

PS: Have you forgotten me? If you have, you deserve to be severely <u>castrated</u>. I have written three letters to you without receiving a response. Now you had better die or forget your old friend.

(Despite the levity, both Woodard and the letter's recipient would perish within 18 months.)

Meanwhile, people in the North were still processing the results of December's bloodbath at Fredericksburg, along with the ramifications of the newly enacted Emancipation Proclamation. Schoolteacher **Martha A. Lingrell (1835–1922)** discussed both with her brother-in-law, who was a Union officer.

Sumnerville, Michigan
January 18, 1863

I think matters have a more favorable appearance for the past week. Since the disaster at Fredericksburg, things have looked gloomy. But reports from

England are very favorable the past week, and the difficulties in Illinois and New York seem to be lulling down somewhat. Large meetings are being held in the former place to quiet the people and sustain the government. The difficulty in Illinois is the Emancipation Proclamation. They don't like so much nigger. And the governor [Horatio Seymour] of New York's excuse is arbitrary arrests made by the President. But I guess the great difficulty is he is, at heart, a Secesh.

While abolitionists cheered as the Emancipation Proclamation went into effect on January 1, many other Northerners were not pleased with it. In one case, it even prompted the wife of a Union soldier to take the extraordinary step of encouraging him to desert the army.

Twenty-year-old **Mary Van Nest (1842–1928)** was home in Ohio with her infant son while her husband was serving in Tennessee with the 120th Ohio Volunteer Infantry. Her remarkably candid letter even included a suggestion for how to do it, indicating that she had given the matter serious thought.

Rowsburg, Ohio
February 1, 1863

If I was you, I would not stay down there and fight for the Negroes anymore, for I would not have my blood spilt for them. This is not an honorable war, anyhow. The men that lives to get home will not have any honor.

Joe, I don't care how soon you desert and come home, and your folks don't care either. They said they wished you would come home. I would not want you to start with those [military] clothes on, but send me word, and I will send you some [civilian] clothes. I can send them in a box and get them expressed to you, and then you would have no trouble to get home, and you might go to some other state and work until the war was over. I would stay where I am, just so I know where you were. I would not care.

Oh! how I wish you would have taken my advice and stayed at home with me. Sometimes, I think it can't be that the one that I love best of all on earth must be so far from me. Oh, Joe, sometimes I sit down and cry when I think of times past and gone forever and never to return again. It is a solemn thought indeed that I may have seen you for the last time. It is hard to tell. I think sometimes I must just start and come and see you, but the distance is too great. It seems awful hard to think you can't come home until the war is over. Oh Joe, desert and come home. If you knew how bad I want to see you, I think you would.

(Despite Van Nest's earnest pleas, her husband did not desert.)

Some soldiers in the Union ranks, including **Henry Bowman (unknown)**, a private in the 126th Pennsylvania Infantry, bitterly opposed the Emancipation Proclamation. He bluntly shared his feelings with a cousin stationed at Fort McHenry in Baltimore.

Grand Army of the Potomac
Camp Near Falmouth, Virginia
March 7, 1863

I was glad to hear that you are getting your discharge. I wished I was in the same place you are in and could get my discharge. They are making arrangements for another fight and expect us to make a move soon as the roads are a little better. I won't go in no battle anymore in my time [period of enlistment]. Before they get me in another, they will have to kill me, for I ain't going to lose my life for the damned black niggers.

Martha Lingrell's letter mentioned earlier continued with an update on the situation in the East.

The latest news from Fredericksburg is there has been no more fighting. The Rebels are fortifying the place, and the opinion is that Burnside will soon make another move. There has been no resignations that you spoke of. I do not think the government attaches any blame to Burnside, but it was owing to a misunderstanding as to who should forward supplies and bridges [pontoons], and they were so long in getting up that the Rebels were too well prepared for them.

Indeed, Burnside was eager to regain the momentum that had been thwarted weeks earlier. He was finalizing preparations to march his army up the Rappahannock River and attack Lee in a different location. But this time, his plans would be undone by something beyond his control: the weather.

It started innocently enough when driving rain blew in from the west in an unusual winter thunderstorm. The rain turned into a deluge. Inside the capital's fortifications, the 138th New York Infantry, the same regiment underage Lewis M. Foster had joined the previous September by lying about his age, became the 9th New York Heavy Artillery. **Walter Guppy Duckett (1841–1909)** also served in that regiment. He expressed to a friend the cynical view of the war that was becoming widespread in the Federal ranks.

Headquarters, Fort Gaines
Outside Washington, D.C.
January 22, 1863

It is a rainy, dreary day. It commenced raining yesterday morning and has rained most of the time since. This morning, when I took the reports to head-quarters, I found the mud nearly to my horse's knees.

Well, John, I suppose you would like to know what I think of the war. I will not say much—only that I am fully convinced that it is a "humbug" or a war of speculation. I find that it is a fine thing for an officer to have plenty of patriotism when at home, but when they get down here, it is played out. Money and position are the only matters of consideration with them here. The more they can rob their "beloved country" (as they call it), the better they are suited. And if you could be in the streets of Washington but for one hour, you would be fully convinced of the fact. Pennsylvania Avenue is constantly thronged with officers of all ranks who put up at the largest hotels and live in the best style, and all this extravagance is at the expense of their "beloved country."

For the past few weeks, we have been busy building barracks and quar-ters, etc. I have now got good quarters (much better than barracks). I have got the tent that Lieut. Col. William H. Seward [son of Secretary of State Seward] had occupied. It is about 10 feet square and affords ample room for Ben and myself. The wall tents are entirely proof against rain.

But there was no protection for the regiment's enlisted men. The storm system was accompanied by severe weather, which made conditions rough for 16-year-old **Lewis M. Foster** and others in smaller shelter-half tents.

Camp Gaines
Outside Washington, D.C.
January 25, 1863

We had a severe rainstorm last Tuesday night. Some of the tents blew down, ours with the rest. Ourn blew down about five in the morning. The wind blowed so hard we could not get it up again. My cap blowed away, and I could not find my shoes in the dark. We had to go to some other tents in our stocking feet through mud ten inches deep. You would have laughed if you had seen us. I told the boys to never mind if we did get wet because it was all for the Union. It is military for a tent to get blown down, and in a whole, everything got as wet as water would wet them.

The ferocious storm struck precisely as the Army of the Potomac was on the move, trapping men, mules, and horses in the harsh elements. Burnside's Mud March was so terrible that many Northern soldiers considered it one of the worst experiences they endured during the entire war.

An **unidentified Union soldier** recounted just how miserable it was.

Camp near Stafford Court House, Virginia
January 25, 1863

We left Fairfax on Monday the 19th and had a very bad march of it through mud and rain. It rained for two days and two nights. We got here on Friday afternoon. Some days, we did not go more than three or four miles and was on the road nearly all day, so you can know that the roads must a been bad. We could a have went farther, but our artillery and wagons could not get along, and we had to keep in a reasonable distance of them.

When we started, the roads was froze up. We got along very well the first day. But after that we had a time. We had to build bridges across creeks and streams so the infantry could cross, but we might as well a waded, for we were wet all over anyhow and muddy. You ought to have seen some of the boys. You could not tell what kind of clothes they had on, for they were mud all over.

Well, we would stop at night and build a fire and make a little coffee and eat a hardtack and perhaps then go on guard as wet as a cat and stand in the rain wet to the skin. But all went off first-rate, all in good humor. Start off in the morning again, the rain pouring down and the wind a blowing and some of them a cheering and some a singing and some a swearing. I took it all calm and patiently, but it went hard for me to march, not having been used to much marching since I left the hospital. But I was always up with the ranks.

The road was lying full of dead horses and mules that we lost in the march—awful, awful roads. Some places corduroy roads for two or three miles for a stretch.

We started with two and some three days rations, but a man can't carry three days rations in a haversack. So we marched five days with about 3 days rations. We had only one day's rations in the wagons, and that was only crackers and sugar and coffee—no meat. The reason we run short was on account of the rain coming on, and we were five days instead of three on the road. But we are where we can get rations now and don't know how long we will stay here.

General Henry Slocum reviewed us yesterday and said to us that we had gained as much praise and had endured as much hardships in this march as any battle that we will have to encounter with. But I will stand all such marches sooner than go in any more battles for I don't care about fighting anymore in this war, for I am down on it now for I believe it all to be a good deal of imposition and speculation. I thought when I left home that I was going to fight for the Union, but I think different now.

The debacle was Burnside's undoing as army commander. On January 25, Lincoln accepted his resignation and turned over the Army of the Potomac to Joseph "Fighting Joe" Hooker.

The news was met with widespread skepticism among soldiers in blue who still missed George McClellan three months after his dismissal. **Thomas Marple (1830–1873),** a corporal in the 91st Pennsylvania Infantry, expressed the opinion of many in the Union ranks to a friend.

Camp Near White Oak Church, Virginia
February 8, 1863

Frank is about right in saying that no general can command this army like McClellan. But our Administration does not want me to think the same way. They must have an idea the way they act that a general sent to command a hundred thousand men can be picked up anywhere. But I think they will wake up one of these fine mornings and find their mistake. The men did not think much of Burnside, and now they think less of Hooker. I know that he was a good general when he had a corps and had somebody to plan for him, but now that he has the responsibility of the whole army resting on him I think that he will fail. I hope that I am mistaken. But time, the great revealer of everything, will show about the amount of it. This war will last until the administration drops the everlasting Negro question and goes to work in earnest, and I think they are to blame that it was not settled a year ago. I tell you the soldiers are tired of the way they have been fooled by the bigwigs at Washington.

Hooker quickly made sweeping changes to improve conditions in the hapless Federal army. His most controversial move involved turning a blind eye to army regulations and permitting prostitutes to follow the troops. Hooker believed that it was good for the men's morale. But not everyone saw it that way. **Benjamin Franklin O'Bryan (1837–1864),** a sergeant in the 140th Pennsylvania Infantry, wrote disapprovingly to his wife, referring to prostitutes with a polite euphemism for practitioners of the "world's oldest profession."

Camp near Stevensburg, Virginia
February 20, 1863

There is no exciting news of importance out here at this time, only there is quite a goodly number of the feminine sex who are out on a visit to the army. I am afraid a great many of them are hard cases who have come out here to ease some of the shoulder straps [officers] of their extra Greenbacks.

I tell you, the staff officers about corps, division, and brigade headquarters are having a gay time this winter. They have erected at corps headquarters a ballroom 10 feet long and 40 feet wide. The one at the division headquarters is 60 by 30 feet. They have dances nearly every night and I suppose all such other debauchery. For I think no other women but hard cases would stay out here.

Then as now, army life was filled with deadly situations beyond the battlefields and hospitals. Risk accompanied even routine military movements. **William Holiday (unknown),** a private in the 3rd Missouri State Militia Cavalry (Federal), told his sister about one such occurrence that winter on the White River in the Missouri Ozarks.

Forsyth, Missouri
March 7, 1863

There was five men drowned in the river the other day. Four of the 19th and one of the 1st Iowa Cavalry. They was crossing the river with forage, and the rope of the ferry boat broke, and she sank with two teams and about 20 men. They all got out but five, and they sunk to rise no more. Also, two wagons and 11 mules sunk to rise no more. Most of the men went down to the river to see it, but I stayed behind because I didn't feel very well. They say it was a harder sight to see them men drown than it was to see the battle-

field at Prairie Grove, Arkansas. I suppose it was a hard sight, poor fellows. None were of our company who drowned. One was in the water but swam out safe.

As Hooker was reorganizing his army in the East, Grant was dealing with a different problem in the West. Fresh off the previous fall's string of Union victories, he had turned his attention to Vicksburg, Mississippi, the hilltop Confederate citadel. It and a similar stronghold 130 miles to the south at Port Hudson, Louisiana, commanded the last Rebel-held stretch of the river, providing a vital conduit for beef and other critical supplies coming from Texas and Louisiana into the Confederate interior.

Anticipating a Union advance from the north, the Southerners had heavily fortified Vicksburg. In late December 1862, Federals led by General William T. Sherman had been transported up the Yazoo River and attacked at Chickasaw Bayou. They were repulsed with heavy casualties. That assault marked the start of the Vicksburg Campaign. Private **Alfred A. Thayer (1838–1878)** of the 96th Ohio Infantry described to his wife what happened next.

On the Battlefield
3 Miles Above Vicksburg, Mississippi
January 5, 1863

They are still firing away with the cannons and pickets all the time. I have been on duty every night but one since we have been here, and when not on duty, we have to lay in the rifle pits. But I don't think it will be long. The Rebel officers tried to get their men to make a charge on us the other night and got them in line, and they swore they wouldn't do it and threw down their arms, and they had to let them go back in their forts. So a deserter told us.

I was a speculating last night. I was on guard to the sutler's, and he was very lazy, and he told me if I would sell a box of gingerbread, he would give me half. I made fifty cents. The bread wasn't very good, but it would do for soldiers. I hardly know what to write more than we are a getting pretty used to the Rebel's sharpshooters. I guess they will be played out after a while.

While Grant was slugging away at Vicksburg, Lincoln was hedging his bets. He authorized an old Illinois political friend, General John McClernand, to recruit a second force for use in operations against Vicksburg. In early January, he superseded Sherman in a murky command situation, and, in a change that initially infuriated Grant, McClernand swung northward. Working in coordination with Admiral David Dixon Porter's gunboats, his men captured Confederate Fort Hindman on the Arkansas River at Arkansas Post, which defended the approach to Little Rock.

George Sifleet (1842–1863), a private in the 127th Illinois Infantry, told his parents about the action. (He would die of disease 90 days later in Louisiana.)

Camp Arkansas Post, Arkansas
January 15, 1863

I came out of the battle without a scratch, but I must tell you that the balls flew like hailstones. We left Vicksburg and came up the Mississippi River till we came to White River [as a diversion]. We run up that river about 30 miles, then stopped and got off the boat and went out in the woods, and they was well fortified there. They had breastworks there and had the advantage of us. But we was too much for them.

We fought them with our gunboats on Saturday night. They throwed shells where we was in camp for the night. We layed on our arms all night in the mud, and the next morning, we started on double quick, and we fought them for about four hours that day. Our gunboats was too much, and they raised two or three white flags, and our regiment's flag was the first flag on the breastworks. We took 6,000 prisoners. 4,000 was there, and 2,000 came in for reinforcement that night. They had left lots of clothes and things. Our boys got lots of everything. This paper was there. Our boys got three or four watches. N. Barner got one, and some of the rest of them got a gold watch, and some of them got pants and shirts and everything.

I suppose you know that I cannot write when I want to, for we have been a tramping through the mud and everything. Our brigade general is no man at all. At Vicksburg, he was so drunk that he fell off his horse. I am writing before breakfast. I must quit and get some crackers.

Private **Friedrich William Charles Heldman (1840–1912),** a young German-born immigrant in the 17th Missouri Infantry (Federal) Volunteers, also described his experience to his brother.

Near the mouth of the Arkansas River, Arkansas
January 15, 1863

The bombardment at Arkansas Post was awful. The whole fort was tore to
pieces. The men in it were nearly all dead or wounded. There were 125 artil-
lerymen in it, and only 20 were left when they surrendered. We took about
600 prisoners and a good many cannons. Our regiment was in the hottest fire
all day. I used 80 cartridges in about two hours, but we did not lose many
men. Our company did not lose any this last time, though we were in a hotter
fire than at Vicksburg [Chickasaw Bayou]. Our regiment lost 3 killed and
about 10 wounded.

Vicksburg is very hard to take. We are just now going down to try
again. I hope we will have better luck this time. If the Yazoo River gets a
little higher so our gunboats can go to work at them, they will find out better.

Those events were perplexing and difficult to follow on the home front, as
Martha A. Lingrell (1835–1922) shared in the letter mentioned before.

I should like to know what you are doing at Vicksburg. One day, we hear the
place is taken, and the next, it is contradicted. The latest papers say McCler-
nand withdrew his forces without the knowledge of Sherman, and there is
likely to be trouble about it.

Trouble did swiftly follow for McClernand. He was reassigned to lead a
corps under Grant, thus ending the potential threat to Grant's command of the
campaign. Still, the problem of how to take the Confederate fortress and open
the Mississippi River remained.

On February 2, the Union ram USS *Queen of the West* ran past Vicksburg's
powerful batteries so that it could disrupt Confederate traffic at the mouth of the
Red River. On February 13, the USS *Indianola* also ran the artillery gauntlet as it
headed downriver to support the *Queen*. **James Giauque (1844–1926)**, a private
in the 30th Iowa Infantry, told his brother about it. He also described another
serious enemy that Grant's men were facing: disease.

Camp below Vicksburg, Mississippi
February 16, 1863

We have had no chance to fight the Rebels here yet. They don't disturb us any
nor we them. The gunboat [USS Indianola*] ran down past Vicksburg the*

other night. Went down to aid the ram that went down before [USS Queen
of the West*]. I guess the Rebs fired many shots at her, but I expect it did not
hurt her. She ran on down, and we could not find out much about her.*

*It has been raining here for three or four days right straight all along.
Looked like it never would stop. I was on picket the other night at a post half
a mile below with three men. It rained, thundered, and lightninged all night
as hard as I ever seen, but I didn't have to stand so I didn't get much wet. We
made us a kind of shelter with blankets. I just laid there and told the boys
when it was their turn.*

*Our company has twenty-four or five men for duty. Other companies
have less. The sick men are all up at the landing. We call them the Quinine
Brigade. It takes a good man to stand soldiering. John Bennett stands it bully.
He don't say anything but is always in a good humor, and a guy for the eternal grit is Levi. He will never say anything about being sick. Spunks up and
gets well though that is what got Ben down when he was on the Yazoo River.
He was so sick he couldn't get along. Still, he wouldn't give up as long as he
could stand. At the same time, boys no sicker than I was played off [feigned
illness] and went to the hospital boat.*

*The men getting homesick is what gets them down most generally. I
believe very little else is the matter with men that ought to be stout enough to
stand it bully. Of course, there is many a man that cannot stand the hardships
of a soldier's life. That steamboating we done some time ago was enough to
kill most anybody. The brigade surgeon says our regiment could go north to
recruit if the colonel would only say so, it being reported unfit for duty. But
the colonel wants to get his name up, I guess, by keeping us here. Of course,
I would like to stay and get in a fight, but the colonel says our sick men will
never get well here.*

Write as soon as you get this, and if you don't get this, write soon anyhow.

As Grant worked out details for a new strategy to take the important Confederate bastion, he was amassing troops on both sides of the river. One Union
contingent kept Vicksburg's defenders occupied above the city, while a larger
number of troops gathered on the Louisiana shore beyond the range of the massive cannons. Among them was Corporal **Robert Boyd (1841–1863)** of the 16th
Ohio Infantry. Writing to a 10- or 11-year-old cousin, he tried to describe things
in terms a child could understand. (Boyd died of tuberculosis six months later.)

Milliken's Bend, Louisiana
March 4, 1863

We are encamped still on the banks of the Mississippi River, which is as wide as from Moreland to Ackerbacks and as deep as from your house to Hindman's. Some places, the river is higher than the country on either side and is kept in its banks by huge embankments as large in some places as the railroad at Wooster and a good deal wider so that one can see steamboats coming toward him, and they appear to be walking right over the land. You have never seen a steamboat. There are a great many things here that would be of interest to you if you could see them, but there is no use in trying to tell you about them, for you would not understand what I said.

If you could see all the soldiers here, you would see as many camps as would cover the land from Moreland to Wooster. The ground is speckled for miles as far as you can see with the white cloth houses of the soldiers. The ground is low and flat everywhere, and the upper deck of a steamboat is the only place one can go to look over the country. The fields are bigger than four of our farms put together, and many of them are full of corn that was never husked. Our army is using it now to feed our mules. Some of the fields are full of cotton that never was picked. Imagine a tall field of buckwheat with big brown stalks as high as your head and those stalks hanging full of bunches of wool so that you could see about half wool and half stalks, and you will have a pretty good idea of a cotton field.

You seem to think we always have a hard time sleeping on the ground. It is not always so. True, sometimes we must sleep right in the mud in the rain and have nothing that is fit to eat. But when we are lying in camp a month or two like we are now, we can fix our camp and tents so that we are very comfortable. We tear down all the board fences and old buildings and make beds up off the ground. Though they are not soft as feathers, we are used to them and sleep quite well, if not sounder, than if we were sleeping in the nicest bed. We live a good deal better here now than half of the folks at home, though nothing would give me more pleasure than to eat a meal with you and Aunty.

Gradually, a plan for attacking Vicksburg began to emerge in Grant's mind. In order for it to work, he would need the assistance of Union naval forces. So a force of seven warships commanded by Admiral David Farragut sailed up the Mississippi River from New Orleans. On the night of March 14, Federal forces on the ground advanced toward the extensive fortifications as Farragut's ships ran the Confederate batteries at Port Hudson. Four were disabled during a spectacular three-hour nighttime battle, including the USS *Mississippi*, which ran aground and sank with a deafening explosion. Two days later, 22-year-old Captain **Albert Jenkins Barnard (1841–1916)** of the 116th New York Infantry struggled to put into words what he had witnessed in this letter to his mother.

In camp near Baton Rouge, Louisiana
March 16, 1863

We were ordered to halt and go into camp for the night, which was about twelve o'clock. At this time, our advance was only two miles from Port Hudson, where they had a skirmish with the Rebel pickets, driving them into the fortifications.

Shortly after this, Commodore David Farragut opened on them, firing at intervals of about ten minutes. We could hear the report [of cannons firing] at our camp, the distance about eleven miles. At ten o'clock, the Rebs replied to the commodore's shots, and then the fight commenced in good earnest. After that, we could only hear a continual roar; no distinct report. It sounded like thunder, and the shells flew thick and fast. They looked like balls of fire, about the size of my fist. One burst in the air, and it seemed as if it tore the heavens. All the rest fell out of sight. This lasted till after twelve, which was the time the boats succeeded in getting by the batteries. This, together with the report that the Rebels was on our right flank with fifteen hundred cavalry and would probably try a flank movement. That kept us awake till two, when the colonel got orders to fall back with the wagons. This looked very much like a retreat.

All were excited and wondered what it could mean. At this time, we saw a bright light up the river and again heard firing. Both kept coming nearer and nearer until by the time we got started, it was just abreast of us. All sorts of rumors were flying through the train. The one that seemed most credited was that a Rebel ironclad was driving our fleet, which had first been damaged by the batteries. After we had marched about two miles, and just as it was getting gray in the east, a column of fire, smoke, and embers rose from the river as if from a volcano, and it was as light as day. All drivers stopped their teams and riders their horses. In about four or five seconds—it seemed an age—we heard a terrific report that shook the earth and frightened the horses and mules. The roar lasted about three minutes. The colonel says it sounded like an engagement, and then all was so quiet it seemed as if one could hear a pin drop. I tell you, I never saw so grand a sight in my life. I wish I could describe it.

In the afternoon, or rather at 1 o'clock, we were ordered to halt, and here we first heard of the success of our fleet and the burning of the Mississippi, *which was what we saw in the morning and what had given us such a scare. I don't mean scare exactly, but we thought we were running, and the Rebel gunboats were after us. Here, we heard also that our whole army was in our rear. A few moments after we halted, we got orders to go into camp where we were. The probabilities are that we will all stay here instead of going back to Baton Rouge. What the next move will be, or when, no one knows.*

Grant knew. And he was busy finalizing details necessary to set his campaign into motion. His soldiers on the far side of the Mississippi went to work building bridges, draining swamps, and constructing roads to carry Union troops through the Louisiana wilderness. Some were even digging a canal designed to cut a new river channel that would bypass Confederate batteries. (It didn't work.) **John Caleb Lockwood (1811–1891),** quartermaster sergeant with the 30th Iowa Infantry, observed all the activity and reported it to his wife and family.

In camp near Vicksburg, Mississippi
March 18, 1863

From indications for the past few days, there seems to be an onward movement toward the grand object of taking Vicksburg. A great many troops have passed our camp with five days' provisions, but what their objective is, we do not know. It, however, looks ominous.

The work on the canal opposite the bend in the river still progresses. One dredge boat now being at work about midway through, though the enemy are trying to harass them as much as possible, and while I write, their cannon is booming about every 10 or 15 minutes, throwing shells from the opposite bank, and although our present camp (having lately moved to a more pleasant site) is about three or four miles distant, we feel the jar in the air though. Up to last account, no damage had been done. There are now about 150 of our men on picket in the immediate vicinity.

Met one of our men from below [the city] who brought up a deserter from the Rebel side. Said he belonged to the battery opposite the canal and escaped in an old skiff, being a conscript [draftee]. Gives a hard account of

Rebel fare [food]—very scarce and very high. Said there are about 2,500 troops in Vicksburg and a good deal of sickness.

Young Barchoff from our neighborhood called to see me today. Said five gunboats have passed Port Hudson, and part of them are coming up. I'm told that our forces have gained considerable advantage in the rear of Vicksburg about where we fought them before [Chickasaw Bayou]. It is now thought there will not be much fighting, yet we expect to be in possession, or have control of, the river soon. Col. Charles H. Abbott was on board one of Commodore Farragut's boats and had an interview with him a day or two ago. Think likely we shall be able to pitch our tents on the hills of Vicksburg 'ere long, which will be an agreeable change from these low grounds.

Likewise, Hooker was moving ahead with his own plans for an offensive against Lee in Virginia. With spring nearing, optimism was slowly returning to his army. **Archibald Brown Cook (1828–1895),** a clerk in the War Department, wrote to his half brother in Pennsylvania that great things were expected from "Fighting Joe."

Washington City
March 14, 1863

We have had very disagreeable weather for about a month, raining and snowing most of the time. I hope we will have nice weather soon so that the Army of the Potomac will have a chance to move. From all accounts, the army is in better condition now than it ever was. General Hooker is very much liked by his officers and men. He has reorganized the whole army since he took command. I conversed with some of the officers a few days ago. They say they are bound to give the Rebels an awful thrashing as soon as the roads get good, which I hope will not be too long. General Hooker is a good soldier and a good man.

I received a notice the other day that my salary would be raised to $1,600 a year commencing April 1, 1863. I expected to be promoted but did not expect it quite so soon.

I am not certain whether I will get home this summer or not, but I will try and get a month's leave before September, if I get off at all. I have some serious thoughts of taking a Maryland lady home with me when I go. What do you think of the idea? Tell Robert to have me some good old rye [whiskey] when I go out next summer.

All winter, Confederate cavalry commander General Jeb Stuart had raided Union supply routes and harassed troops between Fredericksburg and Washington.

On the night of March 8–9, one of the war's most daring exploits took place. Lieutenant John S. Mosby, the "Gray Ghost of the Confederacy," led 29 men deep behind Union lines to the outer ring of Washington's defenses at Fairfax Court House. They captured General Edwin H. Stoughton in his headquarters while he slept and then sped back to Southern lines (along with 32 other prisoners and 58 horses)—without firing a shot. **Edward S. Manley (1841–1875),** a private in the 14th Vermont Infantry, excitedly shared the news with his aunt the day it happened. His account reads like an action-movie plot.

Fairfax Court House, Virginia
March 9, 1863

The first words that greeted my ears this morning were, "The general is taken," and great was the excitement in camp. We did not believe it at first, but soon the report was fully confirmed. Isn't this the greatest thing of the war? The brigade is all excitement. We can't think of anything else.

About three o'clock this morning, a body of about 40 cavalry commanded by one of Stuart's captains [sic] dashed into the village. It was a very dark night and suited exactly to their plans. They surrounded the house where Stoughton makes his headquarters and took the guards (five men with a corporal and the telegraph operator and all the horses) and knocked on the door. His waiter put his head out the window and asked what it was they wanted. They said, "Scouts with dispatches for the general." The waiter next let them in. At the moment he opened the door, six loaded revolvers were pointed at his head. Told that if he made a noise, they would blow his brains out. He had presence of mind enough to take them to every room in the house before he went to the general's room. Captain [sic] Mosby went into the general's room, waked the general up, and said, "General, you are my prisoner. I haven't much time to spare. Put on your things as quick as you can." The general saw that it was a fact. He put on his clothes without a word, and they took him off right through our picket lines, past cavalry, infantry, and artillery, and not a gun was fired nor the sound of a pistol even heard. His brigade knew not a word about it until morning. Capt. Mosby is the name of the Rebel that took the general. He left his card on the table in the general's room and wrote his name on the wall. Wasn't that a pretty bold dash?

It is the general's fault we think that he was taken. He ought to have been at the Fairfax Station, where his adjutant general and his nominal headquarters are. It is the Station and not the Fairfax Court House [some four or five miles away] that the 2nd Brigade of five thousand troops is guarding, and he ought to have been with his men. But at the Court House, he has a nicely furnished large brick house for himself and staff and lives in style, while had he been at the Station, he would have had to live like a soldier in a tent or board shanty, and "Generals must have their ease."

Wasn't it a "big thing" to steal a brigadier general? It's true, it's no laughing matter. But I don't know as it will do any hurt to laugh at it. The general has wanted to go to the front, and now I reckon he'll go to his heart's content. I hope our next brigadier won't allow himself to be stolen by the Rebs.

Mosby was promoted to captain six days later and then to major a week after that. Lincoln is said to have remarked that he did not mind losing a brigadier general because he could make another in five minutes, "but those horses cost $125 apiece!"

The problem of returning exchanged prisoners plagued both sides. The Dix-Hill Cartel had been reached in 1862, calling for prisoners to be traded on an equal basis. Trades followed extensive, detailed negotiations at City Point, Virginia. Once officially exchanged, the soldiers could then rejoin their regiments. The arrangement covered political prisoners as well as combatants.

One such swap involved the release of Edward Eggeling, Jefferson Davis's personal steward in the Confederate White House. He and his 22-year-old niece Eugenie Hammermeister were detained in 1862 by Federal officials while traveling to his native Germany and imprisoned as spies. They were released in March 1863. **Robert Ould (1820–1882),** the Confederate commissioner of exchange, reported the news to authorities in Richmond.

City Point, Virginia
March 17, 1863

A flag of truce boat has arrived with 350 political prisoners, General Barrow [Tennessee Attorney General Washington Barrow] and several other prominent men among them.

I wish you to send me at 4 o'clock Wednesday morning all the military prisoners (except officers) and all the political prisoners you have. If any of the political prisoners have on hand proof enough to convict them of being spies, or having committed other offenses which should subject them to punishment, state so opposite their names. Also, state whether you think, under all the circumstances, they should be released.

The arrangement I have made is largely in our favor. We get rid of a set of miserable wretches and receive some of the finest material I ever saw.

Tell Captain Turner to put down on the list the names of Edward G. Eggeling and Eugenia Hammermeister. The President [Davis] is anxious they should get off. They are here now. This, of course, is between ourselves. If you have any female political prisoner whom you can send off safely to keep her company, I would like you to send her. Two hundred more odd political prisoners are on their way.

Prison life on both sides was far from ideal. Consider the Confederacy's Libby Prison in Richmond. A three-story brick tobacco warehouse, it was pressed into service when large numbers of Federals were captured during the 1862 Peninsula Campaign. By 1863, more than 1,000 captives were crammed inside one large room. Poor sanitation, coupled with the South's food shortages, led to rampant disease and a high death rate there.

On his release, **Henry E. Wrigley (1840–1882)**, a captain and assistant topographical engineer, detailed conditions to a fellow prisoner's father.

Philadelphia, Pennsylvania
September 28, 1863

I arrived here last week from Libby Prison and left your son, Capt. Benjamin Franklin Fisher, enjoying fair health and in good spirits.

The officers are more comfortable than at first. They are confined in four large rooms, 105 feet in length by 45 feet in width, one in the second and three in the third story, and do their own cooking, washing, etc. They are allowed to purchase things outside, exchanging their Federal money with guards at the rate of eleven dollars Confederate for one of Federal money.

There is no prospect of [prisoner] exchange at present, but it is presumed that the Rebels, upon whom the exchange depends, will give way on the necessary points before long.

I saw Col. Meyer of Capt. Fisher's bureau in Washington. He has established a private method of communication with him.

The following is a late order of the Confederate War Department: "All gold sent will be handed to the prisoners in kind—also Confederate money. No more Federal money will be received. That already in the hands of the Confederates will be exchanged (at the current rates in the market) for Confederate money and handed to them." Any further information that may be desired, I will be most happy to furnish.

(Captain Fisher later successfully escaped. Having a background in architecture, Wrigley drew several illustrations of the inside and exterior of Libby Prison for *Harper's Weekly* magazine in the North. Those engravings frequently appear in Civil War books today.)

At the front, Confederate troops still stretched along the hills opposite Fredericksburg, where they had been stationed since November. Above and below the battered town, Union pickets patrolled on the far side of the Rappahannock River while Confederates stood watch on the opposite bank. The men frequently conversed with each other and, when their officers weren't around, even indulged in forbidden trading. **Robert Guyton (1838–1915),** a private in the 139th Pennsylvania Infantry, explained to his sister how it was done.

Camp near White Oak Church, Virginia
April 5, 1863

Enclosed in this letter, I send father a little bit of Rebel tobacco, which they sent across the Rappahannock River the last time our regiment was on picket. They built a kind of boat and rigged it off with sails and would send it over to our side of the river with newspapers, tobacco, and so forth, and our fellows would send them over coffee, pork, and so on. They were very willing to trade anything they had. But when the officers came along, both sides had to stop sending their boats over. Joseph Borland got a piece of tobacco that was sent over in one of their boats, and he gave me this piece. I thought I would send father a chew of the Reb tobacco.

I had one of the papers that they sent over, and I will give you a list of the prices [in Confederate money] of some things in Richmond as taken from the Richmond Sentinel *of March 30th.*

Apples	*$30.00 to $50.00 per Barrel*
Butter	*$2.75 to 3.00 per Pound*
Brandy	*$22.00 to 24.00 per Gallon*
Beans	*$16.00 to 17.00 per Bushel*

Corn	$7.50 per Bushel
Candles	$2.25 per Pound
Coffee	$4.00 per Pound
Dried apples	$12.00 to 14.00 per Pound
Dried peaches	$18.00 per Bushel
Molasses	$10.00 to 12.00 per Gallon
Oats	$6.50 to 7.50 per Bushel
Peas	$12.00 to 14.00 per Bushel
Salt	37½ cents per Pound
Wheat	$4.25 per Bushel
Flour	$28.00 to 35.00 per Barrel

Both sides utilized a Signal Corps to send and receive important messages in the field. It was an intriguing branch of service to **Arthur M. Stone (1844–1912)**, a young private in the 34th Massachusetts Infantry, who wrote his mother from Washington's fortifications about it.

Camp Fort Lyon, Virginia
April 2, 1863

You enquired of me in your letter what the duty of a man in the Signal Corps was. I do not know the whole of it, but I can tell you what little I know about it, that is what I have seen. Anywhere the Rebels is near, the Signal Corps are to signal back to the forts or camps where they are. The way it is done is in the daytime, they have a white flag, and in the center is a square of red cloth. Whenever one of the men sees them signaling, he has a glass he can look through to see who it is to. The way that they signal is by swinging this flag sometimes to one side of them and sometimes to the other, and each way indicates a certain number. And in the night it is done with a light in the same way. Sometimes, at a great distance, they send up rockets. I have heard that it was a first-rate place, and they get extra pay besides, I believe.

Our company is on fatigue. We went up to a new fort they are building on the Potomac and the captain said that we should work there for some time to come. We start in the morning about 8 o'clock, and stay there until about half past 2 o'clock and then come back and have our dinner. After we eat, we begin to clean up for dress parade and inspection, for they must have an inspection every night to see who is the "pretty one." The colonel wants to get his name up as having a very nice regiment. He gets the gains, and we get the pains.

Throughout the war, Union commanders faced two enemies: Confederates in their front and Washington politicians in their rear. Specifically, those serving on the congressional Joint Committee on the Conduct of the War.

Its hearings were held in secret, with reports to the public released periodically. A Federal general who lost a battle or campaign could find himself hauled before the committee and subjected to severe questioning. Members were particularly harsh on Democrats who failed to voice enthusiastic support for ending slavery. And it was frequently a thorn in the Lincoln administration's side for not pursuing the radicals' goals.

Former Army of the Potomac commander (and Democrat) George B. McClellan was one of the committee's earliest targets, as mentioned in a letter from schoolteacher **Emma Graves Shaw (1839–1924)** to a friend.

Providence, Rhode Island
April 12, 1863

Don't you lose your interest in the war sometimes? I get so disgusted that I throw the papers aside and think I won't touch another. But the next that comes compels me in a measure to read all I can find.

Have you read the report of the Committee on the Conduct of the War? Every new development serves to show McClellan in blacker colors. "How not to do it" is the story of the war except in rare cases, and those who do accomplish something are instantly shoved to one side. Unless the Rebels are starved out, I have no faith that we shall end the war until the government is ready for such men as Generals John C. Fremont [a staunch abolitionist] and Benjamin Butler [who declared escaped slaves to be "contraband of war" and thus not liable for return to their owners] and is ready to adopt their principles, carry out their plans, and endorse their deeds squarely and unflinchingly.

How it would rejoice the people to hear of the capture of Charleston, South Carolina! There are some flags flying, but I cannot hear of anything authentic. The Copperheads [pro-Confederate supporters in the North] showed their cards most too soon for success, didn't they? I am glad N.E. [New England] stands squarely for the Union. I see that we may look for a draft before long. I wonder if the Copperheads will dare organize to resist it? It will be their death blow if they do, I fancy.

I have not heard [Irish lecturer] Thomas Mason Jones or [Tennessee political activist] William "Parson" Brownlow. As to the latter, although he is an undoubted Unionist and has suffered for it yet, in other respects, slavery, for instance, his experience hasn't taught him what it ought, according to my notions.

The North took the threat of the emerging Copperhead movement very seriously. The Republican Party responded by rooting out suspected disloyalists from its midst while simultaneously laying the groundwork for Lincoln's coming reelection campaign the following year.

That was demonstrated in a letter from **George P. Stetson (1807–1891)**, chairman of the Penobscot County Republican Committee in Maine. The Stetson family was active in the GOP, as evidenced by their older brother Charles's recent term in Congress, and he was writing to the postmaster in nearby Newburgh. While that sounds like an unusual contact for political purposes today, at the time, all postmasters were appointed by the president and were expected to be reliable party stalwarts.

Bangor, Maine
April 14, 1863

I have been requested to ascertain who constitutes the Republican Town Committee of your town, who is its chairman, and whether he is unquestionably loyal to the [Federal] government. Please inform me of the facts at your earliest convenience.

If there is no Republican or Union Committee in your town, it is important that one be formed immediately of men who are known to be unswervingly true in their support of the [Lincoln] Administration and for the prosecution of the war for the preservation of the Union.

Sometimes, the response to the growing Copperhead threat went too far. After the twin disasters of Fredericksburg and the Mud March, General Ambrose Burnside was given command of the Department of the Ohio, containing Illinois, Indiana, Kentucky, and Ohio. Washington figured he couldn't get in any trouble there.

Washington figured wrong.

The region was rife with antiwar sentiment. Burnside reacted on April 13 by issuing General Order No. 38, a crackdown on basic civil liberties, including freedom of speech and freedom of the press. "The habit of declaring sympathies for the enemy will no longer be tolerated," it proclaimed. Offenders would be tried by military tribunals, not in civilian courts.

That infuriated many people living in the department, including **Mary Jane "Jennie" Cleland (1841–1864)**, who fumed about it to her younger brother serving in the 111th Ohio Infantry.

Defiance County, Ohio
April 24, 1863

I heard that General Burnside has issued a proclamation that anyone who says anything against Old Abe would be subject to imprisonment. I'll say what I please yet. Old Abe is worse than any king.

You see, we have no law to punish anyone but Democrats. The abolitionists can do as they please. They make laws to suit themselves. If they can't whip the South, they must whip someone, I suppose, so that they can keep the power. The Democrats should let them know that they are not going to have things as they please if it can be helped.

The Negro will not fight for himself. He says, "You white men may fight for us." The Negroes are beginning to think they were better off before than they are now, and I believe it is so, for they can never be kept down and behave themselves unless they are in bondage. The blacks are an inferior race, I think. I am willing that they should be freed if their condition could be bettered.

But Old Abe had no business turning the war into an abolition war. If the abolitionists had let slavery alone, I believe it might have been done away with after a while. I think the South are to blame, but there is no use in being so bitter against them. The abolitionists have no mercy for anything. I guess this is enough on the subject. If I write anything that doesn't suit you, just overlook it. Everyone has a right to think as they please.

In the White House, Lincoln privately fretted that Burnside had gone too far. But the commander-in-chief did not countermand the order.

On the Atlantic coast, the North launched a much-anticipated major naval assault on the Confederate port of Charleston, South Carolina, where the war had commenced two years earlier. A powerful strike force was assembled for the attack on April 7. It was led by Admiral Samuel Du Pont and included two new state-of-the-art warships: the 18-gun ironclad USS *New Ironsides* and the experimental monitor USS *Keokuk*. An **unidentified sailor** related his frustration with the outcome to his parents.

North Edisto Island, South Carolina
April 20, 1863

Our fleet of 8 monitors and the New Ironsides *ran in Charleston Harbor. When they came opposite Morris Island, there could be seen a glimpse of fire and smoke burst from the batteries of Forts Sumter and Moultrie. They fired from all these points by signal and at the same time. These shots—some 90 in number—were directed at the monitor* Weehawken. *The greater portion of them struck her but were no more to her than so many hailstones. There were 10 shots put through her stack pipe, but they did no damage as she can do without it altogether.*

The fleet ran by these batteries and forts in line of battle, and none received any damage except the Keokuk. *She was sunk, proving herself a perfect humbug. She was pierced by 98 steel-pointed balls. She was not built in the style of the Ericsson monitors but was of another model. The man who built her commanded her and said he would either sink her or batter Fort Sumter. So he ran within 300 yards of Sumter and cast anchor and only raised it again when he found the* Keokuk *was sinking. He got her out, and she sunk the next day. It is said that the government hadn't any faith in her, and the owners sent her here to test her quality. The crew were saved.*

Our guns fired but a few shots, but when they did give a broadside, it left its mark. They dismounted 2 guns in Sumter and breached her badly. Then Du Pont ordered them to come out of the harbor, and 'twas with great reluctance that the captains of these boats obeyed. They are confident they could have battered down Sumter and Moultrie in a short time. The sailors are also very much dissatisfied with Du Pont. This movement is a mystery to the greater portion of us.

Union land forces in the Charleston area were likewise disappointed in the campaign's failure, as 2nd Lieutenant **Charles Walbridge (1841–1913)** of the 100th New York Infantry wrote to his brother. He also mentioned the ill-fated monitor *Keokuk* as well as hearing about civil unrest that rocked a dozen Southern cities. Supply shortages combined with runaway inflation were making food outrageously expensive in the Confederacy that April, leading to "Bread Riots" from Richmond to Atlanta.

Folly Island, South Carolina
April 18, 1863

I have not seen a paper of later date than the 1st, though there is a paper in camp of the 7th and one at headquarters of the 8th. Captain Payne was telling me that he saw in one of the papers an account of very expensive bread in Richmond. If such riots get into fashion in the Confederacy, goodbye to the present [Davis] Administration.

Do you know whether Jake Davis was in the Keokuk during the bombardment and whether he got off safe if he was? The Keokuk is visible at low tide off the point of Morris Island; the Rebs attempted to meddle with her yesterday morning. But our blockading fleet drove them off.

Despite the fleet's firing, the *Keokuk*'s two massive submerged 11-inch Dahlgren guns were too tempting for the cannon-starved Confederates to pass up. Working at night and at low tide, the pair of prized artillery pieces were eventually recovered and immediately added to Charleston's defenses.

Cannons weren't the only items in low supply for the Confederacy's armies. The food shortages plaguing the home front were equally serious in the ranks as well. The situation grew so grave that Lee was forced to take drastic measures. In April, he dispatched two divisions under General James Longstreet to southeastern Virginia and northeastern North Carolina, where supplies were readily available.

The Confederates besieged Union troops in the town of Suffolk, Virginia, though fighting was light, and little came of it. The mission's real purpose was rounding up food for the troops in gray. As **George Setszer (1842–1863)**, a corporal in the 18th Virginia Infantry, mentioned to his parents, the expedition gained the nickname the "Bacon Raid" among Confederates. (Setszer would die less than 90 days later in Pickett's Charge at Gettysburg.)

Camp near Greenville, North Carolina
April 18, 1863

Washington, North Carolina, is about 25 miles below here on Tar River. We did not intend to take Washington, but all of us thought that we were a going to take it. But all of our wagons was a hauling out bacon all the time we was down there. We stayed down there two weeks, and General D. H. Hill was doing the same thing on the other side of the river.

We got our knapsacks from Greenville yesterday. I don't know how long we will stay here. Rumor says that we are coming back to Virginia, but I don't know whether it is so or not. We have been living on the country ever since we have been here. We haul the corn to the mill and have men detailed at the mill to grind it, and then we have been getting bacon for the army. I expect that we will stay here till we get all the supplies out of this country.

Longstreet's command was eventually ordered to rejoin the Army of Northern Virginia. Although it returned too late to fight at Chancellorsville, the food it brought with it fed Lee's army for two months.

The previous year's trouble with Sioux Indians in Minnesota and neighboring Dakota Territory wasn't finished, and the threat to settlers there remained real in 1863. Several thousand Federal troops were dispatched to the Great Plains to address it. Disgraced General John Pope, who had been vanquished by Lee at Second Bull Run/Manassas the previous year, now headed the Union's Department of the Northwest. Civilian **Warren B. Hill (unknown)** witnessed blue-clad horsemen heading off and told his sister about the sight. (The uprising would eventually end following four battles that summer.)

Des Moines, Iowa
April 21, 1863

Howard has told you about the 6th Cavalry in his letter. They passed through town a few days ago! They are going to Sioux City (pronounced <u>Sue</u> City) to fight the Indians. I suppose you have heard of the depredations of the Indians, how they murdered men, women, and children in cold blood. Well, General Pope, who is in command of this department, sent this regiment to the frontier to quell the uprising of the Indians.

The inhabitants of Sioux City (which is 275 miles N.W. of here) were very much alarmed, and a great many soldiers are there. This 6th Cavalry was a splendid regiment. It has 1,200 men in it, beside a great many horses and wagons which were needed to carry the food, etc., necessary for the subsistence of such a large body of men in crossing the Plains. It is said they were two miles long. There were about 50 buglers in front who played "Buy A Broom" [set to the tune of the popular "O DuLieber Augustin"] as they entered the town. It was a grand and imposing sight.

With their men away in the army, things were especially stressful for mothers at home with young children, women such as 27-year-old **Sarah Ann Bowers Haffer (1836–1904)**. She was raising three toddlers while her husband David was fighting in the 158th Pennsylvania Infantry. As she wrote to him near midnight one Thursday, her loneliness and fear for him, her children, and herself were all painfully obvious.

Cashtown, Pennsylvania
April 16, 1863

I heard that you were 30 miles from New Bern, North Carolina, and were surrounded by Rebels and that you would have to fight your way out or starve. You know how I would feel at hearing such news. I am writing you now, but the Lord only knows whether you will be spared to get the letter or not.

I would like to see your camp, but I would much rather see you coming home. I know it would be more pleasure to us all than anything ever was in this world. It would do me good to see Sammie put his arms around your neck and kiss you like he does me, and I know it would be equally as much pleasure to you, but it's not likely that we will be thus gratified very soon, and it's not worthwhile for us to talk about it. I always think that you will get home again, and you shall not go back again if it takes all we have to keep you at home, for if I had all the world, I could not have any pleasure now.

It is 11 o'clock and the children are up yet. I asked the girls what I should write for them, and they said I should send you a kiss and tell you to send one back. Ellie says you ought to come home, and then you would make her eat her onions. Sammie is hauling the chairs to the table and climbing on them so that I can scarcely write, and when I tell him to quit, he says, "Leave me be!" Not quite as plain as that, but he can talk very near everything now.

I want to finish this letter before I go to bed. I would just as soon write for I have to study [think] about you half the night when I am in bed.

There were men in the ranks who wanted very desperately to go home. They often pulled every string they could to be discharged. This letter from **Jesse A. Sargent (1824–1904)**, a private in the 6th Massachusetts Infantry, sought help in securing his medical discharge. (He didn't get it.)

U.S. Hospital
Hampton, Virginia
May 7, 1863

I am writing to you as I know of no other one that is so well acquainted as you are in the circles which would have an influence to get me discharged. Now sir, if you will try and get my discharge, I think it could be easily done as I am in this place with my right eye very badly affected with ulcers on the ball, and the doctors here have told me that it will not be any better till my time is out. Now I think there is no doubt if you write a letter to me stating my circumstances at home, that my family is dependent on me alone as I have no one large enough to help me, and that I must be very anxious to save my eyesight, you may try for me, saying that I have done my duty in every respect in the 6th Massachusetts until three weeks ago when my eye was affected and it is very bad. I am afraid if I stay until my time is out that I shall lose it. Now sir, with a letter wrote and signed by a man like Senator Henry Wilson or Governor John Andrews, I think that I should get my discharge so as to come home to old Massachusetts to save my sight, which I am afraid I shall lose. If you please, see what you can do. If I can satisfy you for the trouble, I will do it as soon as I see you.
The surgeon's address here is E. McClellan, the head man.

The Civil War witnessed many firsts in American history. Chief among them was the first national military draft. Up to that time, all previous wars had been fought with volunteer forces. While the Civil War began that way, it soon became clear to both sides that armies of heretofore unimaginable size were needed to wage a conflict that sprawled over half a continent. The Confederacy acted first, with the First Conscription Act's passage on April 26, 1862. (A second act came the next year, with a third act approved in 1864 that extended the draft to white males ages 17 to 50.)

The Union soon did likewise. Congress passed the Enrollment Act of 1863 on March 3, with the first draft scheduled to commence that summer. That cast an increasingly nervous pall across the North.

Spring's arrival meant that dirt roads were now passable, allowing active operations to resume in the field. In Virginia, Hooker had spent the winter preparing to go on the offensive in April's closing days. He left a sizable number of troops across the Rappahannock River from Fredericksburg, where Lee's army remained entrenched beyond the town, and secretly marched the bulk of his command upriver to the west, crossing on April 27 and turning to the south. The plan was to swing around and attack Lee from the rear.

The complex maneuver went smoothly at first. Then suddenly, on April 30, the bulk of the Army of the Potomac paused near the crossroads hamlet of Chancellorsville. Hooker lost his nerve and drew his men into defensive positions.

Lee responded by doing the very thing military textbooks said an outmanned force should never do in the face of a numerically superior foe: he divided his army. Leaving a token force in the Fredericksburg defenses, he marched west toward Hooker on May 1. Discovering that the Union army's right flank was "in the air" (meaning that it was not securely anchored to any geographic feature, such as hills or a river, for protection), Lee immediately spotted a strategic opportunity. He once again divided his small army and sent Stonewall Jackson on a roundabout march aimed at Hooker's exposed flank.

Private **Flavius Franklin Kimbrough (1839–1913)** of the 6th Alabama Infantry was writing to his sweetheart when Jackson launched his surprise attack.

Cooking yard near Guinea Station, Virginia
May 2, 1863

I will attempt to drop you a line this morning, as I don't know when I will get the chance again. But you must excuse me if you catch me nodding before I get through, for I have not slept more than four or five hours in the last forty-eight. I am also completely exhausted from marching and cooking. The regiment was formed day before yesterday morning and double-quicked down to our front lines as the enemy were crossing the river. We had not been in the breastworks more than five minutes before Nat Lyon and myself were detailed to go to the rear and cook for the company. We were put with the balance of the detail from the regiment and sent to the rear. We cooked all that evening and night. Next morning (yesterday morning) I carried the rations down to the company, and I had scarcely regained the cooking yard before we were ordered to pack up our cooking utensils and move. We then marched up the lines eight or ten miles and cooked all night again.

I think the battle is about opening, as I hear heavy cannonading on the left while I write. I am going to start to the regiment in about an hour with more rations.

I think the battle is certainly opened, as the cannonading grows heavier every moment. Fear nothing. I know God will protect me.

The fighting that followed was among the war's most brutal. Jackson rolled up the vulnerable Union flank until darkness halted his troops. When the battle resumed the next day, it grew more desperate as the engagement moved into woods and dense thickets. In an eerie forecast of a similar atrocity that would be repeated exactly one year later in the same area, the woodlands caught fire, burning some soldiers alive.

Lorraine Walker Griffin (1833–1907), a private in the 16th North Carolina Infantry, detailed the horror to his sister.

Camp near Fredericksburg, Virginia
May 30, 1863

You ask me how long I was in the fight. I was under the enemy's fire for 7 days. We fought Sunday, and we had nothing to eat from Saturday morning till Sunday evening. We could not eat even if they had anything, for we were fighting all the time. You said something about the woods burning. They was burning some as the cannon fired [ignited] them. We fought through the fires and whipped them back. Took all our men out, but the Yankees did burn. Some of them, they would halloo for help, but we was after our own. Some of them would put the fires out. Some we let them burn till they quit fighting. Then we put the fires out.

It was an awful time. I saw as many as 20 men fall in our ranks at one time from their batteries when we was charging them. Our men run them from a battery, and then they come back and planted their flag on the breastwork, them on one side and our men on the other. Our men took their flag and run them off. Hard fighting, but we whipped them. We fought off 150,000 men with 48,000 and drove them back across the river.

We were reviewed yesterday by Generals Lee and A. P. Hill. We had a fine time.

As the Battle of Chancellorsville was raging, a large-scale cavalry raid led by Union General George Stoneman was harassing Confederate supply lines in the rear of Lee's army. One week after the battle, 22-year-old **Franklin S. Wright (1841–1863)** of the 33rd Massachusetts Infantry told his mother about the fight. (He would be killed in action in Tennessee five months later.)

Camp Near Stafford Court House, Virginia
May 10, 1863

*We raised the devil with the Rebs last Sunday. What a difference in the
two days. Last Sunday, the roar of cannon and musketry was terrible. This
morning, all is still. The Rebs set their loss at 18,000. General Stoneman was
within 3 miles of Richmond and destroyed the railroad, and it is posted there
was not 100 men in Richmond, and if he had known it in time, he might
have gone in and destroyed the place and taken old Jeff Davis a prisoner.
And the Rebs admit that it is so. And they had the impudence to send a flag
of truce to General Hooker asking for rations to feed the wounded. I don't
know the reason why we had to fall back, but I hear that we are to start
again tomorrow.*

While both armies were engaged at Chancellorsville, another battle was
being fought a dozen miles to the east at Fredericksburg. Hooker ordered General John Sedgwick to attack Confederates defending strategic Marye's Heights
beyond the town the next day. On May 3, his men crossed the Rappahannock
River and marched across an open plain—the very plain where Burnside had
been so thoroughly defeated the previous December—though with a different
ending. **Edwin Lawrence (1822–after 1905),** a private in the 77th New York
Infantry, recounted the assault to his sister.

Camp near White Oak Church, Virginia
May 15, 1863

*Early on Sunday morning, our corps (which was all the force near Freder-
icksburg) took its position, which was a line from the city and three miles
below it. Our regiment was deployed as skirmishers at nine o'clock. From that
time till noon were fighting all the time. Then, all of our division charged
on the Marye's Heights—our regiment leading all the rest. We were the first
on the hill, and after we were to it, about two hundred rallied and took two
cannon from the Rebels which they could not get away before we were up
to them. We took a flag [of the 18th Mississippi Infantry] and a number
of prisoners. All of our forces to reach the Heights had to cross a level plain
almost a mile wide before we came to them. All that time we were under the
fire of the Rebel infantry and three of their batteries on the Heights. It was
the most terrific storm of iron and lead that men could stand.*

I am proud of our regiment now. General Albion P. Howe compli-
mented us on the field. This battle was not like the one last fall. This time, it
was the Rebels that suffered.

Chancellorsville was among the war's bloodiest battles up to that time. It
was a Confederate victory and is considered Lee's military masterpiece. But it
came at an enormous cost. Among the casualties was Stonewall Jackson, who
was shot by friendly fire. He was taken to the rear, where his left arm was amputated. Pneumonia set in, and he died a week later on May 10. A special escort of
veterans from Jackson's original command, the Stonewall Brigade, accompanied
the casket. Jackson's loss cast a profound depression on the Army of Northern
Virginia, as **John William Middleton (1835–1907)**, a private in the 27th Virginia Infantry, shared with his aunt the next day.

Camp near Hamilton's Crossing, Virginia
May 11, 1863

You have received all the particulars of the battle before this, and I will not
rehearse them, for it causes sad thoughts. Our loss is estimated from 8 to
10,000. I think it greatly exceeds that number. General Jackson died last
evening. There was a detail made from our brigade to escort his remains to the
train. I am very fearful that the enemy will make another forward movement
when they hear of his death. I have just now heard that the escort will go as
far as Lexington, Virginia. I would like to be on it if they do go up there.

Oh! that this cruel war would close, that we could return to our homes
and our friends. Oh, the gloom that this battle will spread over Rockbridge
County. She suffered greatly. A man made a remark just now that struck
me with force. He said all the original secessionists were getting killed. Oh,
I hope there will not be another man killed. I hope our rulers will come to
their senses and make some kind of a compromise. Anything in preference to
this war.

Just to think, after the hard fighting we did, they do not give us half
enough to eat. We have not eat anything today. They give us praise for gal-
lantry displayed, but that will not satisfy the cravings of nature. I would
advise them to dispense with their praise and give us something more sub-
stantial. I am of the opinion that our stock of provisions are nearly exhausted.
If they do not feed us better, there will be some of the greatest flanking done
[men deserting to return home] that has been done since the war started.

It is reported that the Yankees tried to cross at Kelly's Ford last night but were driven back. Oh, how I dread a second engagement. Some of our officers think that we will move forward in a few days. General James Longstreet has moved up to Gordonsville. If we have to fight, the sooner, the better. I want the war to stop, and I do not care much how it terminates.

Writing a few days after that, Private **Cornelius Smith (unknown–1864)** of the 107th Pennsylvania Infantry told his sister the news. (He was mistaken about Confederate General A. P. Hill, who was wounded but not killed. Smith would die in battle the next year.)

Camp Near Belle Plain, Virginia
May 16, 1863

We have been across the Rappahannock River, and we had a little fun with the Rebels. We wounded Stonewall Jackson, and he died before they got him to Richmond, and General A. P. Hill was killed. The Rebel loss was heavy, and we lost a great many. We are on this side of the river again. The Rebels almost captured our regiment, for we were the last coming off the field. The Rebels were close behind us. We left a great many wounded in the Rebels' hands, and I tell you, I would not like to be one of them.

Another Union soldier heard about the hunger and sadness in the Southern ranks. **Sylvester "Sly" Rounds (1843–1899),** a private in the 17th Connecticut Infantry, likewise mentioned them to his sister.

Brooks Station, Virginia
May 16, 1863

We—or the army—is all quietly laying on this side of the Rappahannock. We have been (that is, our ambulances) bringing off our dead and wounded, having crossed the river with a flag of truce. Quite a number of our company that were wounded and taken prisoner are already paroled and come back to our camp. They say that the Rebs all treated them with kindness and gave them the best that they had for them to eat, which was flour and water. They all say that they were very destitute of food. They took nothing from our prisoners but their weapons. Did not disturb their money or watches. They also said that the Rebs all seemed to be much depressed in spirits on account of Stonewall Jackson's death. I guess he has gone for good this time. If so, they have lost one good general. The [routed] 11th Corps did some good if they killed him, even if they did run.

Our folks that were prisoners say the Rebs were mowed down in windrows, that the battlefield was completely covered with their killed and wounded. They must of suffered much more severely than we did, although they may not like to own it. But one that saw some of it ought to make something like a correct estimation. I guess they got rather more prisoners than we did, but not many more. We captured about 5,000 of their men. They got about 7,000 of ours.

Waiting for word of a soldier's status in the aftermath of a major battle was often torture for loved ones at home. Consider the agony that **Martha Russell (1844–1924)** expressed in this letter to her cousin. Her husband was a private in the 20th Connecticut Infantry, and Chancellorsville was its first time under fire. Russell worked as a housekeeper while he was away.

Prospect, Connecticut
May 11, 1863

I am at last seated to answer your long-neglected letter. I thought of it every day, but when I first received it, I was cleaning house, and now, O! me, the fighting. Seems to me I shall go crazy for the 20th regiment was in the battle. I have seen only the death of two from that company, but quite a number from other companies. I have not known nor done anything for the last week. I cannot work. It makes me just about sick. I forget what I am doing half of the time. Made up my beds yesterday morning without putting on any sheets, and that is just about the way I work. I pity anyone that has got any friends in this war. It seems awful to me to have so many lives lost. I can tell you I am not much of a Republican. Be you?

Augusta, I will try and write a little more as I have a few moments. I cannot bear to think of the thing, but still, I am afraid what news I shall have. It is two weeks since I have heard from him—two weeks this morning since they marched. Such times I never seen in my life as the last week has been.

I advise you not to go to Waterbury to do housework to be made nigger of for the big bugs. I have had enough of it.

Oh! Augusta, Henry has come in and brought me a letter. It is from my dear Charlie! He has been in battle, but come out all safe and sound. He says Frank Matthews was hit by a ball and that Fred Williams, John Platt, and Jim Blakeslee are missing. Whether taken prisoners or killed, he does not know. I do hope they will fetch them back. I cannot help but think of poor Mrs. Henry Platt. I pity her from the bottom of my heart and the rest, too. I cannot be thankful enough to think Charlie is all safe. I wish the rest were.

An inaccurate communication after Chancellorsville triggered wild if unfounded celebrating among Federal forces in the West. Luckless General Ambrose Burnside sent a report to Union troops serving in Illinois, Indiana, Kentucky, Ohio, and Tennessee, erroneously announcing that Stoneman's raiders had captured the Confederate capital. **Charles Howe (1845–1864),** a 17-year-old private in the 36th Massachusetts Infantry, recounted to his parents what happened when that word was received. (Howe died at Andersonville Prison 15 months later.)

Camp near Middleburg, Kentucky
May 12, 1863

Sunday the 10th, I was on picket on the Green River and consequently did not share in the reports of the evening, but I will tell you what happened as it was told to me. About an hour after dress parade, as the colonel of the 36th was standing in front of his tent, a courier from General Thomas Welsh rode up to him at a breakneck speed and handed him an order, then rode away to the other regiments.

Colonel Henry Bowman read a moment and then gave a shout, at which the boys made a rush toward him. All were eager to hear the news. "Hold your wind, boys, hold your wind a minute," says he. "Steady boys," and then he read the order, which proved to be a telegraph dispatch to General Burnsides [sic] from the War Department stating that Richmond was taken and the Stars and Stripes were proudly floating over the Rebel capital. Now, three cheers for the Stars and Stripes quoth Henry. And then the boys set up a yell the like of which was never before heard in Old Kentuck [sic]. I was a mile and a half away, but I distinctly heard all the cheering and drum beating of that night. Every man was furnished with three candles (every man in the brigade). Two were placed on each tent and lit, and the other was stuck into the muzzle of the gun, and the brigade paraded around, cheering, beating the drums, etc. I could plainly see the whole performance, and it was the grandest sight I ever witnessed. Speeches were made by the officers, and "many were the songs that were sung."

As soon as the order was read to the boys, Bowman mounted his horse and rode round to the pickets, and soon fires were blazing on top of the knobs (as the mountains are called here) and all along the riverbank. I tore down about six lengths of Virginia fence and built a rib roaster. It was a noisy night, and I got no sleep at all but slept all day yesterday, or I should have written to you then.

Yesterday, the report came that Vicksburg had surrendered, and 30,000 prisoners were captured. I hope it is true, and then "Goodbye, Southern Confederacy." I want to see Charleston, South Carolina, in ashes before the war ends, for I think that place ought to suffer for its folly.

General Welsh told some of the boys that we should see home in three months, but I don't think we shall quite as soon—not before November, though the war may end next month. What will General Lee's army do now that their base of supplies is captured? Guess dat de Souf ain't quite nuff for de Norf, am it? Well, keep a stiff upper lip, folks, for I can see my honorable discharge now in a short time. I will be at home next winter, and if we don't have one good time, it will be because we don't know how.

Burnside's latest blunder was quickly corrected, though it fed growing cynicism in Union ranks. That, coupled with thoughts of the looming draft, was on the mind of **John Hebron (1842–1914)**, a bugler in the 2nd Ohio Volunteer Infantry, as he confided to his mother a few days later from the massive Union fortifications outside Murfreesboro, Tennessee. ("Old Rosy" refers to General William Rosecrans, commander of the Army of the Cumberland, who, incredibly enough, also held a patent for a soap manufacturing process.)

Murfreesboro, Tennessee
May 25, 1863

I don't think we will move unless Grant does something at Vicksburg or Hooker at Richmond. We have had good news from Vicksburg in the last two days, but I don't know how it will turn out. It may turn out like the last fight in Virginia [Chancellorsville]—the first news we got, our men were in Richmond.

What does Hans [brother Hansford Hebron] think of the Conscript Act by this time? Is he getting scared? I think it is time for him to be making some preparation and get a better thing of it than I have by going on a gunboat or in some brigade band. Or I see Burnside is going to recruit two regiments of heavy artillery for the fortifications around Cincinnati and through Kentucky. Or he might get in some home guard regiment or company guarding bridges on the B&O Railroad. I think he could get in our brigade band as they have no B-flat player in it now. But anyhow, don't go in no infantry or cavalry. Artillery is a nice service—only in an engagement, then it is pretty hard work. Gunboat service is nicer still, as you have no marches to make with a mule's pack on your back. It may be a little confining sometimes and hard work in time of action, but you have plenty of room for to carry as much as you can eat and better than we have here and have a chance to see a Northern state once in a while.

Old Rosy is doing things like an old settler down here. Things begin to look like civilization. He has 5 sawmills in operation, a large soap and candle factory (some of the boys said they seen Old Rosy in there making soap), and he has a large garden worked by convalescent soldiers not able for field duty. He builds his fortifications inside as nice as a man would build a house. Since he has been in command, we have drawed as rations pickles, potatoes, onions and peppers—something we never got before. We don't get them very often now because the quartermaster cheats us out of them.

Both armies in the East spent several weeks licking their wounds after Chancellorsville.

As Lee reorganized the Army of Northern Virginia following Jackson's loss, he also weighed his options. Momentum had swung to the Southern side, and gradually, he began crafting a bold strategy to make the most of it.

Several hundred miles to the west, Ulysses Grant was still focused on capturing the Confederate stronghold of Vicksburg on the Mississippi River. He knew that it was too heavily fortified to take by direct assault. All his previous attempts to advance from the north had met with failure. Now Grant prepared to launch his riskiest offensive to date.

Just as operations were getting underway, the Confederate high command was rattled by an unexpected loss. Adulterous General Earl Van Dorn was shot and killed by an angry husband in Spring Hill, Tennessee. **William A. Ferguson (1831–1902)**, a captain in the 8th Confederate Cavalry, wrote about it to his young wife in Alabama.

Camp Middleton, Tennessee
May 16, 1863

There seems to be but little doing in this part of the Confederacy at this time. All is quiet along our lines. You have seen through the papers an account of General Earl Van Dorn's death—an unfortunate affair it was. General Nathan Bedford Forrest, I understand, is to take his position as major general.

I was out near the enemy's line yesterday and heard a considerable fuss going on in Murfreesboro. Think the enemy are sending troops off from there to reinforce Grant. The arrival and departure of trains and the beating of drums keep up a continual noise. The impression here is that they will make another demonstration on Vicksburg soon. I see no visible indications of a battle here at present, although our forces seem quite busy entrenching between this place and Shelbyville. It looks to me like labor lost, but General Braxton Bragg knows his business.

Ferguson had indeed heard sounds of Union mobilization, but he was mistaken about its purpose. It was not an effort to reinforce Grant; Rosecrans was busily preparing for his upcoming push to both drive Bragg from middle Tennessee and prevent him from sending reinforcements to Vicksburg. (Ferguson was taken prisoner at the Battle of Shelbyville 31 days after the previous letter was written.)

After months of cajoling, begging, and even threatening from Lincoln, Secretary of War Stanton, and General-in-Chief Halleck, Rosecrans finally moved on June 24. He set his 65,000-man army in motion on the Tullahoma Campaign in the southern part of middle Tennessee. His goal was to capture the important rail hub of Chattanooga. That would open the way to Atlanta and, in turn, the Confederate interior.

The campaign was marked by prolonged heavy rainfall. Soldiers joked that "Tullahoma is an Indian name. Tulla means 'rain,' and Homa means 'more rain.'"

Yet the two armies got no respite from the inclement weather. **James B. Cox (1834–1889)**, a sergeant in the 29th Mississippi Infantry, indicated to his wife that an important moment was at hand.

In front of Tullahoma, Tennessee
June 30, 1863

We are lying out here expecting a battle to come off at any hour. Probably by the time this reaches you, the fate of Tennessee will be decided. We have been having some of the hardest rains for the last week I believe I ever saw. We evacuated Shelbyville last Saturday morning. The enemy came in a few hours after we left. They are now about 4 miles of our works here. We have lost all our cooking utensils, knapsacks, and tents. If anyone has seen hard times for the last week, I think it is our brigade.

We went up the railroad Sunday evening to protect a bridge. Just after we passed along about 4 or 5 miles from here, the Yanks made their appearance on the R.R. and ambushed themselves, waiting for the train to return with the troops we relieved. We made a little demonstration, and they skedaddled.

You will not probably hear from me again till after the fight. I could write a great deal more but have not time. I send this by a passenger to Chattanooga to mail for me. I thought you would like to hear from me just before the fight and know I am well. I have backed [addressed] 2 envelopes and give one each to Capt. Barland and H. S. Butler, so if I get killed or captured, they can write you. Keep in good spirits, and if I fall, bear it with as much fortitude as possible. Hope for the best and trust in Providence.

Write to me and direct to Tullahoma. If we get whipped here, our letters will come to us wherever we go. Put the brigade, corps, and division on the envelope. It will be sure to follow us. Ours is Walthall's Brigade, Wither's Division, Polk's Corps. Look out for a good account of it. If I come out safe, I will write to you, my dearest, as soon as possible.

While that was happening, Grant was embarking on his audacious gamble. First, he marched his soldiers below Vicksburg on the Louisiana side of the Mississippi River, safely out of range of the garrison's heavy artillery. Then, on the night of April 16, while Grant's men were slogging their way south, the Union river fleet commanded by Rear Admiral David Dixon Porter slipped by the powerful Confederate river defenses, much the way Porter's adopted brother Farragut had done at Port Hudson the month before. Although the firing was intense, only one transport was lost.

News of that success helped revive the Union's drooping morale. **Charles Kramer Reppert (1842–1921)** mentioned it to his brother, who was serving in the 15th Pennsylvania Cavalry in Tennessee. (He also discussed the newly formed Union Leagues. A semisecret organization with chapters throughout the North, its members encouraged loyalty to the Union and support for the war.)

Pittsburgh, Pennsylvania
April 27, 1863

The news from Vicksburg is cheering. A large fleet of gunboats and transports has run past the batteries. It is thought Grant's army will unite with them and then march onward. It is confidently stated that the rebellion is on the wane and will receive its quietus [death] in two months. God grant it! It would be a happy day to us all.

You have no doubt noticed a change of sentiment in the North lately. The Copperheads are not so rampant as they were. The Union Leagues have a beneficial influence on refuting their denunciation of the war and the Lincoln Administration. They [Copperheads] had better beware for vengeance swift and just will surely come to them for their treason.

When the army and navy eventually rendezvoused, the boats ferried Grant's men across the Mississippi River in early May. First Lieutenant **Morton Willson (unknown)** of the 93rd Indiana Infantry was among them, as he described in this letter to his sister.

Grand Gulf, Mississippi
May 8, 1863

This makes six days we have marched. The boys all stood the trip very well. We crossed the river over into Mississippi. I expect we will keep marching. We have had tolerable slim. But when we get out in the country, we will live fat.

This place has not been taken but a few days. There is about 40 prisoners here now. I think we will march on Vicksburg in a short time. We are some forty or fifty miles below it. We burnt some of the finest houses I ever saw. There was one plantation I suppose we burnt six hundred thousand dollars worth of property. It all went in a few minutes. I was in the cotton gin when it was set on fire. I said, "Let her burn."

It has been very cold for the last two nights. We have no tents nor cooking utensils and not a very heavy supply of blankets, for we thought that we would not need them. Some of the boys them hot days we had at the start throwed away knapsacks and blankets.

I must close, for it is so cold I can't write. It is nearly dark. My arm and shoulder is numb from carrying my knapsack, so as I can't write.

Grant kept moving, fighting the Confederates in a series of desperate battles until they were eventually driven inside Vicksburg's extensive ring of forts and entrenchments. **John Flannery (1843–1865)**, a private in the 72nd Illinois Infantry (Chicago Board of Trade Regiment), updated a friend back home in Schuyler County, Illinois, on the campaign's progress. (Flannery was captured at Franklin, Tennessee, and is believed to have died as a prisoner during the war's closing months.)

Near Vicksburg, Mississippi
June 6, 1863

You have heard before this of the movement of General Grant's army in the rear of Vicksburg and the part taken by the troops of General James McPherson's command in the recent battles. From the 13th to the 18th of May, we were marching and fighting every day. Our company crossed the Mississippi River with 54 men. We have now but 30 left. We had one wounded at Raymond, 3 killed and 5 wounded at Jackson, and 6 killed and 11 wounded in the charge of the 22nd. From the time we left Grand Gulf till we got to the fortifications of Vicksburg, we took 5,000 prisoners and 71 pieces of artillery.

We got here on the evening of the 18th, and on the morning of the 19th, we formed a line of battle, and skirmishing commenced along the line. In the afternoon—in crossing an open field—we had 17 of our regiment killed and wounded. We gained our position close to the Rebel fort, where we remained till we charged their works on the 22nd. We are now 50 rods from the Rebel works, protected by a hill.

We have the Rebels completely surrounded. Each wing of our army rests on the river. General Sherman commands the right, General McClernand the left, and General McPherson the center. They must surrender or attempt to cut their way out, which, if they do, we have every advantage of position and numbers. Our batteries have dismounted all their guns, and our sharpshooters pick off every man who shows himself. We are at work every night building fortifications close up to theirs, and Vicksburg will soon be among the things that was.

The Federals who survived Grant's massed assault on May 22 were stunned by its ferocity. A different type of savagery occurred a few weeks later. For months, the Union supply base at Young's Point on the Louisiana side of the Mississippi had been a gathering place for freed slaves. Some joined the newly created U.S. Colored Troops (USCT).

Confederates led by General Henry McCulloch attacked nearby Milliken's Bend early on June 7, mistakenly thinking that Grant's supply line ran through there. It was guarded by a poorly trained USCT brigade. Although the black soldiers fought bravely and received much praise in the Northern press, only cannonading from the USS *Choctaw* and USS *Lexington* prevented a Federal catastrophe.

James H. Mitchell (1842–unknown), a private in the 47th Illinois Infantry, had participated in Grant's May attack and was with his regiment when it was later sent to guard Young's Point. As he conveyed to his cousin, he did not share the Union's glowing assessment of the black troops' baptism of fire.

Young's Point, Louisiana
June 12, 1863

Our brigade lost heavy in that charge on the 22nd of May on their works. I never was in such a hard fire, nor ever expect to be. We lost nearly 300 men killed, wounded, or missing in our brigade. I never want to be exposed to such a fire ever again. We had to fall back. We stayed at Vicksburg for two days after the fight. We had two or three skirmishes with them and, after marching our brigade nearly to death, they bring us over here to Louisiana, and now we are guarding Young's Point from the Rebels.

They attacked a nigger brigade here the other day [Milliken's Bend] and liked to have cut them up entirely. They drove them to the bank of the Mississippi River, and they could retreat no farther. But the gunboats coming up saved the niggers. The Rebs took some of them prisoner and hung them. The niggers make great brigades. Our boys are anxiously waiting for an account of the fight in the Chicago Tribune. *How many Rebs they killed and how we drove them back, while it was actually the gunboats that done the work.*

(The *Chicago Tribune* strongly supported the Lincoln administration and its policy of arming freed slaves; the last three lines were sarcasm.)

As Grant settled down for an extended siege, a similar Federal investment was underway downriver. A second Union army laid siege to Port Hudson, the same bastion that Farragut's warships had run past a few months earlier. As **Henry Hall Northup (1839–1927),** a commissary sergeant in the 49th Massachusetts Infantry, wrote to his sister, it was a sprawling military installation.

Camp near Port Hudson, Louisiana
June 4, 1863

We are before Port Hudson—the stronghold of Rebeldom. General Nathaniel Banks, with an army of 25,000 consisting of infantry, cavalry, light and heavy artillery, is besieging and assailing the place. The heavy guns from the right, left, and center are constantly pouring shot and shell. This is more than human nature can endure, even by Rebs who have sworn to die in "the last ditch."

I can, of course, give you no description of Port Hudson at present. Formerly, it consisted of a few straggling houses and a grog shop or two. T'was the abode of the poorest and vilest of the Southern poor. The Rebs found it available for fortifications. How they have thrown up banks, dug entrenchments, and made it the stronghold of the Mississippi River. It is now a strong place. The front extends three miles. The sides are from two to three miles. Our force extends around the fort for about 12 miles. The Rebs suffer more or less exposed to the sun, with our shells fired among them, now from the right, now left, now center. They must feel that rebellion is surely punished.

The 27th, a severe fight occurred. Our brigade assaulted the works. The gallant Col. Edwin Chapin was shot dead. The 49th Massachusetts Infantry suffered a good deal. Thirteen were shot dead, 56 wounded, and 3 missing. Only 231 went into the fight. Three companies were on guard, and many were sick. Otherwise, the 49th would have lost more men. The loss was great in proportion to the number of men.

The living here for a few of us is pretty good. If the soldiers discover any cattle that they think will make beef, a crack of the rifle and down it comes. This makes some of the Secesh squirm, but we are in power now. The property of all Union men is respected, but when we come across a family where perhaps the husband and two or three sons are in the Rebel ranks, we show them very little mercy. This looks hard, but an invading army always lives more or less off the country where it is. The enemies of the Union must be made to feel the effects of secession.

Cut off from supplies and reinforcements, Vicksburg was subjected to ongoing bombardment by the besieging Federals. Its population—defenders and civilians alike—faced starvation. They also dug caves in which to take shelter. Then, on July 3, the gunfire suddenly stopped. **Alfred A. Thayer (1838–1878)**, a private in the 96th Ohio Infantry, reported to his wife what he saw next.

In the rear of Vicksburg, Mississippi
July 3, 1863

Well, Annie, there has been considerable excitement here today. The Rebels ceased firing, and pretty soon, they raised the white flag, and one general, one colonel, and one of their staff officers came to our lines on horseback. They dismounted, and our officers took them, and blindfolded them, and took them to headquarters. They stayed there a couple of hours, then led them back and let them go. What their business was, I don't know. Some say to get to take the women and children out of Vicksburg, and some say it is to surrender. But I can't tell. They are fine-looking men. Their names was General John S. Bowen and Colonel Louis Montgomery. I didn't learn the other name.

The forts were thick with Rebels. Our boys was up a talking with them, so we are having a fine time today. I don't know what it will amount to—I hope a surrender.

We have quit picketing in the rear and gone in front. It is a very hard place to picket. We have to go at night and stay till the next night and ain't allowed to lay down while we are there in the rifle pits. The dust is very bad and hot enough to roast a goose. Our guns got so hot that we could hardly hold them, and we had to keep up a constant firing day and night to keep the Rebels from throwing hand shells [early grenades] into our fatigue men that was digging right up to their forts.

[Added the next day]

It is with pleasure that I can write the surrender of Vicksburg. It was surrendered this morning at 10 o'clock, the 4th of July. You ought to have heard the cheering. It made many a heart beat with joy. The Rebels came out of their forts and stacked their arms. The number I can't tell for we ain't got to go in yet and I don't know as we will. I don't know what will be our lot yet but I will write soon and tell you more.

Well, I am badly disappointed. I expected to get in Vicksburg, but we have to start to Black River tonight at 4 o'clock, a distance of 15 miles, up and downhill all the way.

The next day, Corporal **William Kimble (1832–1865)** of the 31st Iowa Infantry excitedly described the fallen citadel to his wife.

Vicksburg, Mississippi
July 5, 1863

Vicksburg is taken, is taken at last. This siege lasted 48 days. They surrendered yesterday, the 4th of July. We took the whole thing just as they was. They had plenty of arms and ammunition, but they had nothing to eat. The soldiers have been living on a small slice of mule meat and an ounce of flour made of peas a day for several days. There is about fifteen thousand sick and wounded, and them that is well is so starved that they could not do much towards the last.

I got a pass this morning and went all over the city. It is a desolate-looking place. There is hardly a building but has had a cannonball or two put through them. There is hundreds of holes dug in the ground for the women and children to shelter in. The Rebels told me that they could not a got along as well as they did if it had not been for fruit. Peaches is ripe and tolerable plenty. I can't tell you how many prisoners we have got here. One thing is certain: we got all that is here, generals and all in a pile. It was a beautiful sight to see all the boats drop down to the city. There is now about 100 steamboats landed in front of Vicksburg.

If they [the Confederates] had a had plenty of provisions and ammunition, the way they was fixed the whole North could not have got them out of there. The most of them is tired of the war, but some hotheads swear they will fight till they die.

There was about 50,000 of our troops ordered out on a march last night. Our regiment waits for one. There is a few of us left in camp to take care of things. They took five days' rations. The Rebel General Joseph E. Johnston is in the rear of us with a pretty good army, and I expect General Grant to take them by surprise.

I can't tell you whether we will be stationed at Vicksburg or not. There is so many guard lines to go through, and it is hard to get a pass just now to go anywhere. But I think they will not be so strict after things get settled at Vicksburg. I think the fighting is pretty much done in the southwest but that does not stop the war. I don't see much prospect of the war ending for a while yet. I am tired of this kind of living myself, but I suppose that I can stand it as well as some others. The weather is terrible hot and the sand would almost roast eggs.

Vicksburg is taken. The Rebs is gone up in this part of the moral vineyard.

To the south, Port Hudson held on for five more days until surrendering on July 9. With the Union finally controlling all of the Mississippi River, Lincoln said, "The Father of Waters again goes unvexed to the sea."

With the Army of the Potomac recovering after Chancellorsville, many in its ranks still missed their beloved former commander. More than six months after his dismal, Union soldier **Henry C. Martha (unknown)** told a friend he wanted to see General George McClellan brought back. His observations reveal the ongoing lack of confidence many Eastern soldiers had in their generals.

[Virginia; location unknown]
May 31, 1863

The weather is very warm and dry, and the sand is drifting like snow. This part of Virginia looks almost like a sand desert. There is no grain or grass growing here. It has been traveled over so much that it is most barren.

I suppose the folks in Vermont are down on McClellan, but they are not here. Only some other generals that did not want Little Mac to have all the praise of putting down the rebellion. If they had gave him reinforcements when he called for them, he would have taken Richmond a year ago. But the Army of the Potomac has not gained a victory since McClellan was superseded. You thought if I was in Vermont and read the papers, I should think different about him. But I have a better chance to know McClellan than those in Vermont that read the papers.

They put in Burnside. He was the man. He was going to crush the rebellion. But what did he do? He crossed the Rappahannock and fought three or four days [Fredericksburg]. Our division was in the center, and our loss was light, but there was hard fighting on the left and right, and great was the slaughter thereof, and we were driven back across the river. And sometime after, we went on a pontoon expedition and worked three days in the mud and then returned to the old camp again. And General Burnside was willing to acknowledge they had turned away a man that was a much better and capable commander of the army than he was, and he was willing to give up his command.

And then they put in old Fighting Joseph Hooker. I am afraid he will get his horns knocked off. But I don't know what he may do yet. I will not write any more on this subject.

With spring winding down, Robert E. Lee was ready to roll the dice once again and try a second invasion of the North.

On June 3, he sent the Army of Northern Virginia marching northward. The Gettysburg Campaign began with an unexpected jolt almost immediately. On June 9, Federal cavalry under the command of General Alfred Pleasanton unexpectedly attacked General Jeb Stuart's Confederates troopers at Brandy Station. It was the war's largest cavalry engagement. The seesaw battle lasted all day, and although it was technically a draw, it marked the first time Northerners had ever fought on par with Southern horsemen. That—and the fact that Lee's army was now on the move—concerned teenager **David Breed (1848–1931)**, writing to his older brother, who was an officer in Hooker's army.

Pittsburgh, Pennsylvania
June 11, 1863

I suppose and hope you were not in the last fight between Pleasanton and Stuart. I believe they are making preparations to guard Pittsburgh from any attack by the Rebs as it would be easy for them, with the present condition of Pittsburgh, to come and take it and burn it to the ground.

Fear spread throughout the North as the gray columns headed out of Virginia. Just four days later, young Breed again wrote to his brother, this time with an urgency that bordered on hysteria. (It is worth noting several things. First, Lee's troops never went anywhere near Pittsburgh. Next, the second letter's tone is a dramatic contrast to the June 11 letter. Finally, mid-Victorians used exclamation points with exceeding rarity. The fact that Breed used so many in his second correspondence reveals both his youth and his fear that his city was at serious risk of capture.)

Pittsburgh, Pennsylvania
June 15, 1863

Pittsburgh in great danger! How does that sound to you? The Rebels are coming!!! How does that sound to you? Pittsburgh to be put under Marshal [sic] Law!!!!!! How does that sound? Coal and Herron Hills to be and are being entrenched!!!!!!!!!! Hurrah for General William T. H. Brooks, major general commanding the Department of the Monongahela. These are facts.

There is great excitement in Pittsburgh today. The Rebels are said to be coming, and General Halleck telegraphs that Pittsburgh is in great danger of a Rebel raid, and General Brooks is ordered to command us. The Rebels are said to be at Hagerstown, Maryland, and coming right on to Pittsburgh, and they are entrenching Coal Hill and Herron's Hill. 2,000 men, I believe, are at work on the entrenchments. Some 100,000 militia have been ordered out from adjoining states, and 5,000 Ohio troops are expected here tonight.

This is the state of things at Pittsburgh. Hurrah for General Brooks! May God keep them off and send them panic-stricken back to their own dominions.

With the military situation rapidly dissolving into a crisis, Hooker was removed from command of the Army of the Potomac on June 27 and replaced by General George Meade. The news spread like wildfire through the ranks, as **Anson Mills (1843–1922),** a private in the 23rd Ohio Infantry, observed to a friend.

Fairfax Seminary Hospital, Virginia
June 28, 1863

I have just heard today of the removal of Joe Hooker from the command of the army. What in hell is that for? Can you tell? Can anybody tell? Only that he has not been able with an inferior force to defeat a superior. I am almost tempted to damn Abe Lincoln uphill and down for it. I suppose that he has some reason for it, or he would not have done it, but it is discouraging. The war will never end in our favor if it is carried on as it has been for the last year.

We have very exciting times here, considering our location. There is a signal station here and a squad of cavalry is also stationed here. They have to go out scouting every night and signal all the daytime. The Rebs are not very far from us. They are way this side of the Court House and have been seen rather too close to us to be comfortable.

A squad of cavalry have just went past bound for a scout. I don't envy them. I have had all that I want of it.

Spirits were high in Lee's army. Writing in July after returning to Virginia, **Stephen Long (1832–1868),** a soldier in the 2nd South Carolina Infantry, detailed the journey leading to the fateful battle to his sister-in-law.

Camp Near Culpepper, Virginia
July 25, 1863

No doubt, an advance was anticipated by the people at home as well as by the soldiers in the army. For my part, I only thought we would make a raid into Maryland and had no idea of visiting the land of Pennsylvania.

Saw plenty of ladies on the road and any quantity of white handkerchiefs to Gainesville and rested about two hours, then marched till night making 21 miles. This was the hottest day of all, and men fell on all sides of the road, being overcome with the heat, some of whom died from sunstroke. So intense was the heat that the rear guard were ordered not to arrest the men who fell behind.

On June 17th, we passed through Ashby's Gap. We met the cavalry here. They had just had a brush with the Yankees and drove them back, for a wonder. Our cavalry have justly gained for themselves the title of "Buttermilk Boys" as they usually fall back when provisions are scarce, or there is a support of infantry near.

From this gap we marched to the Shenandoah River, and here we had a very rough time. The river was very swollen and very swift and it was with difficulty that we could wade it. The water came up nearly to my armpits. Very few of the men took off a thing but, swinging their cartridge boxes on their bayonets, went in with a shout.

Having crossed, we built large fires and having dried off our clothes retired for the night. We remained here until the 23rd of June and went to Summit Point, 20 miles. Here was the first place we got fresh beef to eat since last winter. Several of us made a large kettle of soup and made a hearty supper at half past one at night. Slept till daylight and started for Martinsburg, passing through Smithfield where we were cheered by the ladies. This day we made 20 miles and took up at night.

Next day, we waded the Potomac and landed on Uncle Sam's territory after a march of 16 miles. We were now in Maryland. Started in the direction of Hagerstown. Secesh got beautifully less, and the old fogey's faces began to assume a length out of all proportion to our own people. We began to see young men with boiled [freshly washed] shirts on, which seemed to make our boys feel like the barber's wife in the Alhambra when they found the gold. "Proud to show them my rags."

Reached Middleburg on the Pennsylvania line, gave three rousing cheers for Abe Lincoln, and a lady close by remarked, "Yes, and a rope to hang him." We were now on a turnpike, but the mud was awful, so we took through wheat fields and clover pastures. Orders were very strict, and our camps guarded to keep the men in. Washington's army was tracked over the frozen ground by the blood from their feet. Ours could have been tracked by cherry tree boughs, chicken feathers, and empty dairies.

Passed through Greencastle, where, for ornaments, they had cherry trees, and every tree had a Rebel in it. Brass bands played "Dixie" and "Bonnie Blue Flag." The dogs barked at us, and our wagon trains peeled a merry chime from the old Dutchmen's sleigh bells as they adorned our mules. The old women squinted but gave everything they had, only asking us not to burn down their houses. This showed a guilty conscience on their part and surely they must have taken the Rebels for a set of such people as was furnished to their army of marauders. The Rebel army, though their advance struck terror to the hearts of everyone, behaved very well. Next, we went to Chambersburg, a large town. Passed through on Sunday. A great many turned out to see us pass.

From there, we went to Gettysburg, where the great battle took place.

And so began the largest engagement ever fought in the Western Hemisphere. It also marked both the Confederacy's high-water mark and a shift of momentum in the North's favor.

The battle itself is so widely known and so well studied that an in-depth review of it isn't necessary here. This capsule summary that **Franz Trouts (1836–1863)**, a private in the 11th U.S. Artillery, recounted a few weeks later to a cousin succinctly sums up what happened. (Trouts died in an accident on a railroad bridge in northern Virginia 12 days after writing this.)

Near Shepherdstown, Maryland
August 11, 1863

We have fought the hardest battle at Gettysburg, Pennsylvania, that I ever was in, and I never seen Secesh so completely whipped on as large a scale before. The Secesh outnumbered us three to one on the first two days, but it appears that they hadn't all their forces ready for a fight.

On the third day, the fight commenced in earnest. They opened with their artillery, but we could bring three pieces to bear on every one of theirs. When they found that they could not silence our batteries, they tried their old game of charging, first on our left, then on our right, and then on our center.

But they were met and repulsed or captured on every point. There had been some talk about capturing what is left of the Secession army before they could get across the Potomac, but they managed to get off again.

Likewise, **Jacob F. Mader Jr. (1840–1922),** a second lieutenant in the 61st Ohio Infantry, testified to the battle's severity to his future wife.

In line of battle near Gettysburg, Pennsylvania
July 5, 1863

This is the fifth day we have fought the Rebels with a heavy loss on both sides. We are in possession of nearly the whole battlefield. The Johnny Rebs charged us from all sides but were driven back with great slaughter every time. There was not a spot in our lines that was not reached by their cannon. Our line is in the shape of a horseshoe. We can reinforce either flank in fifteen minutes.

The Rebel batteries had us in a crossfire while lying on the hill of Gettysburg Cemetery. For two days, Captain Garrett, myself, Lieutenant Smith, and 52 men were supporting Dilger's Battery under a crossfire of the Rebels' shot and shell, which made the air hideous with their whizzing.

Our regiment has suffered considerable. Captain Reynolds was wounded and has since died. Doctor Moore had his hip shattered by a solid shot. It is supposed he will die. Captain Bending is missing, and it is hoped he is a prisoner.

From what I can hear, we have taken from 15,000 to 20,000 prisoners. Among them is the Rebel General James Longstreet and other officers of high rank.

I think the Rebs have retreated or are retreating. I am thankful to the Almighty God that I have escaped the iron hail of the invaders of our soil.

(Longstreet was not captured.)

Gettysburg was a rarity in the war's major battles because fighting raged through the town's streets and caught residents in the maelstrom. Among those swept up by the conflict was **Sarah Monfort (1827–1908).** The 36-year-old widow lived her entire life in Gettysburg.

Writing two weeks after the battle to a cousin in Ohio, she struggled at times for the right words as she described all she had endured. Because her account is so riveting and the events were so monumental, it is worth sharing the majority of her remarkable account. Only someone who had seen, heard, and experienced what she did could give such a fascinating firsthand description of that pivotal moment in American history.

Gettysburg, Pennsylvania
July 19, 1863

You have heard of the fearful time we have had. Well, our lives have been spared, which appears a miracle when we think how the shells and bullets showered down among us. I will try to tell you something about the battle, but I indeed do not know where to begin to give you a correct account. I can see from our newspaper correspondence that they all differ. Some of them say many things that really are not so, and then again, the half is not told. I thought I knew something about the horrors of war by reading and hearing those who had fought speak about it. But I knew nothing. We must have it in reality to know something about it. Some families left town. We were thinking about it, too. Well, now I am glad I was at home so I could see for myself.

Monday [June 29], the Rebels were said to be in a large force in the mountainland, their pickets in view of town. Monday and Tuesday, they were to be seen all day taking a spyglass view of our place. They would come as far as the Seminary Hill.

Tuesday [June 30] about 11, our army came into town. Oh, but they were hailed with joy. There were about 4,000 of them (calvary), led by General John Buford. The Rebels then fell back to Cashtown.

Wednesday morning [July 1], I went uptown to see and hear what was going on. Went up on the observatory of the Old Academy (our church) with a glass. I could see our men plainly. Also, the Rebels. Skirmishing with the pickets commenced early in the morning, but our infantry was sent for and came in double quick, ready to fall down by overmarch when they got here. But poor fellows, they had to enter the field.

At 10, the Rebels fired the first shot about 2 miles west of town. Our men had the Seminary Hill. They returned the fire from their batteries. Then commenced one of the bloodiest of all the battles of this war.

The part of our army that was engaged was the 1st and 11th Corps under Generals John Reynolds and Oliver Howard. Reynolds fell when only engaged for about one hour. It set a damper on his men. One of them told me last evening had it been General John C. Robinson that was killed, the men would have given three cheers as he was under the influence of brandy, did not know how to lead his men, and that is why they broke and ran. Reynolds was loved by all.

Our men had the Cemetery Hill and kept it a while. We could see them from the upper story of my house. They had to fall back. Part of them retreated down the old railroad with a column of Rebels on each side firing up on them. Of course, it was death to many. They fell every step as Rebels had them on each side. That afternoon, they took altogether about 4,000 of our men prisoners. It was then that our men took a whole brigade, including General James Archer.

The army gradually grew around the north of town. Our batteries with Rebels to the edge of town, and the enemy occupied the ridge at one time. The enemy was drove over the ridge. We hoped our men could hold it, but soon, we saw them [the Confederates] make an advance and drive our men back with a rush. The battle still raged at 2 o'clock. They were around as far as the Poor House.

I stood and watched them till my eyes pained with gazing at them. The folks were leaving their homes and fleeing to the county, and many of them got in the heaviest of the fighting as they were fighting all around for miles except a space from the right of Boroughtown Road to Taneytown Road. That ground our men held all of the time. One of our officers rode our street at the head of about 50 men. I was at the door. It was when our neighbors were leaving their homes for a place of safety. I said we must leave town. He answered that he would not say we should as it was hard to know what was best. We were in a hard place, but if we did go, we should go to Taney-town Road. I answered I would be needed to take care of our men, his men answered with a shout, "That is what we want! Such women, we need it!"

I then only knew how much they needed us if we could do no more than hand them water from morning till night. We stood at the doorway handing them water when the shells and bullets were whistling over and falling around us all the time. One poor fellow sank down at my door exhausted, said he could go no farther. I got campha water. He attempted to swallow but could not. I worked with him for a while. Took his canteen and haversack off him. After a while, he came to. Never did I see an exhausted person till I saw that man. I stood with him, rubbing and washing him till our men begged me to go to my cellar for safety. I then ran to the cellar where we all stayed till the cannoning [cannonading] ceased, came up, went to the door, and saw the Rebels had possession of our town. Describe my feelings then, I cannot.

It was when our army fell back to Cemetery Hill that my house was shelled with a Rebel shell. It struck the corner, made a large hole, of course, and a tremendous noise. The shell busted and fell on the outside. There was also a minie ball that passed through my balcony and hit the wall in three places. Wednesday night, the fighting ceased early. The Rebels said it would commence early next morning. Well, it did with heavy cannoning.

We set our table for breakfast but did not eat. Left it spread all day. Left our house early in the morning and went across the street to Mr. Warner's cellar. It was dry, and we made a little fire in it. Mother was afraid of mine; it was so damp we took a chill whenever we would go in it. We still went over there whenever we thought there would be heavy fighting, at least when it was in the direction of our street. As we could still see when the army was in motion, that part of it that was in our town.

The fighting did not continue long Thursday morning [July 2], though there was still some shells thrown. Three o'clock was the hour that the Rebels said the battle would commence. We were in a worry all day, knowing something was before us, and we knew not what it would be. At 4, it opened, and oh, it was terrible. There was no cessation from cannoning. One thunder after another. Both armies. There was not often that there was as heavy artillery fighting done. It just appeared as if the earth was being torn to pieces. About 9 o'clock, it became quiet. The muskets kept up occasionally firing all night.

Early in the morning Friday [July 3], they began again. We still heard from the enemy that they were going to have reinforcements, too. That was the day the most terrible infantry fight ever was during the war [Pickett's Charge]. I cannot describe the roar of musket fire and then the awful cheering or screaming. When they charged on our battery on Cemetery Hill, we could hear them. The Rebels would say they would soon hear if it was taken. The cannon would cease, and nothing but muskets heard for a few moments. It was then they had a hand-to-hand fight with some of our men. Then the cannon opened on them. Most terrible again. One of the batteries the Rebels approached, and the one that carried the colors mounted the cannon when one of our men almost cut him in two. At another line, our men and the Rebels had the cannon at one time, each pulling to get it off the field while others were firing in on them. That was the one that General Lee said he was determined to have.

The fight at Roundtop was terrible. That is the hill to the left of the Emmitsburg Road between that and Taneytown Road, about 2 miles from town. You recollect it. There, the dead lie unburied and never can be buried.

Some have fallen down between rocks that cannot be reached. They were put there by the Rebels or else fell as they stood on the edge of the rocks. Horses is not all buried yet, either. Those that fell in our streets the first days of the fight was not buried until the Sabbath. The citizens asked the Rebels to let them bury our dead. They said no, they would do that themselves, but they left quietly and quickly and when our muskets could not see them.

Saturday morning [July 4], we could see no Rebels. They [Union troops] gradually came near town when our citizens gave a shout, and of course, there was general shouting. The Rebels kept the ridge west of town. Planted their battery there to cover their retreat. Our armies could not tell how many there was preparing to shower the town, and of course, the citizens must leave. Oh, how soon our joy was turned to sorrow when our officers rode up and told us to be ready to leave at a moment's warning. But the Rebs only tried to escape with safety.

Monday [July 6], Jane and I walked out to the 11th Corps hospital. All the suffering and distress I saw there was awful. The poor fellows came around us, said we were the first ladies that had been to see them. We handed out cakes and bandages, but it went such a little ways. It made me so sorry that I had so little.

Will try and finish this soon, but I have so much nursing to do. Had two wounded officers with me for 10 days. One was a Captain Frederick Stowe [Harriet Beecher Stowe's son] of Massachusetts. Our church has been taken for a hospital along with the rest of the churches in town, as well as college, seminary school buildings, all of the halls, houses, and in the greater part of the private houses. If the private homes are not filled with the wounded, they are often with the friends who come to look for their dead.

Also, in that first week of July, a Confederate attempt to retake the Mississippi River town of Helena, Arkansas, and relieve the pressure on beleaguered Vicksburg failed. (Ironically, it was being fought as Vicksburg's garrison was being surrendered.)

The trio of Union victories—Gettysburg, Vicksburg, and Helena—revived flagging Northern hopes. They were cheered by **William T. Clark (1836–1911)**, a sergeant in the 79th Pennsylvania Infantry, in a letter to his cousin. He was returning to his regiment in Tennessee after having unsuccessfully tried to recruit a militia company in Pennsylvania during Lee's invasion.

Louisville, Kentucky
July 9, 1863

The 4th of July, 1863, was a day full of happy events for the loyal people of the United States and will long be remembered as a day of inglorious disaster alike to Rebels and Rebeldom. Great victory at Helena, Arkansas. Vicksburg, with 24,000 prisoners, has surrendered. And last but not least, the defeat of the Rebel Army of the Potomac [Gettysburg]. Any one of these would have been severe to Rebellion, but all coming upon that same day, and that day, too, being the anniversary of American independence, will cause two-fold great rejoicing throughout the length and breadth of our land.

Meade cautiously followed Lee's retreating army until it reached its own soil. **William Farrand Keys (1837–1917)**, a private in the 143rd Pennsylvania Infantry, told his brother about the Federal pursuit.

Bealeton Station, Virginia
August 13, 1863

I wrote you a short letter immediately after the Battle of Gettysburg. I do not feel inclined to discuss it now, but if I ever see you again, I will tell you something about it. Those were terrible days—those three—and I thought after they were over that I would rather do almost anything than undergo another such an ordeal.

One day (I think the 12th of July), we crossed Antietam Creek and arranged ourselves in line of battle in a devil of a hurry, I tell you, our brigade in the front. Smoke would spurt out once in a while, and the bullets of Rebel sharpshooters would throw up the dirt at our feet. We sent out skirmishers who soon made the "Johnnies" skedaddle. By next morning at 9 o'clock, Old Bobby [Lee] was safe on the south side of the "Rubicon" [the Potomac]. We followed his trail to Williamsport, Maryland, and found his entrenchments in our front very strong. If we had made an attack, I think it would have proved the last of the 2nd Brigade.

While the skirmishing was going on, a citizen of Funkstown, Maryland, whom the Rebs had robbed of everything he possessed, came out and took a position on our line with gun and equipments to try, as he said, to get a little satisfaction. He blazed away very industriously and with evident delight. Presently bang! whizz! came in one of the shells I spoke of right over his head and exploded in the rear. Ye citizen was startled. His sport began to assume a serious aspect when, bang! goes the Rebel gun again, and once more, the iron message to "get out" went hissing over his head. Ye citizen was frightened, and before the third report came, his coattails were toying with the breeze at right angles with his flying body. He did not go to the rear at double-quick, but as the artillery men would say, he ricocheted—touching the ground once in forty rods and bounding like a spherical 12-pounder shot.

It is an interesting as well as a curious fact—and one that I particularly remarked during the battle—that the battery [artillery] men are perfectly indifferent to shells no matter how thick they come or what destruction they create. But of the little singing "minié ball" they evince a wholesome fear. With the infantry, the case is exactly the reverse. They do not care for bullets but have a dread of shells.

The weather has been, for about two weeks, intensely hot, and we suffer for water, which is poor and scarce. I notice that it thunders and lightnings here with an energy seldom reached in our latitude. Write soon. I have not received a letter for so long from anyone that it would be a new sensation.

At the same time, Confederates tried to view the disaster in as favorable a light as possible. **Stephen Long** concluded his previously mentioned letter on a note of bravado.

Camp Near Culpepper, Virginia
July 25, 1863

Our brigade suffered severely, losing over 700 men. The Yankee papers, with their usual lying, claim a victory. But every day, they come out a little more, and truth like murder will out. They left their position in front of us first, and General Lee gave them every chance to attack his demoralized army, but they did not come. Every issue of their journals shows a greater loss for them than first represented.

So, we are here awaiting further developments. We are now in hearing of the railroad whistle and resting after a march of nearly 400 miles, having undoubtedly left the inhabitants of the invaded country under the strong impression that they will vote for the next president of the United States, an uncompromising peace man.

With both Lee's withdrawal from Gettysburg and Pemberton's surrender at Vicksburg occurring on July 4, the dual victories were greeted with cheers across the North. And they came just as the Union was preparing to conduct its first national military draft. A man identified as **J. N. McBee (unknown)** talked about both to his children.

Putnam, Ohio
July 8, 1863

We have had stirring times here for a week past, especially since last Saturday. General Meade, who superseded General Hooker, fought Lee's whole force, 100,000 strong on the 1, 2, 3, and on the 4th, utterly routing him or at least driving his whole force, capturing 30,000 prisoners and 118 guns.

    On Sunday night at church, it was our quarterly meeting. When I was reading the closing hymn, a dispatch was handed to me saying that General Meade had taken 15,000 prisoners and 108 guns. The elder stopped us to sing the Doxology. After prayer, we closed amid general rejoicing and joyful greetings.

    Yesterday about 2:00 p.m., a herald drove furiously through town saying Vicksburg is fallen—surrendered on the glorious Fourth—so the 4th is now rendered thrice glorious. Some were afraid we might be deceived, but I got our flags out and the bells ringing and the steam whistle we kept up for over half an hour. Last night, we had some skyrockets. Tonight, we are to have more. I wish Harry was here to see the sights.

    About noon today, we had a dispatch saying another great fight is going on between Lee and our forces. Meade is driving them again with great slaughter. The Potomac is up, and there are hopes that Meade will capture or disperse Lee's whole army. That would naturally end the rebellion. There is intense interest to hear the result of these terrible battles. Over 12,000 wounded Rebels are in our possession. This news drives the Copperheads to their dens; not one of them can rise again.

    I finished enrolling two townships [for the draft] yesterday week ago. I had no serious trouble with anyone but was somewhat annoyed by a few butternuts [Southern sympathizers] with lies and evasion, but I believe I got them all. I was 22 days employed.

(McBee was mistaken; there was no second "terrible battle," though the Potomac was flooded, and Lee recrossed it into Virginia with great difficulty.)

The guns were barely silent at Gettysburg and Vicksburg when a new crisis erupted in the North. The Enrollment Act of 1863 went into effect on July 1. The drawing of names for the draft quickly followed.

Within weeks, thousands of men around the North began getting letters identical to this one sent to **Edward Cook (unknown)** in New York State.

Provost Marshal's Office,
12th District, State of New York
September 18th, 1863

You are hereby notified that you were, on the 11th day of September 1863, legally drafted in the service of the United States for a period of 3 years, in accordance with the provisions of the act of Congress, "for enrolling and calling out the national forces, and for other purposes," approved March 3, 1863. You will accordingly report, on or about the 28th day of September, at the place of rendezvous, in Poughkeepsie, or be deemed a deserter, and be subject to the penalty prescribed therefor by the Rules and Articles of War.

 Transportation will be furnished you on presenting this notification at Millerton, on the 28th day of September, or at the station nearest your place of residence.

Protests immediately erupted. The first names in New York City were drawn on July 11. They were published in newspapers the next day, sparking demonstrations that grew into some of the worst rioting in U.S. history. Chaos reigned from July 13 to 16. An estimated 50,000 rioters (many of them Irish immigrants) went on a rampage, killing as many as 120 people and injuring 2,000 more, including the city's police commissioner, who was beaten almost to death. There was also widespread looting and arson; churches and even an orphanage for black children were burned. Damage was tallied at $1.5 million (about $55 million today).

Four infantry regiments were rushed from the front lines to the city. They arrived on July 16 and quickly set about restoring order. **Benjamin Wendover (1833–1915)**, a private in the 126th New York Infantry, was among them. He dashed off a quick letter to his wife the next day.

New York City
July 17, 1863

Our regiment is in New York City now, and the 26th Michigan Infantry.
We came here last night to put down the mob. They are a murderin' and
stealin' everything they can get ahold of. I helped guard the printing office of
the New York Times *last night.*

We have been almost to Richmond, and we was ordered back. We
marched 60 miles in two days. They marched us almost to death. I don't know
how long we shall stay here. I expect that I will have to go back to Virginia.
But I would about die as to go back there again.

For New Yorkers caught in the mob's path, those July days and nights were
filled with terror. **Joanna Mills (1813–1902)**, a 50-year-old resident of Brooklyn,
explained to her daughter a few days later all that had just happened.

New York City
July 19, 1863

So far, we have been the most quiet ward in the city. But we were frightened
enough two nights last week.

On Monday night, we all went to bed and slept soundly while our
neighbors were awake all night watching. Those who know nothing fear
nothing. We had not heard of any intention to destroy that police station
house, so we had nothing to keep us awake. Not so on Tuesday night. Kate
brought me in the news about ten o'clock. George was asleep, and Charley
was out. I debated in my own mind for a few minutes what I should do and
went up in the parlor to take a view out of the window when I saw Miss
Steckle and her friend running as fast as they could up the street with a large
basket between them filled with things. In a few minutes, she was back and
opened the door with her night key and took out another large basket which
had been ready in the hall. I also saw some of the poor people that lived below
the station house taking out things for safekeeping.

I sat down for a minute to think what I should do but could not think at
that time of night of one place that I could trust anything to be any safer than
in my own house, for they might be stolen if not burned. I went up and called
George and consulted him, and we decided to let things remain in the house.
Then I got the key to Joseph's wardrobe as quietly as possible out of my drawer

(so as not to disturb Father) and took out the box Josey left in my charge. At first, George thought it best to put the contents of the box about his person for the mob, of course, snatch everything out of a person's hands, but I told him if he were robbed, then Joe and Tom might think if I had carried the box, it would have been saved. So I decided to put on a large shawl and keep the box out of sight if anything happened. I then took Father's money and put it in my underskirt pocket and John's watch and things in another underjacket and kept my own watch as much out of sight as possible, and everything else I should have had to abandon—even my silver I could not have saved. I suppose, though, we intended to have Charley go in Mrs. Pomroy's, and we were going to break the blind out in your room by your bureau, and George was to hand him other valuables.

But nothing happened, thank God. For two nights, I had my things placed in my pockets and Josey's box done up in an old flannel, ready for a start. On Wednesday and Thursday night, I was not alarmed because there were plenty to guard against the invaders. But on Monday and Tuesday nights, all the policemen were in other parts of the city.

Mr. Farmer, the gentleman in Charley's office, went home on Wednesday afternoon and found he had lost every stitch of clothes he owned and $1,000 worth of silver [$36,000 today] that was in his trunk all burned up in the house in which he boarded. Mr. Bull's brother's house was sacked, and the residents had to leave.

I hope everything will remain quiet now as the rioters have been addressed today in the different Catholic churches, I expect. Kate said the priest talked to them in her church this morning and told them if there were any rioters or any who had been engaged in stealing property, as he knew there were some present, to return it and desist from such a course of conduct as they nor their children would never prosper. He also read them several parables, so I hope Bishop Hughes and the rest of his brethren will have some influence over them.

Although the rioting eventually ended, public anger over the draft remained. The atmosphere was just as divisive in small towns as it was in big cities. **Louisia Rogers (unknown)** described the tension within the former to her husband, who was serving in the 9th Vermont Infantry.

Strafford, Vermont
July 18, 1863

I wish the war would close. Everybody is talking and talking about it. It is
hard times here in the North. They have awful times here about drafting. I
can't tell how they will come out at last. They are fighting [rioting] in New
York and Boston hard. They have not tried to draft here yet. They will next
week. They will have a row [fight] here if they do.

The draft was widely despised—and with good reason. Unlike twentieth-century conscription measures, the Civil War version contained two highly controversial provisions that led to the protest, "It's a rich man's war and a poor man's fight."

The first permitted a drafted man to avoid serving by paying a $300 commutation fee ($11,000 today); this at a time when a common laborer earned about $500 (or $18,000 now) a year. Pennsylvanian **William VanHart (1833–1888)** received a Civil War–era "Get Out of Jail Free" card with this letter.

Frankford, Pennsylvania
September 5, 1863

We, the subscribers composing the Board of Enrollment of the Fifth District
of the State of Pennsylvania provided for in Section 8 Act of Congress for
Enrolling and Calling Out National Forces approved March 3rd, 1863,
hereby certify that William S. Vanhart of Lower Makefield Township, Bucks
County, State of Pennsylvania, having given satisfactory evidence that he
is not properly subject to do military duty as required by said act by reason
of having paid $300 commutation money is exempt from all liability under
this draft.

The other provision allowed a draftee to hire a substitute to take his place. In Watertown, New York, **Edward Walker (1823–1897)**, a surgeon serving on the local Board of Enrollment, informed a draftee that a substitute had been found. (The young replacement enrolled in the 100th New York Infantry the same day this letter was written; he was later wounded and died of typhoid fever in May 1865.)

Watertown, New York
October 9, 1863

Enclosed, please find the receipt for a substitute. I obtained him this after-noon, a good, sound German boy, 22 years of age. Philip Schnauber by name.
I congratulate you on your being able to fill your place in the ranks and would that all men, similarly circumstanced, had taken equal pains. If I can be of further service, please inform me.

The possibility of being drafted brought the specter of war home to North-ern families. Many men began making preparations in case they were called. In July 1863, **George Clay (1840–1918),** a private in the 2nd U.S. Sharpshooters who had just survived severe fighting at Gettysburg, received a letter from his 18-year-old brother, Smith Clay, back home in rural Vermont. Their neighbor was 25-year-old farmer Mendel Wood, whose father had died and left him responsible for providing for his mother and sister. Wood had made Smith Clay an important proposition to which George Clay responded.

Camp Near White Sulphur Springs, Virginia
July 28, 1863

Today I received a letter from you. You said that they had got father's name [for the draft] but had not got yourn. You said that Mendel Wood had offered you three hundred dollars to take his place if they draft him. You wanted to know what I thought about it. You said that you should not take his place till you heard from me, and I hope you will not then.
Now, Smith, let me say one thing to you about enlisting. If I was to home, $1,000 could not entice me to enlist again. There is nothing that there is so much hardship in as there is in being a soldier, and if you was out here, you could not stand it too much and go through what a soldier has to go through and go into battle and be shot as I have seen many a poor fellow.
Now, Smith, you may think that $300 is considerable, but that is no comparison. I would not come out here again if I was at home if Mendel Wood would give me his farm and all there is on it. I hope you and Father will not have to come.
But remember one thing. Don't come unless you are obliged to, and then come and do not grumble. Make the best of it you can. It will be hard enough at the easiest. Three hundred dollars don't pay for one battle. You may be

killed, and you may be wounded and live two or three days and then die. If you had ever seen what I have, you would think that $5,000 might got to the Devil for all you care. I have seen men shot through the stomach and live a long time and then die. And then again, I have seen them shot through the head and never knew what hit them. Then I presume I have seen a thousand with their legs shot off above their knees and some with their feet shot off, and now I will close.

Write soon. This from your affectionate brother George to Smith Clay. Write soon and tell all the news you can think of and I will do the same. Goodbye. I wish this sheet was longer, then I could write more, but this will do this time, and next time, I will write more.

People throughout the North eagerly followed developments as the draft progressed. **Isaac H. Killmer (unknown)** updated his niece, who had moved out of state, on the latest.

Stouchsburg, Pennsylvania
September 28, 1863

The draft of Berks County is now finished for this draft.

Number of Substitutes Accepted	*218*
Exempted for Physical Disability	*326*
Exempted for Other Causes	*181*
Who applied for exemption & failed to receive it	*304*
Drafted men held for duty	*5*
Total number examined	*1,034*
Exempted by payment of $300, commutation fee	*124*
Total number of whole County of Berks	*1,158*

In Lebanon and Schuylkill Counties, they commenced drafting last Wednesday.

I have hopes that this tremendous, cruel war will be over soon. Some people think it will be over soon, but I cannot see any reason to make me think so. If you or George have any idea that it will soon come to an end, I wish you would please let me know the reason what makes you think so. A great many of our people are of the opinion that it will soon come to a close, but their reasons are not strong enough to convince me of it.

Some men took extreme measures to avoid compulsory military service. Army regulations required soldiers to have both front teeth. Private **Edward Mott (unknown–1864),** 5th Connecticut Infantry, had been captured at Chancellorsville and wrote to his mother while waiting to be exchanged.

Parole Camp
Alexandria, Virginia
September 3, 1863

What is the matter with Henry that he can't go to the war? I didn't mean anything when I spoke of Damon's teeth, but a great many have had their front teeth removed so they could not tear cartridge [thus evading the draft].

Not all draftees and paid substitutes turned out to be good soldiers when they reached the front. Some deserted at the first chance they got. The penalty for desertion was death. One instance highlights why the men in the ranks, who were forced to witness military executions, reacted to them with revulsion and disgust.

Privates Edward Elliott and George Layton of the 14th Connecticut Infantry were convicted. **Edward H. Wade (1836–1897),** a corporal in the same regiment, wrote to his younger sister about what happened when the entire command was assembled the day after a raging thunderstorm.

Loudon Mills, Virginia
Near Rapidan River
September 20, 1863

Now I come to a sad part of my letter, but it must be told. Friday, two men belonging to the 14th regiment were shot for the crime of desertion. They were two of the new men and were brought here about 6 weeks ago but deserted in two days after they came here. They were found dressed in Rebel clothes and, after they had had a court-martial, were sentenced to be shot on Friday, Sept. 18th, in the presence of the division to which they belonged. I did not wish to see it, but I could not help it.

At 3 o'clock in the afternoon, the whole division, containing 12 regiments of infantry and two batteries of 6 guns each, were marched into a large open lot. Here, we formed a hollow square. About 4 o'clock, the guards who were detailed to shoot these poor men came marching along slowly, the two prisoners in the middle of the guard, and the 14th band playing a funeral dirge. They reached the graves where the coffins were placed by the side of them. The officer of the guard then read the sentence of the court-martial to the prisoners. The chaplains of the 12th New Jersey and 14th talked and prayed with them and bid them a last farewell. The officer of the guard then stepped to them, tied a white handkerchief over their eyes, and shook hands with them, each on his own coffin. He then went to his guard and gave them these orders: Ready, Aim, Fire! Owing to the terrible storm the night before, the powder in the guns was very wet, and only two guns out of the twenty went off. One of the men was only shot in the arm and the other slightly in the head. But they must be shot, and so they fired again, and they had to shoot 12 different times before the poor men were killed. Oh, it was dreadful to see the agony the poor men were in. One of them got up from his coffin, took off his handkerchief from his eyes, and wanted to shoot himself, he was in so much misery.

After they were pronounced dead, the division had to march past them and look at them. They were mangled terribly, and I hope never to see another such a sight. The men were young—one of them being 22, the other 18. One of the men was a substitute, and the other—a nice-looking young man of 18 who was unable to pay his $300—was drafted and had to come.

This is what comes of the North, for if they would have been brave enough to come [volunteered], there would have been no need of a draft and no substitutes to hire, and there would have been two men more in the Union army. When will the North open their eyes and see their danger?

But I will stop writing on this subject, for it makes me sick at heart.

(Wade apparently wasn't close enough to witness the gruesome conclusion to the bungled affair. Another witness reported, "At last, the provost marshal himself, drawing his revolver, placed the muzzle at the man's head and discharged all the barrels of it. This finished the man, and he fell over into his coffin and never moved again.")

A major change came to the U.S. military in 1863 when the War Department created the Bureau of Colored Troops. Some 178,000 freed blacks eventually enlisted in approximately 175 regiments in the USCT. They served as enlisted men and were commanded by white officers.

Some of the whites were abolitionists. Others transferred to leadership positions in the new regiments in order to rise in rank or for more pay. Yet, some Americans were disdainful of the two races serving alongside each other. They included a young woman identified only as **Callie (unknown),** who urged her boyfriend against becoming a USCT officer.

Madison, Wisconsin
December 18, 1863

You ask me what I think about your accepting a commission in a colored regiment. My first impression was that you ought not to think of going, and I have not changed my mind on the subject. I would rather you would remain where you now are than by endangering your life to receive twice the salary and all the glory you imagined you would have. I do not think, however, that you have the least idea that you would go, do you?

Would you, Alfred, be subject to a draft? You speak as though you would. Now, I would not want you to be mixed up with that class for twice the amount of pay. And then you know how horribly you would be treated, provided you were taken prisoner. But who advised you to send in your name? I hope you will be a little more explicit and tell me your opinion. But don't commit yourself (if you have an idea of doing so) until I see you, will you?

In the Mid-South that crucial summer of 1863, a mounted force of nearly 2,500 Confederate cavalry commanded by General John Hunt Morgan was speeding northward through central Tennessee. It entered Kentucky on July 2. **William Walker (1839–1907),** a musician in the 17th Illinois Infantry stationed directly across the Ohio River from the important military depot of Louisville, experienced the drama of the moment and shared it with his brother. He began by paraphrasing the title of the popular wartime song "All Quiet Along the Potomac Tonight" (a reference to the recent Battle of Gettysburg).

Jeffersonville, Indiana
July 8, 1863

Things ain't so damned quiet on the Potomac.
Our communication seems to be cut off with Nashville via railroad. Morgan is making another raid through Kentucky. Some think he is close to Louisville and coming closer all the time. There was great excitement night before last in consequence of an alarm being raised that Morgan was almost in sight of Louisville. Bells were rung, cannons fired, soldiers formed in line, citizens ordered out to the works to defend the place while the women and

children crowded the streets whispering with white lips, "The foe they come, they come," so to speak.

But all has once more become quiet, only to be raised up again by the news that Vicksburg has surrendered with 24,000 prisoners. If it's only true, it's a big thing. They had a rousing time in New Albany, Indiana, last night over it. Balloons and rockets were sent up. Martial bands paraded the streets. Cannons thundered forth their mighty notes until it seemed the Ohio River was being lifted from its bed.

We expect to start for Nashville today, where you will again hear from me if we get through safe. I would not wonder if we saw guerrillas before we got there. About 100 Rebel prisoners were brought through here last evening from Rosecrans' army. They were stout-looking fellows.

Morgan's command crossed the Ohio River (using two captured steamboats) on July 8 at Brandenburg, Kentucky, and then raced across Indiana and Ohio, having covered more than 1,000 miles before being captured on July 26. The raid so infuriated Northerners that Morgan and six of his officers were sent to the Ohio State Penitentiary as civilian criminals rather than held as prisoners of war.

A few days later, **Sabina Hiatt (1841–1933)** wrote about it in a letter to her younger brother, a private in the 84th Indiana Infantry (who was killed at Chickamauga six weeks later).

Home
[Near Farmland, Indiana]
July 30, 1863

It appears that they have stopped the Rebel Morgan's career, who has caused so much trouble. For now, they have got him and all his men, I guess, and I hope they will not let him live long.

The state militia was called out while Morgan was in Indiana. There was a company went from over south which got in a bad snap. While the brigade was marching around a hill, the ends came together, and they mistook each other for the enemy and fired into the ranks, killing five or six and wounding several. Amongst the killed was William Fortland, who used to live in Farmland. Jim Bates got his arm shot off. That was all that was killed or wounded in that company. It happened in the night. Eli belongs to a company at Melville. I don't think that it will amount to much.

Some 300 of Morgan's men eventually returned to the Confederacy, crossing the Ohio River opposite Belleville, West Virginia. They battled dangerous swirling water as well as Union gunboats and cavalry. Those who made it across still faced harrowing ordeals, including **William Taylor Humphreys (1844–1873)**, a private in Corbett's Light Artillery attached to the 2nd Kentucky Cavalry (Confederate). He recounted his experience to his father two months later.

Office of Subsistence
Demopolis, Alabama
September 30, 1863

I laid on the banks of the Ohio for two nights and days thinking of the awful task before me—that of swimming the river, which after two days' and nights' deliberation and starvation, I concluded to risk my chances on a rail and swim the river which I accomplished in about twenty minutes. I would have surrendered had it not been for you, for I know you would have been almost distressed to death to hear that I was in prison. Poor Capt. James McClain was drowned in crossing the river. I wrote to you that he escaped, but it was another man.

I wrote to you just after I crossed the Ohio River when I told you I thought I was safe, but I was bushwhacked on the road when I got in about 50 miles of our lines. There was some 12 or 15 of them fired on me from the bushes about 30 yards from me. I was standing still at the time, and I cannot imagine how they come to miss me, but I was not hurt at all—only one ball passed through my coat. I was too fast on foot for them after they missed their aim. I was going along, not thinking about them, as the citizens all told me I was clear out of danger. There was 9 of us when they fired on us. The rest were behind, and they caught six of them and killed them. I escaped with the loss of a fine pair of boots which I abandoned in the retreat.

I walked across western Virginia, a distance of 200 miles, to our lines. I have been through the different departments of the Confederate Army since I saw you all last and thank heaven I am well and in better spirits than ever I was.

This place [Demapolis] is full of beautiful young ladies, and all are as rich as cream. I have not been here long enough to have me some new clothes made. I have found it a military necessity to appropriate the captain's broad and gray cloth and ruffled shirts. They do not call a man wealthy in this country unless he has not got about a thousand Negroes and two or three plantations. Ed and I eat in the office and have our meals cooked next door, and two or three Negroes to come and go at our calling. I am afraid if I ever take a notion to go back to the command, I will be perfectly spoilt. We have been very busy here lately for the Vicksburg prisoners rendezvous at this place, but in the future, do not expect as much as they have been exchanged.

Union forces were scoring victories on other fronts as well. In South Carolina's Lowcountry, their attention returned to Charleston Harbor. Using Folly Island as their staging ground, the Federals hunkered down for the long haul in the brutal coastal heat, as **George H. Thomas (unknown–1864)**, a corporal in the 13th Indiana Infantry, told his sister. (He would die in battle in Virginia nine months later.)

Folly Island, South Carolina
July 8, 1863

Our picket is in about one mile of Fort Sumpter [sic]. They keep up a continual shelling of our men all the time, but can't do them much damage as we have good earthworks to protect us. I had the pleasure of seeing two holes shot through Fort Sumpter the other day when we was up there. It was done by a 200-pounder that our men has in range of it. I think it will be but a small job to level its walls. When we are a good and ready, we will have forts built within 300 yards of Fort Wagoner [sic]. Our men is so close to it that they can't use their guns only at night on account of our sharpshooters.

It is still as warm as usual. We cook our coffee in the sand very often without a particle of fire. This may seem like a fish story, but it is a positive fact. I made some as good coffee the other day as I have drank since I have been in the service. Just by putting some ground coffee and water in my canteen and burying it in the sand. The sand is so hot where the sun shines that it would blister your hand almost as quick as it would to stick it into the fire.

Heavily fortified Morris Island defended the harbor's southern and western approaches while also providing cover for the dwindling number of blockade runners that brought desperately needed supplies into the Confederate port.

On July 10, Union forces bombarded the Confederate works there with four ironclads and guns from Folly Island. The next day, General George Strong's brigade landed and captured the lower portion of Morris Island. A sunrise attack on Fort Wagner in heavy fog the following morning failed. **Erwin Welsh (1835–1915)**, a sergeant in the 67th Ohio Infantry, updated his wife on the movements.

Camp at Morris Island, South Carolina
July 14, 1863

We landed on Saturday, the day after the attack, at daylight and passed up the beach about 2 miles, where we have remained ever since. The bombardment ended at 7 o'clock and 27 minutes, and our forces landed and met with but little resistance. They succeeded in charging and taking 3 of the Rebs' forts. The number of guns that we taken was 8 siege, 2 mortars, 1 Manchester gun, and 5 field pieces, a number of mules, wagons, some cattle, hogs, chickens and all their camp equipage. As near as I can learn, we have taken 150 prisoners and 75 Negroes. We captured their hospital with all their medicine and doctors.

They occupy the north end of the island, whilst we occupy the South. They occupy Fort Wagner and Battery Gregg. Our regiment has not lost any. The loss of the rest has been 75 killed and wounded. There was 4 companies of the 7th Maine supported by the 9th Connecticut. The 9th broke and run, and most of the 7th was captured. Their colonel was wounded. We have got forces on James Island of 6 or 7 thousand, and they have been meeting with good success. They have passed up the island and taken Seceshville [Secessionville, South Carolina] and taken 2 of their forts. That was day before yesterday. There has been some firing in that direction yesterday. General Alfred Terry has command of the forces on that island, and General George Strong on this. Our light artillery ran down the beach and sank one of the Rebel transports. She was loading troops on this island.

The Rebs keep throwing shot from Sumter every few minutes. They killed one man yesterday. The boys said that they threw a shot every 15 minutes all night, but I did not hear a shot after 8 o'clock. I guess that I must of slept some. What do you think the Rebs said, that we took them by surprise, that they did not know a word of our batteries being there. They said that they thought that we had 1 or 2 guns there the day before, and they were making preparations to attack us the next day. They would have found a warm reception if they had come. We had 40 guns and mortars planted on the point.

The Rebs have commenced their shelling since I have been writing this. You must excuse the poor scribbling, for if you knew how quick I have wrote it, you would not wonder at the scratches.

On July 18, the 54th Massachusetts Infantry, a regiment of black soldiers, led a second, larger attack on Fort Wagner under cover of darkness. It was repulsed in bloody fighting. (That assault was featured in the 1989 motion picture *Glory*.) It was supported by some 4,000 additional Federal troops, including **Charles A. Lawrence (1828–1894),** a second lieutenant in the 7th New Hampshire Infantry, who was slightly wounded in the engagement. He recounted to his wife what he experienced that summer night.

Morris Island, South Carolina
July 25, 1863

The Charleston Mercury *[newspaper] says the dead of our forces lay in the ditch like sardines in boxes. They buried some 600 of our men the next day. No person who has not been in a battle can have any good idea of the scene that is presented or the sensations felt by the actors in the tragedy or of the horrid reality. When I left the field of slaughter, although suffering great pain myself, I could not help noticing many of the dead. Some lay straight as could be, whilst others were all drawn up in a heap with their head down to their knees.*

But the worst were the wounded. The poor creatures like myself were trying to get out of the way of the shot that was continually poured upon us. I saw one poor fellow that was laying in the water of the sea, and the tide was rising fast, and he could not get up and said that was the best place to lay to be out of the way. I hope that I may never again see such a sight.

The men greatly rejoiced last night when they heard that Lt. Ezra Davis and Lt. Charles Worcester are not dead. Col. Haldiman Putman was instantly killed, the back part of his head being blown off. He was last seen on top of the enemy's works, calling his men to come on.

Edward was unwell, and so he was not in the fight. But he worked hard after he found it was going on in helping off the hurt. By the way of the flag of truce, I learn that we lost not less than three captains. Captain Henry Leavitt was wounded and died at Charlestown [sic] on the 23rd. Capt. Warren Brown was killed outright, and Capt. Jerome House had a ball in his hip, and they cannot find it to extract the same. My company has 17 on the sick list today, besides those that are in the hospitals, and only 13 for duty. Some difference between that and the forty-some we had last week.

Fort Johnson is firing this morning on our men, but I do not know with what effect.

*Give all my friends my regards and tell them that I am well and that
I am ready to meet the enemy again whenever we are ordered to do so, and
I hope the next time we meet him we shall whip him hard. Yes, harder than
he did us at Fort Wagner.*

Realizing that further attacks against the fortification would be futile, the
Federals switched strategy and began trying to shell it into submission. Confederate cannons replied with equal ferocity.

Lawrence, who was promoted to second lieutenant the day after the battle,
was now among the troops besieging Fort Wagner. He told his wife that the
Northerners were confident of success and described the toll that the incessant
artillery barrage was taking on nearby Fort Sumter.

Morris Island, South Carolina
August 30, 1863

*We are slowly but surely gaining, sapping their strength away from them.
We have driven them into Wagner now and well mean to keep them there (I
mean the garrison of the fort). One night last week, the 24th Massachusetts
Volunteers attacked their outer works and drove them in, killing some and
taking 67 of them prisoners, and held the works. Good for Massachusetts. The
night before, the Rebs attacked the Third New Hampshire and was repulsed
by them in fine style.*

    *My company has been under fire a great deal, and yet we have not had
but two men hurt since the fight of the 18th of July, and they were both by the
untimely bursting of a shell from our own guns. George Stevens had his left
arm taken off. He was one of our best men. Today, we have heard that four
more of our missing men [from the July 18 attack] have been heard from. They
are confined in jail at Columbia, S.C. I hope that we shall soon liberate them.*

    *We are at work now to reduce the forts, and Sumter looks like an old
brick building that has had the woodwork burned out of it and a part of the
walls fallen in. Nothing but a heap of bricks on one side, and all the others
badly shattered. The Rebs throw over shot and shell more or less every day,
but the casualties are comparatively few. We are getting used to shells so that
we do not fear them, especially in the nighttime because we are always sure
to see them then. They look like a ball of fire, and they make a very peculiar
whizzing noise which shows us where they are, and so we can get out of their
way, and our men understand that part well.*

A few days later, Lawrence shared how amusing moments occurred even while being bombarded.

Morris Island, South Carolina
September 4, 1863

I sometimes see the most provoking sights, and yet it seems wrong to laugh when the missiles of death are in the air and all around one. I will tell of one instance. A few nights ago, I was at the front in charge of a fatigue party of Negroes. The shells were flying rather too near for safety, and one of the darkies went head first into a wicker basket called a gabion (that is open on both ends) for safety. Just think of it, a man hiding in a basket to get away from a cannon ball. I see many similar incidents.

The Confederates were forced to evacuate Fort Wagner on September 7. Lawrence was finally able to tell his wife that it, along with another strategically important fortification, was now in Federal hands.

Morris Island, South Carolina
September 11, 1863

This forenoon, Sergeant George Corson wished to pay a visit to Fort Wagner, and I went with him. We viewed the works and found them fully as strong as we had thought them to be. Our engineers are at work on them now, and I think they will soon show the Rebs that we shall make Wagner of service to the Union cause by levelling the walls of Fort Moultrie and the other batteries on Sullivan's Island. Battery Gregg is the other point gained. Corson and myself visited it today. It is a strong sand battery on Cummings Point nearest to Fort Sumter. Was built by the Rebs [in 1861] to reduce Sumter with. At the present time, it mounts the same guns that the Rebs put there, and we shall now turn them on the city or any of their batteries that we wish.

Today, whilst I was up there, they threw a shot which struck the top of the fort and bounced away off down the marsh. Fort Johnson threw a shell that burst inside the fort, and the way some of those pieces went down the beach and road was a caution. They went as though they meant to make mischief, and I think they would if they had hit anyone. But I am alright now, thank God. But for His sustaining hand and his protecting power, I should have long since been cut down.

Union artillery began bombarding Charleston with Greek Fire, shells containing an incendiary fluid that would explode over its target and start fires. A massive Parrott cannon weighing more than 12 tons, nicknamed the "Swamp Angel," joined in the attacks. On its thirty-sixth shot, it exploded. Another smaller piece of heavy artillery was brought in to replace it. It likewise had a premature ending, as **J. W. Norris (1840–unknown)**, a sergeant major in the 1st South Carolina State Troops, told his father.

Charleston, South Carolina
October 20, 1863

We are still in Charleston. The Yankees are firing very rapidly and steadily for the past few days—nearly every fire causes the sash on our windows to rattle. They have not thrown any more shells into the city since Monday as they burst their gun.

We have warm weather this morning, but these little cold snaps are very severe on us, and we suffer severely. I had to put on my woolen shirt over the cotton. Tell Mattie [his wife] and Lula [daughter] I have got some straw now and have a straw bed, which does better than sleeping on the floor. But I get very cold before day these cold mornings and would like to have Lula's arms twine about my neck. There are very few nice, clean children in the city. Most of them are dirty and bad-looking. All the better sort have gone out to the country [to escape the bombardment].

I got the provisions sent down. We cook the peas and rice together, and the boys are very fond of them. The government issued to us red peas, which have so hard a skin on them we can hardly eat them at all.

Back in the summer, by late July, the momentum shifting in the North's favor was obvious. For Private **James Henry Clark (1841–1864)** of the 3rd Vermont Infantry, the recent round of Union victories was very encouraging, as he expressed to his brother.

Camp near Berlin, Maryland
July 18, 1863

Isn't it glorious news that we are having lately? Vicksburg, Port Hudson, Helena, Ark., Morris Island, Charleston Harbor, S.C., and last but not least, Gettysburg, Pa., which is one of the most decisive victories ever achieved by

our armies. We are all feeling first-rate over the good news—the first step-
ping stone to taking Fort Sumter is gained. The Rebel horde of invaders are
driven from Pennsylvania and Maryland soil once more, and rest assured,
they will not be anxious to try that again. The last news we heard from Rose-
crans' army, he was closely following Bragg's dispirited and retreating army,
taking many prisoners. And now I would ask if we need be discouraged.
Prospects for the Union cause were never brighter than at present.

No! my photograph does not tell false tales. In regard to my health, it is
excellent and I hope it may continue so while I am in the army. If I am lucky
enough not to be the receptacle of any Rebel iron or lead, I think I shall get
through all right. We have had some very hard marching since we started
from the Rappahannock. One day, we marched some over 30 miles, which
was the day we marched to Gettysburg, Pa.

(Clark did not survive the war; he fell in battle less than a year later.)

The day after capturing Vicksburg, Grant sent 40,000 men led by General William Sherman to drive General Joseph Johnston's Confederate 30,000-man force from central Mississippi and keep the Mississippi River open to Union water traffic.

There was heavy fighting at Jackson, the state capital, in the middle of July. Johnston withdrew on July 16, falling back deep into the Mississippi interior and effectively ending the Vicksburg Campaign. **Joseph A. Briscoe (unknown)**, serving in the 14th Texas Cavalry (Dismounted), described the brief but intense fight to his aunt in the Lone Star State. After so many Southern setbacks and despite his war-weariness, he put the best face on conditions and remained hopeful.

Camp Hardee
Scott County, Mississippi
August 13, 1863

We were on Big Black River at the time that Vicksburg surrendered. We
went from there to Jackson. There we stayed in the breastworks for eight days.
The Yankees tried to flank us, and we retreated back some 40 or 50 miles to
where we are now. There was some of the heaviest picket fighting at Jackson
that ever I saw or heard of. It was like a little battle all the time. We had
two men killed in our regiment and several wounded. The Yanks attacked the
breastworks in front of Breckinridge's Division. Breckinridge's men killed

300 or 400 of them, wounded a great many more, killed two or three colonels, and taken two or three others prisoner. Got three stands of colors.

I reckon you had heard General Lee up in Virginia went into Pennsylvania. He stayed only a short time. He had a big fight with the Yanks. He taken about 2,000 prisoners. The Yanks got about 3,000 of his men, then he came out of Pennsylvania into Virginia. The Yanks got 20,755 of our men at Vicksburg, including officers and all. It is expected at this time we will go to Wilmington, North Carolina, or Chattanooga, Tennessee. I have no idea of when the war will stop, but I hope and trust that it will stop soon, for I want to come home.

I tell you, Aunt Zade, war is a horrid thing. I am mighty tired of it. The Yanks are fully as tired as we are of it. You wrote that Uncle Ned had got tired of Texas. Tell him, if you please, you had better stay there and think more of it than ever, for it is the only state that the Yanks are not in. If he was to see how the Yanks serve people in the other states, he would be satisfied to live in Texas. Tell him he never saw hard times yet. Let him wait until the enemy comes through and takes every horse, cow or sheep and even the chickens, and him and his family wantonly insulted and driven away from their house, and then he will see the beginning of hard times. Every word that I have wrote is the truth and nothing but the truth.

You speak of hard living at home. If you were here to see how we had to live in camp, you would think you were feasting all the time at home. Times is very hard here at this present time, though that is the natural consequence where an army is. It lays waste to everything within 15 or 30 miles, and Zade, the people of Texas ought to be very thankful there is no army or Yankees there to disturb them as an army takes everything as it goes. Times look very gloomy at present into a brighter future.

Even in the midst of military operations in the field, some soldiers would not let blazing heat or rugged terrain keep them from pursuing temptations of the flesh. Young **George Waterman Jackson (1843–1910)**, a private in the 4th Independent Battery, Indiana Light Artillery, wrote to a cousin about the extreme lengths he and his comrades went to for illicit physical activity.

Camp Davidson
Crow Creek Valley, Tennessee
August 18, 1863

I will give you some of the details of our march. We started the morning of the 8th of August at 6 a.m. for to cross the Cumberland Mountains. We went about one mile when we came to the foot of the mountains. Here, we halted for about one hour when the bugle sounded, and we started for the top of this awful mountain. Some of the guns got stuck, and the boys had to put their shoulders to the wheels to keep them out. We marched in this way all day when we camped for the night in this valley about eight miles from the Tennessee River and five miles from Stevenson, Alabama.

There is more [sex] in this country than ever I saw. I was out over the mountain into what is called Little Crow Creek Valley. I was to three secesh whorehouses, the latter house having three whores. There was three of us. We was all on horses, and the mountain was so steep we had to dismount and hang on to our horses' tails to get up the mountains. It was awful hot, but we was after the little skin and didn't feel the heat. I and my partner is a going back tonight. This is one hell of a place for skin, Jim. I wish you could be with me for a little while. We would have some fun.

With prostitution widespread, there was an accompanying spike in sexually transmitted diseases. In some cases, illnesses significantly depleted ranks at the front. Because men and women discussing such private matters was seriously frowned on in the mid-Victorian era, **Benjamin Franklin O'Bryon (1837–1864)**, a sergeant in the 140th Pennsylvania Infantry, used delicate language when telling his wife about it.

Camp near Rapidan River, Virginia
September 21, 1863

You spoke of W. A. West. I learned that he is in the Invalid Corps at Washington City, D.C. If that be the case, he has made a nice thing of it and even has a fair chance to satisfy his anonymous and amorous passions as he can have a fair chance of getting into company with the fair sex. I also understand that he had a secret disease that unfitted him for the service. How true this is, I cannot vouch for the correctness. I got it from one of my messmates who was over at their camp.

Other people took a more spiritual approach to wartime pressures. The Confederate reversals produced a Southern call for divine intervention. General Lee issued General Order No. 83 on behalf of President Davis, declaring August 21 a "Day of Fasting, Humiliation, and Prayer." Among those observing it in Richmond was widowed **Mary Barclay Kirby (1811–1891)**. The aunt of General Edmund Kirby Smith, commander of the Department of the Trans-Mississippi, she wrote to her son, a young engineer serving on his cousin's headquarters staff in Shreveport, Louisiana.

Richmond, Virginia
August 21, 1863

Today is our time of prayers, fasting, and humiliation. I trust it will be kept all over our Confederacy and that God, in His mercy, will look upon us and deliver us from our enemies and grant us peace.

I received a long letter from your Aunt Fanny last week. She is in Madison, Florida, at Mr. Putnam's—Judge Benjamin Putnam's brother. She says before leaving St. Augustine, the last letter she received from your cousin Edmund [Kirby Smith] was dated 1st March—one year five months ago—but a few days before she wrote me, she had been much gratified by a letter from Cassie [Kirby Smith's young wife].

She and your Aunt Helen have been shamefully treated by those miserable Yankees. In January, General David Hunter sent an order that they, with some officers, should be conducted over the lines beyond the pickets. At the time, your Aunt Helen was confined to her bed quite ill, your Aunt Fanny an invalid not able to leave the house. A statement of these facts was made to General Hunter by a Yankee surgeon and also by Dr. Peck, your aunt's physician. He gave them permission to remain and said they should not be molested. In the face of all this, Col. Joseph Hawley, who commands at St. Augustine, sent them an order to leave, only giving them 24 hours' notice. They had to leave, of course, and it would be impossible for me to tell you all the annoyances and discomforts they had to endure. I am thankful they are out of the enemy's lines, although it is a hard case to leave all their property in the hands of such enemies as we have to contend with. "But vengeance is mine, sayeth the Lord. I will repay." I cannot believe that a righteous God will allow such acts to go unpunished.

Your Aunt Fanny is very desirous to come to Richmond, and I have written to her mentioning the price at which I can get her board for her, *which will be $100 per month, washing and servants' attendance included. It may exceed that during the winter as fuel will be very high. That is a cheaper board than she could get anywhere in Richmond but with me. Most of the boarding houses are asking $100 for day board. The hotels, $10 per day. I do not know what we are to do if the price of everything continues to increase. Your sister yesterday had to give $45 for a pair of shoes.*

Your brother saw Col. Larkin Smith a day or two ago. They were compelled to leave their home in the North Carolina mountains and go to Childsville to live on account of the Union men and deserters in that neighborhood. They threatened last fall to burn Col. John Palmer's house and destroy all his property.

The same day that letter was written, one of the conflict's worst atrocities occurred. The savagery along the Missouri–Kansas border was a war within a war. Deadly violence had been raging there for a decade. Pro-Southern guerillas and pro-Northern partisan Jayhawkers and Red Legs robbed, killed, and burned with reckless abandon. After outrages were committed against their families, Quantrill's Raiders burned the abolitionist stronghold of Lawrence, Kansas, on August 21, killing 164 men and boys. The violence only intensified after that.

Writing from Missouri a few months later, pro-Southern **Leonora Dickson (unknown)** described to her grandfather in Kentucky what life was like in a land terrorized by guerilla warfare.

"Dixie Land"
Lafayette County, Missouri
December 1, 1863

Things are quiet now with us. Yesterday, there was some excitement about the "Red Legs" making a raid through this part of our country. I hope for the best. The enrollment of the "Americans of African descent" is going on rapidly in Lexington, Missouri. It is thought the quota of this district will be made up of such. Pa's boys have enrolled to fight and have left us to get along the best way we can. None of the women have left, but we would not be surprised any time if they were to leave. They think it is very hard to have to go to the woods and cut wood. We have very little of our crop gathered in. Pa feels quite broken down when night comes.

Everything bears a good price here. Mules are very high, ranging from $135 to $200. Pa sold his for one thirty-some and a half and has nothing in *the world to get about with but one horse. He would not have parted with his if he had thought he could keep them. Our neighbors lose horses every night [to theft].*

Desertion was a serious problem for both armies. Punishment ranged from shaming (wearing signs labeling them as deserters, head shaving, and being drummed out of the army) to imprisonment and even execution. Several Maine regiments were especially hard hit in 1863. **Edwin Cobb (1844–1927),** a private in the 5th Maine Infantry, was sentenced to hard labor in the remote Florida Keys for deserting. He wrote to his colonel that he and a comrade had experienced a change of heart. (Cobb eventually returned to the regiment and lost an arm in the Battle of the Wilderness the following year.)

Fort Jefferson, Florida
August 24, 1863

I take this opportunity to let you know where I am, for I don't think you know anything about it. Tyng Libby and I was sent to Washington and put in the Old Capitol Prison. We stayed there for about three weeks and were sent to this place. This place consists of about 10 acres, all of which is covered with a brick fort and it is surrounded by water. It is a hot, sickly, lonesome place.

There is 10 men here from the 121st New York that have written to their colonel, and he obtained their pardon. They expect to go back to their regiment every day. There was 105 of us sent here, and there has been a number of them died and a number of them pardoned. And we have made up our minds that we would like to come back to the regiment and do our duty as men. And if you cannot do anything for us, I should like to hear from you. We have written letters to the boys in the company but have received no answer. We still remain your obedient servants.

PS: Tell the boys in Company D to write us.

On the Gulf Coast, the Federals tried to invade Texas in early September. The French had seized control of Mexico, and the Lincoln administration worried that the newly installed Emperor Maximilian might provide an avenue for desperately needed supplies to enter the Confederacy.

However, 60 members of the Jeff Davis Guards, manning six cannons in a single fort, pulled off the most lopsided victory of the war. On September 8 at

Sabine Pass, located near the Gulf of Mexico on the Texas–Louisiana line, the handful of Southerners successfully fought off a Union invasion force of 5,000 soldiers, four gunboats, and 18 transport ships. Grateful residents of Houston, Texas, raised funds and presented medals to Guard members—the only medals awarded by the Confederacy during the war.

Yet not all the recipients cherished them. Three months later, an **unidentified Union naval officer** wrote his mother on Christmas Day about some men who came aboard his ship.

U.S.S. Seminole
Off Sabine Pass, Louisiana
December 25, 1863

We had deserters came off yesterday. We saw a boat pulling directly off from the shore toward us at noon. They arrived and proved to be five men stationed at the fort here. Three of them had the medals presented to them by General John B. Magruder for bravery shown on the 8th of September in the action at this place. The medals are old Mexican dollars filed down and engraved on one side, "Sabine Pass Sept. 8 1863," on the other, "D.G." which means "Davis Guards" and a Catholic cross. They belonged to a company called the "Irish Texans," and Irish Texans they are, too, I can assure you. They hadn't been on board more than two hours before they had turned everything into Greenbacks. Their medals they sold for five dollars apiece, and their money [Confederate] they handed out by the handful. We asked them what percent they wanted for it. One of them says, "Faith, take it an' give us what ye likes for it; the whole boonch av it won't buy a bottle o' whiskey," and they had some three hundred dollars. One of them had on a coat he gave two hundred and seventy-five dollars for in Houston, which could be bought in the North for about eight or ten dollars.

The way they got out, they got permission to go and shoot ducks, which the commanding officer saw fit to give them, and when they got down by the lighthouse, they found it was foggy, so they put out to sea.

One poor old fellow came off a week ago or more who had been in the swamps running away from the Rebs for two months. There was a reward offered for his head, and he found they were after him with bloodhounds, so he came off nine miles in a dugout. Poor man, I pity him; had to leave his family behind and everything that belonged to him.

It is horrible down here. They have to keep one company to guard another, and the cavalry are scouring all over the country, driving everybody between the ages of 16 and 60 into their army, and if he refuses, they shoot him at his own door. If you could hear the curses that they call down on the heads of the leaders in this rebellion, 'twould make you shudder.

The war kept grinding on as summer drew to a close. Union General Ambrose Burnside took Knoxville, the key to eastern Tennessee, on September 2. The Confederacy suffered another serious setback a few days later.

In one of the war's most skillfully executed movements, Rosecrans demonstrated above Chattanooga, while simultaneously sending three corps across the Tennessee River in Alabama to the southwest of the city. He then moved below Chattanooga, threatening to cut its essential rail link to Atlanta.

The Tennessee River was a formidable obstacle. The large-scale flanking movement was made possible thanks to military engineers. They erected wooden pontoon bridges that allowed Union troops to cross. But constructing them wasn't easy, as **Perrin V. Fox (1821–1910)**, a captain in the 1st Michigan Engineers and Mechanics regiment, told his wife.

Bridgeport, Alabama
September 4, 1863

Companies A, D, and part of G and L started for Bridgeport to build a wagon bridge across the river. Immediately commenced the bridge, which is 1,220 feet long. The water in the deeper places is six feet. About 200 feet was bridged with pontoons. Commenced work at six in the morning. Worked all day and night. Got it ready to cross at 10 o'clock Tuesday. As the heavy wagon trains passed over, the boats being lower than the bents, drew them a little each time until at 4 o'clock, part of the bridge fell with teams on it. Not a very serious accident, only one mule drowned. Went to work again and had replaced 200 feet when at 8 o'clock p.m. it fell again. Went to bed tired out. Next morning went at it again and at 1 p.m. had it completely and thoroughly braced. Near 1,000 wagon teams have passed on it, and it stands very well.

General Rosecrans, with most of his army, has crossed the Tennessee River, and the Rebs must fight or skedaddle very soon. Our army has never appeared to be in so good condition. General Ambrose Burnside is in supporting distance, and you may expect good news from this department soon.

Bragg was forced to evacuate Chattanooga on September 8. Although Rosecrans had achieved his strategic goal, he had overextended himself and would soon suffer severe consequences for it.

A few days after that, Federals commanded by General Frederick Steele brushed aside Confederate troops under General Sterling Price and captured Little Rock, Arkansas. The loss of yet another state capital, combined with ongoing Federal operations in Charleston Harbor, was a blow to sagging Confederate morale. Conversely, they added to the Union's growing list of encouraging news, as **George Dwight Knox (1837–1908)**, a private in the 3rd Minnesota Infantry, told his family.

Little Rock, Arkansas
September 23, 1863

We have late [recent] papers to the 11th, which state Chattanooga, Tennessee, is in our hands, and Bragg (flower of the army) again is on the skedaddle. Rosy [Rosecrans] has again outflanked and out-generaled him. Also, the evacuation of Morris Island, Forts Wagner and Sumter, and that Charleston, South Carolina, will soon fall.

Many people shed tears of joy when the Stars and Stripes were hoisted over the [Arkansas] State House. I will here state that the 3rd Iowa Cavalry raised the flag while the fighting was still going on. Everyone singing at the top of their voices,

"Rally round the flag, boys, rally once again; Shouting the Battle Cry of Freedom."

The citizens said it was a grand affair. We captured the U.S. Arsenal with a large supply of ammunition, none of which was injured. The Rebels had men stationed at the arsenal and other places in the city to burn them, but our cavalry dashed in so sudden that they barely had time to escape. The steamboats that were burned [on the Arkansas River] they did not set fire to themselves. They paid a Negro $10 each for firing them. The Negro is now here and has Confederate rags to show for his incendiarism.

We have rumors of another engagement between Lee and Meade's armies [in Virginia] and that Lee was badly repulsed, but nothing definite in regard to it. There is also a rumor that it is the opinion of Lee and his leading officers that peace will soon be declared in favor of the U.S. These are rumors only. We take them for what they are worth, no more.

(Knox was mistaken on one point: Fort Sumter and Charleston remained in Southern hands.)

The situation was becoming dire for the South. But the Confederate high command had a trick up its sleeve. As Chattanooga was being given up, General James Longstreet was leaving Virginia to join Bragg's army in northwestern Georgia. He took with him two divisions, one extra brigade, and a 26-gun artillery battalion on the 775-mile journey through the Carolinas, over to Atlanta, and up to join Bragg and the Army of Tennessee. The lengthy trip through the Confederate interior took three weeks.

W. O. Ruddock (1840–1876), a private in the 23rd North Carolina Infantry detached to hospital duty far from the front, knew all about it. He also mentioned to his uncle how non-Virginians fighting there felt unappreciated.

General Hospital No. 2, 2nd Division
Danville, Virginia
September 15, 1863

There is several divisions of General Lee's army going West, Hood's, Pickett's, and McLaws's Divisions, and ordered all the men belonging to their commands that are able to have transportation to be sent forward. I have heard of no other division having gone. I heard that my (Rodes's) Division was going. If it does, I suppose I will get another long train ride. I would like to see the Western country and study the geography of it a while. I am tired of Virginia, in fact. The North Carolina soldiers get very little credit for what they have done here.

I heard a few days ago that Pettigrew's Brigade had went back to North Carolina to take up deserters. That will be very light duty, I suppose, but I don't think very desirable. But I would be willing to perform almost any kind of duty if my brigade could only get there. But the men would not be satisfied. It seems that every place we go, we think it is the worst place. It is natural for mankind to not be satisfied. The better they are treated, the better they wish to be treated.

(While he knew the gist of what was happening, Ruddock's news wasn't completely accurate. Pickett's shattered division was still recovering from its mauling at Gettysburg and did not accompany Longstreet; neither did Rodes's Division.)

At the same time, two Union corps were likewise sent from Virginia to reinforce Federals in Tennessee. In the letter to his wife mentioned earlier, **Benjamin Franklin O'Bryon (1837–1864)** said that soldiers in Meade's army were itching to attack the Confederates.

Camp near Rapidan River, Virginia
September 21, 1863

There is heavy firing on our right, and we have 8 days' rations of hardtack in our knapsacks and may be called into action. It is reported that Lee has reinforced Bragg with two corps. If that be so, you may look for active movements in the Army of the Potomac, for if there ever was a time to strike a decisive blow and ruin old Lee's army, I think, then this—the time has arrived.

I want you to give the news in general, especially what they think of the Rebellion by this time and how the Copperheads are getting along. I suppose they are kicking up quite a mess. Would to God we had the opportunity of hanging the sons of bitches for they are the ones who are prolonging this war. If it had not been for the Doughface Democracy [congressmen who did not oppose slavery] of the North, we never would have been in this war. They are the cause of the land being draped in mourning. They are the cause of all this inhuman butchery and sacrificing of human life. They are the cause of all this public debt and enormous taxes which will be imposed on the people and they are the whole cause of the ruination of the country, of all mean and deluded men as Northern traitors. I think after the coming fight, if we prove successful, the President will offer an amnesty to the disloyal states to all who will lay down their arms and hang the [Confederate] leaders.

The lead elements of Longstreet's reinforcements began arriving in northern Georgia on September 17, two days before the start of one of the conflict's bloodiest battles. Chickamauga was second only to Gettysburg in number of casualties. The Confederates attacked but could not break the Union lines on September 19. The next day brought one of the war's biggest blunders. Erroneously told that there was a gap in his lines, Rosecrans shifted men to fill it, thus creating an actual gap—just as Longstreet's men were launching an assault at that very spot. The defeated Federals were swept from the field and fled back to Chattanooga. Only determined resistance by General George Henry Thomas (known afterward as the "Rock of Chickamauga") prevented Rosecrans's army from being annihilated.

Bugler **John L. Hebron (1842–1914)** of the 2nd Ohio Volunteer Infantry notified his mother a week later.

Chattanooga, Tennessee
September 26, 1863

I am still safe through another bloody battle. After skirmishing with the Rebels for several days, we attacked them in earnest on Saturday and held them pretty level. They took our battery (Loomis' old battery), but McCook recaptured it in the afternoon. But they came near capturing our brigade on Sunday. The Rebels must have had 2 to our 1—about half of the Richmond army was here, so prisoners say. This battle was worse than Perryville on the Steubenville boys. Alex Surls was killed early in the engagement. John Neas was wounded and taken prisoner on Sunday. They gave us thunder, driving our whole line and taking lots of prisoners.

We have a picket fight with them every day. I guess there is no danger for us here. We are a little too well-fixed for them.

An **unidentified Federal soldier** in the 89th Ohio Infantry described to a friend the battle's frightening conclusion.

Camp near Chattanooga, Tennessee
September 29, 1863

We had to wade a little river [Chickamauga Creek]. It was better than knee-deep. Then we had to lay down in line of battle and lie there all night, and the old man came pretty nigh freezing.

Sunday morning, we heard them fighting on our right. And it wasn't long until we started in that direction. About 10 o'clock, they began to shell us to keep us back. It was dangerous, but I couldn't help laughing to see the boys running their heads in the grass when a shell would come over. We pushed ahead until we got where they wanted us.

Layed there a few minutes, then was ordered up. You never heard such yellin' in your life. Just as we got to the top of the hill, the Rebs began to pour the bullets at us. And for one hour, we could hear nothing but the roar of cannons and musketry. Then the Rebs fell back a little.

We got to rest about an hour, and they came up 4 or 5 deep, and as fast as we would shoot them down, they would close up. I suppose it was the hardest fight that has been during the war. We got all mixed up. I stood behind a tree and shot at them until they came within 10 steps of me. I looked along the lines, and they were driving our right and left—over half of our boys were out of ammunition. We kept falling back a little at a time until they had swung pretty nigh around us. I seen there was a chance to save myself, and I got out. If I had been 5 minutes longer, it would have been all over for me. Thirty of us were in the fight, and only 5 came out. I only got one wounded man out.

Our pickets and theirs are now within 300 to 400 yards of each other. The Rebs have tried our lines 4 or 5 times last week, but we put them back. One night, we killed 25 of them and only lost 4 or 5 of our men. We don't get to sleep very much now, only in the daytime. We have to get up at 3 every morning and stand in line of battle until after daylight for fear they might slip in on us. We have got 3 or 4 pretty strong forts built and miles of breastworks. If they try it here, they will find it won't fit very well. Old Rosy [Rosecrans] sent a flag of truce to Bragg Sunday morning to get permission to go after our wounded.

One incident during the battle stuck with a young Yankee. **John Gray (1841–1930),** a corporal in the 101st Indiana Infantry, was detailed to an artillery battery and shared it with his little sister.

Camp of the 19th Indiana Battery
Chattanooga, Tennessee
December 5, 1863

A few days ago, we were threatened by the Rebel force, but today, we are safe even without pickets. I learned to despise danger since the fight of Bloody Chickamauga because I considered if it was possible to come through such a storm of death missiles, it was even possible in the future.

I will tell you of a "little drummer boy" who belonged to the 75th Indiana Infantry. He was short-legged, fat, and hearty. His age was not over 13, but was exceedingly hardy and stood long marches. But when he sometimes gave out, he would come to our battery with his haversack filled with crackers and his little knapsack filled with "nicknacks" and "scarcities" as he called his load. He frequently rode along with us, but when the fight of Chickamauga began, he jumped off and said, "I must go to my regiment and see the fight." Brave as a lion, he feared nothing. It is the place of drummers to be hospital boys to carry the dead and wounded off the battlefield. These boys pile their drums up in a stack, and having red tape around their arm, this little drummer could not carry much but showed his willingness by offering to help.

He came off the field with us Sunday night but found that he had left his drum. So he started back after it, and just as he got hold of it, the Rebels fired at him, also crying out, "Halt! Let that drum alone." But he picked it up and walked up to a big tree and broke the drum to pieces, saying, "There old drum. The Rebels won't make music out of you for me to march behind as a prisoner." They took him. He is not yet exchanged.

(The drummer described was possibly young Almon Beneway, alias Albert Walton, who spent 14 months in Confederate prisons in Andersonville, Georgia, and Florence, South Carolina.)

Chickamauga was such a serious Federal rout that some observers lost sight of a significant fact: although victorious in the battle, Bragg didn't achieve his strategic objective. **Warren E. Perkins (1838–1879),** a first lieutenant in the 2nd Massachusetts Infantry, noted that to a friend. He was serving alongside a regiment of black soldiers, the 1st Tennessee Infantry (African Descent), and he observed that in racial matters, emancipation didn't mean equality in the eyes of many whites.

On camp 4 miles north of Decherd, Tennessee
[Modern-day Estill Springs]
October 6, 1863

We picket the railroad to Winchester. There is some apprehension of an attack on Rosecrans's communications, as it would be useless to attack him in front. There, his position is secure. People down here don't seem willing to admit that he has suffered a defeat. They can't see the difference between a victory and a decisive victory. Undoubtedly, Bragg was victorious, but his victory was not decisive because he didn't drive Rosecrans out of Chattanooga.

There do not seem to be any other troops here except the 11th and 12th Corps and Rosecrans's army. No reinforcements have arrived from Grant, and I have not heard of Burnside's juncture.

There is not much to eat here except sutler's canned stuff, and that you know always has a bad taste, unlike what comes from home. I am not very likely to get what I want here, but I can live very comfortably with occasional help from home.

We have a nigger regiment here which has just been raised. Their camp is next to ours, and this morning, I went over to see guard mounting. They are very green, officers and men. The officers are all white, of course. Our men don't show the slightest ill will but seem very much amused at their new neighbors. If we had a joint picket, and our privates were put under nigger sergeants, it might make trouble, but I don't believe they will try anything of that sort. Black and white troops have no natural enmity, if they are kept separate.

As the fighting raged on, daily life was difficult for people living in the path of the great armies, especially those in the Border States of Kentucky and Missouri, where control frequently changed from one side other. Many residents there survived by being ambivalent, as **John F. Moore (1833–1907)**, a second lieutenant in the 10th Kentucky Cavalry (U.S.), mentioned to his parents.

Lexington, Kentucky
October 23, 1863

We are now encamped in the fairground. A lovely spot, but much abused by the Rebels. Just before I sat down to write this letter the officer of the day came to my tent and requested that I should go with him to an adjoining woods where the colonel thinks he will move the camp this afternoon. While there, three young girls came out of a house and spoke to me. One of them asked if I would give her my beautiful horse. I asked her if she was a Union lady. If so, she should have my horse if I should happen to be killed by General John Hunt Morgan. But she said, "When the Rebels are here, I am a Rebel. When the Union army is here, I am Union." We talked for a long time on the subject but could not agree. The Rebels are expected back here every day, and I should not be surprised if they would pay us a visit.

Once again, the war on the Missouri–Kansas border displayed its unique brand of brutality. On October 6, Quantrill's Raiders attacked a small Union fort near the little town of Baxter Springs, Kansas. Although unable to capture it, the raiders happened on a passing column of troops escorting Union General James Blunt as he was relocating his headquarters to Fort Smith, Arkansas. The raiders wore captured blue Union uniforms, allowing them to take the Federals by surprise, killing those who tried to surrender. In all, 103 Union soldiers and 10 civilian workers were killed; two raiders died.

The incident horrified people throughout the west, including **Isaac Hardacker (1843–1873)**, a private in the 32nd Iowa Infantry. He wrote to a friend while recovering from illness at a military hospital.

Madison, Wisconsin
November 5, 1863

That was rather a serious affair that happened near Baxter Springs to Capt.
Conkey's company. Those boys that went from our neighborhood got killed
before they were down there long. It does really seem too bad that men must
be sent down while young and in good health by a band of lawless traitors,
but our homes must be secured and traitors punished and it stands everyone
in hand to do something.

In Ohio, captured Confederate General John Hunt Morgan and his officers languished in the state penitentiary. The previous December, the 38-year-old Morgan had married 22-year-old Martha "Mattie" Ready, the daughter of a Tennessee congressman. Now the newlywed bride was a refugee in southwestern Virginia, hoping for her husband's release from prison. Private **W. O. Ruddock (1840–1876)** of the 23rd North Carolina Infantry described meeting her.

General Hospital No. 2, 2nd Division
Danville, Virginia
November 4, 1863

I had the honor of taking tea with Mrs. General Morgan last evening at
Colonel Withers'. She has been stopping there for some time. She has the
reputation of being very lively, but she seemed to be in very low spirits at
tea and went to her room from the tea table. She is a fine-looking woman.
I understood she asked some ladies to call on her if they would condescend to
associate with a lady whose husband was in the penitentiary.

We are looking for about six thousand prisoners that are to be sent here
from Richmond to be taken care of. I don't know where they will store them
away. I don't think I could pack six thousand Yankeys [sic] in what room that
is vacant here. I don't suppose they are particular as to their comfort.

Mattie Morgan did not have long to wait; her husband and six others tunneled out of the penitentiary three weeks later and escaped to Confederate lines.

As summer gave way to autumn, Lee and Meade waged the Bristoe Campaign, a series of back-and-forth movements through central Virginia that included extensive marching and a few minor battles but yielded few notable results for either side.

In the West, the Union army was now besieged in Chattanooga. Bragg's forces occupied the mountains and ridges surrounding it, cutting off all supplies. Food for men, mules, and horses grew dangerously low. On October 16, Lincoln dismissed Rosecrans and replaced him with the victor of Vicksburg: Grant.

Also that month, Ohio voters rejected Democrat Clement Vallandigham for governor. The former congressman was a prominent leader of the anti-war Copperheads, who wanted an immediate peace agreement with the Confederates. Ohio was one of several states that held off-year elections at the time, and the results were a boost to the Federal war effort.

It all was discussed by a Federal soldier identified only as **Oscar S. (unknown)** with his cousin.

Germantown, Tennessee
October 25, 1863

Well, Hiram, what do you think of the military changes that have taken place? I think it is just alright. General Grant is just the man who can make old Bragg climb for tall timber if he takes the field in Chattanooga in person. In regard to our affairs in Virginia, that is such a complicated institution that I cannot find any head or tail to our army. According to the papers, Meade and his army was trying to get away from Lee, and now today, Lee is trying to escape from Meade, who is in hot pursuit at the rate of two miles per day. If they keep on marching backwards and forwards as they have done heretofore, I should think that there would be little of the "Sacred Soil of Virginia" for the Rebs to fight for.

I should think that the Copperheads in the North would feel down in the mouth over the late election in Ohio, Indiana, Pennsylvania, and Iowa. The cause must be greatly on the increase for those states to give such a Union majority. It was more than I expected. Vallandigham can now give up his "waiting and watching." I should think that the last call of the President for 300,000 more men would make them squirm greater still, but the best thing of all will be when they commence to draft them. I think that they have given too long a time for volunteering by just one month.

Likewise, Private **Alvah Jay (1842–1915)** of the 102nd Illinois Infantry also commented to his father about the new general leading the army in which he served.

Camp LaVergne, Tennessee
November 1, 1863

You will see by the papers of the change of commanders over us. Some of the soldiers are making a big blow about it, but I expect it is all for the best. We do not know everything that happened at the Chickamauga fight. General Grant is a successful general.

 Colonel Franklin Smith has been trying to get us seven shooting guns, but we have not got them yet. I hope he may succeed. The four companies that are here have all got horses now. I expect we will go on a scout soon.

As Grant assumed command in the West, the Bristoe Campaign was underway in the East. On November 7, Federals crossed the Rappahannock River in central Virginia, driving off Confederate defenders on the southern bank at Kelly's Ford. That forced Lee to abandon his plans for going into winter quarters around Culpeper, choosing instead a safer site south of the Rapidan River in Orange County. **Joseph Green (unknown)**, a captain in the 30th North Carolina Infantry, related to his wife about the engagement and the increasingly scanty supplies Lee's men were receiving.

Camp near the Rapidan River, Virginia
November 10, 1863

We had a fight last Saturday. We was on picket at Kelly's Ford on the Rappahannock, and the Yankees came to cross. We was off a piece from the river, and we started down to the river. They fired into us with artillery and small arms, and you may know we had a rough time of it. And about the time we got down to the river, we got orders to fall back, and we had to march very near all night and wade two or three rivers, and you may know it was cold. We have got in camp now close to the Rapidan River. I can't tell how many men we lost. I heard we went in with 600 and come out with 260. We lost a good many of our regiment, and the Second. They was the only two that was in the fight. You said you wanted to know what I got to eat every day. I get a pint of flour every day, and it is made up with cold water. No grease nor salt to put in it. And I get a pound of beef a day, they say, but we don't get that much. Our rations is very light. We draw bacon once a while but not very often and we have a stomach to fill a good deal more than I get. And I think it very hard that I can't have enough to eat. After the march I tried to buy something to eat, but I couldn't buy anything.

Please don't think hard of me for not paying the postage for I will send you something to pay it with. So no more at this time for it is very cold and I have got to get wood.

Of the war's many distinctions, the creation of federal cemeteries was among the saddest. The first one opened in 1862; within a year, the number had grown to 12. As preparations were being finalized for a ceremony dedicating the new Soldiers National Cemetery in Gettysburg, Pennsylvania, on November 19, organizers realized that they had neglected to invite President Lincoln. He was belatedly asked to make "a few appropriate remarks."

Writing to a friend in New York, wealthy businessman **John A. McAllister (1822–1896)** easily dismissed the event.

Philadelphia, Pennsylvania
November 16, 1863

Sorry I cannot go to Gettysburg on Thursday. We are too busy to permit my leaving.

With that, McAllister missed hearing one of the most famous speeches in history.

At Chattanooga, the Federals' position was precarious. Confederate artillery still ringed the city, shutting off the delivery of supplies. Horses and mules were dying of starvation. Things weren't much better for the human warriors.

Grant wasted no time getting down to business. His top priority was bringing food and forage to his besieged command, which he achieved by opening the "Cracker Line." The first step was pushing back Confederate outposts from the Tennessee River, as **John L. Hebron (1842–1914)** of the 2nd Ohio Volunteer Infantry described to his mother.

Chattanooga, Tennessee
October 31, 1863

There is nothing new here in the way of fighting, although they had a pretty brisk skirmish a few days ago driving the Rebels from along the river so we can get rations up the river with a boat we have here. We are still on half rations, but we expect to get full rations in a few days as the railroad is completed to within 15 miles of here, and the railroad is two miles from the river at that point, and we will have the boat a running in a few days.

Jacob Summers, who was wounded at the Battle of Chickamauga, died at General Hospital at this place on the night of the 27th. He was wounded in the back of the knee, and the doctors couldn't get the ball out.

Grant's next step was getting reinforcements. And they came rushing in from both the East, troops under Joseph Hooker, and the West, William Sherman's command. Meanwhile, Longstreet's troops marched off to reclaim Knoxville from Burnside. The situation soon became serious for Federals there, as **John W. Cleland (1843–1912),** a corporal in the 111th Ohio Infantry, related to his sister.

[Cumberland Gap, Virginia]
November 24, 1863

Rumors last evening were that the army at Knoxville was surrounded and had only 10 days rations, but there was reinforcements coming to them from Thomas's department. If they should reach Knoxville in time, it would probably save the place.

Bragg's army still ringed Chattanooga's southern and eastern sides, its cannons focused on it from towering Lookout Mountain and across the length of nearby Missionary Ridge.

One of Sherman's soldiers, **Edwin Wallace Atwood (1840–1871),** a private in the 8th Missouri Infantry (Federal), later recounted to his sister his experience being redeployed across 425 miles.

Chattanooga, Tennessee
December 1, 1863

We have had a long and tedious march since we left Camp Sherman in the rear of Vicksburg. We left there on the 27th of September and arrived here at Chattanooga on the 22nd of November. Our army corps was ordered to open the battle the next day without even one day's rest for the men. But notwithstanding their long and late nightly marches through the rain and mud, they went to the field of strife and carnage without a single murmur and full of confidence as to the results of the victory.

We are only getting about two-thirds rations, and the horses and mules are dying of starvation. There is no way of getting supplies, only by the Nashville and Chattanooga Railroad, and it is not completed farther than Bridgeport, Alabama, which is 36 miles from here, and the railroad cannot furnish full rations to the men, and thus animals have to go without forage.

First Lieutenant **Elson M. Misner (1841–1914)** of the 145th New York Infantry had followed Hooker from the East. He had a dim view of his Western comrades, which he made clear to his sisters.

Santallion, Tennessee
November 19, 1863

We will soon have provost work [the Civil War version of modern Military Police] for the whole 15th Army Corps and two Divisions of the 16th, passed through here for the front during the last week. They were under the command of General Sherman, and I must say a worse lot of scamps never were seen. They were little better than a thoroughly organized mob. No discipline or order was being observed. Stragglers lined the roads and mountains for miles, and the houses of citizens, good Union men, were burned, robbed, and the inhabitants plundered indiscriminately. If they are a sample of the great Western Army, I pray that we may never change our name. It is rumored that General Sherman has been placed under arrest for allowing these proceedings, for plundering and straggling are the two most serious enemies known to military law. In the Army of the Potomac, the penalty is death. But such wholesale straggling never has, moreover never will be, permitted in that Prince of Armies. No general or other officer would hold his commission a great while who would countenance such gross violations of civilized warfare. (As [humorist] Artemus Ward has it, "nuff sed on that subject.")

You have, I suppose, heard of the capture of Lookout Mountain and how General Hooker's army did their work. We were not in that fight for which I am thankful, and as I am not actually spoiling for a fight, why you will probably see with what grace and ease I can forgive old Fighting Joe.

(Misner was mistaken; Lookout Mountain had not yet been seized from the Confederates. He most likely heard about skirmishing at the base that was reported to headquarters.)

The mountain was completely taken five days later when Hooker's troops stormed up the daunting heights. A few days after the action, **John Caleb Lockwood (1811–1891)**, quartermaster sergeant in the 30th Iowa Infantry, described to his family how the engagement earned the nickname the "Battle Above the Clouds."

Camp near Bridgeport, Alabama
December 10, 1863

At the taking of Lookout Mountain, our regiment was stationed one night near its summit where it was so steep they had to brace themselves against trees and stumps and their bayonets stuck in the ground to prevent them from sliding down the precipice. For several hours, they dare not make fires for fear of the sharpshooters of the enemy on the summit above them, and they suffered from cold. But that night, or early next morning, the enemy evacuated. They had, however, stubbornly resisted the approach of our troops, and I am told that during the fight, a fog or clouds intervened between those fighting below and they who occupied the summit, thus protecting our troops from the fire of the sharpshooters. It reminded me of the cloud that protected the Israelites from their enemies of olden times.

While we lay encamped in Chattanooga Valley, it was interesting to see the clouds floating along between us and "Lookout" and below its peak. As we crossed over one-fourth of the way up with our wagons, it was more like a staircase than anything I had before witnessed, the mules fairly scrambling up ledge after ledge of rocks. Along this road, the Rebels had built forts to shell the city and valley below. Our forces are now busily engaged in rebuilding the railroad from here to Chattanooga so that supplies may be more readily conveyed to our army stationed there. General Rosecrans must have had a hard time to get supplies while hemmed in by the enemy as he was. I'm told that five thousand mules died there—mostly starved to death, I suppose. Our teamsters ventured out and confiscated forage for our animals, or they, too, would have gone hungry. They also got flour, meal, and meat that the Rebs had left in their haste. They were building winter quarters about two miles out from Chattanooga, but we soon spoiled their calculations when the "Vicksburg Gophers" got after them. Some who had fought against us at Vicksburg told our boys after being taken prisoners that they recognized the yell when our boys charged on them. I believe they are more afraid of the Western troops than the "Star Boys" (the XII Corps) of the East, thousands of whom had been lying there in sight for months past.

The victory gained here is a severe stroke on the Rebels, and I do hope may hasten the crushing out of the rebellion and that the plans now maturing will bring them to terms—that next spring will open with restored peace. "So mote it be."

The next day, it was Missionary Ridge's turn. Sherman's troops attacked the northern portion. Later, Thomas's men were ordered to take the rifle pits at the base of the ridge. But acting entirely on their own, they kept charging up the slope until they sent Bragg's army fleeing into nearby Georgia, leaving behind a large amount of artillery in the process. That fight, coupled with Longstreet's failure to retake Knoxville a few days later, left the Union firmly in control of Tennessee.

In the letter mentioned earlier, Private **Edwin Wallace Atwood (1840–1871)** described the situation.

We have had a very hard fight, but as usual, Generals Grant and Sherman, with the help of Generals Thomas and Hooker, completely whipped and defeated General Bragg and his Rebel crew at all points. It was reported the day before yesterday that we had taken 22,000 prisoners and 86 pieces of artillery, but I think the numbers are magnified as they generally are at first.

I do not think it will take long to run Bragg so far that he will never find his way back here again, and then we will probably go back to our own department or go on and join Burnside's army for the purpose of sending Longstreet on a journey southward to join his friend in misery and disaster General Bragg.

Likewise, Private **Charles W. Strickney (1844–1904)** of Taylor's Chicago Battery was clerking in Sherman's headquarters when he dashed off this quick note to his brother that almost reads like a telegraph dispatch.

Chattanooga, Tennessee
December 2, 1863

I must tell you the news. Last Wednesday gave Bragg a handsome whipping, driving him away from Mission [sic] Ridge. Captured 40 to 50 guns, mostly brass, hundreds prisoners. Follow him up next day as far as Ringgold, Georgia. Next day, whipped again. Went no farther. Troops coming back. Bragg probably retreated to Dalton, Georgia. Longstreet been besieging Burnside at

Knoxville. Sherman, with 4th Corps and 2 Divisions of 15th Corps, some 30,000, gone up Tennessee River to Burnside's relief. News today, Longstreet been repulsed by Burnside and retreating. Must go to Virginia; can't retreat south. We'll cut South in two soon. If Meade would whip Lee now, end the rebellion. No more fighting till spring.

As 1863 drew to an end, the Union naval blockade was growing stronger than ever. Blockade-runners had an increasingly difficult time getting in and out of Southern ports. Those that were captured—and their cargo—were sold as prizes. The proceeds were then shared among the officers and men on the ships that caught them based on rank. Many sailors diligently made sure they received what they had coming.

In the closing days of 1863, **Reuben Rich (unknown)** wrote to Washington concerning his share of claims money. (During the period mentioned in the letter, the USS *Juniata* stopped five ships, including one loaded with Southern cotton and another carrying much-needed chemicals for the Confederacy.)

U.S. Steamer Wachusett
Charlestown Navy Yard, Massachusetts
November 26, 1864

Will you have the goodness to inform me if the proceeds of prizes taken by USS Juniata *from March to December 1863 are yet ready for distribution? If they are, will you please forward me an order to have my share as Acting Master's Mate credited to me on the books of the ship?*

Not only did the blockade deny the Confederacy badly needed materiel and supplies, but the capture of blockade-runners was a financial loss to the investors who had put their money into them, as this letter from attorney **Thomas Andrae (unknown)** in the increasingly important port city of Wilmington, North Carolina, shows. It was written to an investor in Richmond. (The *Ceres* had been launched in England only a few months earlier. Arriving at Bermuda in November, she received a coat of light paint, then continued on with her cargo in her maiden attempt to run the blockade. She ran aground at the mouth of the Cape Fear River near Wilmington and was set on fire by her crew. Sailors from the blockading USS *Violet* put out the flames and refloated her. The *Ceres* was then taken to Prize Court and sold off.)

Wilmington, North Carolina
December 7, 1863

I am sorry to inform you of the loss of the "Ceres." She got on shore, coming into this port early yesterday morning, and was burnt in order to prevent her from falling into the hands of the Yankees. <u>Nothing,</u> to our knowledge, was saved.

The year ended on a high note for the North, as captured in a brief note that Lieutenant Commander **Andrew Wallace Johnson (1826–1887)**, captain of the USS *Unadilla* on blockade duty off the coast near Savannah, Georgia, quickly scrawled to a Union colonel stationed nearby.

USS Unadilla
Tybee Roads, Georgia
December 3, 1863

I make haste to send you the good news. The dispatch vessel that came in this morning with our mail, etc., informs us that Meade is on his way without opposition and that the ironclads are ready to go up in the harbor at Charleston. Burnside has also achieved a big victory [Battle of Fort Sanders and ending the siege of Knoxville]. A salute was fired in honor of our successes at Charleston.

Everything looks encouraging. Things seem to be coming to a fine point—as the Irishman terms it, "an airy one."

And so the bloodiest year in American history up to that point ended. While the Confederacy had suffered serious reverses, the war was still far from decided. Strong Southern armies remained in the field, the South's will to fight was unbroken, and—perhaps most important of all—the leader of the Union war effort was up for reelection in the year ahead. Would Northerners vote to continue the conflict, or would war-weariness prevail?

1864

"I sometimes get very disheartened,
but hope for the best."

BY THE WAR'S THIRD WINTER, AN ANNUAL ROUTINE HAD BEEN ESTABLISHED. Commanders on both sides now understood the folly of trying to move large armies during the coldest time of the year. Frozen roads made maneuvering almost impossible, rain and snow could create nightmare situations overnight, and canvas tents provided little relief from frigid temperatures. Union and Confederate forces hunkered down in winter quarters where soldiers kept warm inside miniature log cabins. While their generals planned and prepared for the spring campaigns, men in the ranks rested and swapped stories, dreamed of home, and secretly dreaded what would come when the days grew warmer.

In northwestern Georgia, Sergeant **Leander Calfee (1839–1910)** of the 54th Virginia Infantry was serving under a new commander. General Joseph Johnston replaced Braxton Bragg as head of the Army of Tennessee on December 27, 1863. Writing to his brother back in the Old Dominion, Calfee could already see what spring would bring. (Two weeks later, Calfee was hospitalized with a severe illness. He recovered in time for the Atlanta Campaign.)

Camp Extra Billy Smith
Near Dalton, Georgia
January 10, 1864

We have had some very cold weather for the last 12 days, but as most of the troops here are in winter quarters, we prefer cold weather to warm, wet weather. It gets so muddy here when it rains. It turned warm and rained a few days back, and I never saw so much mud at any place as was about Dalton. I thought some days I could hardly get back when I would go after the mail. From what I can learn, this is a very cold winter. I see the papers speak of it being very cold in Richmond and other places in Virginia.

I think the cold weather has stopped all military operations in the field for the present time. There is not likely to be much fighting done this winter on our northern front. The Yankees appear to be recruiting and reenlisting their armies. They are also thought to be completing their lines of communication between Chattanooga and Nashville and accumulating large stores at the former place for spring operations.

It appears from all I can read that the enemy intends to make a desperate effort to overrun us next spring and summer, and if our people don't wake up to the danger, they will succeed. Congress appears to be making a feeble effort to increase the efficiency of our army by putting principles of substitutes into service, but it looks very much like locking the door after the horse is gone. I am afraid it is too late for them to do any good now. If they had done this last year and carried it out in good faith, it might have availed something. But it will not do much good now.

Both sides struggled to keep their ranks filled with troops. That put added pressure on those at home who performed what are today called "essential service" jobs. Consider this note signed by an **unidentified staffer** at Keatinge & Ball, the premier engraver of Confederate currency, stamps, and bonds, to retain a valued worker.

Columbia, South Carolina
January 18, 1864

Mr. William Hussung is employed by us on work for the Treasury Department. His services are all important to us in the prosecution of the work. We beg that his detail may be continued.
   Keatinge & Ball

The manpower shortage wasn't the only problem plaguing the South as 1864 got underway. As the Union naval blockade's ever-tightening grip on its seaports intensified, Confederate engineers became increasingly innovative. They constructed the *David*, a semi-submersible torpedo boat, at Charleston, South Carolina. It had attacked the USS *New Ironsides* on October 5, 1863, causing some damage. That success spurred the production of additional "Davids" there.

News eventually drifted to the Federal lines, where officers anxiously wanted to know more about it. Lieutenant Commander **Andrew Wallace Johnson (1826–1887)** wrote to a Union officer outside Charleston in late January, eagerly seeking intelligence.

> *USS* Unadilla
> *Tybee Roads, Georgia*
> *January 23, 1864*

> *Deserters from Charleston report that the Rebs are building 25 torpedo boats with which to attack the ironclads in the harbor. Several of them are already launched, and the one which made the recent attack on the "Ironsides" is also ready for service. They are all waiting for an opportunity to make our Tars navigate the ethereal regions. Should any refugees or deserters arrive at your post, will you be kind enough to afford to me an opportunity of "pumping" them [for information] as to these infernal contrivances?*

Just three weeks later, the Confederacy's ultimate secret weapon made naval warfare history.

The CSS *H. L. Hunley* sank the USS *Housatonic* in Charleston Harbor on February 17, 1864, making it the first submarine to sink an enemy vessel. The *Hunley* also sank in the attack.

Amid that backdrop, the blockade's effects were being painfully felt inside the Confederacy. Store shelves were growing increasingly bare as a Southerner identified only as **Alfred (unknown)** noted to his wife in North Carolina during a visit to Richmond. Shortages would only worsen, and prices would shoot up even higher due to hyperinflation in the coming year.

> *Ballard House [Hotel]*
> *Richmond, Virginia*
> *January 31, 1864*

> *I have looked in almost every drugstore in town for a brush for baby, but so far have not been able to find one. Miss Margarch will get the zephyr [a fine cotton gingham] for you if it is in the city, but she fears it cannot be found. The flannel, starch, sugar, etc., can be had. I have bought you some good laudanum, paregoric, some sausage (smoked), some ox marrow pomade, and some other little fixings. I think I will bring you some nice soap, too.*

No Birdseye in town—Wortham looked everywhere, so you must buy slated tablecloths, if so, at auction. A case of Birdseye is to be sold in Petersburg on the 17th of February at a big sale, and I will write tomorrow to try to get three pieces of it at whatever it sells for.

Everything is high here. Board at the Ballard House is $20 a day, and in private boarding houses, it is $200 to $300 a month. I do not know yet what Miss Kate Reginault will do for hire, but she will get a nice place.

I am sorry, my darling. You wanted so very little, for it would have given me so much to have gotten the things for you. Nothing gives me so much pleasure when away from my sweet little wife as to get things to please her. I miss you very much, darling, and have a terrible time getting on my braces [suspenders] every morning.

A few weeks later, Richmond was rocked by one of the war's most controversial events. On February 28, Union horsemen launched a raid aimed at the Confederate capital. They were repulsed in sharp fighting a few days later. The Federal commander, Colonel Ulric Dahlgren, was killed. A major scandal erupted when orders were found on his body that went far beyond the accepted rules of war. **Mollie Gilmore (1842–unknown)** told the details to a relative.

McGaheysville, Virginia
March 8, 1864

Suppose you have heard ere this of the "on to Richmond" the Yankees have made again. But thanks be to the Holy One, they have been foiled, and some have been taken prisoners and some killed. There was a Yankee colonel killed. On his person was found the entire plan of the raid. They were to liberate the prisoners, hang Jeff Davis and his officers, set fire to the city, and depart in peace. Caused quite a sensation throughout our country. Stole a great many Negroes and horses, burned all the flour mills they came to.

I really dread the spring campaign, for I think there will be very hard fighting. Hope this year will end the war, and we may soon hear of peace, independence, and liberty hurled over our dear Confederacy with widestretched wings.

How far up the Valley do the Yankees come on their raids? I feel so uneasy about them, for they are carrying on their warfare in the most inhumane manner possible. Burning and plundering seem to be their whole desire.

The Dahlgren Affair was so serious that General George Meade personally assured General Robert E. Lee that the matter was not sanctioned by the Union army. Northern newspapers insisted that the orders were a forgery. But Southern skepticism lingered. The war was entering a new phase of increasing brutality.

One of the conflict's lesser-known yet fiercely fought engagements occurred early in the year. Although the total of 10,500 troops on both sides was relatively small, its almost 2,000 combined casualties rank it among the bloodiest battles for the number of troops involved.

In February, Union General Truman Seymour landed his small army at Jacksonville, Florida, as planned. But without informing his superiors and with very little preparation, he proceeded through the sparsely populated countryside toward Tallahassee, the state capital. The Confederates met the Federals at Olustee (also called Ocean Pond) on February 20 and defeated them, forcing Seymour back to his coastal base. **Reuben T. Wells (1835–1902),** a private in the 115th New York Infantry, recounted his disgust with the debacle to his wife.

Jacksonville, Florida
March 3, 1864

I suppose you have seen in the papers about our fight. Well, you can believe about half of what you hear and see in the New York papers. Our fight on the 20th was a hard-fought battle, for we lost half our men. The bullets flew so thick that it seemed almost impossible for anyone to escape unhurt. But I never got a scratch. There is a good reason, for I was in the rear with the wagon train. But the balls were plenty there, and now and then, a shell and some grapeshot exploded. I expected not to see any of our boys again.

It is shame on the general [Seymour] that did us in, not knowing what he was doing nor where he was going. They never tried to find the enemy's strength nor position but rushed in regardless of all danger. The Rebs made a trap for us and got us in it, so we got licked and badly, too.

The cavalry and mounted infantry have taken all the prisoners and cannon except one jackass battery our men found in the woods by the river where the Rebs burnt up a steamer of cotton. Deserters come in every day and say the Rebs have a heavy force, but they dare not advance for fear of the gunboats. We have this place well-fortified.

This is a damn poor country. I wouldn't give 65 cents for the whole state.

The widely reported defeat underscored the fact that the North was facing a critical situation in early 1864. With no end to the war in sight, the three-year enlistment for tens of thousands of soldiers was due to expire that summer. An aggressive campaign was launched to encourage officers and men to sign up for another three years as veterans. Large cash bounties and a month's furlough for a visit home were offered to all who reenlisted. Prominent citizens in many communities wrote letters urging men to remain in the army.

Those appeals sometimes worked. Other times, they didn't. **Enoch Franklin Piper (1838–1920),** a private in the 4th Maine Infantry, was among those who had had enough by 1864. His reply to one such request to stay with his regiment is so eloquent that it deserves quoting at length.

Near Brandy Station, Virginia
February 15, 1864

I have thoroughly considered the subject and have concluded not to reenlist, at least for the present. I am aware, sir, that the bounties offered by our state and the general [Federal] government are ample, and perhaps I need them as much and even more than many others. Yet, sir, this fighting simply for moneymaking purposes is wholly repugnant to my feelings. If a sense of my duty to my country will not induce me to fight her enemies, money will fail to do so.

I do not wish you to infer from my refusing to reenlist that I have sickened of our cause and that I am willing to sit down and see the rebellion pushed through to a successful termination without the least effort on my part to stay its course, for such is not the case. Were the Northern states drained of young, able men such as are required for military purposes and our armies so reduced as to be unable to meet the enemy successfully, then would I willingly and cheerfully forego the comforts of civil life and enter the service there to remain until the rebellion was no more. But the North has no lack of men. There are thousands there as well able to endure the privations and hardships incidental to a soldier's life as any of those who are now in the field, and it is highly proper too that they should contribute something to the cause of this country. That country whose blessings they have ever enjoyed and which has ever protected them in their every right. And now that country is assailed, its very existence threatened by a reckless and implacable foe.

I reiterate that it is highly proper that those who have enjoyed its prosperity should now come to its rescue. I contend, sir, had it not been for a certain class of the North, this struggle might have been successfully closed 'ere this. I refer to that vile, treasonable, aye denounceable class termed Copperheads. If they had at the breaking out of the war supported the government and presented to the South a united North, and shown the Rebels from the first that all hope of aid from the North was vain, our national affairs at the present time would be in a far more satisfactory condition than now. But they pursued a far different course. Every act of the Lincoln Administration was characterized as weak; they denounced the government upon every occasion and threatened openly to resist its authority if an attempt was made to execute the laws of the land. They were never satisfied except when Union armies were beaten and Northern blood caused to flow as freely as water. Such lies have been the course of this party. I charge upon them the responsibility of prolonging the war. Now, if they desire liberty, let them come into the field and help secure it. I do not feel it my duty to do their work for them.

(Less than 90 days after writing those words, Piper was seriously wounded in the Wilderness/Overland Campaign. He eventually mustered out of the service that July.)

Large cash bounties were offered to new recruits. State and local governments frequently chipped in with additional bounties of their own. The money was intended to enable working men to support their families while away at war. To collect it, veterans, recruits, or their heirs were required to file a bounty claim. And sometimes those applications got tangled in government red tape.

Lawyers advertised their services in bounty and pension claims in much the same way today's lawyers use TV commercials to promote their assistance with personal injury and disability cases. Yet sometimes, those inducements didn't turn out to be as advertised. In his reply to an unsatisfied client, attorney **William Van Marten (unknown)** backtracked on his ad, explaining that he specialized in bounty rather than pension claims and that "free" wasn't really free after all.

Washington, D.C.
March 11, 1864

You entirely misapprehend me. I say I collect such claims as I obtain for clients free of cost. I have obtained your pension, and if you want me to collect it, I will do it free of cost. You confuse the two terms "collect" and "obtain." Besides, this whole paragraph, as you will see, has reference solely to bounty claims and not to pensions. Yet it is right and is not susceptible to the construction you give it.

I have so much to do in this line and for which I get paid that I can't spend the time to work for nothing. I think on reading my circular [advertisement] again, you will see the difference between collecting and obtaining, as I have there used the terms, and then feel like withdrawing your remark that I designed to use "sharp practice." This voluntary effort to collect is accepted by nearly all my clients, and I collect from 1 to 2 thousand dollars a day without charge. I supposed it was understood what my fees were to be, that they were half the legal fees and in no case less than $3.

As the conflict dragged on, daily life, with all its complexities and problems, also went on. **John W. Houtaling (1836–1905)** had enlisted as a private in the 95th Illinois Infantry in late October 1863; married in Belvidere, Illinois, on December 31; mustered into the regiment on January 6, 1864; and quickly marched off to Mississippi. Writing to his new wife a few weeks later, he hinted that they had wed under less-than-ideal circumstances and touched on two taboo topics for mid-Victorians: abortion and sexually transmitted diseases.

Vicksburg, Mississippi
February 28, 1864

I was very sorry to hear that you had been sick while at Rockford for I know you could not enjoy your visit much. And I was sorry to hear that you thought you was treed (as you call it). Very sorry indeed. But still, I think you are alright, although I am no judge of such matters. If you are sure that you are in a bad way at this present time, I wish we could get rid of it in some way if it would not injure your health.

Most of the boys are well, although there is some contagious diseases in the army. There is some of the boys here had the mumps and the measles, and some other diseases that I will not mention now but may in some future time. You can guess what it is if you try very hard.

Well now, if the above is not pretty stuff to write to a nice young woman, then I am fooled. But what of it, for it is to my companion for life and probably we will know each other better in some future time. Now Kate, when you answer this letter, I want you to consign it to the flames so that it will not be seen by anyone except yourself, and you will oblige me.

Prolonged separations sometimes led to marital infidelity. An **unknown Union soldier** in Sherman's army asked his wife for details about a fallen comrade's wife.

[Location unknown; date in 1864 unknown]

You spoke about the hard talk that was afloat. Tell me what it is. Really, it is too bad that Van was out here and since died and a wife at home doing wrong, probably very intimate with some man. It is awful to think of how she must feel now if she is guilty. Since Van has been in the service, he done well by her sending all his money home, did not spend any unnecessary at all, and often talked about her and the children.

That same soldier also wrote his wife about his own physical difficulties being apart.

Emma, I will tell you my dream that I had last night in my lonely slumbers was the thought that we were in Ohio where Messer lives below the Corners, and there went to bed as real as we ever did, and the balance you can judge for yourself. Oh, how I do wish it had only been so, but lo, when I awoke found myself lying in my little tent way down here in Georgia. Often do I dream similar dreams, but when I wake am disappointed very much. Oh, were that I could enjoy myself today and better tonight. You must not get angry at my talking so because I cannot help it.

On March 2, President Lincoln dramatically ramped up the Union's war effort by appointing Ulysses Grant a lieutenant general, the first American to hold that rank since George Washington. He was also named general-in-chief, giving him command of all Union armies. Grant spent a few days conferring with his replacement in the West, General William Sherman, then hurried to the East. While Meade would remain commander of the Army of the Potomac, Grant would travel with it and oversee its operations, making it Grant's army in all but name.

He immediately stood apart from his predecessors. Writing later that year, **William Addison Hosford (1837–1912)**, quartermaster of the 2nd Connecticut Heavy Artillery, described what made his new commander different in a letter to his mother.

City Point, James River, Virginia
September 9, 1864

General Grant's headquarters are here, and like a true soldier, he lives in a tent. He is a very plain man, seems always in deep study. Often converses with the common soldier and as freely as with commissioned officers and is the favorite of all who know him.

Grant was determined to succeed where McDowell, McClellan, Pope, McClellan again, Burnside, Hooker, and Meade all had failed. While his Confederate opponent, General Robert E. Lee, was widely acknowledged as a brilliant strategist, Grant planned to use the North's superior numbers to his advantage. Even before the spring campaign began, Private **Edson Emory (1833–1915)** of the 2nd Vermont Infantry could tell what Grant intended to do, as he described to his brother back home. Another brother, **Philo Emory (1836–1864)**, was also a private in the same regiment and added a short postscript. (Philo would be killed in fighting 71 days later.)

Brandy Station, Virginia
March 30, 1864

General Grant's headquarters are at Culpeper. Our army is reorganized into three Grand Divisions—Sedgwick the right, Hancock the left, and Warren the center. Grant has not reviewed us yet but probably will soon. Reinforcements are coming in as their camps are to be seen as far to the rear as the eye can reach.

There will be a desperate struggle made in Virginia by Grant—one side or the other will get terribly whipped. Grant is massing an army of over 100,000 men. His intentions are to outnumber Lee, and there is where his head is clear, for I think Grant knows his generalship is no better than some of his predecessors has been; therefore will rely on superior numbers. The clash will be terrible, you may depend, and too, as soon as the going will admit. You may calculate that you will hear of some of the bloodiest battles of the war! —Edson

We have had a cold, bleak, rough day. I think the campaign will commence as soon as the 20th of April. Grant is massing a great army here— probably more than 100 thousand men, and a great battle will soon be fought. Mother must keep up good courage. —Philo

Confidence was likewise strong in the Confederacy as the spring campaign drew near. One Southerner, in particular, had high hopes after meeting with the commander in chief.

Viewed as major American historical figures today, it is difficult now to fully appreciate the intense vilification that both Abraham Lincoln and Jefferson Davis experienced during the war. However, **John Sneed (1822–1901)**, a former Tennessee attorney general who had briefly served as a general in his state's forces early in the war, expressed to his cousin how he had a change of heart after sitting down with the Confederate president.

Greensboro, North Carolina
April 10, 1864

I have been much of late in Richmond. Everything looks encouraging, and men speak confidently of the prospect of closing the war this year. I saw the President and had a business interview with him. He is looking well. He impressed my mind, which had been prejudiced against him, as being a very remarkable man. Now that I have seen and judged him in person, I positively like him. I had always admired his administrative abilities—but there is that about him when his official cap is on that impresses all about him with the idea that he is a very extraordinary man. Calm—always self-poised— quick to apprehend—prompt to execute—with more upon his brain—and yet the coolest head amid the millions of sufferers around him. He seemed to me the very man of God's nomination to "ride upon the whirlwind and direct the storm." Add to this that he is a devoted Christian, and you have the "highest type of man."

March 1864 marked an important political milestone. Lincoln's term would end in exactly 12 months. So would his presidency should he not be reelected in November's election. And at the moment, a second Lincoln term was far from a sure thing.

In fact, **Dewitt Davis (1833–1915)**, an attorney and Republican Party activist, told a friend that he was already sizing up possible presidential replacements.

Milwaukee, Wisconsin
March 31, 1864

I have just returned from a Republican state convention at Madison called to nominate delegates to the Baltimore [national] convention. Lincoln seems to have the inside track, though there is no very great enthusiasm for him. I would prefer [General and former House Speaker] Nathaniel Banks, or [Treasury Secretary] Salmon Chase, and perhaps [General and 1856 GOP presidential nominee] John C. Fremont. I think there is some doubt whether Mr. Lincoln will be nominated at Baltimore. I think I perceive a growing reaction in the winds of the people against him.

While the Union was swelling the ranks of its armies at the front, thousands of soldiers were detailed on service missions behind the lines. Duty there was light, and the men looked for ways to fill their days. As 17-year-old Private **Henry Wilkins (1847–1910)** of the 123rd New York Infantry, who had enlisted at the age of 15, wrote to his aunt, he passed his time with the same sport that teenagers still play today.

Camp in the wood
Warren County, Tennessee
March 25, 1864

We have very good weather down here now. We have not had snow enough to make the ground white, and it is as warm now as it is in May up there. The last of January, we went 60 miles from camp in companies and was gone one month. Two companies had to guard a lot of hands [workers] while they took up a bunch of railroad track that was 40 miles long, and they have got two-thirds done. I expect we will have to do some such thing all summer. They find our regiment very good for such things. We play ball every day, and it gives us a very good appetite to eat Uncle Sam's hardtack and salt pork.

I have not got any more of them photographs but will get some taken as soon as I get a chance. We do not get a chance very often unless we are marching through some town and stop to get dinner or some such thing or other.

Across the North, major cities competed with one another by holding special fairs to raise money for the U.S. Sanitary Commission. The charity supported Federal troops in the field by providing stationary and envelopes, medical supplies for the sick and wounded, soap and other necessities. The largest was New York City's Metropolitan Fair, which raised more than $1.3 million (about $47 million in modern dollars) for the war effort from April 4 to 23. An **unidentified woman** recounted the massive event to her brother.

New York City
April 11, 1864

Our time has been much taken up at the Fair here. They made half a million last week!!! There are two buildings. In the International Department, the ceiling is filled with flags of all nations, and every other one is the Stars and Stripes. The names of different great battles are over the booths from which things are sold by the ladies.

But the other building is much the largest. There is a fine band playing almost constantly, a floral temple is in the center, and the greatest quantity of fancy articles you imagine all around for sale. There is a trophy room which is crowded with interesting things. Flags that have been through many battles and some captured ones, balls, cannons, etc. etc. The Curiosity Shop is also intensely interesting. There is the table General Washington eat off from, a pincushion made from a piece of Mrs. Washington's wedding dress, etc., etc. Then foreign things, a Chinese shrine, a coat of mail, Peter Stuyvesant's court dress, etc., and more than I can remember. There is also a picture gallery, which is the finest collection of paintings ever exhibited in this country. We have been every day for a few hours and still find things of interest to see and to buy.

Of the approximately one dozen Sanitary Fairs held in the North, one carried special significance to Unionists. Lincoln had passed through Baltimore in disguise overnight while traveling to his 1861 inauguration. The deadly Baltimore Riot followed weeks later. With the president and city each eager to make amends, Lincoln spoke at the opening ceremony, and Baltimore went all out to show it was solidly behind the Federal war effort, as **Ann M. Sears (1826–1919)** wrote to a friend.

Baltimore, Maryland
April 25, 1864

Our Sanitary Fair was opened last Second Day [Monday] by the President, since which time it has been crowded day and night. I believe thus far they have done as well as it was expected. It is to be continued through this week, and being so near Washington have had visits from the members of the Cabinet, Congress, and foreign embassies.

Secretary of the Treasury Salmon P. Chase was present Saturday evening, but he passed through the hall, bought some articles, made a speech, and was presented a beautiful sofa cushion while I was in the New England Kitchen, so I did not see him. He was accompanied by a son of the President.

Three years ago, when soldiers were shot down in our streets, who would have thought of such a change, and more particularly in regard to the colored troops? There have been great numbers of them encamped near the city, and they occasionally make a fine parade without being molested in the least.

I had a letter from George Evans last week. They are still in Germany. They, with other Americans and some Germans, celebrated the 22nd of February [Washington's birthday] in good style. Those abroad who feel an interest in our country are anxious for the reelection of President Lincoln. Our men did not vote for him at first, but are ready to do so now.

We could hear the puff, puff, puff of the cannonading all day yesterday. A great number of troops are passing through. Everyone is looking forward with a great deal of anxiety to the coming campaign, feeling that it is to decide the question. Let us hope and pray that Grant may be as successful on the Potomac as he has been elsewhere. Last week, I saw two returned prisoners, one from Libby Prison, the other from Belle Isle. They say they would not like to spend another summer there.

(Sears was mistaken; Treasury Secretary Salmon P. Chase actually visited the fair with his son-in-law, Senator William Sprague IV, not Robert Lincoln.)

That spring, Confederate General Nathan Bedford Forrest led a cavalry raid deep behind Federal lines into western Tennessee and Kentucky. His goal was to disrupt Union supply lines and communications ahead of Sherman's anticipated advance into Georgia. On April 12, he attacked and captured Fort Pillow, situated on a bluff overlooking the Mississippi River above Memphis. It was garrisoned by 600 Federals, about half black and half white.

A massacre reportedly occurred in the engagement's closing moments. Union survivors claimed that some Confederates shouted, "No quarter!" (meaning that no prisoners would be taken) and shot blacks who had surrendered. In all, some 221 Federals were killed and 130 wounded compared to 14 Confederates dead and 86 wounded.

News of the incident sparked outrage in the North—including a congressional investigation—and was extensively reported in the press.

Amos Gorrell (1837–1928), a private in the 18th Ohio Infantry, who was still recovering from the wound he had received at Chickamauga six months earlier, shared with a friend how the incident revealed much about racial attitudes within Union ranks.

Nashville, Tennessee
April 17, 1864

About all the news we have here is the capture of Fort Pillow and garrison by the Rebel General Forrest. It appears that the colored soldiers suffered severely when they fell into his hands. I hear some of our soldiers, some too who are particular advocates of the policy of arming Negroes, say that it would be a fine thing if all the Negroes were served the same way. Whenever I advocate the policy of arming Negroes, I will have to advocate the policy of protecting them, not only as human beings but as American soldiers, also.

I think the capture of Fort Pillow might have been prevented. Forrest has been threatening that portion of the country for the last two weeks, and I can't see why a fort, right on the Mississippi River, could not have been reinforced in time to save it. I fear there is too much interest taken in the upcoming political campaign to do justice to our military campaigns.

John L. Hebron (1842–1914), a bugler in the 2nd Ohio Infantry, mentioned to his mother how the affair reflected the war's deepening brutality.

Graysville, Georgia
April 28, 1864

It appears the Rebels have hoisted the black flag from the way they used our prisoners—both black and white—at Fort Pillow. They took six of our men down at Ringgold, Georgia, all white men, and shot them and then punched them full of holes with the bayonets. If that ain't showing no quarter, I don't know what is.

We are laying under marching orders all the time now, but we may not make any move for a month yet till them militia get ready anyway. But when the army does make a move, there will be something done. I don't think we will have much to contend with down here as there is no Rebel force here but Bragg's old army, which is reduced to almost nothing.

With Forrest still operating in Tennessee, Sherman fretted that the Confederate cavalry chieftain would strike near Nashville and hamper the essential flow of supplies to the Federal army. Union General Samuel Sturgis was ordered to neutralize that threat by drawing Forrest away from middle Tennessee.

Known to his opponents as "That Devil Forrest" and to his admirers as the "Wizard of the Saddle," Forrest used his cavalry as mounted infantry. He rushed to northern Mississippi, where Union forces were gathered at Brice's Cross Roads.

As **Joseph Bovee Hughes (unknown)**, lieutenant colonel in the 38th Mississippi Infantry (Mounted), told his brother, Forrest boldly attacked a larger force.

Okolona, Mississippi
June 13, 1864

General Forrest has gained (so says report) another complete victory, and I am told such skedaddling was never known before in the Yankee army. The fight began about 8 miles west of Baldwin near the X roads.

I was ordered to Tupelo, Mississippi, last Saturday with a detail of prisoners. All but one man in my detail left me at Tupelo and went home, some with and some without leave. I could not turn the prisoners over at Tupelo and had to bring them to this place. However, I have had no trouble with any of the boys. They all seem willing to return to camp. I had to impress one guard outside of the regiment. E. C. Hunter of the 3rd Kentucky. He is all a soldier. You will, when he arrives, fix up his papers all right and send him back to his command without a delay.

(Hughes's brother would be killed in the Battle of Nashville six months later.)

For the first time in the war, Union troops were either moving or preparing to move on all fronts. In early March, a coordinated offensive with the goal of driving Confederates out of the Trans-Mississippi region got underway. Union forces in Arkansas headed south, while troops led by General Nathaniel Banks pushed up the Red River toward the strategic Confederate stronghold of Shreveport, Louisiana.

Nicholas Belveal (1839–1926), a private in the 33rd Iowa Infantry, urged his wife to remain optimistic.

Little Rock, Arkansas
March 13, 1864

We are ordered to march in the morning. We are to take nothing but one change of clothes, one woolen blanket, 1 gum blanket, 1 blouse coat, and 40 rounds of ammunition. I don't know how far we will go. I guess we are to cooperate with General Banks and General James Blunt from Fort Smith, Arkansas, and the report says there is a force coming up the Red River with some gunboats. The boys all seem to be in pretty good spirits and willing for the march.

We can't take our paper and ink. I don't know when I will get to write you again, but I want you to keep in good heart. Well Mary, if you don't get any more letters from me for a long time don't get discouraged.

John P. Schuyler (1844–1864), a corporal in the 160th New York Infantry, was among Banks's troops. He wrote this letter to his sister.

Camp in the Field
Near Machintaugh, Louisiana
April 4, 1864

We are now on the march. We are at Machintaugh [Natchitoches] some 70 or 80 miles above Alexandria. We are now lying still for 2 or 3 days. We have marched 232 miles. We march about 15 miles a day. Our cavalry have took some prisoners. We, I think, are bound for Shreveport. We expect to have a gay old time up there of some sort. I can't tell how it will go, but we calculate to take it. Of course to be sure, certainly we do, yes we do. Tell the children I will write them a letter if I ever get into camp again.

Schuyler did not get to write another letter; he was killed five days later in the Battle of Pleasant Hill. Banks was defeated at Mansfield. When the fighting resumed the next day at Pleasant Hill, he was able to withstand renewed Confederate attacks and then began retracing his steps. **William Shakespeare "Shake" McKinley (1842–unknown)**, a private in the 1st Indiana Heavy Artillery, didn't sugarcoat the loss to his father.

Baton Rouge, Louisiana
April 15, 1864

We have had a big fight. In a few days you will get the particulars of the battle. It will give us the best of it. I hope that the people will think so. But I can tell you that we are whipped and badly whipped. The 13th Army Corps are demoralized, and the 19th Corps will have to fight the next battle. The Rebs took Nimm's entire battery—the best battery in the service. Our loss is 3,500—two generals and four colonels among the lost. We took five hundred prisoners. The Rebels have concentrated their whole force on the west side of the river at one place. They are 50,000 strong while we are 40,000.

There are still many Rebs along the river. We were fired into coming down, but nobody was hurt. Our men had a skirmish at Port Hudson. We lost a small piece of artillery.

The dismal campaign ended with a final setback for the Federals at the end of April. Banks believed he could still salvage victory. Pausing at Alexandria, Louisiana, he had sent word for General Frederick Steele in Arkansas to bring his 14,000 men to him. But Steele was compelled to fall back toward Little Rock. As he was marching that way, he was attacked at Jenkins' Ferry by Confederates led by General Sterling Price.

George Dwight Knox (1837–1908), a private in the 3rd Minnesota Infantry, updated his parents on what happened.

Pine Bluff, Arkansas
[circa mid-May 1864]

There has been some exciting times in this Trans-Mississippi Department for the last two weeks. Banks and Steele have both fell back. There is a report current here that Steele came up to Price on the 29th on the south side of the Saline River. Price attacked him while he was endeavoring to cross. The engagement lasted 5 hours. Every time our boys charged the Rebs, they gave way. Price was defeated and compelled to retreat, the loss unknown but heavy on both sides. Steele captured several pieces of artillery and 800 prisoners. Our wounded took the boats for Little Rock. Price is retreating in the direction of Camden. Gov. Stephen Miller [of Minnesota] sent a doctor from the state to attend to our wounded.

Banks is now at Grand Encore, Louisiana. Steele fell back to Little Rock, received reinforcements, and is again making a forward movement on Price. Banks is censured, Steele is not. Banks has few admirers in this department. There is hope he will be superseded.

By late May, Banks's army was back on the Mississippi River, where it had started nearly 90 days earlier. The reputation of Banks, a former Massachusetts governor, congressman, and Speaker of the U.S. House of Representatives, took a profound beating following the campaign that Sherman later summed up as "one damn blunder from beginning to end."

Grant removed Banks from command in the field. However, he retained command of the Department of the Gulf (in an administrative capacity) despite serious reports of widespread corruption and unsanitary conditions. That made the problem of bad morale even worse, as **Adolph M. Leve (1830–1903)**, a private in the 38th Massachusetts Infantry, explained to a friend.

Morganza, Louisiana
June 8, 1864

Heard from Allie only a few days ago and was surprised to hear that he is soldiering again, and if it was not for only 100 days, I should have thought the boy was crazy. I hope, however, that his 100-days experience will not prove so severe as the last 100 days I have spent in this department.

Marches and countermarches, interrupted occasionally by a battle, was the order of the day. This department has had some hard experiences of late. We have suffered great reverses, which I hope that the successes in Virginia will counterbalance. What is most absurd of all is that our great General B. [Banks] places a guard on Rebel property wherever we are supposed to pass on our march. Not only this, but he also furnishes them with the very means to carry on a successful war against us. He supplies them with quartermaster and commissary stuff while our men and beasts are kept on half rations on hard marches and fighting. The Western men have no confidence in Banks. They call him "Corporal or Quartermaster Banks." I am under a firm conviction that if popular prejudice was not in his favor owing to his position as a politician, he would have been removed from this department long since.

The corruption in this department is enormous. Permits [for trading cotton and other items] are forged in New Orleans, Baton Rouge, and everywhere by wholesale, and goods are imported into the enemy's lines, with provost marshals and officers in authority being in league with speculators and enemies having previously been gained over by means of large bribes. Almost 22 months of our service has expired, and I am longing for the day in which I shall see Old Massachusetts again. Then, if they shall ever catch me way down South again, my name is not A. M. Leve.

Imagine yourself encamped in a lonely God-forsaken place called Morganza on the banks of the Mississippi. At our first stay, we had to contend against both sun and dust, which is very annoying, especially on our frequent excursions called reconnoissances in force. But of late, we have had heavy rain every day for 9 days, and in front of our regiment's stores, a large bayou or mud puddle has arisen, rendered noxious and unhealthy by the filth thrown in by an unruly soldiery. No Sanitary Commission (so much boasted and talked about) nor any other makes its appearance. The effect of this nuisance is very bad. It has really impaired my health.

(The War Department initially resisted pressure to dismiss Banks. The Lincoln administration didn't want to be seen firing a famous—and well-connected—political figure ahead of November's elections. However, the problems grew so severe that Banks was eventually relieved of command in September.)

Tension rose in Virginia as winter gave way to spring. In Richmond, **Margaret Barclay Kirby (1839–1904)** shared her concerns with her younger brother, who was serving at the Confederate Trans-Mississippi Department headquarters in Shreveport. With the Union fully controlling the Mississippi River and mail service interrupted, the letter's opening reveals how Southerners had to rely on correspondence being carried by hand from one theater to another. (Margaret's twin brother, Lieutenant Colonel Edmund Kirby of the 58th North Carolina Infantry, had been killed at Chickamauga seven months earlier.)

Richmond, Virginia
April 10, 1864

The gentleman Col. DeShield expects to leave for Texas in a day or so. I have determined to write you this morning so that any letter may be ready for him to deliver at any time.

Sammie and little Alex are now in the country at Mrs. Hill's in King William County. We expect them back on Saturday. We feel anxious for her to return as I have no doubt the Yankees will be coming up, and Mrs. Hill's *place is entirely at their mercy. I almost dread the opening of the spring, for they are making such vast preparations to come against Richmond, and while I cannot believe they will succeed in accomplishing their purpose, still we know so many precious lives will surely be sacrificed and so many hearts made desolate. Our churches were all crowded on fast day. Dr. Moses Drury Hoge preached for us. At night, Dr. John Lansing Burrows preached in the <u>theatre</u>. He was requested to preach there, thinking great good might result from it, which I hope may—although it seems almost sacrilege to preach in a theatre. The building was crowded to its utmost capacity.*

Col. John Palmer has been to Richmond on business. He stayed a few days. Last Thursday evening he spent with us, and we expected him again Saturday evening. Brother David went down to the hotel for him, but the night was very stormy, and he was suffering from a severe cold and was afraid to venture out. Cold is a serious matter with him; as you know, he has been threatened with consumption. So we were denied the pleasure of seeing him again before he left. He spoke so affectionately of our dear brother. Said he loved him as his own brother and felt his loss deeply. He enquired after you.

Blythe is still a prisoner. I saw Mr. Cravins last week. He is among the last returned prisoners. He says they were treated very badly, but it seems to agree with him, for he was looking very well. Mother is now at the Treasury Department, where she is kept very busy. Give our love to Cousin Cassie and Edmund [Kirby Smith]. I sent you a letter from Kate Kirby carried by flag of truce—did you get it?

Joseph Lee Kirby was known for his ability to get correspondence across the South, as evidenced by this request from **Georgia Anna Tucker Stubbs (1838–1894)** for his assistance in sending a letter to her husband serving hundreds of miles away in Virginia. It also reveals the great difficulty people faced in communicating across the Confederacy with regular postal service disrupted.

Monroe, Louisiana
June 12, 1864

In a recent letter from Mrs. Harlan Kirby, she assured me that if I would enclose letters to my husband under cover to you, they would be forwarded across the Mississippi. If you will send the one enclosed east, you will confer a great favor on the writer.

Far to the north, Grant was attending to final details as he prepared to put his massive army in motion. **Willis D. Golin (unknown)**, a Federal staff officer, told a friend about it. He also reflected the derogatory attitude many Eastern officers held for their newly arrived commander from the West.

Headquarters 6th Army Corps
Office of the Inspector General
April 21, 1864

Yesterday, the 6th Army Corps was reviewed by Lieutenant General Grant and Generals Gouverneur Warren, Winfield Hancock, David Birney, and John Sedgwick, who commands the corps. I have seen General Grant before. I look on him as a "lucky" man, a man who has done much for the cause and country. But he never saw any fighting compared to the <u>Army</u> <u>of</u> <u>the</u> <u>Potomac</u>.

The review was a splendid sight, as far as the eye could reach. Regiment after regiment with bright and glittering bayonets, the men marching with the most exact precision. The corps (which consisted of 30,000 men) took two hours to pass a given point. After the review, the generals and their respective staffs came to headquarters and had a "big" time. Some got tight [drunk], and some did not. The 1st New Jersey Band was in attendance and dispensed the most excellent music for the benefit of the officers.

Sherman, the new commander in the West, was a different personality from his predecessor. He was described in this letter written later in the year by **Robert Bell Stewart (1839–after 1910)** of the 15th Ohio Volunteer Infantry.

Nashville, Tennessee
December 6, 1864

Enclosed is a photograph of General Sherman, a very true picture, though not as good a one as I would have liked to have had. His whiskers are short and sandy, and there is a kind of nervous twitching about his mouth and a fierce twinkle in his eyes. He is very slim and a little stoop-shouldered.

In the closing days of April, Sherman began moving troops into position for his long-awaited drive to Atlanta. Writing to his brother from northeastern Alabama, **Lycurgus Mechling (1841– 1919)**, a private in the 53rd Ohio Volunteer Infantry, was eager to get going.

Scottsboro, Alabama
April 30, 1864

The spring campaign has commenced here in this department. We are now under marching orders—have been ready to march for two days—and last evening, we had orders to be ready to march this morning at 6 o'clock. But we did not start, and I think now that we will not leave till tomorrow or Monday. It is a general movement along the whole line, and the cry is "Onward to Atlanta!"

I think from the movement that our Corps (15th) will go by the way of Rome, Georgia—about 40 or 50 miles west of Dalton, Georgia, as there will be a fight at Dalton if the Rebels have not evacuated and I believe such is the report that the 15th Corps is to be on the right of our line and we will move on Rome for the purpose of flanking the enemy at Dalton. There is a very large army in and along the line of Chattanooga, and all are under the same orders that we are, for there was some cavalry came through from Chattanooga and brought that report.

It is now high time that our armies were on the move, for the weather is getting so warm it will soon be difficult for the men to march and so much the worse for the poor fellows that must fall in the coming conflicts. I see by the papers that General Grant is making provisions for the wounded before the battle and is not waiting for them to be killed and wounded and then begin to prepare for their comfort. It is the desire of all the soldiers here that he may be successful in the coming campaign, as they all feel that if he makes a successful move and serves Lee as he did Bragg, Richmond will be ours, and we feel able here to drive Joe Johnston from Dalton and Atlanta. And I believe that all of the fighting can and ought to be done this summer unless our armies meet with disaster and defeat, which I think cannot happen when we have as good men at the wheel as we now have with Grant at Washington, and W. T. Sherman in the West—two of the best generals of the day. And from the reports of the papers, I think we will keep Honest Old Abe where he is. He will receive the hearty support of the soldiers here—all that will be allowed to vote.

I fear from all accounts of the fight at Pleasant Hill, Louisiana, that our men were worsted. Some papers give the victory in our favor, and some against us. If such is the case, it will give the Rebels more courage and will help to raise their drooping spirits.

In looking over the papers, I see that the recruiting of the colored men is going on with vigor. There are four regiments being raised at Chattanooga and some at other places. We will soon have a large army of the colored troops, although we have none with us, and as far as I can learn, I do not think that the government intends to put them in the front. They will be more for garrisons of forts than anything else, although I would be pleased to see them in the front. They might just as well stop a Rebel's ball as any white man. They have done some brave fighting in some instances and enough to tell that they will fight. And why not let them do it—fight for their liberty as we have to do?

Mechling was a tad premature; Sherman did not launch the Atlanta Campaign until May 7.

Back East, Grant also began moving, commencing his push toward Richmond on May 4. He sent the Army of the Potomac directly into central Virginia's tangled underbrush, an area that previous Union generals had generally avoided called the Wilderness, and immediately fought there. In some of the war's worst terrain for fighting, regiments and batteries struggled to maneuver into position, with men often firing into woods without even seeing the enemy. As had happened in the same vicinity exactly 52 weeks earlier during the battle of Chancellorsville, flames again raced through the thickets, burning alive wounded soldiers who could not escape.

Richard Thomas Lombard (1839–1925), a captain in the 16th Massachusetts Infantry, described the engagement in a condolence letter written to a fallen fellow captain's brother a few days later.

Bivouac in the Field
Fifteen miles south of Fredericksburg, Virginia
May 17, 1864

On the morning of May 6th, we entered a thick wood and there met the foe in superior numbers. We, the 16th, fought them until our support was gone, both on the right, left, and rear, when Lieutenant Colonel Waldo Merriam (who has since fallen) gave the order to "fall back." A few moments before that order was given, I saw Capt. Joseph Hills fall. I was within ten feet of him. I saw him place his hand on his left breast and utter a sigh. A member of his company said, "In a moment, all was over." It was impossible to rescue his body.

We have lost a large number in killed and wounded on this campaign. We had one man mortally wounded this morning. Lt. John Woodfin fell within a few feet of Captain Hills. Lieutenant Colonel Merriam was also killed on the 12th inst.

The din of battle is still upon my ears. At some future time, when the campaign is over, I shall give you a fuller account; but at present, we are within the range of the enemy's guns, and I have but a moment to spare.

With Grant's much-anticipated offense finally underway, news of it spread rapidly, but not always accurately. By the end of the first day's fighting in the Wilderness, word had reached Washington. An **unidentified Union soldier** stationed in the fortifications encircling the city related what he had heard in a letter to his father.

Fort Reno
Washington, D.C.
May 5, 1864

As you have heard that I had started for a battle, I will tell you that I have not and don't see any sign of it. The report is that Grant has had a fight with the Rebs and that he has whipped them and is a following them up toward Richmond.

They say that Grant has taken 40,000 prisoners and 35 pieces of artillery, but that is almost too good to be true. The boys feel first-rate tonight. If we move from here, I will write. They say that if Grant takes Richmond, we shall go there to defend it.

But Grant had not "whipped them." Lee had fought him to a standstill. Although casualties were horrific, the Union commander pressed ahead and swung toward the Confederate right flank. An equally savage battle followed at Spotsylvania Court House from May 10–13. Among the casualties was General John Sedgewick, the highest-ranking Union general killed in the war.

As the armies were slugging it out there, General Philip Sheridan led 12,000 horsemen in a raid behind Lee's lines that targeted Richmond. Derided today by some historians as an unsuccessful sideshow to the main Union offensive, the raid did result in the death of Confederate cavalry General Jeb Stuart in a small battle at Yellow Tavern.

Despite the staggering casualties, the Army of the Potomac remained confident as Grant kept it in motion. Developments were coming so fast that **Albert Church Brown (1843–1922)**, a private in the 16th Maine Infantry, barely had time to scribble a quick note—and nothing more—to his aunt.

[Virginia; location unknown]
May 17, 1864

We are south of the Rapidan River in the county of Spotsylvania in what is called the Wilderness, and I think we are getting a little the best of the enemy. I am still alive and well. Have been in several engagements and escaped the bullets so far. I will write again as soon as I can.

In the first half of May alone, Grant lost nearly 31,000 men killed and wounded at the Wilderness and Spotsylvania. Lee lost approximately 18,000. North and South alike were stunned by the extent of the carnage. As a result, Grant suddenly had a new nickname: "The Butcher."

Private **Daniel Joseph Taft (1842–1924)**, 82nd Pennsylvania Infantry, had recently arrived in Virginia after having guarded the prisoner-of-war camp on Johnson's Island in northern Ohio. He expressed to a friend his shock at the bloodshed.

Camp near Belle Plain, Virginia
May 17, 1864

They have been doing a wholesale business in slaughtering men within the last two weeks. The roads to Fredericksburg are lined with such of the wounded as can walk, and the ambulances and supply trains are all loaded with wounded. Every house in Fredericksburg is said to be filled with the wounded.

The three regiments of our brigade, which left Sandusky, Ohio, about three weeks before we did, are all killed, wounded, or taken prisoners but about 250. But few from these regiments were captured except the wounded. General Alexander Shaler, commander of the brigade, was wounded and taken prisoner. You can judge where our regiment would have been had we been relieved in time to be sent with the others. But it is not too late yet. I expect we will soon be relieved from here and sent to the front.

You have no idea of the amount of troops that are passing through here to the army daily. This is where all of the prisoners are brought from the front. Since we landed, we have been kept here to guard the Reb prisoners, which now number about 6,000—more are coming in and being sent off every day. Yesterday, 1,300 were sent to Point Lookout, Maryland. I tell you, they are hard-looking cases.

Keeping Grant's massive army replenished with men and supplies was a massive undertaking in itself. Soldiers from a wide array of sources were pressed into service. **Egbert B. Buzby (1842–1932)**, a corporal in the 138th Pennsylvania Infantry, was recovering from an injury he had received in the Wilderness two weeks earlier. He vividly described the scene behind the lines to his mother.

Camp Belle Plain Landing, Virginia
May 22, 1864

I have seen a great many regiments going out to the front. It is very lively down at the Landing. There is hardly standing room for an idle person. Everybody appears to be on important business, and it must be done in the shortest period of time imaginable, and the crowd of wagons, mules, Sanitary Commission men, teamsters, niggers, cavalry, wounded men, officers, and guards make a great deal of noise and confusion.

My wound has healed up finely, though it is very tender yet. If I had to march much, I could not stand it. I arrived here last Tuesday from Camp Distribution in Alexandria, Virginia. About 400 of us got on board a steamboat and had a pleasant ride down the Potomac River. The place where we are at is called Belle Plain Landing. All supplies are hauled from here in wagons to Fredericksburg and from there to the army.

We are kept here because Grant sent word that he didn't want any troops sent out front except regular organized regiments. They have organized a brigade of soldiers here for picket and guard duty and for the protection of the supplies, which the Rebs and guerillas need badly and would like very much to get hold of. It is called the Provisional Brigade. This brigade is composed of paroled prisoners just from Camp Parole in Annapolis, Maryland, convalescents from different regiments, reenlisted men whose furloughs have just expired, and recruiting parties who have been at home recruiting. It is somewhat of a mixture. I believe every regiment in the Army of the Potomac is represented here.

The many battlefield deaths that spring brought sad tidings to thousands of homes. **Hannah Burrows (unknown)** related the bad news to a friend.

Greenville, Connecticut
May 18, 1864

I now take my pen in hand to let you know that Alonzo Cushman is dead. He was shot last Monday. He was shot through the head. They had a letter from his chaplain today. Caroline wanted I should write to you for she had got so much writing to do tonight. If they can get his body, they will let you know in time enough to come to the funeral. They are a going to try to get it. I hope they will. They sent a lock of his hair. In the letter, he [the chaplain] wrote that he [Cushman] was buried between two pine trees, and his grave was marked.

If we hear anything more about Alonzo, I will write to you. You must excuse my writing tonight, for I am so nervous.

Recovering the remains of a loved one killed in battle was important to soldiers' families. But it wasn't always possible, as Private **John Lobdill (unknown)** of the 117th New York Infantry wrote to his fallen tentmate's sister.

Before Richmond, Virginia
November 21, 1864

Susan, I know how to appreciate your feelings in regard to your brother. I should be glad to do anything that is in my power toward sending his remains home if it were possible. But as circumstances are, I could do no more than write to those who attend to such business, and it would be better for your folks to make the arrangements themselves. I can't go to where he is buried, and even if I could, the body could not be expressed without being put in a metallic coffin and sealed, for they will not send them without. I have enquired as to the amount it would cost, and it would be over $137 [$5,000 today].

While Grant was pressing into the Wilderness, another offensive was underway south and east of Richmond. General Ben Butler's 33,000-man Army of the James moved up the James River on May 5. Its goal was not capturing the Confederate capital, but rather cutting the vital railroads leading into it from the south.

Although the Federals met with some initial success, the push stalled after a series of small but sharp battles. The Confederates eventually counterattacked, essentially bottling up Butler at his base at Bermuda Hundred.

Charles William Hobbs (1844–1924), a corporal in the 13th New Hampshire Infantry, described the brief, fruitless campaign to a friend.

Near Petersburg, Virginia
May 18, 1864

A week ago today, we had a pretty hard fight with the Rebs, and our brigade gave them a good thrashing. But they drove our men on the right of us, and we had to fall back. They charged us 3 or 4 times, 4 columns deep, but we gave them such a fire that they had to fall back. Our company took 13 prisoners that day.

The Saturday before, we were out skirmishing and had quite a lively time with the Reb sharpshooters. They pelted us hard as we crossed an open field, but we were none of us hit. Then we came to some woods, and according to skirmish rules, each man took a tree or stump and watched for them. It is a rather exciting business to stand behind a tree, look out to see a Reb, and have a bullet plunk into a tree in front. But then it would be our turn to give him a crack while he was reloading. We were in plain sight of the Rebel fort [Fort Darling] near Drewry's Bluff, and when we were skirmishing, we were within rifle shot of it.

You can't think how much good your last letter done me. It made me feel more like fighting the Rebs than ever before. I have seen enough of their works to make one feel rather ferocious toward them. I saw them set the woods on fire where our wounded lay and then fire on us when we went to take them out. That is hardly civilized warfare.

Enough of war. I wish there was no such thing known. All I want is to get home in safety.

And still, the killing raged on. Grant kept inching closer to Richmond, and Lee kept blocking him. The Federals made desperate assaults in early June at Cold Harbor, just a few miles beyond Richmond's outskirts. It proved to be another bloodbath for the attackers. Prospects for success were so dim some Yankee soldiers even sewed their names and regiments onto their uniforms in advance to aid in identifying them after they were killed.

Cyrus Willis (1837–1906), a private in the 58th Massachusetts Infantry, was still shellshocked when he wrote about it to his wife three days later.

Within six miles of Richmond, Virginia
June 6, 1864

It is hard for me to write about this bloody battle. They opened on us from their hidden entrenchments with grape and canister, poured on our defenseless forces such continual showers of leaden hail as has not been endured by our troops before. The Rebs was commanded by Generals A. P. Hill and James Longstreet, and it is said they had the best of their army with them. They fought like demons worthy of a better cause.

We stood our ground without faltering for fifteen long hours, the longest I ever saw, although we were busy at work with all our might firing. Our regiment fired over 200 rounds to a man. It was not until after 8 o'clock that the firing ceased. We laid on our arms there that night, and oh, how soundly did I sleep. It was so calm and still. I thought of home and loved ones there who perhaps were interceding our Heavenly Father on my behalf and to whose prayers I am indebted for my safety. I can think of no situation when one must feel the need of our Heavenly Father's care and protection as amid the cruel and bloody screams of war. Yet many, very many, are thoughtless, profane, and wicked. Such curses and swearing I have never heard as I've heard here, even in battle. (God forgive them.)

June 7th
I had to leave off writing yesterday and fall in. We were attacked again, and quite a furious fight came off between the Johnny Rebs and our skirmishers. The consequence was that we moved a short distance and built works. Was up till 3 o'clock in the morning. We feel the necessity of the defense, and it would astonish one to see how soon this is done. We are expecting a fight today. The Rebs are throwing occasional shells at us. I dread it, but let it come. The sooner it will be over. We have joined our forces with General Benjamin Butler's and there can be no stopping now. But oh, at what cost will it be even if we are successful?

We lost in our last battle the 3rd of June, 19 killed, 73 wounded from our regiment of 273 men. Our lieutenant colonel was wounded, the major killed, two captains and a second lieutenant. In our company, 3 were killed

and 9 wounded, some of them mortally. Sergeant E. Howard was wounded,
we fear mortally. He was by my side when he was struck.

We are well, only tired out. Now, dear Clara, give love to our dear par-
ents and brothers and sisters. I never thought so often of them.

Willis was correct; the Army of the Potomac had made contact with Butler's forces. Realizing that he could not take Richmond by direct assault, Grant
changed tactics. He moved his troops south of the James River and targeted the
key rail hub of Petersburg, some 20 miles below the Southern capital. Both sides
quickly entrenched and settled into the longest, most intense siege of the war.

At the same time, one of the war's great oddities was concluding. In the fall
of 1863, Russia's Atlantic Fleet had suddenly appeared in New York Harbor, and
a squadron from its Pacific Fleet docked in San Francisco. At the time, Northerners viewed it as a show of support from an important world power for the
Union war effort. While Czar Alexander II did side with the Federals, he had
another secret reason for the move: he was worried about a possible war with
England and France over an insurrection in Poland and wanted to prevent his
warships from being frozen in Russian ports that winter. So, he sent them to the
warmer waters of the United States.

Coming from half a world away, the Russian sailors were a great curiosity.
William Harrison Dunham (1841–1934), a private in the 8th New Hampshire
Infantry, described their visit to his brother as the fleet prepared to head home.

Cambridge, Massachusetts
June 1, 1864

The Russian fleet has arrived in Boston Harbor and are the lions of Boston.
The city authorities are doing things up first-rate for them and are showing
them all the sights. They are to visit Cambridge this week, also Lawrence and
other places. They have got some fine-looking vessels and are worth going to
see. They lay off Lewis and Commercial Wharf and are watched by a large
crowd of persons.

The Virginia Campaign is proceeding first rate, and General Grant is
within 5 miles of Richmond, and I suppose the siege of the place has commenced
before now. Hope he will take it before many days. General Lee appears to be
afraid to risk another battle and continues to fall back into his last entrench-
ments. News from there has been very scanty for the past week, but we shall
not have to wait long for some if the Rebels will only stand and fight.

The amount of personal property damaged and destroyed during the war was immense. Among the casualties was Arlington, General Robert E. Lee's estate on a hillside overlooking Washington, D.C. Federal authorities intentionally made the grand house uninhabitable by turning its lawns into a vast burial ground, transforming it into today's Arlington National Cemetery. Union forts in the southern ring of Washington's defenses also crossed the property, causing immense damage. **Cyrus Liggett (1834–1908)**, a private in the 166th Ohio Volunteer Infantry, served in a 100-day regiment that garrisoned the fortifications. He described the impact on Lee's home and the less-than-ideal conditions there.

Fort Richardson
Near Arlington House, Virginia
May 29, 1864

I seat myself this morning to let you know how we are getting along in this God-forsaken land. It appears more like Hell on Earth than anything I can think of. I will tell you this—it's no place for a young boy to be nor an old one neither if he respects his family.

We are on Old General Lee's property now, and I have not seen one rail fence since we have been here. There are hundreds of acres laying here going to the commons and no kind of grain being raised scarcely, but all kinds of fruits. We can see Washington every day from here. Oh! how I wish you could see the Capital House [Arlington House] and the nice yard and the pool of water with those yellow fish in it.

I don't want to make a public talk of it, but when I get out [of the army] this time, I will stay out if it takes my last dollar.

The army is getting along. I suppose you get more correct news than we do. They say that Grant is within 8 miles of Richmond, but you can't believe one word you hear here. I will tell you the truth about it. We are starved sick here, living day after day on two hardtack and a little colored water, cold coffee without sugar or cream. I have seen my dogs and your dogs eat more and better than we get sometimes—that is the truth of it.

Yet amidst all the hardship, there were also moments of humor. Union soldier **A. B. Walker (unknown)**, presumably a clerk or staff officer in St. Louis, wrote a parody of a military order requesting photos from two sisters under threat of a court martial. (It was entirely tongue-in-cheek.)

Special Order No. 108
Headquarters, Department of Missouri
May 29, 1864

Notice is hereby given to one Jane Pierce, also one Caroline Pierce, sister of
said Jane, both of the town of Manchester, county of Ontario, state of New
York, are ordered to transmit to these Headquarters without delay a true
and correct likeness of themselves. If said persons do knowingly and willfully
neglect to comply with said order, there will be a court martial immediately
ordered to investigate the conduct of said ladies.
    By order of Maj. General Rosecrans
    Department of the Missouri
    (Official)

In Georgia, there had been six weeks of nearly nonstop action as Sherman thrust into the Peach State. His army faced stubborn resistance from Johnston's Confederates every step of the way. There was much maneuvering through rugged mountainous terrain, several large battles (Rocky Face Ridge and Resaca among them), and continual skirmishing.

Private **Robert Bell Stewart**, 15th Ohio Volunteer Infantry, recapped the campaign's opening weeks to his sister.

Cassville, Georgia
May 22, 1864

We have been fighting more or less every day and marching. One of the great-
est foot races of modern times has very suddenly ended at this place. General
Johnston could not stand the pressure, and so he had to run, and we followed
as hard as we could till we got here when the whole Rebel army vanished
like smoke. I do not know where it has gone to, but perhaps General Sherman
does. At any rate, we start in search of it tomorrow.

    I guess the general opinion is, though, the Confederate army as an orga-
nization has been entirely destroyed, different parts of it sent off to different
points. There is one thing very certain, if Johnston had kept it together much
longer and tried to get to Atlanta with it, the men with the army he has now
would have gobbled him up like a duck would a frog. I hope we will go into
Atlanta. All the Rebel army here can't stop us.

Why, so far, we have one of the finest and easiest campaigns we ever had. It has been nothing but fun. Of course, it has been rather serious sometimes. We have lost some men. At Rocky Face Ridge, we lost some while on picket. The Rebels were on the rocks right above us, and we, as well as they, had to keep hid all the time. Anyone who showed himself might be hit. I stuck close to 5½ feet of hillside and behind a pile of rocks too—as close as I ever care about again—for 16 long hours.

Well, they packed up and got out of Dalton and us hard after them. Passed them too hard at Resaca, and they turned on us. We were in it long enough to fire 40 rounds of ammunition and were under fire several other times. But they soon turned the other way, and we took quiet possession of the town—some thousands of prisoners, guns, and any quantity of cornmeal. We had hardly got into town before three or four trains of cars came in loaded with pontoons and bridge timbers, for the Rebels had burned the railroad bridge over the Oostanaula River. In a short time, the army was over and on the heels of the Rebels and drove them fighting all the way this far. Thousands of acres we have spoiled. The country behind us is a burning desolation. The towns are all deserted.

They had breastworks to fight behind all the time, for the whole country is fortified between here and Dalton. The railroad is finished to this place, and the cars come in regular. We had not been here 12 hours before the cars came up loaded. This is Yankee progress for you. We did not give the Rebels time to destroy the road.

But the whole country and everybody is looking to Grant at Richmond and cannot see Sherman. You do not see whole columns of the papers filled up with news from Sherman. It is all Grant and Richmond. Well, I am satisfied that it is so. We are able to hold our own and a good bit more down here. I want Grant to have all the men and means he needs, for he has his hands full. I never saw this army in such high spirits as it now is. We have good health, plenty to eat, and enough of fighting for the spice to make everything interesting. We know just what force Johnston has and that we can just drive them as we wish.

Twenty-year-old Private Henry Smedley of the 101st Ohio Infantry was among the 1,665 Federal casualties in the Battle of New Hope Church, Georgia, on May 25. Replying to one of his son's comrades in Company K on receiving the news, **Hiram Smedley (1819–1899)** expressed the anguish that thousands of parents, North and South alike, felt that spring over leaving a fallen son's body so far from home.

Jacksonville, Illinois
June 9, 1864

Sad, sad news does yours of the 26th bring to us. Is it so, is it so? Tip, I thought I was prepared for the worst, but I find I was mistaken. I cannot at present think of letting my soldier boy's remains lay in that accursed land which I believe God has forsaken. Oh, Tip, can I get him home as soon as you get this?

 If you have not before, write me the particulars of his last moments. I heard he was never well and when he left Bridgeport, Alabama, that he dragged along worn out by fatigue until the summons came which relieved him from his troubles. I wish you would gratify me enough to pen me all the particulars once he left Bridgeport. I heard a few hours before he went into battle that he seemed rather dispirited. Do let me know all, and what I most desire is to have his dear body, if possible, although you may be far from the field on which he fell.

 If this reaches you, still I want to hear from you fully. I want you to tell me the place of his burial, how far from the railroad, how far from Dallas, Georgia, what direction from Dallas, and whether anyone lies beside him and how many. In fact, give me as many particulars as possible. If I can possibly get a pass beyond Nashville, I think of trying to go get his remains. I want you to write me whether the cars run as far out as Dallas, if not how far they run. I would be much obliged if you or some of his friends will see that his little effects are faithfully cared for until such time as they can be sent home. Please give me probabilities whether it is possible under all the circumstances his body can be brought home. I cannot think of leaving him in that land of sin and rebellion.

 Tip, when you write, let me know whether it was possible for you to give my poor boy a rough coffin for his burial. I know it is out of the question in many cases. Let me know the truth.

By early June, the two armies had reached the last forbidding entrenchments some 20 miles northwest of Atlanta. Although Sherman had advanced more than 70 miles, this final chain of mountains crowned with Confederate cannons stood between him and his goal.

Don Carlos Newton (1832–1893), a captain in the 52nd Illinois Infantry, was on duty when news was received of a high-level Confederate casualty that he told his wife about.

In the woods at the foot of Lost Mountain, Georgia
June 15, 1864

Our corps is about one mile in our front and is banging away with artillery and has been all the morning. They get no reply from the Rebs—only an occasional shot is fired by the skirmishers. General Sherman was out here yesterday afternoon, and someone of his staff said to him, "General, they have pretty strong works up there." His reply was, "Let them keep them. I ain't going there." The right wing of the army seems to be swinging in upon them, and I think before night will have them flanked so they will have to leave and find another "pozish."

Marietta, Georgia, is said to be just in the rear of the mountain, and the general impression is that we will occupy it before tomorrow night. But it may be longer. I don't think General Sherman is in any hurry. He don't act so but takes everything as cool as if he had all the time to take Atlanta that anyone had.

Within three days, four full companies of Rebels have come in our lines at this point and gave themselves up. They came with their officers. They report that there is a whole brigade over there who are trying to get away and that in their regiment—300 strong—but two men in it who are Rebels enough to want to fight anymore for a fallen cause. This can all be taken with considerable allowance, as deserters from any army are not the most reliable people in the world. Where there is so much smoke, though, there is pretty sure to be some fire, and I am of the opinion that a great many of the rank and file are pretty much sick of it and would be very glad to see the thing effectively wound up one way or the other.

A company that came in last night report that General John Bell Hood was killed. This was the report last night, but this morning, I am informed that it was General Leonidas Polk that was killed. He was the Episcopal bishop who turned his cowl into a sword and went in as a Rebel general. I don't think many will mourn him or any other man who will turn traitor to his country and leave the work of his heavenly master to do so. If such men don't go to Hell, there is no use in having any such place.

5 P.M. We moved about 2 P.M. one mile to the left near the railroad and are still here. There has been a good deal of artillery fighting all day but nearly all from our side, the Rebels only replying occasionally. About 4 this afternoon, we captured 425 prisoners—parts of the 31st and 40th Alabama Regiments and a good many others have come in during the day. With them was a colonel and a major and captains and lieutenants enough to match—quite a haul. They say they weren't hard to catch.

16th. The last prisoners in say it was General Polk that was killed—that a solid cannon shot passed right through his body, killing him instantly.

A few miles away, Southern soldiers mourned Polk's loss. **Asahel W. Thompson (1838–1864),** a private in the consolidated 6th/7th Arkansas Infantry, updated his sister. (He was wounded in the Battle of Atlanta five weeks later and died the following month.)

Near Pine Mountain, Georgia
June 16, 1864

I am sorry to inform you that General Leonidas Polk that commanded a corps in this army was killed dead on the field yesterday. His left shoulder was torn off with a shell. He was killed on the right of my division.

We are in line of battle, and the enemy are in a half mile of our line. Skirmishing are going on all the time, day and night. While I am writing, the cannon are belching forth their war whoop from the invader in front of our lines. We are waiting for the Yankees to advance on us, which we expect them to do soon. It is thought they will advance today. They are maneuvering from the way they throw their shells.

Our rations are not very plenty, but we can make out on them. We get nothing but bread and meat. You must answer in haste. Give me the latest news from the 8th and 6th and 26th Arkansas regiments. If you do not get a letter every week from me, it is on account of the mail as it is not regular from here to the railroad. We are on the extreme left of our line of battle, and that throws us five miles from the railroad. You can give Aunt Wineford some of the buttons if she has any use for them, as she is always making new pants. The postage for the buttons was very high, and [Confederate] money is not worth much.

Sherman advanced a few more miles, then was stopped by the greatest physical barrier of all: Kennesaw Mountain. In late June, he tried to break the Confederates' heavily fortified entrenchments. **Henry Harrison Orendorff (1840–1910),** a private in the 103rd Illinois Infantry, was in the attack, which he shared with his brother.

In front of the enemy
Near the foot of Kennesaw Mountain, Georgia
June 28, 1864

Yesterday (June 27th) was another bloody day with us. Our brigade was again called on to lead in an assault on the enemy's works, which we did, but were repulsed with heavy loss. I never want to see another such a charge as the one of yesterday. The enemy had very formidable works, and our men crawled right up to them, but they were too much for us. A little stream about 50 yards in front of their works that we had to cross is said to have actually run red with blood. I crossed and recrossed the stream but did not notice it running with blood, but do not doubt it as there were a great many men shot right in the hollow. I feel very thankful that I came off without getting hurt. I hope and pray that I may always be so lucky. I don't know why it is, but our brigade generally has to lead in a charge. I hope it will not be so in the future.

Orendorff's wish was granted; the attack at Kennesaw Mountain was the last time in the campaign that Sherman ordered a frontal, massed assault on a heavily fortified position.

Across the lines, the victory caused Confederate hopes to rise. Still, **Thomas Bailey (1832–1904),** a surgeon, shared his concerns with a fellow army surgeon.

Field Infirmary, Manigault's Brigade
Marietta, Georgia
June 28, 1863

Yesterday, there was <u>tremendous</u> cannonading going all day, and I hear we were successful in repulsing the enemy with immense slaughter. It is said that General Patrick Cleburne informed General William Hardee that the dead and wounded Yanks lay in heaps in front of our works to a greater extent than under similar circumstances at New Hope Church. I also heard that we had a great force of the enemy in a gorge where they could neither retreat nor advance and that General Benjamin Cheatham intended to attack them last night. But I have not heard that the attack was made, and everything is comparatively quiet today.

I am painfully excited about affairs in Virginia. There is such a complete silence on the part of the newspapers. This is attributed to the fact that the telegraph wires are cut. But enough time has elapsed to have heard ere this.

There was a report that Lee has gained a great victory and that Beauregard has attacked them on the right and that Lee has caved their left and center. Such a dispatch, it is said, has been privately received by General Joseph Johnston. Many believe it, but this time, I am very, very doubtful.

Our medical fraternity is much as usual. We have a hot brick store for an infirmary when we might have got a pleasant and commodious building on the outskirts of this town. Such is the usual conceit of our chief surgeon, who disregards the rest of the medical officers of the brigade. We have had very few wounded since we have been here. Only one amputation performed in 34th Alabama in upper third femur, and I think recovery very doubtful.

Truly friend after friend departs [died]. It is time for the awful drama of blood and carnage to come to an end, and I feel very hopeful that the God of Battles will be on our side. I feel more cheered up here than I have been. It looks like Johnston has at last made a stand. I am very concerned about the situation near Petersburg, Virginia, and truly hope that the rumors may prove true.

As you may not have seen it, I send you Sherman's wicked letter. It shows what we are to expect from such monsters as General Benjamin Butler and himself.

Still, the mountainous obstacle remained in the Federals' way. That, coupled with the upcoming presidential campaign, was on the mind of Private **Thomas Hine (1838–1897)**, 39th Ohio Volunteer Infantry, when he wrote to his sister.

Kennesaw Mountain, Georgia
June 29, 1864

I only have one vote for Old Abe and Andy [Johnson], but if I am spared and have a chance, I will give them that. What say you? Am I sound?

Well, we have finally run against a circumstance—that is, the Kennesaw Mountain. We have been here in rifle pits for some 8 or 9 days within musket shot of the Johnnies on the side of the mountain where we can't get up to them, and they dare not come down to us, for they could not get back any more than we can get up now. So you see, things are at a standstill. Our right and left have closed in on them considerable, but not enough to flank them. Musketry can be heard at any moment in the day or night on the skirmish line. Therefore, we are having some few wounded every day and occasionally one killed along our lines.

Day before yesterday (Monday), we made what might be termed a general attack—our right and left being engaged in force, the center only making a demonstration to keep them from massing their forces in their center on their flanks against us. But from what I can find out, our right and left both were repulsed with quite a heavy loss. We have had artillery duel with them after duel, but what effect our shells have on top of the mountain, we do not know. But one thing is certain, their shells do us no harm. We are so close to the mountain that they can't depress their guns to hurt us, and then our artillery makes it too hot for them. When they commence to fire, they don't more than get forty at it till Mr. Johnny has to run his cannon back over the mountain where our gunners can't see them. Now, within the last minute, not less than twenty cannons have fired, and no response from Johnny. I think we have thrown iron enough on this mountain to make one as large.

Judging from the 4th Corps moving out with ten days' rations accompanying a team of pontoons this morning, I think a new base of operations is being introduced. You will, in all probability, hear from it in a few days, and I think favorable. I have no fears but what we will eventually succeed in getting them out of Kennesaw, and then their advantage over us will not be so great in position between here and Atlanta.

Hine was correct; Sherman eventually flanked the Kennesaw Line and crossed the Chattahoochee River, forcing Johnston to retreat into the Confederate defenses encircling Atlanta.

On July 17, President Jefferson Davis finally had enough of Johnston's defensive strategy and fired him, turning over command of the Army of Tennessee to the more aggressive General John Bell Hood. **William Jere Crook (1838–1881),** a major in the consolidated 13th/154th Tennessee Infantry, shared his thoughts about the change with his sweetheart (and future wife) in South Carolina the day the news was made public.

In the field near the Chattahoochee, Georgia
July 18, 1864

The army and the country was startled this morning by the official announcement that General Johnston had been relieved of command of this army and that General Hood was to succeed him. This unfortunate occurrence has caused a cloud of gloom to settle on the face of every soldier in the army. General Johnston was the idol of the troops, and all had the most implicit confidence in his capacity to successfully lead us to a glorious and triumphant victory.

I hope it will all be for the best, but I confess I can't see the wisdom of such a course. It seems from some cause that this is an ill-fated army. I think it is a strange time to have a change of commanders right in the very presence of the enemy while they are ever thundering at the very walls of the Gate City of the South [Atlanta].

General Hood is a young man of fine promise and great boldness. His promotion to the command indicated there will be an early [soon] and bloody conflict. He will not retire but will meet upon the field of carnage and measure strength with our country's foes. I feel that a few days at most will herald to the world a glorious victory to our arms; or the broken shattered ranks of the Army of Tennessee will tell a tale of sorrow and blood that will cause mourning in almost every home in this southern land of ours. That God may be with us and grant us victory and safety is my earnest constant prayer.

This twilight hour is disturbed by the sudden roar of the enemy's cannon and the crack of the sharpshooter's rifle. Everything has been unusually quiet, we occupying one side of the Chattahoochee River and the enemy the other. The news is that they have crossed the river to our right. I now hear very heavy cannonading in that direction, and we have been ordered to be in readiness to move at a moment's notice. We are all packed and ready to move . . .

The order to march has come.

Likewise, many Confederate civilians were also displeased by the change in commanders. **Mary Barclay Kirby (1811–1891),** one of the dozens of "Treasury Ladies" who signed Confederate currency by hand, commented on the shakeup in a letter to her son serving in Louisiana.

Treasury Department
Richmond, Virginia
August 5, 1864

Captain Dannet (I think you know him; he boarded with your Aunt Ellen, is a nice little fellow) called to see us with Mr. Allen. He is on his way to join Hood's army at Atlanta. Johnston's removal from command has given much dissatisfaction, and the President is much censured for his conduct towards him. I hope we will not suffer because of this change. The situation of Atlanta is a concern me, but I trust that God in mercy will listen to the prayers of His children, which are constantly ascending to His throne and, by His own almighty power, defend us from our enemies.

Mr. Allen will tell you that your Cousin George Peakin was wounded near Petersburg. It was a great mercy he was not instantly killed. The ball passed in near his ear, taking off a small portion of it and striking the bone passed out of his neck behind. He was wounded by a sharpshooter while going with a flag of truce.

Hood wasted no time lashing out at the Federals. Just four days after taking command, he attacked at Peachtree Creek, then again two days later in the Battle of Atlanta, where the fighting was so severe that it involved hand-to-hand combat. **George Washington Sheldon (1845–1864),** a private in the 47th Ohio Volunteer Infantry, was writing to his parents when the latter engagement began. It was a letter he was unable to finish.

In Line of Battle near Atlanta, Georgia
July 22, 1864

The Rebels abandoned their first line of works last night, and we moved forward this morning. We are now within one mile and a quarter of the city. The artillery is keeping up a constant roar from both sides. Several shells have landed near where I am sitting. There is a 12-pound spherical case shell lying close to me. It came within 3 or 4 feet of Bill Orr while he was picking blackberries. It was filled with musket balls.

[In different handwriting]

July 23, 1864—Mr. Sheldon. Dear sir, I sit down to inform you of our sad disaster yesterday. Shortly after your son George stopped writing, the enemy moved on us in solid column and, after twenty minutes of heavy fighting, they took our works. We clubbed muskets with them, but they overpowered us, and we were driven back in disorder. Our company lost 20 men. Your son is a prisoner.

As I said, we were driven back nearly one and three-quarters of a mile and rallied. General John Logan rode along the line and cheered up the boys. He said he would have a rally before the sun set. We formed in line of battle, and when the signal was given, we moved forward and retook the works and as many prisoners as they took from us. Their dead lay thick around our works. We expect them to try us again this evening. If they do, they will find it more of a task than they did yesterday.

Our regiment lost 107 men. Our company lost 20 men killed, wounded, and missing. Our lieutenant colonel was wounded and taken prisoner. One of our color bearers was killed, and the other was wounded. The Rebs got hold of our flag, and one of the guards killed him and brought the flag off the field. The staff of the [regimental] battle flag was shot in two 4 times, and the Stars and Stripes were shot in two pieces. Neither one has got a staff now. We have the 5th sergeant to command the company. I believe I have said enough. As your son was a bunkmate of mine, I thought it my duty to write and inform you of his capture. —Wm. H. Orr

(Sheldon was taken to Andersonville Prison, where he died of chronic diarrhea seven weeks later.)

Both the Battle of Peachtree Creek and the Battle of Atlanta were Union victories; both had very high casualties. Union General James McPherson was among those who fell on July 22, as Private **Robert Bell Stewart**, 15th Ohio Volunteer Infantry, wrote to the folks at home.

1.5 miles north of Atlanta, Georgia
July 23, 1864

I saw Atlanta the other day from the top of a tree. It was about two miles off. I could not see much of the city, however, for trees. The forests seem to come close up to the town.

General Hood took command of the Rebel army a few days ago and is now reported killed and his body in our possession, but the report is doubtful. I hope it is true. Prisoners stated it. Generals Carter Stevenson was also reported killed and William Hardee wounded, and William Loring in command. One thing is certain, they lost some of their big officers, and a big lot of men on the 20th [Battle of Peachtree Creek]. Nearly 500 were buried by our men. Hooker lost about 2,000. Only one division of our corps—Newton's— was engaged. He lost but few. We could hear the fighting and see the smoke of the battle from where we were and were expecting a break to be made on us. Nearly all afternoon, heavy fighting was going on far on our left.

They tried Hooker on the right and failed yesterday. They tried McPherson on the left and failed, though I have not yet heard the particulars. We looked for them to try the center in the evening, but they did not. They may yet. But if they do, they will please us very much. Our lines now nearly invest the city and will do it in a day or so if the Johnnies only remain long enough. They are now in, I think, their last ditch about Atlanta.

The Johnnies kept shooting all night, too, and from every direction but did not hurt anyone. We did not shoot any but lay low. The Rebels have a great horror of our artillery. It just makes them burrow in the ground while we do not fear theirs much. There is one of our cannon companies sending some compliments over to the Johnny Rebs—Boom, Boom, Boom, goes six guns. Bang, Bang, Bang goes six shells right over in the Rebel lines, and I'll bet they hunt their holes quick.

Thursday Evening. General McPherson is reported killed. I am afraid it is true. There are 1,000 dead Rebels unburied on the battlefield of yesterday. Wish it were 100,000.

Stewart was correct; McPherson had indeed been killed. He was the second-highest-ranking Union general killed in combat and was adored by his men. The news was noted in another letter written the same day by Sergeant **Ebenezer Hudson McCall (1841–1922)** of the 80th Ohio Volunteer Infantry to his sister.

Allatoona, Georgia
July 23, 1864

We feel gloomy this morning on account of hearing of the death of General McPherson. However, we do not fully credit the report. He was certainly one of the ablest generals in the Army. A sight of him is enough to make one love him. He is so kind, modest, and unassuming, and always has a good word for the poor soldier.

We hear heavy firing this morning—said to be at Atlanta. It sounds like "distant thunder." A report came a few moments ago that our troops are occupying one portion of Atlanta and Johnston's the other.

Tell Mother she need have no more fears about the Secesh women destroying me, as I am far removed from those threats with females, and I couldn't think of wasting my affections on any Georgia woman that I have seen. They are certainly a deplorable-looking set, and the ones I have seen appear to be bordering on starvation. Many of them come into our camp to trade blackberries and such garden vegetables as they have for our flour, coffee, sugar, and meat. I believe I told you I was "messing" with the captain! He buys potatoes, green beans, and such other extras as come in.

I hear the boys say McPherson's body was brought through on the cars. What a loss his death will occasion to our arms. The cars were loaded with prisoners.

Three days later, **Don Carlos Newton (1832–1893)** wrote to his wife about a brawl among the big brass at Union headquarters. (It should be remembered that General Thomas Sweeney had only one arm, having lost the other in the Mexican War.)

Near Atlanta on Battleground of the 22nd
July 26, 1864

Everything has been very quiet since the battle [of Atlanta]—so much so that our generals yesterday had to get up a plug muss [a fight for a fireplug] to keep their fighting blood down.

General Grenville Dodge, General Thomas Sweeny, and General John Fuller (who commands our 4th Division) sat talking over the battle yesterday when the relative merits of the 2nd Division were being discussed, and General Sweeny was expressing a little dissatisfaction as to the amount of credit which General Dodge awarded his division. General Sweeny claimed all the honor while Generals Fuller and Dodge claimed the 4th Division was entitled to as much if not more credit than the 2nd, they having lost 380 and our division only 280 odd. General Sweeny charged the 4th with breaking, and General Fuller called him a liar. General Sweeny called him a son-of-a-bitch and told him he could whip him. General Dodge intervened, and General Sweeny called him a coward and a thief. General Dodge slapped his mouth, and General Sweeny knocked him down. General Fuller then intervened, and General Sweeny downed him, and so the disgraceful scene went on. The result is that General Sweeny is under arrest and has been sent to Nashville for trial.

The fact is both divisions fought like heroes and turned three times their numbers of Rebels back and are entitled to equal credit. General Fuller's division lost the most because it was longest in the fight from the fact of our being the furthest off and the longest in getting to the scene of action.

We have again moved to the right flank of our army and today are only two miles from Atlanta. We are nearly to the only railroad the Rebs have left. Last night there was a very large fire in Atlanta. We expected to find the Rebs gone this morn, but they are not.

Hood attacked one more time at Ezra Church and was beaten back again. The campaign then turned into a lengthy siege, with both armies coiled around Atlanta in lines of trenches and earthen forts. **Marcellus Ovando Messer (1842–1938),** a corporal in the 19th Ohio Volunteer Infantry, described the earthworks in a letter to his younger brother at home.

Camp Before Atlanta, Georgia
July 27, 1864

We dig, chop, or carry logs and rails nearly all the time. So you see I am kept in a poor condition to write to anybody. The cannon and musket balls are whizzing over our heads all the time. Those that come low enough and hit are stopped by our breastworks, which save many lives.

Our works we have strengthened in most every way, fixed up in front of the works everything we could to stop the onward march of the Rebels if they see fit to charge us, which is not likely, as our position is a strong one naturally, and with which we have added to it, it would be madness for them to try to take it. Last evening, the regiment was formed in front of the colonel's quarters where he read to us the official report of killed, wounded, and prisoners on our side, and the killed and prisoners on the Rebel side in the last two fights in front of Hooker and Newton and McPherson [Peachtree Creek and Atlanta]. The killed and prisoners of the Rebs is more than our total loss, and when you add that there is at least five wounded to every killed, the Rebs must have lost over 15,000 men. They cannot stand more than one more such loss.

As both sides settled into the trenches, Sherman's cavalry chief, General George Stoneman, led three mounted brigades on a raid to liberate Union prisoners at Andersonville in late July. It ended with Stoneman becoming a prisoner himself. **Jacob F. Mader Jr. (1840–1922),** a captain in the 61st Ohio Infantry, told his girlfriend that the news was greeted with disbelief in Union ranks.

In the trenches near Atlanta, Georgia
August 9, 1864

It is rumored here that General Stoneman was captured not far from Macon, Georgia, but it is not credited here by the officers generally.

Our artillery has been booming away today at the rate of five shots a minute, and the skirmishers keep up a constant firing on the skirmish line which keeps up a kind of excitement which is necessary while laying so close to the enemy for we know not what moment we may be attacked. We have very good breastworks here, which are about twelve feet thick and an abatis in front twenty feet wide, and I think if the Rebs ever come up, they will meet with a warm reception. Just now, a minie ball whizzed above my tent, shot by some Rebel sharpshooter.

The report about Stoneman was true. After a running skirmish, the Union horsemen were deceived by Confederate cavalry. Two brigades slipped off to safety, while Stoneman, his aide, and 600 Federals were captured on July 31. The Confederates seized enough captured horses to remount a brigade. Stoneman was the highest-ranking Union general taken prisoner during the war and was held for three months until Sherman personally requested his exchange. **Samuel Welch (1837–1918),** a corporal in the 51st Ohio Infantry, didn't bother masking his disdain for the general to his brother.

Near Atlanta, Georgia
August 17, 1864

Stoneman's expedition to the rear of Atlanta was a complete failure. His main object was to liberate our prisoners at Andersonville and Americus, and a good many of his men left here with two sets of arms and accouterments— one for their own use and one for the prisoners. The plan was a very good one. But instead of putting arms into the hands of the prisoners, they got their arms taken from them and were taken prisoners themselves. However, only a small portion of the command was taken, and Stoneman with them.

The general opinion among speculating men now is that it was a good thing that Stoneman was taken. But this is always the case when a general fails. No one ever heard tell of any good that he [Stoneman] had ever done before. But if reports are true, he certainly got justice. It is said that he allowed his men to scatter in all directions, to forage and pillage, and while his men were out, every fellow for himself, he was attacked.

Week after week, the siege dragged on in the blistering Georgia heat. Conditions were equally bad in the Confederate lines, as **Hugh Garland (1837– 1864),** colonel of the consolidated 1st and 4th Missouri Infantry (Confederate), told a friend. He also revealed how the Confederacy was gradually becoming threadbare and broke—literally in this case. (Garland was killed 90 days later at Franklin, Tennessee.)

Headquarters 1st Missouri Infantry
In the Trenches at Atlanta, Georgia
August 12, 1864

The enemy have approached nearer to our pickets, and both sides keep up a continual firing. In a few days, I fear we will have to keep close in our trenches and won't have the easy time we've had for the last two or three weeks.

Enclosed, I send you certificate and power of attorney from Colonel Robert Bevier to purchase cloth for him [for a uniform]. If you have any money to spare, please purchase the cloth for him, and I will be responsible for it as soon as I can draw money from the paymaster, who at present is without funds.

Some Union soldiers had difficulty seeing Sherman's end plan for capturing the beleaguered city. In the same letter cited previously, **Samuel Welch** of the 51st Ohio Infantry shared his confusion with his brother.

It is hard to tell what the program is for taking Atlanta. The Rebels are for-tified along the Macon Railroad for several miles so that our lines will have to be very long to reach it. Our right wing is within shelling distance of the railroad, and the cars have not come in for ten or twelve days. Our spies say that the women and children are all removed from the city and that every man that stays there carries a musket. The dwelling houses are all empty, and the most valuable furniture has been removed.

There are some reports in circulation since yesterday evening that our corps is to be taken to the extreme right, but they are only reports, and it is hard to tell whether there is any truth in them or not. There is no doubt that a corps is needed on the right if Sherman expects to cut the Macon railroad. But if our corps is withdrawn from its position, our railroad will be exposed to raids as there will be but few troops left on the east side of the road.

General Joe Wheeler is now trying his hand in our rear. They captured a thousand head of cattle near Marietta a few days ago, and the report come in last night that they were in the vicinity of Dalton and Tunnel Hill. I don't think they can do much damage as there are but two bridges between here and Dalton, and it seems as though they have passed both of them.

There has been no move made for several days. Nothing going on except skirmish firing and cannonading along the lines, and we have got so used to that that we seldom take any notice of it.

During lulls in action, soldiers looked for ways to pass the time. Some wrote to the forerunner of "lonely hearts clubs," which matched men in the service with women at home wanting to write to them. Union soldier **Arthur Clemmair (unknown)** sent this reply to a woman who called herself simply "Cora" in Clarksville, Ohio. (Note that much like today's online dating, correspondents took measures to safeguard their identity.)

Headquarters Military Division of the Mississippi
Memphis, Tennessee
July 7, 1864

I am pleased to learn that my note of introduction was interesting enough to elicit a reply. I can hardly conceive how it was that you selected my letter from the many as for one of your correspondents. I'm such a poor letter writer at best. I have written to many unknown correspondents, and, without flattery, I must say your letter pleases me better than any I have yet received. I am very well pleased with your description and like to see ladies display some degree of gayety and enjoy innocent amusement. Don't like to see young ladies at sixteen appear older than their mother. I also have a good ear for fun and am naturally lively, talkative, and quick on perception of human nature.

You wish to know my former place of residence. My home is in McDonough County, Illinois. Illinois is my native state, Cora. I can hardly write at all this evening. I think perhaps the reason is that I am a little homesick. If you know anything about the complaint, you will surely sympathize with me. I am, like you were when you wrote the letter before me, am tired of writing. Have been writing in the office all day.

If I have failed to meet your expectations, don't despair. Hope to do better after better acquainted. Please give me your true name in my next letter. I shall be happy to hear from you again soon.

Young lovers separated by war kept in touch via letters. It should be remembered that many soldiers were barely 20, so a good amount of their correspondence involved what today is called teenage drama. Take, for example, **Charlotte Temple Elliott (1844–1901)**. She wrote to her boyfriend (and future husband) James Harvey Tegarden while he was serving in Tennessee in the 137th Indiana Infantry, a 90-day regiment.

Union Pine Grove, Indiana
June 22, 1864

You said you expected that I would hear from a letter that you had written and sent back to this neighborhood. I can guess who it was to, as you said it was to some person whom I didn't like. I know who it was for. I don't know how anybody could like a person who talks as she did. I haven't forgotten how she talked about the veteran soldiers yet, nor do I expect to soon. Have you forgotten what she said? The words was, "I don't like anybody but the veteran soldiers" and more that was a great deal insultinger than that. But, Jimmie, I expect she told you she never said it from what I have learned a few days ago. As I haven't time to give you a short sketch of what I have heard, I will just wait until you get home, and then I will tell you. I don't think hard of you for writing to who you please, for that is a free privilege for all. I hope I don't write to any person that you dislike. If I do, just let me know, and I will tell them goodbye.

Other soldiers took solace in more intimate companionship. They included First Lieutenant **Thomas Rutledge (1841–1864)** of the 33rd Missouri Infantry (Federal), who used a Victorian euphemism for prostitutes in this letter to a friend while also relating news typical of young men's interests. (Rutledge was mortally wounded six months later in the Battle of Nashville.)

In camp near Memphis, Tennessee
June 12, 1864

I got acquainted with a gay fancy woman from St. Louis a few weeks ago. She has been sitting up to the boy, swears eternal fidelity, won't take money, and insists on my staying with her every second night. With my usual generosity, I have accepted.

Three soldiers were shot [executed] here for committing rape upon an old lady in this vicinity.

McFadden has been engaged in all the recent fights in Georgia and was O.K. at last accounts. I am tired of writing to him and never receiving an answer. Grandy has cleared $6,000 since he has been in the service. I do not believe that Carrie cares a damn for Fay; she married him for his money. No, young McKibben is unmarried as yet and has no prospects. Have not seen Mary for a year. Lucy is a brick. She told me she married to escape the unbearable tyranny of her aunt. Says your unworthy cousin Tom was her first choice. How is it that the day of my marriage seems further distant than ever?

Some women at home wanted to see their gender serving on the front lines. However, most men didn't share that view. In fact, Sergeant **Israel Markham (1825–1872)**, 7th Illinois Cavalry, told his cousin that he disapproved of women being near the army in any capacity.

Memphis, Tennessee
May 28, 1864

You think that the women could crush the rebellion. I think they are generally very good at suppressing the rebellious disposition of their husbands, but tears and smiles would have but little effect on these Southern Rebels—especially if administered by the wives and sisters of Yankee soldiers.

I would like to see a regiment of lady cavalry with extensive hoops armed with saber and carbine mounted on dashing steeds on dress parade, but I would not like to see them (if Northern girls) charge on a Rebel host for fear some of them would fall into the arms of the Rebels. How provoking that would be to us. It would create more excitement than the nigger question. Women do not appear to be in their element here in the army. A man in our regiment tore down his wife's tent yesterday, sent her off, and went to the barbershop and tried to borrow a razor to cut his throat. The cause? Jealousy.

I went out yesterday two miles to arrest one of our soldiers. He had married a poor girl and was living off from his father-in-law—a poor, feeble old man. He would not do anything for himself or anyone else. I found the family in a wretched condition in a miserable tent. The soldier's wife had the measles bad. They have been married for about four weeks. He had left that morning, telling his wife that he was never coming back. Women almost invariably get into trouble when they get into the army.

In Virginia, the Army of the Potomac and the Army of Northern Virginia were likewise adjusting to life in the trenches.

Many soldiers stayed abreast of war news from other places, like the sinking of the famous commerce raider CSS *Alabama* by the USS *Kearsarge* near Cherbourg, France, in June. It was noted in this letter home by First Lieutenant **Theodore Frelinghuysen Vaill (1832–1875)** in the 2nd Connecticut Volunteer Heavy Artillery (which was serving as infantry).

Petersburg, Virginia
July 8, 1864

We have just received news of the defeat-sinking of the Alabama, *and it makes us glad—especially as it happened in the eyes of all Europe.*

The weather is very hot here but endurable as long as there is no marching to be done. We had a very hard rain at Belle Plain on May 18th, another when across the North Anna River on the 25th of May, and since that, we have not seen a gallon of rain. But as our supplies come from afar, we are not troubled about the drought here.

The recent railroad raiding by our forces has been pretty serious for the Rebels. They will, of course, repair the damage at once. But I think we can tear up very much faster than they can lay it down, and Lee cannot stay in Richmond without those two railroads constantly open. The northern "invasions" are probably small affairs intended to distract Grant's operations here.

The "invasions" of the North that Vaill mentioned weren't true invasions on the scale of the 1862 Maryland Campaign and the 1863 Gettysburg Campaign. Yet it was a serious incursion by Confederate forces.

Details surrounding the *Alabama*'s sinking emerged. While docked in France for repairs, the *Kearsarge* arrived off the coast. Captain Raphael Semmes impulsively sailed out of the harbor and gave battle. He escaped to England as the raider sank.

That, along with news of Confederate troops entering Maryland, occupied many of the thoughts that Federal Corporal **S. B. Crane (unknown)** shared with a friend.

Deep Bottom, Virginia
July 10, 1864

That is good news about the sinking of the Alabama *by the* Kearsarge. *I think the* Alabama *got more than she bargained for when she sent a challenge to Captain John Winslow, and it was a job done up in good shape. It is too bad that Captain [Raphael] Semmes got away. But don't you think that it will cause some trouble? The U.S. will probably demand his surrender to us and, if refused, it will make trouble.*

I don't think the Rebels will make much by raiding into Maryland. They will be all the nearer to the Northern prisons, where we will transport them when they are captured, for most of them are going to be taken. They have got General David Hunter there, and he is no fool. I have been under him and know a little something about him. There will be some good news pretty soon, and when the news does come, it will be big.

We passed the Fourth of July here on picket and a dull time we had of it. We could see the Johnnies sitting on their picket posts doing nothing, only looking at us and as harmless as little children. We were only about a hundred and fifty yards apart.

The soldiers are in the best of spirits and are confident of a speedy end to the war, and they put up with all the hardships without finding any fault. The position of Grant's army is so that pretty soon, he will compel Lee to come out and fight him, and then they will get what they didn't bargain for. We can hear the big guns of Grant's army thundering away at Petersburg, making slow but sure progress toward the time when they are going to let the soldiers go home not on furlough but to stay.

Despite Crane's upbeat tone, the South's Maryland incursion was growing increasingly alarming to Northerners.

There had been heavy fighting that spring in Virginia's Shenandoah Valley, nicknamed the "Breadbasket of the Confederacy." To divert attention from its rich farmlands, Lee dispatched General Jubal Early there with some 15,000 men. In movements similar to Jackson's campaign two years before, he drove back the Federals as he advanced down the valley, then moved into Maryland, where he was victorious at the Battle of Monocacy.

While Early's movements didn't have much direct impact on Grant's operations at Petersburg, they did cause nervous jitters among Northerners on both the front lines and the home front. Schoolteacher **Rebecca Hand (1834–1914)** shared with a friend, a Union army surgeon, her struggle to understand developments. She was also concerned by the war's sharp increase in the destruction of homes and personal property.

Albany, New York
July 12, 1864

I have not been able to make up my mind yet as to what this raid is going to amount to. Reports are so conflicting. My belief is that were not the election of the president so near, you would all be called back to protect Washington. It will hardly do now to reenact the role of McClellan's campaigns [in 1862] by recalling Grant. So, recourse is had by the militia. [New York] Governor Horatio Seymour is doing all he can to appear to do something while doing nothing, and as he is adept at that, he succeeds very well.

The news of the last few days makes it seem possible that Baltimore may, for a while, come under Rebel domination. I think we are compelled to own [admit] that Grant's getting south of the James River is not the only successful strategic movement of the present campaign. Some ultra Administration folks here argue that it is a good thing that the Rebs have come north. "It weakens Lee's army, gives us a chance to capture the whole force sent here," etc.

But I can't see it in that light. I confess to being too ignorant of military tactics to see where an advantage is to be gained from having our railroads destroyed, trains stopped, passengers robbed, soldiers and officers taken prisoners, cars, bridges, private residences, etc. burned. The burning of private property has, from the first, appeared to me a wanton and useless procedure. Instead of weakening the enemy, it only strengthens them by exasperating and embittering them still more.

I am by no means a "Peace Man," but I am and always have been opposed to the unnecessary destruction of property. When you get hold of the leaders, punish them as they deserve to be punished; but as far as possible, mitigate the horrors of war and do not increase them. If I remember rightly, I believe we inaugurated the house-burning policy, and as retaliation is the order of the day, we have no right to complain if the Rebels make us feel what it is to see our dwellings, etc., destroyed when they can get at them.

Grant's soldiers were also closely monitoring Early's movements. Captain **William Washburn (1840–1922)** of the 35th Massachusetts Infantry confidently predicted Union victory in Maryland to his sweetheart. But he was also distressed by an unpleasant act of military discipline.

Near Petersburg, Virginia
July 13, 1864

The colonel and Captain Draper have gone to witness an execution of a major in the Second Brigade. I think I'll not increase the crowd that will undoubtedly be there by my presence. By "execution," I don't mean shooting or hanging. I'll explain myself. A major has been convicted by a general court-martial of cowardice, and General Burnside has sentenced him to have this sword broken, his straps torn off and buttons cut off in the presence of his regiment, and then to be sent to the Dry Tortugas [in the Florida Keys], there to work out the remainder of his enlistment. This is the second case of the kind during this campaign. Isn't it a terrible sentence? It seems to me if I were in his shoes, I should want to go to the picket line and give the Rebel sharpshooters a fine shot at me. I shouldn't want to live with such a disgrace upon me. And then there is his family. What must be their feelings? It seems too hard.

By the papers, I see that Lee's invasion is meant as a "big thing," to use a slang phrase. It has now assumed much larger proportions than first anticipated, but the result will be proportionately glorious to our arms. In my opinion, something of the kind had to be done to keep the Rebel army together. Its morale has become so low that a dazzling prize, no matter whether obtainable or not, had to be held up to induce the rank and file to a little further exertion in order to gain time in hopes that something in the meanwhile will show up.

Something will turn up, but not to their advantage. The Sixth Corps, General David Hunter, General Darius Couch, and General Franz Sigel, each with large armies, will suddenly turn up where they least expect them. And it is the impression here that but very few of the invading forces will return to Dixie. Goodbye, General Lee, I think your star has nearly set.

They say our communications are out, that General Grant's army is isolated from the north, and that a large portion of Lee's army is between Washington and Baltimore. I wonder if the enemy knows that the Sixth Corps is in Washington, besides the very large number of Veteran Reserve Corps regiments recently organized, to say nothing of numerous militia organizations? If they attack the city, I should say no. But they will not attack the city; they know too much for that.

They will demonstrate against it until their cavalry has succeeded in devastating the northeastern part of Maryland. Then, they will begin a retreat. No doubt that will be their program after discovering the strength of Washington to resist an attack. But will Generals Couch and Sigel and Hunter and Christopher Auger allow that program to be carried out? I think not. They [the Confederates] will not get a great way on their road homeward before encountering obstacles requiring more wisdom and force than they possess to surmount. Everything looks hopeful. This gives the soldiers of this army confidence that the desperate movement is the last struggle of the rebellion and will die out as suddenly as it grew.

What a time for the Copperheads! They will continue until the capture or dispersion of the Rebel army, and Grant has proven his claim to be superior to Lee, "the ablest general of the world." What a time that will be for the slimy Copperheads!

As I write, the artillery is at work in the front in a very lively manner. It may get round to us before sundown. We were expecting hot work very soon. Everything indicates an early move. I have no fear for the result.

Early knew that Grant had stripped Washington's fortifications of thousands of heavy artillerymen for use as infantrymen, so he pushed on toward the Union capital. **Hiram Weller (1843–unknown),** a private in the 6th New York Cavalry, was among the Federal troops awaiting him.

Lincoln Hospital, Washington, D.C.
July 10, 1864

I am detailed here to dress the wounds and give out the medicine. I am pretty busy, you may believe. There is some stirring news here this morning. It is that the Rebels are all around Washington and that they drove our forces into Baltimore. General Philip Sheridan arrived here last night with our cavalry, and I think the Rebels will have some fighting to do in a few days, for when he gets at them with our cavalry corps he will make them fight, and I would not be surprised if the Rebels did not leave in a worse fix than when they came in Maryland.

Tell Mother that she had better not start for here now, not until the Rebels are driven out of Maryland, for it would not be safe. I expect they will try and cut the railroad between Washington and Baltimore, therefore she had better not start.

It is all quiet in the Army of the Potomac at present, but in a few days, there will be such a move the Rebels never heard of. There was about 30,000 troops left New Orleans for some point, and I would not be surprised if they were for Grant.

Weller was incorrect; Sheridan was not dispatched to the capital at that time (he arrived later), though Grant did rush reinforcements there. They arrived in the nick of time because Early's command reached Washington's outskirts on the evening of July 11. The Confederates attacked Fort Stevens, coming within a whisker of entering the capital before being forced to withdraw.

In a situation reminiscent of First Bull Run/Manassas three years earlier, Washington residents watched the fighting from nearby sidewalks. Lincoln witnessed the battle from inside the fort and within Confederate rifle range, making him one of only two sitting presidents to come under fire in wartime. (James Madison was the other during the War of 1812.)

A soldier in the 147th Ohio Volunteer Infantry, identified only as **Jake (unknown),** gave a full account to his sister.

Fort Ethan Allen, Virginia
July 16, 1864

I suppose you have heard about the Rebs being down here and attacking Washington. The first skirmishing we heard was last Sunday, and then there was skirmishing until Tuesday when, early in the morning, they began their bloody work of fighting. They continued the fighting more or less all day. I was out on picket that day. We had a nice view of the battle—that is, the portion we could see. The smoke ascended in black, heavy clouds, and occasionally, we could see a shell burst in the air. A little before sundown, the Rebels made a charge on our men, but they fired their large siege guns, and the Rebs were drove back with heavy loss. Such a noise! It shook the very earth.

Old Abe was in the fight. Some of the Reb's sharpshooters were concealed in a house, and they was shooting at him, and he told our men to set it afire. It was a house that cost several thousand dollars. That was about dusk. The flames shot upward, and the conflagration illuminated the country for miles around. They kept up their firing until after nine o'clock, when it gradually died away.

It was a very pleasant evening. The moon was shining brightly, and it was almost as bright as daylight. Everything was quiet except the hooting of the owl, the solemn note of the nightingale, and the noise of the cavalrymen as they galloped back and forward on the outer picket lines. But while everything was so quiet here, what a scene of carnage and bloodshed there was 5 miles from here at Fort Stevens. There some were lying on the ground wounded, dying, and filling the air with their shrieks and groans. They had no smooth pillow to rest their feverish brows. They had no tender hand to refresh their parched lips or to administer to their wants. But such are the evils of war. The Rebels then retreated that night, and they have not troubled us since. We was expecting an attack here, but I think they have skedaddled.

With that, Early's Northern incursion ended as his army returned to Virginia. But **John Evans Kinder (1830–1877)**, a private in the 131st Ohio National Guard (a 100-day regiment serving behind the lines), told his wife that the Confederates missed nabbing a major prize.

Fort Federal Hill
Baltimore, Maryland
July 15, 1864

The great Rebel invasion is played out. The latest news is that they had crossed the Potomac on the retreat. Their great object was supplies for Richmond and Lee's army. They only fought General Lew Wallace at Fredrick and Monocracy, Maryland, to get him away from the Potomac in order to get their spoils safely over. The object of threatening this city and Washington was to get us to draw our men here and at the capital—that is, for us to act on the defensive until their trains of captured cattle, horses, and supplies were safely run off down the Shenandoah Valley. Then they would safely cross and follow in a consolidated body and keep us back, which they could successfully do as they had a good strong force, and we could not gather in time a sufficient number to overhaul them.

They were disappointed in getting the large wagon train that they wanted—the one that Sigel was starting from Martinsburg for Hunter. It was first sent to Frederick and from there here. It now is safe under the guns of our three forts. It was a grand sight to see it pass us. You can imagine it—say five miles of teams of six mules, all loaded. Also, two thousand head of beef cattle. The government stores here in the city were all loaded on steamers and ships and sent out in the bay for safety so if the Rebs did get in, they would get nothing but private property.

No doubt, they have got a large amount of supplies through the country as they took everything they could find from friend and foe, but their friends they paid well in Greenbacks, as they robbed Union men of all the money they had. Their leader and most of the principal scouting portion of them were Marylanders and knew the roads well and the political status of all they visited. When I tell you that this state is very little over half Union, you will know that it is not much trouble for Rebs to go about. I am told that Baltimore has more men in the Rebel army than in the Union army.

While I write this, I am hearing sweet music from a brigade band. We were serenaded last night by the band of one brigade, and another came and is staying with us. They are the bands belonging to the troops that came here from the South to help us.

Still, many Confederates were encouraged by Early's campaign, as Corporal **Thomas Burriss (1833–1867)** of the 4th South Carolina Infantry expressed to his sister.

In the trenches near Petersburg, Virginia
July 13, 1864

Skirmish fighting goes on day and night on the part of the lines we are now occupying. The enemy gains no advantage and is not likely to while he remains in front of Petersburg. It is very certain that his army is suffering in the extreme, as they have to use river water, and haul it several miles in barrels through the hot sun. The river water is more impure than any you ever saw. Tidewater affects the river at Petersburg, and it is quite apparent that the water must be most disagreeable. I believe the days have run as warm as any I ever experienced in South Carolina, something quite unseasonal for Virginia. Our men are standing the intense heat and extreme dry weather remarkably well. We have an abundance of good water, although it is not very pleasant getting it when the Yanks are firing upon the spring.

It is not very likely that we will have such an easy time during the entire summer. The report is quite current that we will go into active campaign soon. It is not prudent for a soldier to say when or where our campaigning will be, but if I should return an opinion, I would say that the field of our most active operations will be outside of the state. The whereabouts of General Richard Ewell's Corps (Early's command) have been a great mystery to the people of the South and the whole Yankee nation. If he accomplishes all he aims at, you will all be more surprised than you have been.

I must say that the future is more inviting than it has ever been before. Our enemy is much more dispirited and has fewer inducements, while our army is larger and more efficient than it ever was before. General Lee is more confident, surely, than he ever was. He ushered one-third of his men into Maryland and can send a goodly number of soldiers to any portion of the Confederacy as reinforcements. If the people at home would believe us when we assert that the Yankees are a weak and unstable race, fighting without any object in view, then they could plainly see the beginning of the end of this inhuman war.

I am increasingly of the belief that no more serious fighting will take place before this city. It is a characteristic of the Yankee never to fight two great battles on the same ground. There is no doubt now but that England, the great ally of Denmark against Prussia and Austria, will soon be involved in a most serious war, and certainly this will, in some measure, stop the effusion of blood upon our continent. England will need all of her surplus population in her own ranks, and our cruel neighbors (the Yanks) cannot recruit their ranks so easily. From my observation, a large majority of the new troops in the Yankee army are made up of foreigners.

One result of Early's attack on Washington's outskirts was the immediate mobilization of hundreds of clerks in the War Department for the capital's protection. Among them was **William Atwood (1844–1871),** who had previously served for 18 months in a Pennsylvania artillery battery, writing to a friend in Pittsburgh who had likewise served a hitch. (Atwood also revealed how discreet one had to be when living in a Border State and the hassles associated with commuting to work.)

Washington, D.C.
July 30, 1864

I suppose you have heard that ever since the raid here, the War Department clerks have been formed into companies and have drilled every evening. They have now been formed into a regiment of 10 full companies with a complete regiment organization. I was a corporal in Company F, but last night was appointed commissary sergeant. We have a very pleasant non-commissioned staff, and I think we would get on well together if we ever have to take the field. We are not mustered into service, but there is some talk of doing so. They are going to uniform us, however, and draw non-commissioned officers' swords, sashes, etc. About one-half of the regiment has seen service, and they drill pretty well; they will do good service if we ever get the chance. The field officers are all Regulars and understand their "biz." We are only going to drill twice a week after this; that is plenty in this hot weather.

I am living out in Bladensburg, Maryland, now and like it very much. We have good country fare, plenty of milk, cornbread, etc. There is a fine sulfur spring near the house, and we take our nips regularly. The swimming is splendid, with good places for diving, and one can get a good night's sleep, which you can't do in the city these hot nights. There are three or four girls in the family, and we play euchre occasionally. They are pretty strong Secesh but keep quiet about it, and as we avoid all political subjects in our conversation, we get along pretty well together. I am much better satisfied than I was in the city. The days we drill, it hurries us somewhat to get to the cars in the evening, and that is the only inconvenience we have.

I have not been drafted yet, nor do I want to be either. Strong efforts will be made to fill it this time, and I hope they will succeed. I am liable to the draft, not having been two years in the service.

Those "strong measures" that Atwood referenced to fill state quotas for soldiers included offering hefty enlistment bounties. Additionally, as the war dragged on, men willing to serve as draftees' substitutes were able to ask—and get—increasingly high fees. Consider the news that **George W. Burt (unknown)** relayed to his father, serving in the Union army in Virginia.

Oswego, New York
August 26, 1864

I found out last night something about recruiting. They have recruited 206 men in the county; only 54 are credited to the city. I could not find out how many substitutes they had mustered. Chapel was down here yesterday looking for a substitute. He offered Tom Densmore $1,300 [more than $45,000 today] for one, and he was to get one this morning. But I do not know whether he got one or not.

With ever more men on both sides being drafted, resentment grew in the ranks toward those who were sitting out the war at home. An **unknown Union soldier** in Sherman's army shared his resentment with his wife.

[Location unknown; date in 1864 unknown]

Will the Copperheads in the North keep still? I think the draft took some of them, such as the Rev. A. J. Hyser and some others, and the stay-at-home

Republicans such as Wise Long and Tom Berlin. Bully for him. I hope that he will have to carry a knapsack that will weigh one hundred and fifty pounds and only have half rations. I do hope he will come to this regiment. We will learn him how to soldier. It is different than staying at home and talking about it. I do hope every man that is drafted must come.

Throughout 1864, significant cash incentives for enlistments and reenlistments continued to be offered. When federal, state, and local bounties were added up, they could total hundreds of dollars (thousands today). That created the crime of "bounty jumping," where a man would enlist, collect his bounty, and then disappear and enlist again under a different name in another location, repeating the illegal process while reaping illicit gain. At one point, it was believed that there were 3,000 professional bounty jumpers in New York City alone. In some cases, rewards of up to $300 ($11,000 today) were offered for their capture.

Late in 1864, brothers **Alexander McFarland (1844–1871)** and **James McFarland (1832–1902)** wrote to their brother George, who worked in a dry goods store in Troy, New York, about a suspicious character. (Perhaps tellingly, Alexander had a sketchy past himself and had served time in a military jail earlier in the war for desertion.)

Jackson, New York
December 26, 1864

Alexander wanted me to write you concerning Jim Skinner—a deserter and bounty jumper who is skedaddling around these parts. Alexander saw him today and had a talk with him. He said he was in Brooklyn going to school, but I doubt it. Alexander would like to have him arrested if his name is on the list [of bounty jumpers] and wanted you to find out if he had enlisted in the Black Horse Cavalry and deserted from it. Please write immediately and give us your opinion about it. I think it would be nothing more than right that he should be arrested. —James McFarland

I saw Jim Skinner and had a talk with him. He told me that he was going to school in Brooklyn. I told him I was going to Brooklyn. He said that he would go Monday if I would, so we set up a time to go. He thinks that I am alright with him. You talk with the provost marshal and tell him that he is a deserter and a bounty jumper and, if necessary, I will come down as soon as you get an officer to watch for the train. When it arrives, he will surely come to Troy, and I ain't sure but he will be big fool enough to think that I will go to Brooklyn with him as I talked very sweet to him. You see about it, and if there is any chance we will have him. —Alexander McFarland

While fighting raged on the battle lines, guard or garrison duty wore heavily on soldiers serving in the rear, where prolonged inactivity was almost too much to bear.

Amos Gorrell (1837–1928), a private in the 18th Ohio Infantry, recounted to friends how tempers sometimes flared in such conditions.

Chattanooga, Tennessee
August 21, 1864

This is a dark, gloomy Sabbath. It is raining. Has rained more or less every day this month except one. My messmates (five in number) are all in their bunks. Some sleeping and some reading the papers, which the chaplain distributed this morning. The monotony of camp life weighs heavily upon soldiers on a morning like this. They are all housed up in their shanties, some reading, some sleeping, some writing letters, some singing a familiar air, some playing cards, etc. while the trickling of the rain on the rooftops of our shanties frequently brings to mind remembrances of a rainy morning at home before the "cruel war." But enough about wet weather, as we have had plenty of it.

Yesterday, two soldiers of a company, an old soldier and a recruit, had a little fight. All hands stood aloof and let them fight it out. The old soldier came off best, but neither of them was hurt much. They are both a little quarrelsome. Once, about a year ago, I made a comrade behave himself by slapping his chops.

For those at the front, the fighting ground on. Ulysses Grant was an innovative general in many ways. Having seen firsthand at Vicksburg how tedious and costly a prolonged siege could be, he was on the lookout for new ways to break the stalemate at Petersburg. He decided to try something that he had attempted—unsuccessfully—the previous summer, but on an even larger scale this time.

In a tremendous security lapse, Captain **William Washburn** shared details in his previously mentioned letter.

Petersburg, Virginia
July 15, 1864

The army is in splendid condition and anxious to advance on Petersburg. About next Wednesday, their wishes will be gratified. At the same time, about five tons of powder will assist the charge very effectively, so it is thought. You've seen one of those earthquakes gotten up by little boys for the amusement of the big boys, generally on the Fourth of July? The earthquake that will take place about the middle of next week in front of Petersburg will be upon the same principle. Somebody will advance in the world. His descent, though, will be nearly as rapid. It will be a surprise party to that general, whoever he is, who is making his headquarters at a certain house on a hill under which the mine has been dug. Look in the papers for full particulars.

It seemed that everyone in the Union ranks knew that something was up. Private **Calvin Hopkins Cleaves** (1844–1870), 9th Maine Infantry, also shared rumors of the coming attack with his cousin.

In the front trenches before Petersburg, Virginia
July 25, 1864

We expect to see stirring times before I shall get an answer to this missive. 'Tis about certain that something will soon be done here. If there is an advance made, the fight will be hard for the enemy is well entrenched. But there may be in use the same policy that Grant used before Vicksburg—undermining forts. 'Tis whispered around here that he is undermining two forts, but no one seems to know about it in this regiment, at least.

Rained like sixty last night, and I took some cold. When I got up this morning, I felt very still and chilly, but after having a hot breakfast (coffee and baked beans) and a good smoke, I feel as the Dutchman expresses it, "Much petter ish goot." The Rebs are throwing some shells, but if they don't depose their compliments in too close proximity with myself, I shall finish this in spite of their noise. Yesterday, they threw one very saucy shell which killed one man and wounded four, two of which belonged to the 9th.

Our folks, I think, have the most artillery and mortars, and they know how to use them pretty well, for occasionally, when the Rebs open fire on us, our batteries concentrate their whole fire on the offensive guns and mortars and effactually "dry 'em up."

Occasionally, the boys on picket have some fun. They'll agree not to fire and then jump out of their holes, swap coffee and tobacco and throw lumps of dirt at each other, get to talking about the war, and sometimes get mad and have a fistfight.

The much-anticipated assault finally came early on July 30. Some 8,000 pounds of powder exploded at 4:44 a.m. underneath a Confederate brigade and battery. Federal troops then attacked. The ensuing Battle of the Crater was one of the war's greatest disasters. **Daniel Hicks Hopping (1817–1868),** a private in the 24th New York Cavalry, pulled no punches when describing it.

Before Petersburg, Virginia
August 1, 1864

We received orders to fall back to the skirmish line, pack up at once with orders to rest until three o'clock [in the morning], and then be ready to march with nothing but our arms, haversacks, and canteen. It began to look ominous of a battle.

We started at three directly for the front and in the direction of Petersburg. We halted and found a large force of the 9th Corps massed for an attack on the enemy. We waited until the sun was about rising when we were startled suddenly by a convulsive movement of the earth and a dull, heavy explosion. Almost simultaneously, one hundred pieces of artillery belched forth, pouring tons of shot and shell into the enemy's front lines of earthworks. The ball had opened. A Rebel fort had been blown to atoms.

Standing in front and close to their front line of works, before the enemy had time to recover from the effects of the explosion, a division of the 9th Corps had charged on their front line and carried it. The enemy had now become fully sensible of what was transpiring and opened on our men with grape and canister and musketry from their second line, but wholly regardless of danger, they soon reached the second line and carried it. But it was done at a fearful cost of life.

A terrible artillery duel was going on, dealing death on every hand. Our division held what they had gained until ten o'clock when a division of colored troops was ordered in to relieve them and charge on the third line. They went in and advanced near the third line when the black rascals broke and ran like sheep. That decided the battle. The day was lost. The enemy charged on them and soon had taken back all we had gained. With the exception of the

explosion of the fort, they stood where they did before the battle commenced.
I am informed the fort contained two regiments with a general and his staff.
The fort presented a horrible sight when our troops reached it. Men mangled
in all ways imaginable.

    I have it from good authority that our loss is 5 thousand—3 of white
and 2 of colored troops in killed, wounded, and prisoners. I suppose we have
lost more in prisoners than the enemy have. Yesterday at 4 p.m., Burnside
asked for a truce to bury the dead and remove the wounded. But for some
reason, it was not granted until this morning at 8 o'clock. It lasted four hours.
It was a hard sight to see them lying on the field within a few rods from our
works and could render no assistance. Many died, no doubt, which might
have been saved could they have received help, but such is the fortunes of war.

    I have not space to give you a description of this battle as I would like to.
I would like to see what the press says about it. Please send me a newspaper.
I had some pretty close calls that day, but am all right yet.

    I consider this campaign a total failure.

For the men on both sides, conditions in the trenches were terrible. They
were only marginally better in camps behind the lines. Those encampments were
far from the idyllic scenes shown in period lithographs.

Thomas Franklin Brownell (1842–1901) was a college student who volunteered with the U.S. Christian Commission, a private organization that provided
supplies, medical services, and religious materials to Federal soldiers. He spent
several weeks visiting the Petersburg front while supervising the commission's
work there. He described the deplorable conditions to his cousin.

Before Petersburg, Virginia
August 7, 1864

I can tell you what my first idea of a camp was from the view I got from the
side of the covered cart I rode up to my present station in. Take an irregularly
shaped piece of the country about ten miles long and two miles wide, about
half woodland, burn two-thirds of said woodlands, and leave blackened
stumps. Then, throw in any amount of dirty tents, mules, enormous meat
carts, contrabands, and flies. There's your camp. To make the semblance still
better, harness to each of the covered meat carts six mules, put a contraband
on the pole one, and arrange them in strings of twenty or more each. Let them
go in every direction, and these will be "army trains." Have a lot of solitary

horsemen riding to kill on every side, and finally make everything dusty, hot, and disagreeable. Pitch the tents in squads here and there, and the picture will be complete. But you must remember that this applies more strictly to the portion of the field to the right wing near the base of operations at City Point, and the nearer to that, the more mules, flies, and confusion. But the farther you go in the other direction, the less men you see.

It's odd, but here are two armies of perhaps 100,000 each, and they do not see each other. A man that shows his head above the ridges or ramparts on either side gets popped by a sharpshooter. Everybody keeps out of sight behind batteries and in rifle pits, or way in the rear.

I am sitting on my bed, writing on my knee from the U.S.C.C. [U.S. Christian Commission] tent at the 18th Army Corps Hospital. This hospital has about 1,200 in it. While I am writing, about 200 are coming in from the extreme front. Lots of sick folks in this family. Think of it—12 died last Wednesday night, and every night at sundown, there is a squad that goes out and buries those who have died since the previous sunset.

Uncleanliness was not limited to the front. Brownell's older sister, **Josephine Brownell Chase (1836–1898)**, also served with the Christian Commission as a volunteer nurse at a military hospital in Washington. While both armies made major efforts to move sick and wounded soldiers to medical facilities in their respective capitals, conditions inside them were often appalling by today's standards.

Washington, D.C.
August 14, 1864

I think I told you that we were stationed at the Mt. Pleasant Hospital. In my ward, there are sixteen or eighteen men—two of them sick with fever, three with chronic diarrhea, one with rheumatism, one wounded in the groin, two in the head, two with arms off, the rest with amputated legs. Two went home on furlough last week. Three are going this week. We, of course, feel most interested in our particular wards, but we have access to all the men in the hospital.

We went into the gangrene ward the other day to see if we could do anything for them. Poor fellows. I pity them. I think the air was more impure than any place we have been in. We don't mind it very much after we have been in a few minutes.

The "boys" are not getting along very well. It is so hot this week. Such quantities of flies I never saw. Some of the boys' faces, as well as bodies, are literally covered. They have to have a fan to keep them off, but some are so weak that they soon get tired. Each one ought to have someone to sit right down by their bedside and attend all of the time to them. It seems as if we could not do anything for them—there is so much to be done.

The "regular" nurses, I don't know what to think of. We went into a ward the other day, and one was sitting and rocking away, hemming ruffling. In our hospital, we have not seen them doing one thing for the soldiers. We meet them occasionally walking through the halls, trying to fan themselves and keep cool.

One incident at a field hospital almost defies belief. Writing from near Petersburg to his niece, **Thomas Franklin Brownell** described a remarkable occurrence. He also caught the sound of something worth noting. A great religious revival had swept through Lee's army in 1863, and its effects were still being felt the next year.

Before Petersburg, Virginia
August 14, 1864

The Rebs opened fire on the [Dutch Gap] canal from four or five different points and made things hot for two hours or so. A rather curious calamity happened during the engagement. A hospital steward had his arm shattered by one of the shells. He was placed upon the amputating table, and the surgeon began to operate for the purpose of cutting off his arm. While thus engaged, a shell came, killed the man on the table, and took off the arm of the surgeon. They came over here to get our surgeon to take his place.

The other side of the Appomattox River is in the hands of the Rebels, and by walking to its banks, we can frequently hear what is going on. They are having a revival over there, and in the evening, they can be heard singing, shouting, and praying. That seems odd, doesn't it?

The almost endless slaughter and seemingly hopeless stalemates at Petersburg and Atlanta had spiraled both the Union and the Confederacy into a profoundly deep collective depression. The North's presidential election was now less than 90 days away, and war-weariness was in full force. Many people had simply had all they could stand of the bloodbath. Republican Lincoln, running this time on the National Union ticket, vowed to see the war through to the end. Democrats nominated General George McClellan. While "Little Mac" personally distanced himself from his party's platform, which called for an end to the conflict, many Northerners believed that electing the Democrats would stop the fighting.

The situation was highly uncertain.

Lincoln proclaimed a "day of national humiliation, fasting, and prayer" on August 4. To some observers, it seemed more an act of desperation than divine supplication, as Union soldier **T. B. Lisle (unknown)** disparagingly told his wife.

Fort Delaware
Pea Patch Island, Delaware
August 4, 1864

Well, this is the day that Old Abe appointed for Thanksgiving, but I must say that his followers or none others are paying any attention to it here. I suppose the next thing will be a ball at the White House.

> *Soon with conscripts [draftees] we'll be marching,*
> *with dark frowns upon our brow;*
> *Soon with niggers we'll be voting,*
> *Who would vote for Abram now?*

War-weariness was felt in the ranks as well. Private **Daniel Hicks Hopping (1817–1868),** who had witnessed the carnage at the Crater, was ready for it to be over regardless of the outcome.

Before Petersburg, Virginia
August 16, 1864

We are holding the line where the charge was made on July 30th [Battle of the Crater]. There has nothing transpired recently in our vicinity of much note. The usual picket and artillery firing is kept up. A few men are killed or wounded every day.

Do the abolitionists still say use up the last man and the last dollar to subjugate the South? If they do, they had better shoulder the musket and turn out en masse and come down here. I think they would find it quite a different affair. I believe the best military men in the Federal army are convinced that it's time to have peace otherwise than by fighting, and that it can be done honorably to both parties. I think it a poor argument to say that after we have sacrificed millions of human lives and almost impoverished the country, that we must fight it out even if the country is ruined beyond redemption.

For my part, I have seen enough of fighting and enough of the war as it has been carried on. I am for peace, and I know that I am speaking the sentiments of the mass of the Potomac army. The sacrifices and sufferings of the Army of the Potomac in this summer campaign have been sufficient to establish peace to the country if the conduct of the war had been just and right, and I hope the All-wise Being who ruleth the universe will put it in the hearts of the people of the nation to see that peace is better than war, and that might is not right.

Writing from Washington, clerk **William Atwood (1844–1871)** didn't bother hiding his despondency to his friend at home.

War Department
Washington City
August 19, 1864

We have had a week of constant rain here, and you know it is not very pleasant to have to tote an umbrella every place you go. I am in hopes it will be cooler soon. I have never suffered so much from heat in my life as I have this summer. The average state of the thermometer has been 96 degrees in the shade. You ask how the prices of clothing are here. Well, they are outrageous. You cannot buy a decent suit for less than $60 [more than $2,100 today], and not the best of stuff then. I find prices here a good deal higher than they are in Pittsburgh, and they don't make up goods nearly as well as they do at home.

I saw a lot of prisoners last night, and they say that if this war is not ended before the fall, the soldiers in the South will stop fighting, that this thing is about played out, etc. The same feeling seems to exist in the North, I'm afraid, and take it all together, I believe the war will be over very soon now. If our armies don't gain some material advantage before Election Day, I am afraid Lincoln will stand a poor show for being reelected. There is a strong Peace Party rising in the North, and they will try and stop the war at all hazards. We will see stirring times before long. I am like you, I don't know what is going to become of us. Patriotism seems to be completely played out. I sometimes get very disheartened, but I hope for the best.

Hospitals were overflowing with wounded soldiers. That meant that the mail was overflowing with letters bringing news that the recipients did not want to hear. **Margaret "Maggie" Creath (unknown)** got one of them. She had been banished from her home in Missouri to the Deep South in 1863 for her outspoken support of the Confederacy and sent this letter to an unknown gentleman. (She described Captain Hugh M. Pollard from Monroe County, Missouri, who had died in Griffin, Georgia, on August 21 from wounds received in the Battle of Atlanta.)

Marion, Alabama
September 1, 1864

The letter bearing your signature containing the sad and afflicting news of the death of our mutual friend Capt. Pollard came to hand yesterday, and I hasten to reply, knowing you will wait to hear from me. I am greatly shocked that he should have died as he wrote so hopefully in the short letter received from him after the amputation.

He was a generous-hearted, brave little Missouri brother, for he always addressed me as his adopted sister, and I felt an attachment for him inasmuch as his home was near mine, and he seemed perfectly wrapped up in the idea of meeting a Missouri lady friend. Early last spring, on the opening of the campaign, he wrote and requested me, in case of an accident, to take care of his clothing and army effects for his mother and sisters, which I promised to do with pleasure. Anything expressed to me belonging to him will be preserved with sacred care until an opportunity is afforded me to convey them safely to his relatives. The sword you will please preserve, as he spoke with special care about preserving that for his sister.

I am very grateful to you for your kindness in writing me about his death and last words, which will be greatly prized by his friends. In the midst of life, we are in death. Life is a mere span and warns us all to be ready for the coming hour.

It is said that necessity prompts creativity; it certainly was responsible for one of the war's most daring operations. In late August, Lee informed Richmond that his food supply was nearly exhausted. Two weeks later, scouts reported that a large herd of cattle was lightly guarded on the James River a few miles from Grant's headquarters. General Wade Hampton ordered 3,000 Confederate troopers (including "several certified Texas cattle thieves") to seize it in what came to be called the Beefsteak Raid. They struck at 5:00 a.m. on September 16, making off with 2,486 head of cattle, 11 wagons, and 304 prisoners. Lincoln called it "the slickest piece of cattle stealing" he had ever heard of. It was also mentioned in this letter that **Leonard A. Gay (1836–1914)**, a sergeant in the 4th New Hampshire Infantry, wrote to his brother.

Near Petersburg, Virginia
September 26, 1864

There have not been any movements down this way—only the Rebs moved on a drove of twenty-five hundred head of cattle that belonged to the U.S. and moved them off without much trouble. They done it up brown. I don't think we can find any fault.

I have just learned that we are to be on the move again tomorrow morning at four o'clock. We have left the front and moved to the rear. We are going to get paid this week. Then we are going somewhere–the Lord only knows where. Some say to the Weldon Railroad, some to North Carolina, but I shall let you know in my next letter.

Then, seemingly in an instant, everything changed. The turnaround began so slowly that few people recognized it at first.

On August 5, Admiral David Farragut led his Federal fleet into Alabama's Mobile Bay. The monitor USS *Tecumseh* was hit by an underwater explosive device, sinking with the loss of 94 crewmen and making Farragut famously exclaim, "Damn the torpedoes! Full speed ahead!" As a result, Fort Morgan, which protected the city, was captured 18 days later.

That not only closed Mobile as a port for Confederate blockade-runners but also marked the start of Lincoln's dramatic reversal of political fortunes. Ensign **Hiram Parker Jr. (1841–1918)** described to his mother how a comrade came to be on the ill-fated warship as well as Lincoln's improving political situation.

U.S. Steamer Louisiana
Pamlico Sound, North Carolina
September 28, 1864

Potts spoke of the attack on Mobile as being a grand affair. He also confirms the death of my old shipmate Ensign Frederick Barlow. Barlow was not ordered to the monitor [USS Tecumseh*], but her engineer being sick, he* *offered his services and was accepted. He was expecting to go home shortly but did not think it was to be his long home. How little we know of what is before us. And what a change in our destiny small occurrences make. Potts says he is tired of the Navy but will remain in it till the war is over. A great many that I know are of the same mind.*

Abe's prospects are brightening, and I think he is to be our next President. Providence permitting.

A few weeks later came a development whose significance no one could deny. Sherman's army swung south of Atlanta, cutting off its last major links to the rest of the Confederacy. Hood was ultimately forced to evacuate, leaving on the final road available to him. The mayor surrendered the city on September 2. Captain **Don Carlos Newton (1832–1893)** wasted no time telling his wife the big news.

On the battlefield of Lovejoy, Georgia
September 3, 1864

Atlanta is ours. We have met the enemy in 6 more pitched battles and have defeated them with tremendous slaughter in both. We have pursued them to this point, 25 miles below Atlanta, and are still pursuing them. We have destroyed 25 miles of railroad on this and the West Point Railroad and captured from 5 to 7,000 prisoners, killed and wounded from 5 to 7,000 more, and put them to utter rout. I tell you, we all feel glorious. As I write, for miles on either side, the boys are making everything ring with their cheers, and although the skirmishers still keep up the crack of the rifle in front of the Rebel works and the cannons still boom, all are more than joyous, happy.

Prisoners are coming in, in small squads all the time. The Rebs have made another stand here and may detain us for a few days. But I think the campaign is practically over for the present. General Sherman issued a congratulatory order this morning to the troops that we occupied Atlanta and said the Rebels burned and destroyed 80 carloads of ammunition.

We took part in the battle of the 31st [Battle of Jonesborough], and although under a very heavy fire, I had only one man wounded, and he only slightly. In that battle, we repulsed them terribly, and our whole loss did not exceed 2 or 300, while theirs could not have been less than 3 to 5,000. A Rebel surgeon I captured at Jonesborough said they brought in over 2,000 wounded there, and that was not near all as large numbers were brought in our lines. Rumor has it 8,000.

The night of the 1st, I was brigade Officer of the Day and had charge of the picket lines in front of Jonesborough. During the night, I charged the Rebel picket line and drove it a mile and into the outskirts of the town. I haven't had the balls fly any thicker over my head in this campaign than that dark night of the 1st while you were fast asleep in your soft bed. The next morning, I got up and went at them again. But they were gone, and I went in and took the town of Jonesborough. I got in soon enough to fire on the rear of a train of cars just going out and to capture a hospital with 30 or 40 wounded, half a dozen or so of Rebs, 30 or 40 stands of arms, and a caisson with ammunition. Although I had about 300 men, the Rebs made a pretty strong opposition to our advance. I did not have one wounded or hurt—only myself, and I run my knee against a stub and made it black and blue. I marched yesterday, though.

I have been over looking at 200 or 300 prisoners that are in one pile over here—dirty, greasy-looking cusses and from their looks I should say pretty tired of rebellion.

Give my love to my brother-in-law and tell him to come down here and see how he likes to hear the whistle of the bullets.

After 90 days of nearly nonstop marching and fighting during the hottest time of the year, Sherman's army paused for a much-needed rest. At the same time, the city's residents were adjusting to a new life in an occupied city. Writing two days after his twenty-first birthday, **Thomas P. Carver (1843–1916),** a corporal in the 98th Ohio Volunteer Infantry, described to his father an unpleasant surprise that some Atlanta women experienced.

Atlanta, Georgia
September 21, 1864

All our extra baggage that was sent to Bridgeport, Alabama, last spring has just been brought up. This looks as though we would get to rest in camp for a while. Our communication is still bothered some. We don't get our mail. The line is so long it is hard to keep open being 470 miles from here to Louisville, Kentucky, our base of supplies.

I did not tell you the joke we got on a lot of citizens of Atlanta and the towns to the south. While our army was encircling the city and shelling it, some of the women left to get out of the way of the shells that were visiting their houses. So when we commenced evacuating our line of works, they thought the Yanks were gone. So, several hundred women came up in the cars to have a jollification over the retreat of the Yankeys [sic]. The first thing they knew, the Yanks were on the south side of them and holding the railroad, so they had to be taken. Sherman has sent all the citizens away. Those that would take the oath [of allegiance to the Union] were sent north, except soldiers' wives. They had to follow their tribe. The women did not like to leave. There was great crying around. They did not go away as happy as they had come back.

The loss of Atlanta was serious enough for the Confederacy's commander in chief to visit the troops in person. Sergeant **William Hooper (unknown)**, 62nd Tennessee Infantry, told his wife about it.

Palmetto, Georgia
September 28, 1864

Maggie, I have more news to write you than one letter could contain. Hood is now at Palmetto on the Montgomery & Atlanta Railroad. President Davis left here last evening having stayed two or three days. He made us two speeches whilst here, encouraging and reviving the troops. He spoke at some length, recounting our many hardships, fatiguing marches, our victories and defeats, and the bright future that awaited us if faithful only a short time yet. Senator Howell Cobb of Georgia, Governor Isham Harris of Tennessee, and General John Bell Hood also made speeches, all intimating that we would soon march into middle Tennessee. The supposition is that we will go by way of Blue Mountain and Gadsden, Alabama. If so, I think we will do so soon.

On August 31, the 226 delegates who were gathered in Chicago's Amphitheater for the Democratic National Convention nominated George McClellan as their party's presidential nominee. (McClellan, who was 37, and his 39-year-old running mate, Congressman George Pendleton, remain the youngest ticket of any major political party.) The so-called Peace Democrats wing of the party favored a negotiated settlement in the Union's favor to end the fighting. That would have involved making compromises with the South. **James Nicholas (unknown)**, a private in the 118th Ohio Infantry stationed outside Atlanta, said that many men in uniform didn't support that approach.

Decatur, Georgia
September 16, 1864

McClellan is the nominee at Chicago. He has some supporters here. All the Rebels that we have taken prisoner say that this presidential election will decide the war. If McClellan is elected, they say the war will last some longer. For they think that he will give them some favorable terms. While if Old Abe is elected, they know his terms. So they will have to give up or fight for four years longer, and this they can't do. They look a great deal at movements of the Peace Men in the North for help and say that the Peace Men will resist the draft and that there is still hope for them.

I hope that there won't be any trouble about the draft, for it is every man's duty to help. But damn this Rebellion which we hold now by the throat. I have changed my views on the nigger question and, like Old Abe, say set them all free.

Sir, the slightest knowledge of arithmetic would prove to any man that the Rebels' armies cannot be destroyed with the strategy proposed by the Peace Men. It would sacrifice all the white men of the North to do it. There are now in the United States service two hundred thousand black troops in the field defending and acquiring territory to the Union. The peace strategy demands that those be disbanded and turned over to their former masters and restored to slavery. The black man who now assists Union prisoners to escape from a fate worse than death would be turned over to our enemies to gain the good-will of their masters. I say "Never."

The shift of momentum in the North's favor that began at summer's end with the Battle of Mobile Bay and Atlanta's fall increased during October on all fronts. After the Washington raid, Early's Confederates withdrew into northern Virginia to protect the Shenandoah Valley. Grant sent a new Union commander there and ordered him to pursue a radically different strategy. He ordered General Philip Sheridan to make the valley a "barren waste." There was such wanton destruction of farms, mills, railroads, and bridges that survivors remembered it as "The Burning." It was also a foretaste of what Sherman would soon inflict on Georgia.

In a series of battles, Sheridan made Early fall back. Writing from the Petersburg front, Sergeant **Charles W. Smith (1838–unknown)** of the 1st Connecticut Heavy Artillery reacted to news of the Battle of Tom's Brook in the Shenandoah Valley, where Sheridan routed two Confederate cavalry divisions.

City Point, Virginia
October 13, 1864

There is glorious news from Sheridan again this morning. Every victory that we gain now will be so much help toward reelecting Old Abe as well as toward putting down the Rebellion.

I still remain at City Point playing the part of a gentleman soldier with nothing to do, which is hard work for me. You know that I have a great inclination for work, especially when I can't help it. There has been considerable fighting in this army for the past week, resulting in no particular advantage to either side. But the great and final struggle must soon come, which will decide who is to occupy Richmond this winter.

Six days later, Early caught Sheridan in a surprise attack but was ultimately defeated in the decisive Battle of Cedar Creek. It was also a pivotal event in that fall's presidential election campaign. **Charles Miller (1843–1912),** a young private in the 140th New York Infantry serving at Petersburg, was thrilled by the news, as he explained to his sister.

Camp Near Poplar Grove Church, Virginia
October 22, 1864

Only for a moment, reflect and look back and see what has been accomplished within the last few days by Sheridan in the Valley. On the evening of the 20th, a dispatch came to every corps headquarters, which was read off to the troops along the line, that the enemy had attacked Sheridan's left and driven him 4 miles. But getting his cavalry together, he sent them on the enemy's flank, at the same time rallying his troops to defeat the Rebels finely, capturing 43 pieces of artillery and a large number of prisoners, etc.

Last evening, we received another dispatch that he (Sheridan) had found the enemy and captured 50 more pieces of artillery and 1,600 prisoners. Is not that cheering news to every loyal heart? We hear the news when so great a victory is in our favor sometimes before you do, as it is immediately telegraphed to corps headquarters and a dispatch written off and then taken to divisions and battalions, then to regiments, where it is read to the troops. All of the cheering you ever heard never can begin to compare with what took place on receiving intelligence of such a victory.

General Gouverneur Warren has just passed up the line. Heavy cannon-
ading has been kept up on our right for some days past. In the evening, the
shells can be seen passing from one side to another. They look beautiful but, at
the same time, are not very pleasant to those over whom they explode.

On October 2, President Davis named General Pierre G. T. Beauregard to
head the newly created Department of the West. Although little more than a
paper appointment, the move cheered many Southerners who had long considered Beauregard one of their favorite commanders. That opinion was evident
when **Mary Barclay Kirby (1811–1891)** wrote to her son in Louisiana from
Columbia, South Carolina. The Confederacy had relocated its Treasury Note
Bureau (the Treasury Department's currency printing operation) there that summer, and Mary—along with many "Treasury Ladies"—moved with it. She also
passed on some motherly advice about her son's military frustrations.

Columbia, South Carolina
October 13, 1864

Mr. Stovall was at home also on furlough being not on duty in Alabama;
has something to do I think with Atlanta. Everyone, however, seems more
hopeful now that Beauregard has been placed in command of that army.
Everything is quiet around Richmond at present. All the men are in the
field. Your brother was at home, having been quite sick from being so much
exposed on duty below the city [at Petersburg] during the warm weather. He
has had chills but is getting better. I fear they will have some hard fighting
around Richmond before a great while. God has heretofore been so merciful
in protecting our dear home from our despicable enemies that I trust he will
continue to be with us and again drive them back in shame and confusion.
But it makes me sad, my son, when you speak of your Cousin Edmund
[General Kirby Smith] not doing for you as you think he ought. You must not
feel so but be satisfied to do your duty wherever he places you. I know you are
faithful to those duties, and if you could only know what a relief it is to my
mind to feel that you are safe, and still doing what you are required to do,
you would not complain, I am sure, but willingly commit your ways unto the
hands of Him who directs your steps so that He will spare you to return to
be a great blessing to me. What do I care for your promotion if you are taken
from me? Would not I rather that you should remain as you are, I am sure
you ought not complain. Very few rank as high as captain at your age, and if

your life is only spared, I do not care if you remain as you are until the end
of this horrid war. If you wish to remain in the army, then promotion will
come quickly enough. So, for my sake, be satisfied, my dear boy.

Far to the west, Confederate forces led by General Stand Watie scored an
important victory on September 19 in the Battle of Cabin Creek in the Indian
Territory (modern-day Oklahoma). The Southerners attacked and captured a
Union wagon train, netting about $1 million ($36 million today) in desperately
needed food and supplies. They also took 130 wagons and nearly 750 mules.

Watie was the only Native American on either side to attain the rank of
general. He was congratulated for his victory by his nephew, **Elias Cornelius
Boudinot (1835–1890),** who served as the Cherokee Nation's delegate to the
Confederate Congress. Boudinot also relayed political news about assisting
Confederate refugees in getting clothing and medicine as winter approached.

Paris, Texas
October 16, 1864

The whole country is loud in praise of General Watie. The Northern papers
make it out even a more signal success than you did. They say that "Stand
Watie had 4,000 men" and that their loss was over 300 men besides losing
300 wagons, etc. Aunt Sally [Watie's wife] and the children are all well and
are rejoicing in the "dry goods and groceries." News is good from Missouri
and Richmond.

I wrote you advising that you call the [Tribal] Council and recommend
the appropriation of some amount of money for the purchase of medicines
and cotton cards. I will have $50,000 appropriated [by the Confederate
Congress] as soon as possible after I reach Richmond, and if any person should
be sent across the [Mississippi] River for the purpose indicated, it will not be
advised for him to take more money than needed to pay his expenses. But he
should be authorized by act of Council and a letter or order of the Treasurer
to receive the money.

The legislature of Arkansas, which has just adjourned, appointed one
million dollars in Confederate money for the purchase of medicines and cot-
ton cards for the refugee district of that state. I believe all the national funds
could not be better expended than in purchasing articles which might enable
our refugees to clothe themselves. I have just returned from Rusk County and
will leave this place tomorrow for Richmond via Washington, Arkansas. I
am sorry that I could not get to your command.

The "good news" from Missouri concerned one of the war's most quixotic campaigns. Commencing in late August, Confederate General and former Missouri Governor Sterling "Old Pap" Price led some 12,000 troops and 14 cannon out of northeastern Arkansas. Price believed that he would be joined by thousands of recruits when he reached Missouri. With his ranks thus swelled, he could then attack St. Louis and arm the volunteers with guns taken from the massive Federal arsenal there.

It was a slow, plodding campaign. Price barely managed a little more than 100 miles in six weeks. After a costly victory capturing an insignificant Union fort at Pilot Knob on September 27, Price realized that St. Louis was too heavily fortified to be taken. He headed west with the goal of seizing Jefferson City, the state capital. But it also proved unassailable. So he drove his men farther westward toward modern-day Kansas City. As he did, Union forces pursued him from the east, as young Private **Samuel Myers (1845–1884)** of the 49th Illinois Infantry informed his parents.

California, Missouri
October 14, 1864

We have been on a hard march for the last week, and we all stood it first rate except our feet. My feet got so sore that I could hardly walk, and I guess we will start out in the morning again after Old Pap Price. He has been a cutting around here through Missouri, and we are going to see if we can't stop him. They say he is out at Boonville. That is about twenty-five miles from here. We marched from St. Louis to Jefferson City, and then we got on the cars and came out here to California, and we will march through to Boonville. It is very hard marching through Missouri over the hills and rocks.

I got a letter from Atlanta, Georgia. It was from William Snider, and he said he was well. It was dated September the 22, and I got it the 30th. It came through from Atlanta in eight days, and Will said the old Stars and Stripes waved over Atlanta.

Likewise, Federal forces were also heading toward Price from the west. Private **Columbus Griffith (1839–1907)** of the 2nd Kansas Cavalry didn't hide his disappointment at missing the action or his concern for his family in this letter to his sister.

Fort Leavenworth, Kansas
October 18, 1864

I am still in the stable, though most of the troops and General Samuel Curtis and his staff is gone in pursuit of Old Price in Missouri. But they would not let me go. There is 25 of my company here now. That is nearly all that is left of them. They got here three days ago and are starting for Missouri this afternoon. There is 200 of them in all. I went and asked to be relieved to go with them, but they told me no, so I have to stay here. But I don't like to do it.

Price is about 75 miles from here with 30,000 men, and there will be hard times here this winter. I am expecting all the time to hear of a raid on southern Kansas, for there is sure to be one, and if I only had my family out of there, they might have the country for all I care. But Anne is unwilling to leave, and I suppose I shall leave them there and trust to Providence. I have not heard from her for some time. They was all tolerable well when I last heard from there.

Price was eventually defeated at the Battle of Westport on October 23, ending both his raid and the last major fighting in Missouri and the Trans-Mississippi Theater. With Federals nipping at his heels every step of the way, Price's retreat southward along the Missouri–Kansas state line was burdened by a cumbersome wagon train. He had captured 18 pieces of artillery and a large amount of supplies, which he insisted on hauling back with him. That seriously slowed his battered little army, allowing it to be beaten once more at Mine Creek and yet again at Marais de Cygnes, Kansas, on October 25.

With Price fleeing for safety to the south, Federals in Arkansas were racing to intercept him, as **Isaac Taylor (1834–1909),** a captain in the 3rd Minnesota Infantry, noted to his wife.

DeValls Bluff, Arkansas
November 17, 1864

General Frederick Steele has sent all of his cavalry for to try and intercept Price. But I think Old Pap Price will arrive safely at Camden, Arkansas, with most of his booty. His expedition has proved a failure, and no doubt he had to destroy a large amount of his booty in Missouri. We are being reinforced here by General Elias Dennis' Division from Port Hudson and New Orleans. I think this augurs an early movement by General Steele in the spring on Price.

Back in Virginia, with Lee's and Grant's armies hunkered down for the long haul around Petersburg, a pesky problem persisted for both sides: fraternizing with the enemy. The siege's static positions kept Federals and Confederates in close proximity. Although both sides officially forbade it, there was brisk but illicit trading of Southern tobacco for Northern coffee, newspapers, and other items that soldiers often lacked.

However, those clandestine meetings did not always end well, as **George A. Spencer (1844–1914)**, a private in the 7th Rhode Island Infantry, told his parents.

Poplar Grove Church, Virginia
November 4, 1864

As the boys was exchanging papers day before yesterday [with Confederates], the brigade officer of the day came along. He would not let the boys change any more, but thought he would go and change, and the Rebs clawed [captured] him and took him to Richmond. The boys are all glad of it. He was a captain and belonged to the 36th Massachusetts.

Families of soldiers taken captive often had difficulty communicating with their loved ones. Consider the lengths that a woman in southern Alabama, identified only as **CLR (unknown),** went to in order to send a letter to her brother held in the Union's notorious prisoner-of-war camp at Johnson's Island in Lake Erie near Sandusky, Ohio.

Bladon Springs, Alabama
October 9, 1864

Mr. Ward and family leave for their plantation on the Mississippi River on the next boat, and he has kindly promised to have a letter mailed in Memphis for you, so I will have the sweet assurance that one of my numerous epistles will reach their destination. We have only received two of the eight you have written home. You have no idea how much your precious letters are prized by us all. They are our only source of pleasure in these dark days that try men's souls. Last night, I dreamed you was returned home, and I was in great trouble about your returning to the army.

Jimmie says Harry wants to go to Johnson's Island. I wish he was with you. All of the servants [slaves], as well as your many friends, are much concerned about you, so you see how much happiness you have at stake. I hope this will urge you to take good care of your health.

Papa received a letter from General William Hardee saying he had made special application for your exchange, but General Sherman replied he had no authority to exchange anyone not immediately under his control. General Hardee also wrote to L. B. Lippincott of Philadelphia to send you two hundred and fifty dollars. Papa thinks you had better draw it as you need it, as you can bring nothing from prison. I hope you will respond promptly to the general's letter. I feel we can never repay such kindness.

Time passed on slowly for men languishing in prison camps. **William Henry Luse (1837–1904)** was one of them. The lieutenant colonel in the 18th Mississippi Infantry was captured at Gettysburg and sent to Johnson's Island. He escaped on January 6, 1864, and was recaptured the next day. Luse wrote to Virginia Miller, a Southern sympathizer from a prominent Washington, D.C., family. (The entire text of the brief letter appears below; prisoners were limited to writing only one page. The original envelope bears a rubber stamp indicating that it was inspected by a military censor before being sent to Washington.)

Johnson's Island, Ohio
November 6, 1864

Both your last letters received. Have been forced to postpone writing longer than I should have; we have but two letter [writing] days per week, and as I have been so fortunate as to receive four or five letters directly from home, you can understand how anxious I am to write while there was such prompt mail facilities, and I know you will congratulate and pardon me.

Our friend, Capt. Joseph Sessions, was sent through a few days since with sickness. Have some hope of being exchanged soon myself in the same way, so you may judge my health is not good as has been. Lieutenant McCaskill of Colonel Erasmus Burt's old company wishes to know if you can send a letter to Leesburg, Virginia, for him. Remember me to your father's family and believe me your true friend.

Conditions inside prisoner-of-war camps were often almost as difficult for the guards as they were for the captives they watched over. Both sides deemed the camps of secondary importance when it came to distributing food and supplies. Consider what **Addison W. Tarr (1833–1917)**, a private in the 19th

Regiment Veterans Reserve Corps, described to his sister. He was a guard in the dead of winter at the prison camp in Elmira, New York, a place so terrible that it was nicknamed "Hellmira."

Elmira, New York
December 13, 1864

We are in this city guarding Rebels. We have about nine thousand prisoners here and expect to have a lot more very soon. Our duty is somewhat hard and discipline strict and rations very poor. We are living in tents now, and it is cold as the devil here. We have about six inches of snow on the ground. Some of the Rebs froze to death the other night. I woke up the other morning and found my blankets all covered with snow and froze stiff, so you see, we are getting a little of a soldier's life. But I am a little better off today than I was last week, for I have got my tent fixed up pretty well and have got a little stove in it. We have got the "A" tents. I have got a kitten in my tent to make it seem like home. I expect that we shall stay here all winter and we shall have pretty tough times.

We don't get enough to eat, and I have got an appetite like a hog and can eat raw pork or anything else I can get. I thought some of coming home this winter, but I guess that I shall stick it out until my time is up. Besides, I have no home to come to.

As horrific as conditions were in Northern prisons, they were often worse in those of the South. Hampered by few supplies and a poor transportation system, the guards and camp staff fared only marginally better than the men imprisoned here. Writing shortly after his release and return home, **John B. Freeman (1840–1868)**, a private in the 13th Michigan Infantry, recounted his ordeal in this letter to his family.

Roxanna, Michigan
June 27, 1865

I enjoy the opportunity of once more being in God's country and having the privilege to write what I like. I was a prisoner for a long time—from the twentieth of September '63 until the twenty-eighth of April '65. I was wounded and captured at the Battle of Chickamauga. I was wounded in the left shoulder and back so that I could not get away, or they would not have got me. I was then taken to Richmond and remained there until the 12th of December, then went to Danville, Virginia, and remained there until the fourteenth of April, except for a little while when I ran away. I got out of prison for 14 days and was very near to our lines.

We arrived at Andersonville [in southern Georgia] on the 20th of April, where I remained until I again ran away, was caught, and brought back and put in the prison. I run away from the hospital where I had been for 7 months. I then remained with the other prisoners until we came to our lines and a hard-looking set we was, of course, for we had wore the same old clothing for near two years—dirty, ragged, and lousy with naught to shelter us from the sun or storm—not even a blanket—nothing but the sand to lay on. It was not hard at all, was it? The second time I run away, I was caught by their hounds.

All the 21st Ohio boys that were in prison were with me, and many of them died. James Copus' boy, little Joe Copus, he left the hospital last fall. I told him when he left that if he got through, he should let you know about me as I was working in the hospital at that time and had something to do with the sick and dead. They died very fast. I have saw them carry out as high as 172 dead bodies in a day that died in 24 hours. Through July, August, and September, there was not a day passed, but there was 152 died. I must stop. I will send you a couple of songs that I helped to compose in prison.

One of the war's most unusual footnotes occurred on October 19, when nine Confederate soldiers raided the town of St. Albans, Vermont, near the U.S.–Canadian border. The goal was to divert troops from the front lines to protect the border from similar incursions. The raiders robbed three banks of $208,000 (more than $7.5 million today) and engaged in a gun battle with locals before retreating across the border. The attack was big news in the North, as **Ada Hubbard (1845–unknown)** told an acquaintance in the Federal army.

La Grange, Ohio
October 23, 1864

Rebels from Canada have made a raid into Vermont and done a great deal of damage. That is the second time they have been over to see what they could do. The first time, they tried to free the prisoners at Johnson's Island [prison camp], but they failed in that for they were too strongly fortified there. They thought they would try somewhere else next time.

In Georgia, meanwhile, the two sides spent several weeks recuperating after the bloody Atlanta Campaign. Ever audacious, Hood swung his army around the city and marched north, followed closely by Sherman, essentially retracing the movements they had made six months earlier in the opposite direction. That temporarily cut rail service to Chattanooga. For the second time in as many months, people in Atlanta were again facing hardship. Corporal **Charles Van Waggoner (1845–1913)**, 141st New York Infantry, decried conditions in the occupied city to a friend.

Atlanta, Georgia
October 29, 1864

We have been doing guard duty here in the city since the 29th of last month. There is four regiments of us doing this detached duty—the 107th New York, the 66th Ohio, the 19th Michigan, and ours. We are guarding commissary stuff. It is a very nice kind of duty—all indoor work. Our regiment is now in command of Capt. Elisha Baldwin. He is pretty strict with us, but I guess that it is all right.

We have not had but four mails in about three weeks now, for the whole of Hood's army got round in the rear and cut off our railroad communications. But Sherman, after the two pretty severe battles with him at Big Shanty Station, succeeded in driving him away again. But they had no more than got the track repaired again when they [the Confederates] cut it again between Tunnel Hill and Tilton, destroying about 30 miles of track.

So, there was no through trains for about three weeks, and there was not much provisions here to begin with, so it cut us pretty short. They reduced our rations by half. There was two trains loaded with provisions came in the first of the week, but there are so many mouths to feed besides the soldiers—that is the refugees—that things are getting mighty scarce again. But let the wide world wag as it will, we'll be gay and happy still.

I was to a concert here in Atlanta at the Theatre Rooms the other night. It was very good. It was given by the band of the 33rd Massachusetts Infantry.

I think it would do me good to see Theodore Spencer marching along under a knapsack about as large as a decent sized cook stove. He was one of those fine young chaps as was never a going to enlist. Which do you think it was that drew him out—a sense of duty to his country, or a large cash bounty?

Hood and Sherman then pulled back from each and went their separate ways. Sherman withdrew to Atlanta and made plans for his next movement, while Hood headed into northern Alabama and prepared for an offensive of his own. He would invade Tennessee.

When Confederate intentions became obvious in late October, Sherman dispatched the Army of the Ohio under the command of General John Schofield to join the Federal forces being mobilized to defend the major Union supply depot at Nashville. But it was an arduous journey.

As Corporal **Robert Bell Stewart (1839–after 1910)** of the 15th Ohio Infantry described to his sister, it also produced an odd parade of vehicles.

Pulaski, Tennessee
November 2, 1864

On the 2nd of October we were snugly and comfortably living in camp at Atlanta, unsuspecting of anything. Today, we are 260 miles from there by the way we have come. I expect we have marched a good 500 miles in all.

Very suddenly, late one wet morning before daylight—Thursday morning last—we got orders to march that evening. After a hard march of 20 miles through mud, we encamped at Alpine, Georgia. Only our corps was on the march in that direction. Next day, we marched to Lafayette, Georgia, over 20 miles, and on Saturday, we encamped at Cassville, four miles from Chattanooga, Tennessee. We were pretty sure we were coming to Chattanooga when we started but had no idea what for or where we would go from there but hoped we would stay there a few days at least. But arriving in town, there were engines and cars innumerable. I counted over 30 engines with steam ready. We started to think something was going to be done with us, and when our division marched around and loaded on the trains, we knew we were going somewhere.

Well, the cars started. Six trainloads of soldiers towards Stevenson, Alabama. We were not delayed any until we came near Bellefonte, Alabama. There, the tracks had just been cut by guerillas. So, we cooked supper while the track was being repaired. It was dark when we got started again, so wrapping my blanket around me I laid down. It was pretty hard sticking on sometimes as the top of the cars was not level, and I had nothing to put my feet against, but I stuck on as hundreds of others did and slept pretty well. It was a good wood, and we were not delayed any and went along I thought furiously sometimes.

We landed at Athens, Alabama, stacked arms, and got breakfast and were pretty sure that there we would stay a short time. About noon, we got orders to draw a very light day's rations, all there was to be had, and started for Pulaski, Tennessee, 33 miles north. We had all sorts of rumors about Generals Hood and Nathan Bedford Forrest, and the day before, Forrest attacked Decatur, Alabama, and was repulsed by the 12th U.S. Colored Troops. We marched that afternoon about 10 miles and encamped. Started next morning at 4½. Waded Elk River. It was awful cold, too, and deep. At Elkton we got onto a good pike.

We had neither wagons nor ambulances along with us nor any artillery. Only 60 rounds of cartridges and no grub. However, we captured three wagons, teams, and drivers trying to hide in the woods. These were brought along, and at Elkton, Tennessee, we gathered up more than a dozen wagons, buggies, carriages, etc., anything with wheels and would haul a soldier and knapsack so that by the time we arrived at Pulaski, we had quite a train all loaded. It was a curious looking sight: old horses and mules, old buggies and some nice ones too, all loaded with soldiers. There were a good many recruits with the regiment with tremendous knapsacks, as all recruits have. And 20 or 25 miles a day was too much for them. Our company was rearguard and had to keep up all stragglers. I think I could have got as many overcoats as I could have carried by just asking for them, but you never see an old soldier carrying an overcoat.

Then, the way the hogs did suffer. There were hundreds of good hogs in the country, and we had no meat. It was against orders to leave ranks, especially to go off and shoot hogs or get anything at all. It was the duty of the rearguard to prevent all this, but it was bang, bang, bang, bang and squeal all around us the whole day. Every time we would halt there would be a lot of boys coming up with pieces of hog stuck on their guns or thrown over their shoulders. If they could not carry the whole hog, they would take the best portions of it and leave the rest. By night, everyone had plenty of fresh pork.

We got to Pulaski by 3 o'clock p.m., having marched 24 hours. We have heard nothing from Sherman since leaving Chattanooga. We are now under General George Thomas, independent of Sherman. I do not know whether our whole corps will come here or not. There is none but our division here yet.

This town has been a real Secesh nest but what difference does that make to us? I guess they are very well satisfied with Yankee rule. It is about 80 miles by railroad to Nashville, so we are in close communication with the outside world. It was good news we had from Sheridan a few days ago

[Battle of Cedar Creek]. But it was nearly a serious disaster. Only a few days until the election. The Rebel army down here, whoever commands it, is doing all it can to trouble Sherman and spoil the election. It is electioneering for McClellan, but I do not think it will gain many votes.

As Stewart indicated, November brought one of the war's most important developments. It happened not on a battlefield but at the ballot box, as Second Lieutenant **Thomas Munhall (1841–1893)** of the 11th Illinois Cavalry indicated; he even suggested a radical idea for the time.

Vicksburg, Mississippi
November 7, 1864

Tomorrow is Election Day, and oh! what a responsibility is resting on the voters in the North. Perhaps the fate of our nation is resting upon them. We have gained many brilliant victories in the field, but the one which will be gained tomorrow will surpass all. There is no doubt in my mind who will be elected. Lincoln will receive the largest majority which has been given to any president for a number of years. Tis too bad that the Illinois soldiers have not the privilege of voting. I think, in this case, the ladies should be permitted to vote; what say you?

Lincoln was indeed reelected the next day by the comfortable margin that Munhall had predicted. For the first time in American history, soldiers from half of the Northern states were allowed to vote in the field. As Private **George C. Marsh (1832–1865)** of the 1st Michigan Sharpshooters wrote to his brother two days later, that played an important role in securing Lincoln's victory. (He was killed in action less than six months later.)

Camp near South Side Railroad, Virginia
November 10, 1864

I received your letter today and am glad to hear that you are all well and you are a true Union man. The election passed off very quietly here, and I think that the boys have done pretty well for Honest Old Abe. I will give you the figures of every regiment but one in the 2nd Brigade.

	Lincoln	McClellan
1st Mich. SS	*91*	*37*
2nd Mich.	*60*	*21*
20th Mich.	*121*	*34*
60th Ohio	*93*	*41*
50th Pa.	*79*	*36*
	444	*169 = 275 Union majority*

I see by the papers that your state has probably gone Republican. It is quite still times here now, and we have not had much fighting lately, and they are building log huts for winter quarters. Six Rebels gave themselves up and came into our camp this morning, and I think more will follow their example.

Lincoln's reelection meant that the war would continue until the North won. Abolitionists read something more in the victory, as Isaac Taylor of the 3rd Minnesota explained in the letter mentioned earlier.

The good news we have received—Lincoln is elected—triumphantly elected. Slavery is forever dead, and through the patriotism and energy of our people, the Union will now be restored. This will be a dreary winter for Rebels. Lincoln has enough power in his hands now to crush this rebellion. He has an overwhelming majority in both houses of Congress. Nearly every state in the hands of the administration [Republican] party, and a thunderous majority of the people ratifying his present administration will all give him a power hard to resist. And more than all this, he is laboring in a righteous cause. The most cheering of all is that the Border Slave States are fast wheeling into line, and will all soon be able to dress in line with the most ultra Abolition States. Copperheads will, in a very few years, deny that they were ever anything but abolitionists. The Negro may not and will not be much benefitted by the change, but the country will be ten-fold better off.

With Lincoln's presidency now secured, it guaranteed that the North would continue fighting. Sherman moved ahead with his plans to "make Georgia howl." In mid-November, he burned Atlanta to the ground, then launched his 62,000-man army on his infamous March to the Sea. Writing shortly after the campaign's conclusion, a Union sergeant identified only as **Jonathan (unknown)** described the widespread destruction to his siblings in California.

Camp at Savannah, Georgia
January 21, 1865

We left Atlanta on the 16th of November. Had a very pleasant march, it being such good weather. We had to carry in our knapsacks three days' rations and everything to cook with. This regiment had to build roads for the wagons and destroy railroads. We destroyed over 100 miles, burned the ties, and twisted the iron. We destroyed everything. Burnt the houses, barns, cotton and corn, killed all the hogs, chickens and turkeys to eat, and drove off all the cattle, mules and horses so there is not much left. Now, we want to go through South Carolina and do a little worse there.

"Sherman's Bummers," as his men called themselves, took particular pleasure in torching the homes of prominent Southerners. They included the residence of such eminent Georgians as Howell Cobb (a former governor, U.S. Treasury secretary, Speaker of the U.S. House of Representatives, U.S. senator, and president of the Provisional Confederate Congress) and Herschel Vespasian Johnson (another former governor and U.S. and Confederate senator as well as John C. Breckinridge's running mate in the 1860 presidential election).

Andrew Beach Coffinberry (1837–1907), a captain in the 1st Michigan Engineers and Mechanics Regiment, gleefully recounted the wanton wholesale destruction along with the fighting as Sherman neared the Atlantic coast.

Savannah, Georgia
January 1, 1865

We had a great deal of sport in the South and were very fortunate with all our hardships. Poor Warren Heald was left at Ogeechee Church near where the Little Ogee meets the Ogeechee River. He had not been well before leaving Atlanta but was unable to keep up with the regiment. He died Dec. 6 of fever and diarrhea. Dec. 10, a brave boy of Company H fell victim before a Reb battery 4 miles from the city. It is a great wonder no more were killed. They shelled us some little time. We were in an exposed position where they had good range. I was within a few feet of Robert Brown when he fell—he has two brothers in the company.

We have had a long, tedious march and our way from Atlanta here is marked by many piles of ruins—villages, plantations, houses, barns, cotton presses, etc. being laid in ruins while the "iron ribbons" over which the Rebs used to ride and move their armies and supplies are twisted into augurs, the ties burned, and all bridges destroyed.

I had the pleasure of eating peanuts and sorghum at the plantation of Howell Cobb and then seeing it burn. That is the houses, quarters, etc., of which there were many. I had chicken and sweet potatoes from H. V. Johnson's farm, and then we sacked the place.

Four weeks later, Sherman's army reached its objective. **Lewis Buckley (1842–1915),** a private in the 68th Ohio Volunteer Infantry, wrote about it to a lady friend at home.

Near Savannah, Georgia
December 14, 1864

We started from Atlanta on the 14th of November and came here on the 4th of December. We are now lying in the rear of Savannah. We have surrounded the city, and they are sieging at it. I think that this won't last long before they take the place. They can't stand those large guns that they have playing on them.

There is lots of fun here in the army. The Rebels, they send a shell now and then, and the boys have a good time dodging shells that the Johnnies send over. I was to the river yesterday and saw a boat that runs on the ocean. I never saw one before this time.

In Tennessee, the race was on for Nashville and its massive storehouse of supplies. Hood's underfed and ill-equipped army headed north from Tuscumbia, Alabama. The Confederates nearly cut off Schofield's withdrawal to join Thomas at Spring Hill, which involved one of the most bizarre incidents of the entire war. A large contingent of Hood's army was lined on hills along one side of the Columbia Turnpike leading to Franklin, Tennessee, the only route available to Schofield's troops. On the night of November 29, the blue soldiers literally passed directly in front of the Confederates, who—incredibly—were not ordered to attack. Writing about it a few days later, Corporal **Robert Bell Stewart** of the 15th Ohio Infantry could scarcely believe what had happened.

Nashville, Tennessee
December 3, 1864

After dark, we withdrew. When we came along about midnight, the Rebel line was within 500 yards of the road. We could see them quite plainly. Our two divisions passed by them without being disturbed—whether they were afraid to attack us or whether they thought they were getting us in a fix, I do not know. At any rate, it was one of the strangest things I have seen during the war. Some officers told us they were Rebels, but we could not believe it at all. But we found out afterward that it was so.

After passing by the Rebel camp a mile or so, we halted, having come onto our train. If anything ever deserved cursing or got cursing, it was that train. I do not think there was a man who would have fought to save the train. Well, we built a hasty barricade and, at three o'clock, lay down to sleep. Got started again at daylight. Rebels appeared on our flanks and came within gunshot. Just ahead of us, they pitched onto the train and destroyed several wagons. They were soon driven off but hung on our flanks until we reached Franklin. Here, we stopped for breakfast, and our division crossed the Harpeth River and formed a line where we lay till evening. The Rebels, in the meantime, had come up and formed their line.

And so the stage was set for the brief but bloody Battle of Franklin on November 30. Six Confederate generals were killed while leading a series of furious assaults in a pyrrhic victory for the South. Robert Bell Stewart continued detailing what happened.

You have heard of the Battle of Franklin. Our division was not engaged, but we could see the whole thing until the smoke hid everything from our sight. It was a very bloody repulse to the Rebels who thought to carry everything before them, and how near their desperate bravery was to being successful, the thousands dead and wounded tell. Nothing but the stern invincibility of our troops prevented the destruction of our small army and the loss of Nashville and its stores.

About 4 o'clock, they moved to the attack. We were in a good position to see, but the smoke shut out all but the deep, continuous roar. Until dark, the battle raged. Then, the sound ceased. We knew the Rebels had gained nothing. Our brigade had to cover the retreat that night. We moved down to the bridge, and there waited till the whole army had crossed. Then, as soon as the pickets were all across, we fired the bridge and awaited to see it burn. Before we left, however, the Rebels had come onto the opposite bank, and after a while, a volley was fired into them, and we set off in a hurry.

Stewart and the other Federals reached the safety of Nashville and Thomas's army the following day. There, they dug in and prepared for yet another battle, as he reported in yet another letter home.

Nashville, Tennessee
December 6, 1864

We are engaging ourselves in making it hard for the Rebels. Their line in front of us is within 600 yards. No other place is within gunshot. We keep batteries playing on them here all the time, and they have to keep very low; they use no artillery at all. I cannot think what Hood's objective is. He certainly does not intend to seize the place. Any attempt to capture it by storm would be a worse failure and greater slaughter than Franklin. I think he has a nut to crack that is going to hurt his army.

Regular details of citizens and clerks and government employees are kept at work all the time, with a great many citizens volunteering to work.

It was amusing out here last Sabbath. Many citizens thought a good place to spend the day would be on the lines looking at the Rebels, but no sooner were they out here than they were furnished with spades and picks and set to work in their fine clothes and all. A couple of fancy young clerks with their ladies in fine tack drove up to the first line from the city and were halted and set to work for an hour on the promise that they would be permitted to go to the frontline where they could get a good view of the Johnnies.

So, they worked their hour fruitfully and proceeded on their way, rejoicing. But no sooner had they arrived at the desired spot than a gentlemanly guard with a bayonet took them in charge, furnished them with tools, and sent them to work. After an hour or so, they were told that by going to yet another place, they could get a splendid view of the Rebels, but they had seen enough and drove back to town.

A bitter ice storm struck Nashville the next day. When the weather improved on December 15, Thomas attacked. He pushed back Hood, then prepared to deliver a knockout blow on December 16.

When the action resumed that day, **Luther Lee Parks (1837–1864),** Second Lieutenant in the 13th USCT, wrote to his wife as the fighting raged around him. What makes his letter extraordinary is that he wrote up until he was killed in action, barely 30 minutes after finishing his final sentence. It is an exceptionally rare example of a soldier describing the very battle in which he died as it was happening.

In Line of Battle 2½ miles from
[the state] Capitol Nashville 12 PM
December 16, 1864

We have advanced 1½ miles from our position this morning. Our skirmishers are ½ mile in our front. Our regiment has not yet been engaged except for the skirmishing company. The battle has been heavy on the right within ¼ mile of us. Our brigade battery has thrown some shells and shot. The 13th, being the right of our brigade, rests upon the Franklin Railroad and ¼ mile east of the Franklin Pike. The Rebels are retreating, and all goes well. We are looking for a decided victory.

The hardest fighting has been on the right flank. There is much artillery and occasionally heavy musketry. I judge from the direction of the firing at this moment that we are turning the enemy's left flank. If we succeed in doing so, they will be badly whipped between the Franklin Pike and the Cumberland River.

1 PM

We have advanced one mile, and for the last ½ hour our brigade's line has been under heavy fire of artillery. Our skirmishers are at work. Shot and shell dropped around us, and thank God we are all safe. We (the brigade except skirmishers) are lying down, and our artillery has ceased only to move out. I have confidence in my company. They say they will not disgrace themselves. Whiz, there goes another shell. Came over but went by. Too hot to write more now.

2 PM

In the same position but will move up immediately. Skirmishers relieved, and others moving to the advance. Constant artillery from our guns but little reply except by musketry. In a few moments, I think we will be engaged in a terrible battle. God protect the right and give victory to our arms.

The Battle of Nashville was one of the most conclusive victories of the entire war. The Army of Tennessee was effectively destroyed as a potent fighting force. What remained of it limped back southward, with General Joseph Johnston soon returning as its commander once more. **John W. Houtaling (1836–1905),** a private in the 95th Illinois Infantry, updated his wife during a pause in the Federal pursuit.

Duck River, Tennessee
December 23, 1864

Well, Kate, the battle is fought, and the victory is ours. We have fought Mr. Hood & Co. in his fortifications and scooped him high and dry with a very small loss on our side for the amount of troops that were engaged. The 95th Illinois had only one man wounded in the regiment. The battle commenced the morning of the 15th of December and ended the night of the 16th, but still, we are after him yet and are taking prisoners every day. Hood has lost some 12 or 15 thousand men killed and wounded and prisoners. Our loss is probably 15 hundred in killed and wounded.

We are about thirty miles from Nashville now. Left there on the 17th and have been on the road ever since. But today, we lay over. The weather is somewhat cold. The ground is frozen quite hard. It has rained and snowed every day (except today) since we started out. We are not out of the sound of cannon yet. I can hear the booming towards the Tennessee River. I expect we will leave here tomorrow morning. There is a very large army now on the move.

Kate, I have had another streak of bad luck on this march. I have lost my knapsack with all my clothes and little necessaries, besides your photograph and five of my own, and my detail papers, and everything except what clothes I have on, and these is the poorest I had for I knew we was going on a march and it was very muddy. I suppose you will say, "Well, if you cannot take care of my likeness, I won't send you any more." Well Kate, I think it was stolen off the wagon by someone. I may possibly find it yet, but I don't have much hope.

In Virginia, the siege of Petersburg dragged into its sixth dreary month with no end in sight. Eighteen-year-old Private **Morgan Horfius (1846–1903)** of the 211th Pennsylvania Infantry related to his parents how arriving at the front was a jarring experience.

Camp near Petersburg, Virginia
December 2, 1864

It is a curious place. There has been a big fight here since the war broke out, and the graves are thick as can be. In some places, the dead men's feet is sticking out of the ground. It is a sickening sight. God grant it will soon be over.

Since I last wrote we have been on the march and I hadn't time to write. We went first to Petersburg, then to the extreme left of the line, which is about 7 miles left of here where we were put into the Ninth Corps. Then we marched back here, which is about 2 miles to the right of Petersburg and only half a mile from the Rebel line. There is a railroad runs from City Point to the front of our line, and it is only a short distance from our camp to it. We don't know when we will have to leave here. The report is that we belong to the corps which is going to Charleston, South Carolina. Burnside is the commander of ours, and he won't fight in Virginia. As soon as I know where we are bound, I will write to you again.

For many veteran soldiers, those who had served two or three years, the war was growing increasingly weary. Some also became deeply cynical and sarcastic as a result. For example, consider what **Frank Haynes (unknown),** a private in the 1st Maine Veteran Volunteer Infantry, wrote to his cousin.

Camp in the field near Petersburg, Virginia
December 21, 1864

I am out here in this Great American Nigger Show and can't say as I like the performance any too well. But don't expect to get out before my time is up. Haven't had any fightin' yet. Was out on picket guard the other day. Saw a lot of the Johnnies. They wanted us to go over and get some whiskey, but we did not see fit to take up with [accept] the invitation. A lot of niggers came in right from Petersburg. They said the Rebs was on the point of starvation again for the 999th time. Probably, if they are, they will capture a lot of our trains next.

There was a report in camp last night that old Jeff Davis was dead. If that is so and Old Abe will go do likewise, there may be some prospect of peace. I find that the soldiers are not so full of fight here as when they are at home. I hope if there is another call for men, those that voted for the war [Lincoln's reelection] will respond, young and old.

If any of you are so lucky as to be drafted, get a substitute by all means. For a man is not used as well as a dog until he gets to his regiment, then it is not much better. I have seen the time since I started in this show that a hog pen would be a paradise compared to this.

The year's final days saw two momentous events. One occurred on December 23, which **Isaac Rowe (unknown)** shared with his brother.

Black River, New York
December 25, 1864

We are having very good news from the army, and we have just heard of the occupation of Savannah, Georgia by Sherman. The leading men of this state think we are seeing the beginning of the end of the rebellion. Some say it will not last over six weeks. So might it be. I shall be glad when this rebellion is crushed, and it looks to me that the end is at hand. Copperheads here are as tame as kittens.

The other took place on the Atlantic coast, where the Federals were focused on closing the port at Wilmington, North Carolina, the Confederacy's last link to the world. From its docks, blockade-runners carrying cotton departed for Europe and returned filled with desperately needed arms and supplies. Outside the city, powerful Fort Fisher guarded the approach on the Cape Fear River.

On Christmas Eve and continuing on Christmas Day, the North launched a coordinated land–sea assault to capture the massive fortification. But as this letter from an **unknown Union naval officer** to a friend shows, things didn't go as planned.

USS Vicksburg
Off Wilmington, North Carolina
January 1, 1865

We have had some very lively times down here of late, the attempted capture of Wilmington, but which proved a <u>total failure</u>.

We left Fortress Monroe (in Virginia) on the 10th inst. and met a fleet of about 80 ships of war engaged in bombarding Fort Fisher, which guards one of the entrances to Wilmington. We joined in immediately and, after a heavy cannonading from the fleet, drove the enemy from the fort. General

Benjamin Butler's troops had previously landed a short distance north of the fort, and it was their turn now to march into and take possession of the works. But for some unaccountable reason, he refused to cooperate and would not let his troops hold the fort, and as a natural consequence, the fleet ceased their firing, and the Rebs entered their fort again.

All behaved well during the fight, as far as I could see, for my station during an engagement is about six feet below the water line, and you may depend on it, I remained as cool as a cucumber, for I was certain that a ball could not come into close proximity with my worthy person. I managed to gather up enough Dutch courage during the fight to go on the gun deck on two occasions. But I made my visits as short as possible as I had no particular relish for the smell of powder or the whistling of the bombs. I have charge of the steam pumps during action, and I had about 50 offers from the other engineers to exchange stations, but knowing I was in a safe part of the ship, I respectfully declined to accept their generous offers.

I have a very small opinion of General Butler, and it is known that the cock-eyed beast never did any good wherever he went, save ill-treating women and stealing, for which he is talented.

Blood-soaked 1864 limped to a close. Tens of thousands of families on both sides had one fewer relative that holiday season.

It had been a grueling, gruesome year. It had also been a very close call. The North's will to carry on the fight was pushed to the breaking point in August, only to rebound dramatically by November.

The Union would not give up, and the Confederacy would not surrender, so they headed into the coming year with each side determined to hold on until the bitter end unaware—despite all they had been through—just how bitter the end would be.

1865

"I wonder what it all meant."

THE WAR'S FINAL YEAR COMMENCED AMID BRIGHT OPTIMISM IN THE NORTH and dark determination in the South. Having held on so desperately for so long, there seemed no alternative to either side but to see the conflict through to its conclusion. The question was swiftly shifting from how the war would end to when and where the finale would come.

For the Federals, it was a stunning change of fortune. Just six months earlier, it had seemed distinctly possible that war-weariness might determine the outcome. Yet as January commenced, many Northerners were still mentally processing the sweeping turn of events.

Benjamin Shaw (unknown), a Quaker working in the Adjutant General's Office in Washington, was among them. Writing to a friend in Pennsylvania, he seemed almost in awe of all that had happened.

Washington, D.C.
January 15, 1865

I have not yet congratulated thee upon the brightness of the dawn of the New Year to the nation soon to be followed, let us hope, by the perfect day, never to be clouded by the darkness.

How we have grown in the year that has just died. Its dawn was contained with doubt and doom. New disaster followed delay, and "hope deferred" was beginning to induce that sickness of heart which even the patriot at times cannot withstand. Rosecrans at Chattanooga, Seymour at Olustee, and Banks in Louisiana had dashed our fondest hopes. At almost every point, our __armed__ enemies were exultant and defiant giving argument to the __unarmed__ opposition in our midst [Copperheads], which soon began to organize and clamor for peace. How it plotted treason is well known. Loyalty feared, and from good causes too, that the results of the approaching contest at the ballot box would bind it hand and foot and deliver it to its enemies.

Now, thanks to God, came the turning point. The courageous virtue and patient hope of the nation revived. Earnest, loyal, good men begged for victories in the field, and our armies were put in motion. Sherman commenced his triumphant march to Atlanta, and Grant plunged into the Wilderness through which his eagle eye discerned the Rebel capital. Then came the series of battles and victories which will cause the name of Sheridan to be remembered as long as the Shenandoah waters its valley. Lastly, Sherman gives us Savannah and Thomas Hood winks the unlucky Rebel general, which were more than we needed, for in the meantime, we had peacefully at the ballot box reelected our freedom's standard bearer [Lincoln] and shown the undo the strength of republican institutions.

I have another victory as important as any, though bloodless, the casting off of the bondsman's shackles [slavery] in Maryland, so lately followed by Missouri and Tennessee, and which herald the universal manumission of all the oppressed by which the present Congress will consecrate its last hours. Can anyone who is loyal to himself and country but rejoice over the years work or fail to read the inevitable future of our nation—regenerated eternal?

The North resumed its effort to capture important Fort Fisher outside Wilmington, North Carolina. The fiasco there two weeks earlier made an infuriated Grant relieve General Benjamin Butler for failing to follow orders. After being replaced by the more reliable General Alfred Terry, Butler then rushed to Washington to explain himself to the Joint Committee on the Conduct of the War. (Although with Lincoln's reelection secure, radical Republicans in Congress were now more disinclined than ever to coddle inept political generals.)

As Terry and Admiral David Dixon Porter prepared for a second joint land–sea assault, **James J. Tarleton (1827–1900),** a Southern businessman inside Wilmington, clearly saw the writing on the wall, as he related to a friend in Florida.

Wilmington, North Carolina
January 15, 1865

I regret to return you unfavorable news about an adventure in cotton for your friend Burns, as it pays better than anything else. But the freight room on ships is eagerly taken up by parties interested in the steamers [blockade-runner owners], and there is no chance for outsiders. The Yanks, however, have again landed here and are entrenched on [nearby Confederate] Point. They siege Fort Fisher, where they are burrowing like rabbits. I have little hope of driving them away. This will stop business here as they command the Cape Fear River even without taking Ft. Fisher.

The only remittance I can recommend [for exchange] is sterling [silver], and that is at very high rates. Should he propose to do so, he can remit the money to me by express, and I will endeavor to invest it and remit as he may direct; if not through here, I can get it out through Charleston.

On the very day those words were being written, two important things happened. First, Butler testified to Congress that he hadn't attacked Fort Fisher because it was—in his words—"impregnable." Second, while he was offering that excuse, news of the fortification's capture arrived. Butler left Capitol Hill with egg on his face, and the Confederacy was now cut off from the world.

Mamie Bates (1838–1919) recognized that Butler was in dire straits in this letter penned three days later to her husband in the Union army. She also noted the passing of the man remembered for speaking for two hours at the dedication of Gettysburg National Cemetery just before Abraham Lincoln's famous two-minute address.

East Brighton, Massachusetts
January 18, 1865

Butler has got himself pretty well into a scrape, hasn't he? Fort Fisher is captured, and so much more is gained while Butler is stating his reasons for not taking it is the work is done. It seems as though it is about time for the Rebels to give up the contest. We still have some strong forts to take before Wilmington is reached, but what will the Rebs do without Wilmington for supplies?

The funeral of the Honorable Edward Everett takes place tomorrow, and I suppose it will call together a large number of people. I would like to go to the funeral, but I dislike a crowd—unless you are with me.

David T. T. Litchfield (1842–1869), a musician in the 134th Massachusetts Infantry, wrote to his mother how word of Fort Fisher's capture caused celebration in Union ranks surrounding Petersburg.

Camp Holly, Virginia
January 22, 1865

*I wish you could have heard the firing about here on the day the news came
that Fort Fisher had been taken. It sounded like a perfect roar of thunder. All
the bands in the department were ordered to play.*

The exchange of prisoners resumed in late January after having been suspended for nine months. A Union soldier identified only as **George (unknown)**
witnessed a prisoner swap in progress from a distance in Virginia. He also wrote
to his sister about having visited both a captured Confederate warship and a
Federal one that had participated in the attack on Fort Fisher. (Mentioning the
latter two months after the fortification's capture indicates Northerners' pride in
the victory.)

Defenses Bermuda 100, Virginia
Bermuda Front
March 10, 1865

*Since I began scribbling, I have seen a good deal. I was on the lookout or sig-
nal station tower that is 130 feet from the ground, and we had to go all the
way by ladder. I could see the church spires in the city of Richmond. I would
see a Rebel gunboat quite plain with the naked eye. Then I looked through the
glass and would see them exchanging prisoners. I would see very plain the
Rebel gunboat that our boats sunk while we were home on furlough.*

I have been on board the gunboat Saugus. *It was built after the style of
the* Monitor *and carries two large guns—one weighs 41,330 pounds and
the other 41,310. The smallest one of the two I crawled into. I went in so far
that I could not get myself out. The boys caught hold of my heels and pulled me
out. I wanted to say that I was in the gun that knocked (or helped to) Fort
Fisher into a mess. They are awful guns.*

*Then we got in a boat and rowed alongside the large [captured] Rebel
ram* Atlanta. *The captain wanted us to go aboard, so we went nearly all
through her. She is a very large craft, built just like the old Rebel* Merrimack.
*We stood out on deck in sight of the Johnnies and in range well, I might say,
under the Rebel Howlett House Battery and played "The Star Spangled
Banner," "Hail Columbia," "Yankee Doodle," and several more airs. But the
Johnnies did not care to shoot at us. I guess they didn't want to wake up our
gunboats, for they are a rough plaything when once set to going.*

With the war's end approaching, some widows in the North were encountering bureaucratic headaches when they applied for a pension. In certain cases, it was difficult if not impossible to document what had happened to their husbands as required by law. The lawyer representing one of them reached out to Dr. **William Johnson Dale (1815–1903)**, surgeon general of Massachusetts, for help cutting through the red tape. His response shows the challenges applicants sometimes encountered. (Thomas Taber, a corporal in the 16th Massachusetts Infantry, was captured at the Battle of Mine Run and died at Andersonville Prison on or about October 9, 1864, from "scurvy and want of food and proper treatment." His death was confirmed in a sworn statement from a comrade also confined there.)

Commonwealth of Massachusetts
Office of Surgeon General, Boston
January 7, 1865

I have the honor to inform you in answer to your communication of December 14, 1864, a memo of which we put on file, that we have a report of the death in Rebel prison at Andersonville, Georgia, of Thomas Tarbox, Co. E, 16th Mass. Vols. October 19, 1864. We have examined the muster in rolls of Co. E, 16th Regiment on file in the Adjutant General's Office and find that there is no such name as Tarbox on those rolls. We regret to inform you that, in our opinion, this name is wrongly reported by the exchanged prisoners who furnished our agents with the information, and we think the report may mean Thomas Taber instead of Tarbox.

We asked the editor and reporters of the Boston Herald *(which paper published an account of Taber's death) where they obtained the information but were unable to ascertain that fact. We would recommend that you address Lieut. Col. Gardiner Tufts, Massachusetts Agent at Washington D.C., who perhaps may be able to furnish you with some additional information.*

With a combined total of more than 3.2 million men in uniform during the war, both governments were deluged with correspondence, desperately seeking information on missing loved ones. The letters they received in return often contained news the family did not want to hear.

Consider **Joseph Richards (unknown)** of Pittsburgh, Pennsylvania. His son James was drafted in the first week of 1864 and mustered into a heavy artillery battery. When Grant became general-in-chief, he turned many of those units into infantry regiments and marched them off to fight. James Richards was captured at the Battle of Cedar Creek, Virginia, on October 19. When his father did not hear from him, he wrote to Washington and was answered with the following form letter.

War Department
Adjutant General's Office
Washington, February 2, 1865

In reply to your communication of the 27th of January, 1865, I have the honor to inform you that James M. Richards of Co. H., 5th Regt. N.Y. Hy. Arty. Volunteers appears, from the latest information received at this Office (dated December 31, 1864), to be as follows:

> *Prisoner of War Oct. 1864*
> *~~A letter will reach him if directed to:~~*
> *I am, very respectfully,*
> *Your obedient servant,*
> *Sam'l. Breck*
> *Assistant Adjutant General*

(Four days after Breck's letter was written, James Richards died in the Confederate prison camp in Salisbury, North Carolina.)

In the war's final months, the Lincoln administration continued emphasizing the abolition of slavery as its motive for waging war. But not all Union soldiers supported that. They included **Jacob D. Row (1835–1910)**. The LaPorte, Indiana, resident had been drafted in September 1864 and became an unwilling private in the 17th Indiana Cavalry. He spent most of his time in uniform, "playing off" as he called it, and spelled out his intentions in this letter to his wife.

Cavalry Corps Hospital
Gallatin, Tennessee
January 22, 1865

I am still in the hospital, and I am perfectly well and hearty. I do not know where my regiment is now, and I don't care, neither. I am satisfied if they keep me in the hospital, and if they sent me to my regiment, I tell you I shall not stay with it long. The first chance I get, I will parch a lot of corn in salty grease and eat a good deal of it, and that will make me the diarrhea. Then, I will get the piles again. Then I will tell the doctor it is altogether from riding so that he will send me back to the hospital again. I am bound not to do Lincoln much good in regard of freeing the Negroes if I can help it.

In late January, many people began saying the word they longed to hear above all others: peace. Francis Blair Sr. was an aging Washington insider. (He had been part of Andrew Jackson's informal "Kitchen Cabinet," and Blair House across from the White House was his home.) With one son who had been Lincoln's first postmaster general and another a Federal general, he was close to the Union president. Blair persuaded Lincoln to allow him to visit the Confederate president in hopes of negotiating an end to the conflict, which he followed up with a second trip. **Sylvester "Sly" Rounds (1843–1899),** a private in the Veteran Reserve Corps, mentioned it to his sister.

Trenton, New Jersey
January 24, 1865

I see Old Blair has gone off to Richmond again. I can't see into his frequent visits to Old Jeff Davis. It means something, but whether it will ever amount to anything or not is more than I can tell. I wouldn't wonder that any moment, peace commissioners would be appointed, and before we know it, the South would be back again in the Union. I believe the hard fighting for this war has been done. Now, it is coming to a fight of words more than blows, and after that comes peace.

As Rounds suspected, Lincoln and Davis agreed to a conference, the first and only such meeting of the entire war. Negotiators met on February 3, 1865, aboard the steamboat *River Queen* in Hampton Roads, Virginia. Lincoln and Secretary of State William H. Seward, representing the Union, sat down with Confederate commissioners Vice President Alexander H. Stephens, Senator Robert M. T. Hunter, and Assistant Secretary of War John A. Campbell. Although the talks were cordial, the delegates could not find terms that each side could accept to end the fighting. The meeting ended with no results.

Writing from South Carolina, **Mary Barclay Kirby (1811–1891)** discussed it in the following two letters to her son, a young officer serving on her nephew General Kirby Smith's staff in Shreveport, Louisiana, 750 miles away. With thousands of Union troops between them, Confederate mail service was disrupted, and Kirby's letters had to be carried by hand.

Columbia, South Carolina
January 27, 1865

It has been a long time since we heard from you and still longer since we have had any opportunity of writing you. Today, as I left the Treasury office, Sue Johnson told me she could send a letter by a friend of hers who will leave Monday for Shreveport who will be the bearer of this.

How do you feel about Confederate prospects across the Mississippi River? Everything on this side has looked dark for the past month. The fall of Savannah and Sherman's march through Georgia with so much ease have caused the people of South Carolina to feel rather uneasy about their state. I very much fear that Charleston will next be prey to Yankee rule. Today, the rumor is that we are to have an armistice of six days and that England and France are going to recognize us on the Fourth of March. But I have long since ceased to put much faith in any help from them. I think all help must now come from a higher power.

Columbia, South Carolina
January 30, 1865

We hear many rumors about peace today. I understand three commissioners have gone to Washington to try and bring about some measure to that effect. God grant they may succeed. They are Hunter of Virginia, Stephens of Georgia, and Campbell of Alabama.

I wrote you hurriedly, my precious boy, a few days ago, but hearing today that Major Douglas would leave for the other side [of the Mississippi River] and knowing you were with him, I thought I would write a few lines to enclose you some Richmond papers received here today. They are not as late [recent] as I could wish, but I thought you might find something interesting in them. The mails are so irregular, Major Douglas will be able to give you all the late news about recognition [of the Confederacy by Britain and France], etc.

We received a letter from your sister Helen. They had all been sick. She with a sore throat, and the doctor also was laid up. I think I told you a shell passed through his house. I wonder how he feels now about the war since the Yankees paid him such a visit?

People in the North likewise waited to learn what the talk of peace might produce. **Frank Smitt (unknown)** wrote this letter to a friend serving in the army.

Newport, New Hampshire
February 11, 1865

I do earnestly hope that these rumors of peace may amount to something defi-nite and real, but I fear, very much fear, that they will not. What think you?

Yesterday, for the first time, I saw a person who has been held as a pris-oner by the Rebels. His name is Davis. He was connected with the Ninth Regiment, and last spring, he was taken prisoner. He was at Andersonville for seven months and, as a consequence of exposure and lack of care, food, and clothing, he became very ill. He was exchanged late in the autumn or early in winter and reached his brothers in Croydon, New Hampshire. The first few times father saw him, he had not the faintest hope of his recovery. But he began to improve and has continued. Poor fellow; he looked as though his sufferings had been great. Isn't it awful to think of the suffering and woe that this war brings? I suppose the half is not known—nor will be till the day when all things are revealed.

The Union's vastly superior numbers finally forced the South to take a step that had been unimaginable at the start of the war. By February 1865, the Confederate Congress was considering allowing black slaves to serve as soldiers. The measure would become official in March. By then, it was too late to make a difference.

Arming slaves was a highly divisive issue within both the Confederacy itself and its army. One soldier who strongly opposed it was **Benjamin H. Anthony (1836–1910)**, a private in the 11th Virginia Infantry. Writing from the trenches at Petersburg, Anthony also suggested to his younger brother that he join the partisan rangers led by Colonel John S. Mosby, who led raids behind Federal lines.

Petersburg, Virginia
February 22, 1865

How do you like the idea of putting Negroes in the field? Of course, you are opposed to it, which any sensible man ought to be. Company B was in a furor, and two months ago, they swore by all that was good and holy that they would leave the day that Negroes was put in the field.

I see from the papers that you will have to go into the army. If I was you, I would go to Mosby immediately. You know that I would like to have you here with me, but you will not be half as much exposed to enemy fire as you would be here. I wish I had gone the day I started to Camp Lee [in Richmond] as a great many did. But I was foolish, and consequently, I have got to tough it out here.

Just three days later, Mosby's operations were mentioned in this letter home from an **unidentified Union soldier** writing from outside Washington. It came as Grant was amassing men for a new season of fighting.

Camp Briggs, Virginia
February 25, 1865

Our commencing active operations again in all the armies and warm times may be expected before long. One of the trainloads of recruits that went down to the front the other day was fired into by some of Mosby's gang, but no damage was done. Of course, I was not on board, but some of the boys of our company were. We expect to be detailed before night for the front again.

With spring's arrival, people on both sides prepared for the resumption of active campaigning in the field—and for the casualties that would inevitably accompany it. The challenge was doubly difficult in the Confederacy, where manpower, materiel, and other vital resources were rapidly dwindling. Communication was disintegrating, too. Many Southerners clung to one last desperate hope: European intervention on the Southern side, as expressed by this **unidentified Confederate officer**.

Macon, Georgia
March 2, 1865

Not pleased with military status of affairs at present. Still hoping something will turn up from "above" or across the waters that will deliver us as children of Israel.
I wrote you previous to my leaving Columbus, Mississippi. At that time did not expect to come through Mobile, Alabama. Remained at Mobile for two days and nights. Could not ascertain where you are. You will please write to me at this place and inform me whether or not you have been able

to get the cloth account you got from me. If so, I owe you for 2½ yards I got from you.

In the Deep South, bad weather delayed Sherman's departure from Savannah, Georgia, by a month. He commenced the Carolinas Campaign on February 1 and divided his command into the Army of the Tennessee and the Army of Georgia, with cavalry screening his way. Sherman feinted, making the Confederates unsure if his goal was symbolically important Charleston or Augusta, Georgia, forcing them to stretch their depleted forces even thinner.

Instead, he marched between the two by heading toward South Carolina's state capital in Columbia. An **unidentified Union artilleryman** informed his family of the army's hard trek from the Georgia coast to the Old North State's interior.

Goldsboro, North Carolina
Near the Neuse River
March 28, 1865

The campaign was one long to be remembered by the army under Sherman. Only those who have gone through it can form any idea of it. We were for two months without hearing a word from the North except now and then through the Rebel papers and during that length of time, we drew only six days of government rations—the rest of the time having to depend entirely upon the country, many parts of it being poor and not being even able to produce more than would feed the few scattered inhabitants, let alone the great army under Sherman. You can know that we were hard up at times— sometimes not even parched corn—and at the same time rains and mud up to our knees and still raining. For miles along the road was stuck full of mules and wagons swamped. These kinds of roads and times lasted for near two weeks after crossing the pontoon bridge at Sister's Ferry into the godforsaken region of South Carolina.

We then struck on better roads and in a better country. We at length come to Columbia, the capital of the state, which we entirely destroyed. And from that place on to where we are now, we have had fine times and plenty to eat. We got plenty of flour and meal, and we waste more smoked ham than we eat. On the Savannah Campaign [Sherman's March to the Sea], we considered ourselves lucky to get plenty of fresh pork to kill, but on this march, we got plenty of it in the smokehouses all ready.

As noted, on taking Columbia on February 17, most of the city was destroyed in a massive fire. Two weeks later, **Mary Margaret Pugh (1814–1887)**, a member of a Southern plantation family, informed her sister in Georgia about deteriorating conditions inside the Palmetto State.

Sumter, South Carolina
March 4, 1865

I suppose you have heard the sad news that Columbia, Charleston, and Wilmington have fallen to the enemy. Perhaps you may know more about it than we do, as nearly all of our information has been gathered from Negroes.

We did not apprehend much immediate danger, but the first thing we knew, they were marching through our state. Great excitement has prevailed. They divided into three columns, Sherman taking the left for Charlotte, Kilpatrick the center for Cheraw, and Slocum the right for the interior. They have been to Camden and burnt several houses, James and Mary Boykin Chesnut's, General Joseph Kershaw's, General John Kennedy's, and some others I do not remember (they burn all the houses of those who were members of the 1860 Secession Convention), then went to Bishopville where they stripped a good many of provisions, Negroes, and stock of all kinds. The militia has not been called out at all, and I believe a great many of the men have taken to the swamps and left the ladies to take care of their homes.

When Columbia was attacked, your Charles [a slave], Mr. Furman, Jim and Ned and Tim were over there at work on the fortifications. Hattie Nettle's Alfred [another slave] was pressed into service and left behind; he was with the Yankees several days. Miranda sent us word by him they had taken part of her silver and jewelry, but she hoped they had enough provisions left to do them. The neighbors clubbed together and hired a guard to protect their property.

The old State House was pulled down, and the new one was battered down. Nearly all of Main Street is in ashes. We heard twelve hundred and one houses were burnt, and thousands were rendered homeless. Another rumor says nine-tenths of the city was burnt, only about sixty houses left. We hear that Mayor Thomas Goodwin and Dr. Gibbs have taken the Oath of Allegiance. They wrote over to Sumter, South Carolina, the people were starving and begged them to send some provisions over, which has been done, I think. The old Baptist and the Methodist Churches were burnt. Sherman made them a speech and said it was not his intention to burn the town, 'twas done by some of his men who entered the place before he did.

They gathered a quantity of gold and silver in Columbia, more than they have done anywhere else. Alfred says that when they would go into a house, they put something in the door (I suppose a magnet) that would point to the valuables. They searched all boxes and trunks. Miranda did not write by Alfred, as she feared it might fall into the hands of the enemy. They offered Alfred a great many inducements to go with them, but he resisted all.

Mr. John Nettles has moved his family up. They were obliged to leave the Lowcountry on account of the Negroes. They rebelled and refused to work. On one plantation, where there were one hundred Negroes, only one could be made to cut wood. [Federal] Soldiers are passing about constantly, and horses are being impressed for service. We have let another one go, the black pony. Yours have not been interrupted. The Mannings sent their horses and mules and Negro men to Lynches Creek, and they were all captured.

'Tis rumored that General William Hardee has been relieved and Joe Johnston has taken command. We have also heard the rumor that General Lee has gained a great victory over Grant and that we had lost five thousand men. Affectionate love to you and the doctor and many kisses to the dear children. Tell the Negroes howdy.

As Sherman kept moving northward, there were eleventh-hour changes in the Confederate's top command structure in February. Congress created the position of general-in-chief, to which Robert E. Lee was quickly appointed. And General Joseph Johnston was ordered to take command of the Southern forces in North Carolina with instructions to concentrate his men and stop Sherman.

Johnston rounded up all the troops he could find, then boldly attacked near Bentonville on March 19. Two days of heavy fighting in less-than-ideal terrain followed until the Confederates were forced to withdraw. **William L. Johnson (unknown)**, a private in the 116th Illinois Infantry, detailed the wretched conditions to his brother.

Goldsboro, North Carolina
March 27, 1865

We had a hard time last week on the 19th. We was within 30 miles of this place and was moving on as far as possible when the Rebs attacked our left flank. They threw all their combined force against it. Our division was at the rear of our corps, and we did not start until 12 a.m., and we could hear heavy cannonading on our left from 10 o'clock until sundown. We marched until midnight. When we got to camp, we got different orders. We had not a bite of breadstuff for two days, and nothing but a little fat meat and coffee, and it was not very plentiful. At midnight, we got orders to march back on the same road to reinforce the left flank.

We started back. Oh, was it dark and muddy. We marched all night, and the next morning we arrived at our destination. There we got some meat and coffee for our breakfast and got in line, and of all mean places you ever saw, that was one of them. There was a swamp for 3 miles, and it was full of greenbriers, swamp rushes, and water knee-deep. The Rebs would send a peace commissioner [an artillery shell] over into the swamp, which was very disagreeable, especially when they got too close. The 30th Ohio and 6th Missouri [Federal] regiments of our brigade was skirmishing. They lost several killed. At sundown, we got up to the Rebs, but it was a disagreeable place to stay in the water, and we could not throw up dirt earthworks for the water. So we done the best we could with all the logs. There we laid all night.

On the morning of 21st, our regiment was ordered out on the skirmish line before daylight so the Rebs would see us. Still nothing to eat. We all got the best cover we could and then we commenced shooting at the Rebs and them at us, and to make it more disagreeable, it started to rain and continued to all day and night. We heard we would be relieved at night, but they could not get any regiment to relieve us. So we had the stay there that night. We heard they was going to draw rations, so one of the boys and I went back to the [wagon] train and drew them (some moldy crackers and coffee) and started back to the regiment. It was dark and rainy, and after going through a swamp for a mile, we got lost. Then we took a new start and found the regiment at midnight. The boys was glad to get some things to eat, for we had no bread for four days.

The Rebs was pretty bold. They attempted to charge us three times but fell back again. All night and day kept up a steady fire, and the morning of 22nd they left, and we came here. We are on the Newbern Railroad in Goldsboro.

Two days later, Sherman's men reached Goldsboro, North Carolina, connecting with Schofield's command from Wilmington. **James A. Stewart (1842–1927),** a private in the 98th Ohio Infantry, recounted the reunion in a letter to his sister.

Goldsboro, North Carolina
March 27, 1865

How glad the boys was when Sherman's army arrived at this place. They gave their old leader a hearty welcome. Also, too, the boys that they had been with through last summer's dangerous campaign [the Atlanta Campaign]. We look quite dirty and ragged by the side of them. But they knew how to make allowance for that.

It is hardly worth my while to give you an account of our march through the Mother of Rebeldom [South Carolina]. Suffice it to say we left her in ashes. A black mark that will take years to rub out.

You have heard that I was detailed at corps headquarters as one of General Jefferson C. Davis' escort. The duty is very light, and it is much nicer riding and having my knapsack hauled than walking through the mud and carrying everything. There are 12 of us in a mess. We get our cooking done at a citizen's house. It is much nicer than cooking for ourselves, but it seems very strange to have a woman cook for us and to eat off a table.

Despite all they had been through, the Federals were confident of ultimate victory, as the aforementioned letter of the **unidentified Union artilleryman** continued.

Old Billy Sherman is in full command of both armies—that is, his own and Beauregard's [actually Johnston's]. He leads his own men and drives the other. I think our next campaign will end in Richmond—that is, if the Rebels do not evacuate it. If they do, it is hard to tell where we will go. For my part, I don't care where we go. We can show Old Lee a trick or two he never knew. This is now an awful strong army.

Even as the war was commencing its closing act, many Confederates clung to visions of victory. They included **L. N. Halbert (unknown)**, a quartermaster in Forrest's Cavalry Corps in remote western Alabama, who insisted to a friend that Southern independence was still possible.

Camp Robertson
Plantersville, Alabama
March 13, 1865

Tomorrow, our general will be here, and then our fate will probably be known. Whether we will be disbanded or remain in the field. Let it be as it may. I am content, for it is our duty to submit to authorities. This is our war, and better to die in the discharge of duty than be defeated and subjugated. All we have depends on our ability to whip the fighters, and I think every true patriot will be up to doing it, and he who does otherwise is an unworthy citizen of the South.

The Yanks, it seems, are having their own way in Carolina now, but I am not cast down. General Lee will, I believe, integrate a new system of warfare, which will make the year's campaign a successful one. His plans are known only to himself and his councilors, and we outsiders should, as far as is in our power, rally to his side by fully complying with the requirements of the law. For it is by our doing this that he can be enabled to carry out his plans successfully. Trust in God, do our duty, follow our leaders, and fear no evil. Dance less and pray more if we wish for success.

One of the most unpleasant duties that soldiers on both sides faced was witnessing military executions. Even with the war's end in sight, death sentences were still carried out for serious offenders. **Charles A. Tripp (1845–1902)**, a private in the 4th New York Heavy Artillery, one of many such regiments that had been turned into infantry, told his father about it.

[Virginia; location unknown]
March 21, 1865

The other day, we was drawn up in a hollow square around the gallows where took place the execution of a deserter. He had been caught in the act of deserting to the enemy twice.

We have had several division reviews by Generals Andrew Humphrey and George Meade. It is a rather nice thing to see, but my view was limited. We have had several sham brigade charges, and one boy fell down and stuck his bayonet into another's arm, a pretty bad wound.

Well, Father, what do you think of the war now? Do you think it will close this summer? We down here think we will see the end of the fighting this campaign. We thought just so last spring, too. Six days more and I will have been to the front one year.

In Virginia, gray ranks were stretched precariously thin in the trenches surrounding the increasingly crucial rail hub of Petersburg. It had to remain open if Lee's Army of Northern Virginia was to have any chance of fending off the vastly larger and better-supplied Army of the Potomac. The two sides had been locked in siege warfare there for eight months. Yet this letter to his uncle, written by a young Confederate soldier identified only as **Billie H. (unknown)** just days before being forced to abandon Petersburg, was remarkably upbeat.

Camp 54th Regt. [North Carolina Infantry]
In Ditches Near Petersburg, Virginia
March 21, 1865

I like our position very well. We can't be flanked here. It will take straight-up fighting here to rout us. We have three rows of chevaux-de-frise in front of us and are making more. We are under fire of the old mortar guns all the time.
Our boys and the Yanks have made an agreement not to fire on each other in less than six days. They wanted to know the other day if some of us would buy some tobacco and come over to trade for coffee. They holler at our boys sometimes when sharpshooting is going on and tell them not to shoot so close near them, for they don't try to hit us, and many throw rocks at each other. We are only 50 yards apart at some points from each other. I believe if it was not for our officers that our boys and the Yanks would meet and play ball, for they are perfectly friendly.

As spring arrived, Grant began pressing toward Petersburg. He even invited Lincoln to see operations in the field for himself, with the commander in chief arriving on March 25.

It was all tremendously exciting to **Charles S. Woolston (1848–1865)**, a private in the 3rd Pennsylvania Cavalry, who witnessed a dramatic Confederate assault on Fort Stedman. He had enlisted the previous November at age 16, joining the command at General George Meade's headquarters at Petersburg, where, according to its regimental history, it was "constantly at the front, acting as escort to Generals Grant and Meade, filling gaps in lines of battle, and performing the arduous duties of an emergency command." The teenage Woolston and other recent recruits were put on provost duty, escorting prisoners, carrying dispatches, and acting as sentries. (Although Woolston avoided the fighting, he died of disease in a Richmond hospital on June 11, 1865, shortly before his seventeenth birthday.)

Headquarters Army of the Potomac
Petersburg, Virginia
March 26, 1865

We had heavy fighting yesterday in the morning before daybreak. They charged our lines below Fort Hell [Fort Sedgwick] and captured our breast-works and a fort and turned the guns on us, and we charged and took them back with about 3 thousand prisoners. Our regiment moved to the scene right after daybreak and took charge of the prisoners and brought them to headquarters. We got to headquarters about noon, and right after—while we were a guarding them—President Lincoln and Grant, Meade, and staffs made their appearance while they were riding all along the lines and where they had fought at Hatcher's Run.

I was to City Point about 12 o'clock with 800 prisoners. Our regiment took about 4,200 to the Point yesterday. The troops is a moving into the works now. Things look like hot work today, but don't worry about me. I am all alright. I can tell you all about the war when I get home.

In southern Alabama, General Edward Canby's 45,000-man force headed for one of the Confederacy's few remaining cities: Mobile. Cut off from the Gulf Coast since Farragut's victory in the Battle of Mobile Bay eight months earlier, it was protected from overland approach by strong fortifications outside the city, which was precisely where Canby's troops were moving.

There was extensive fighting in the first week of April. **Otis Whitney (1821–1901),** a captain in the 27th Iowa Infantry, updated his wife on the movement in a hasty letter from the scene.

Camp at Fort Blakeley, Alabama
April 9, 1865

Last night, just before sundown, our forces opened fire on Spanish Fort and captured a small fort within the outer works, but could not hold it as it was commanded by the other fort and also by gunboats. At midnight, a general assault was made, and the entire work was captured with only 5 or 600 prisoners, the greater part of the garrison having escaped before the assault was made.

It is now 1½ P.M., and before dark we expect to make an assault upon Ft. Blakeley. It is the general opinion that the garrison is very small and that the fort is being evacuated. Still, there may be ample force to man the guns, and the gunboats may be there, in which case we may meet with a warm reception. If I can, I will inform you of the result without delay.

PS: Have received orders to be ready to move with company at 3 P.M. with one day's rations in haversacks and with blankets but not tents. Do not know where we are going.

Fort Blakeley and its 4,000 defenders surrendered around 5:30 p.m. that day. Mobile was evacuated on the night of April 11. The Federals entered the city on April 12—the fourth anniversary of the war's start.

Events began unfolding at a blinding pace. On Sunday, April 2, Grant ordered a major assault on the thinly stretched Confederate lines at Petersburg, shattering Confederate defenses at long last. **William Henry (1832–unknown),** a private in the 8th New York Cavalry, was part of the attack. (Henry was illiterate and had a comrade pen this letter to his parents.)

Petersburg, Virginia
April 3, 1865

I got to this place yesterday, and I got there just in time to be in the fight. We charged the breastworks. General Philip Sheridan rode out and took off his hat and said, "Give it to them boys!" and the men charged the breastworks with a yell that you could hear for miles around.

We took a great many prisoners, and I got off without a scratch. But I had my horse shot from under me, and I got a little hurt from the fall.

When we got in the city, we saw a nigger a trying to rob a dead officer. I told him to stop, and he would not, so I drawed my pistol and fired at him but missed him. Then, my friend John H. Rose took his pistol and shot him through the leg.

The sergeant is very kind to me. He wrote this letter for me, and I hope to be able to write myself soon as my friend is going to give me writing lessons. I am as big a Democrat as ever. If I could see you now, I could tell you what I thought of niggers.

Grant's breakthrough forced Lee to notify President Jefferson Davis that his army could no longer defend Richmond. The Confederate government evacuated that evening, and the capital fell the next morning. This letter from **Judith Blackburn Alexander (1796–1866),** written the following day, expressed what many Southerners were feeling at that moment. Living in a rural area between Richmond and Charlottesville, she was receiving scattered bursts of information that were not always fully accurate. While she heard that the Confederates had been defeated in the Battle of Five Forks on April 1, the general killed in fighting the next day was actually General A. P. Hill. She was writing to her young cousin, a lieutenant in the 6th Virginia Cavalry.

Near Caledonia, Virginia
April 4, 1865

It is said we have lost ground after a brave battle. Thank God that it was bravely fought. I begin to expect defeat—such odds are against us. Well, if we fall, we fall nobly.

April 5—I have just heard that Richmond is evacuated and General Lee's brave son is killed. No papers; only reports from those who left as the mayor went out to make the surrender.

It is the Lord, oh may he spare you, my cousin. We can get to Heaven under Yankee domination; may we meet there. But it is so desolate to have no relation of my own near me and not to know who lives to weep over our country. If we are to fall, to die as a separate people, to mingle among those who hate us, we must love one another the more, and must stand more firmly in Southern honor and truth, and pray; it may be, even yet, we may be free, the Lord knows the beginning and end. I can scarcely think.

PS: General John Gordon, I hear, not General Lee's son, is killed. He stood next to Stonewall Jackson. Alas!

The mood was completely opposite in the North, where **Horatio (unknown),** a Federal bureaucrat, described what happened when the news of Richmond's capture reached Washington. (The new vice president, Andrew Johnson, had appeared to be intoxicated during his inauguration four weeks earlier, an incident to which the writer obliquely refers.)

Ordinance Office
War Department
Washington, April 5, 1865

What splendid news we have got from Grant. Monday morning about 11:00, we heard cheers from the War Department, and all had rushed over to see what was the matter, and when we heard that "Richmond was ours," didn't we cheer.

I never saw such enthusiasm in all my life. It beat everything. Why we fairly yelled with joy, even hugged and kissed each other. No more business for that day. We were done for. Everybody got drunk, many with liquor, all with joy. We called out Sec. of War Edwin Stanton, Vice President Andrew Johnson (he wasn't drunk but full of truisms), Senators James Nye and Preston King, Secretary of State William Seward, General Benjamin Butler, and anybody who could say a good thing so that we might cheer and yell to get off some of our extra weight of joy and good feeling. We never had so many friends to shake hands with before. We were everybody's friend.

Our fighting is mainly over now. God be thanked for bringing us out alright.

Downtown Richmond was now a smoldering ruin. The retreating Confederates had set fire to warships and military supplies as they withdrew to prevent them from falling into Federal hands. The blaze spread, destroying much of the business district. On April 4, President Lincoln and his young son Tad spent a few hours walking through the captured Confederate capital.

Gilbert A. Tucker (1831–1884), a first lieutenant in the 10th New Hampshire, was among the very first Federal troops to enter the captured city. (The 13th New Hampshire Infantry, the 29th Connecticut Colored Infantry, the 36th U.S. Colored Infantry, and the 5th Massachusetts Colored Cavalry also claimed the distinction. Because the regiments advanced on four different roads, it is easy to see how each believed that it had earned the right to claim to be "first.")

Richmond, Virginia
April 6, 1865

As we all feel so well about taking Richmond, I will try and tell you something about that city that we all have been trying for so long. The 2nd Brigade, 3rd Division, 24th Corps, their skirmish line was the first in the city. We can say that the 10th was the first men in Richmond and then the Negroes, for they didn't have so far to go. We started on the morning of the 3rd and came as fast as we could walk. The men were very tired and couldn't have come so fast, only for the excitement. We never stopped after we started, and the men with their knapsacks on their backs.

The city was on fire, and it was near done in by the Rebels. They blowed up the gunboats and destroyed everything they could before they left. The fire made horrid work, but as soon as we could, the fire engines was at work putting out the fire and made out to stop it.

I was in Old Jeff's house [the White House of the Confederacy] yesterday and also the Capitol and Libby Prison, where there has been some of our men died. The city is a dirty place. But we shall now make it look better. There appears to be a great many Union men here, and they say they are glad that we have come.

Our boats came up the James River on the 4th day [of April], and Old Abe came and walked the streets of Richmond. It is the most demoralized city I ever saw. The citizens all say that since we have come, it seems more as it did before the war broke out. It is boring round the streets. And the Rebels will not take their own money. I will send you a one-hundred-dollar bill and two rings that came out of the city of Richmond. The Libby Prison is full of Rebels now. I think the fighting is about done. This has been a glorious time for our troops.

Things grew even more "glorious" for the Union a few days later. Lee surrendered his army at Appomattox Court House on Palm Sunday, April 9. **Ansel Lothrop White (1835–1910),** a first lieutenant in the 19th Maine Infantry, dashed off a short note to his mother on that historic day.

Headquarters in the Field
Appomattox Court House, Virginia
April 9, 1865

I scribble these few lines while sitting in the saddle to let you know that I am alright. The rebellion has given up. General Lee, we think, will surrender before night. If he does not, we will annihilate his whole army (what he has got left of it), which is very small. We are within one mile of him and have given him battle since we got them from their works at Petersburg.

Generals Grant and Meade are in the house directly opposite from me. I got into the Rebel's lines yesterday. But by running my horse very fast, I escaped, only receiving a few shots after me on my retreat. Inform my friends I am all safe.

Three days later, White wrote to his mother again, this time on the blank side of a Confederate document.

Farmville, Virginia
April 12, 1865

It was one of the happiest days the army ever experienced on the 9th of this month. The men could not say or do enough. They threw up their hats and jumped on them and acted like insane men. We have just arrived at Farmville after a long and tedious march of 20 miles, and as the mail leaves here tomorrow at daylight, I thought I would drop you a line. Even if it had to be done on Rebel paper.

You, of course, are having great times in the North over our splendid victory. Just think of it. Lee's army is no more. The rebellion is crushed. Johnston's army is a mere nutshell if they should attempt to hold out any longer. In my opinion, they will give up.

We are going to Burkesville Station tomorrow and probably will remain several days to get ready for action if General Johnston organizes any of us to silence him. I wonder if the people in the North will have any use for the Army of the Potomac any longer?

I am well, but very tired as we have done very rapid marching, and the roads are in terrible condition. We recaptured all of our men they took during this campaign. If I had been taken the other day, I should have been released before 48 hours with only the loss of my clothes and gun. Enclosed, find some Rebel money. I had $6,000 worth of it.

Lee's surrender triggered celebrations across the North. In Washington, major public buildings were lit with gaslight in a "grand illumination." Lincoln, who had recently suffered a nasty cold, gave a short talk from a second-floor White House window on April 11. It was the last speech he ever made.

Among the hundreds of people gathered on the lawn below to listen was **John Holmes (unknown)** of the 14th Veterans Reserve Corps. The young woman to whom he wrote appears to have been a pen pal who corresponded with soldiers. (The account of Confederate General Nathan Bedford Forrest's capture was untrue; it indicates the wide range of reports and rumors that were circulating at that moment.)

Capitol Barracks
Washington, D.C.
April 12, 1865

You once expressed a doubt about news reaching Waterford, Pennsylvania. You even thought that the fall of Richmond would not reach you. But doubtless, you have heard of the said event many days since. You must also have heard of Lee's surrender, and ere this reaches its destination, I confidently expect that the surrender of Johnston will be flashed along the wires.

News has just come in of the capture of the Rebel General Forrest.

There was a Grand Illumination of the city last night. I went up to "see the sights" and also to hear His Excellency President Lincoln make a speech. He gave evidence of his late indisposition—but his speech was grave, short, manly, and to the point. He seemed to realize that a momentous issue was at hand, for he did not indulge us with any of his celebrated jokes. His enemies have stigmatized him as a "vulgar joker," but last night, in his speech, he gave ample testimony that he is also a wise statesman. The latter part of my letter is uninteresting to you, perhaps, but the evening was dark and disagreeable, so I cannot descant upon the few ladies present—their dress, etc.

Washington was still celebrating when the festivities came to a crashing halt two nights later. **Jacob F. Mader Jr. (1840–1922),** a captain in the 61st Ohio Infantry, was in town to cut through red tape in advance so that his regiment could be paid before mustering out. He and a fellow officer decided to relax by watching a popular play that Friday night. Mader described what came next to his fiancée.

Washington City, D.C.
April 16, 1865

I was present at the theater when President Lincoln was shot, and I seen the cowardly villain as he jumped out of the opera box with a drawn dagger in his hand and as he ran across the stage hallooed "Sic Semper Tyrannus" (So perish tyrants) and was out of sight in a second passing through the back door, mounted his horse, and I believe was soon no more to be known.

Lincoln died at 7:22 the following morning. A few hours later, **Enoch Leavitt (1844–1907)**, a private in the 2nd Ohio Cavalry, wrote these lines to his sister. (Although it was believed at the time that Secretary of State William H. Seward—who was also seriously injured the same night as Lincoln—would die, he survived.)

Newton USA General Hospital
Baltimore, Maryland
April 15, 1865

Joy unspeakable is in this moment turned to deepest mourning. The national heart has for some time been aroused to its highest pitch of excitement in rejoicing over the glorious success of our national arms, the establishment of peace, and the supremacy of our national emblems. But in one moment, sorrow hath come to our jubilant people as fast as the wings of lightning can carry the sad news. Abraham Lincoln—our President, he whom the nation feels proud (in view of his admirable capacity and undying devotion to the cause of our country) to bestow upon him the highest honors of our nation—is murdered by an assassin. Who can describe the infamy of the atrocious act? Also, Secretary Seward, by the same assassinating plot, is mortally wounded. In this infamous act, he whose very life has become distinguished for his acts of kindness and mercy is murdered by one who has been an object of his benevolence. Is there a place in the "blackness of darkness" deep enough for such a perpetrator?

The shocking news was flashed nationwide by telegraph, including to Union troops in the field. However, the information sent to them through military channels arrived in bits and pieces. Writing to his cousin from southern Virginia, **John M. Lovejoy (1843–1900)**, a corporal in the 121st New York Infantry, tried to keep up with developments.

Camp of the 121st Regt. N. Y. S. Vols.
Near Burkes' Junction, Virginia
April 15, 1865

When you was writing the letter now before me, I was in the field shouting and feeling glad over the victories God seen fit to crown us with. Today, we all feel to mourn to hear of the attempt to murder our President. I hope he will live.

Our present situation now is all one could ask for. General Joe Johnston, who commands the only Rebel army left, is now in a tight place between the victorious armies of Sherman and Meade, Ord, Sheridan, and Thomas. He has not a place he can fall back to without fighting for it, and we hold the railroad, and soon his supplies will give out. He must fight, surrender, or else disband his army, and we may look forward to a speedy termination of the war.

Reports have just come (I do not know whether they are official or not) that Mr. Lincoln is not dead but that his wound is a very dangerous one. I hope he may live to pass sentence on his would-be murderer. He is a good man, and I believe he has done what he could for the good of his country.

Sunday Evening.
Another report has just come in about the President. It is that he died at 9 o'clock this A. M. ("Unofficial").

The nation, North and South alike, had never experienced anything like it. Lincoln was the first American president to be assassinated. Coming as it did at the Union's moment of triumph, many people had a difficult time accepting it.

Even those who had deeply disliked Lincoln in life—and there were many of them—were now swept up in profound sorrow over his passing. Consider **John Wesley Folsom (1832–1910).** Writing to his older brother in New Hampshire barely 48 hours after Lincoln's death, he explained how his small town had held a somber service the day before. It was among the hundreds of similar ceremonies held around the North that week.

Greencastle, Indiana
April 17, 1865

Yesterday (Sunday) was the most gloomy day I ever experienced. More sad countenances, more solemn expressions, and more solemn performances than I ever witnessed before. All on account of our national calamity. You and I have both seen the days that we would be glad the presidential chair was vacated, and we would not much care how. But times have been changing since and I don't think either of us would wish it, at least in the manner it was by the assassin.

Friday was a great day of jubilee, and Saturday was a day of great mourning. Sunday there was an address by Rev. Dr. Fisk in the college lot and a procession formed of Masons, Odd Fellows, college boys, four churches, and citizens which took ½ an hour to pass a given point with muffled drums and bells tolling with muffled tongues and flags dressed in mourning and it was the most solemn sight ever witnessed.

John Wilkes Booth, a handsome and popular stage star, had pulled the trigger. At that moment, he became the most hated man in America. This letter from teenager **Edgar B. Clark (1848–1927)** is typical of the feelings shared by many in the days following Lincoln's murder.

Charlotte, New York
April 23, 1865

The nation has met with a sore bereavement by the sudden death of our President. I hope they will find the vile assassin who perpetrated the hellish deed and make him stretch hemp on the first tree that they come to after they catch him. J. Wilkes Booth, I suppose, is the assassin. When I was in Rochester, I got his photograph just to see how the scoundrel looked. He is a pretty good-looking fellow—too good to commit such a crime.

As incredible as it sounds today, some people expressed happiness at Lincoln's murder, even within the Union army. They were a small minority, and things did not go well for them when their extreme views became known. **George Warren Campbell (1830–1874),** a private from Indiana in the Veteran Volunteer Engineering Corps stationed in Tennessee, witnessed it firsthand. He wrote about it to his brother (who had been wounded at Gettysburg).

Chattanooga, Tennessee
May 2, 1865

We were rather jubilant over the fall of Richmond and Petersburg and the surrender of Lee's army. It is hardly necessary for me to tell you that the death of our President cast a gloom over everything, with the exception of a few Rebels and butternuts. There were a few Rebs collected together at a house near the camp of Company I of this regiment the evening of his death and were having quite a jubilee over the sad intelligence. But their rejoicing was of short duration. Company I went for them as soon as they found out what they were doing, thrashed the men and sent them to the military prison, turned the women out of doors, and fired [burnt] the house.

There were a few men who bear the name of "soldier" who rejoiced at the death of the President. Such are now working on the most public streets of Chattanooga (or at least all such that are near this place) with a ball and chain attached to one foot, or rather ankle, and a card tied to their back with these two words, "Assassin Sympathizer" printed in large letters on them so that every person that can read or spell may see for what they are working there for. They ought to have their heads shaved and be drummed out of the service.

As soldiers hunted for Booth and investigators rounded up his accomplices, dozens of innocent people were also taken into custody, falsely accused of having been conspirators. One of them was **John D. Reamer (1816–1866)**, a clothing merchant in Hagerstown, Maryland. He was held in a Washington, D.C., prison for nearly a month. Although eventually exonerated, he was forbidden to see his 16-year-old son before the boy died after an illness. Reamer was utterly dejected when he wrote to his wife.

Carroll Prison
Washington, D.C.
May 22, 1865

I received two letters from you. You asked me about clothing to dress our dear son for the grave, but before I could answer, he had need for them. You know that I never object to anything you do. I hope you done all things well. It was a great task for you without my assistance. I do not know how you could perform it and particularly now in your situation.

I feel like a heartbroken and ruined man—nothing to care for. Never wish to see those low scoundrels who is the cause of our trouble. I hope I may get revenge. This is Monday, and nothing to cheer up a poor broken heart. No sympathy here except from fellow prisoners. They wouldn't grant me a parole to attend the funeral of my son.

I will not say when I will be released as we know nothing about it. I have been told by several persons in authority here that it would not be long. If I had committed any crime, I could submit; but as I am innocent, the stroke is very severe.

Now, as our dear son is dead and in his grave, there is still another great trial that must soon come. Write to me until the last moment. May the Lord deliver you safely through is my constant prayer for you.

(When Reamer returned to Hagerstown after taking the Oath of Allegiance, his business was destroyed and his health ruined. He died of consumption less than a year later.)

With his capital gone and the Confederacy's major army having handed over its arms, Johnston knew he couldn't hold out. After a series of lengthy negotiations with Sherman, he officially surrendered on April 26 near Durham, North Carolina. He also surrendered all remaining Confederate troops still serving in the Carolinas, Georgia, and Florida—89,270 men in all, the largest surrender of the war.

One history-making event after another had unfolded that April with the speed of a string of firecrackers exploding. The war that had dragged on for four bloody years wrapped up in four weeks. Writing to his mother on the last day of that especially momentous month, **John M. Lovejoy (1843–1900)** of the 121st New York Infantry almost had to remind himself that it had all actually happened.

Camp Near Danville, Virginia
April 30, 1865

Four weeks ago today I was in the battle before Petersburg. Three weeks ago, General Lee surrendered the Army of Northern Virginia to Lieutenant General U. S. Grant. Two weeks ago, we was greatly grieved to learn of the assassination of Abraham Lincoln. One week ago, we left Burkesville Station to defeat Johnston.

Our march of last week from Burkesville Station to Danville—a distance of about 125 miles—was made in five days. When we left, it was reported that the Rebel General Joseph E. Johnston was 160 miles from Danville and was marching towards that place. When we reached here, his command was only 40 miles away at Greensboro, North Carolina. Next day, we received official reports of his surrender on the same terms as General Lee. It is said the march of the Sixth Corps to Danville was the cause. If so, I am satisfied.

We have done it, and now we are here in comparative quiet. It is not at all probable we will remain here long for it is a long way to bring supplies, and they have to come from City Point by rail, and the railroad needs much repairing. It is greatly out of order. I now feel more confident than ever that our fighting is done in this rebellion and hope soon to visit our homes and greet our families again in peace.

Johnston's surrender was not without controversy. Believing that he was acting in Lincoln's spirit of a gentle reconciliation, Sherman offered terms that far exceeded those that Grant gave to Lee. When the agreement reached Washington, the Federal high command was irate. Secretary of War Edwin Stanton secretly leaked the terms to newspapers to embarrass and humiliate Sherman. The whole affair was distasteful to Captain **Peter Collins Sears (1842–1919)** of the 33rd Massachusetts Infantry, who mentioned it in his letter home.

Cloud's Mills Near Alexandria, Virginia
May 21, 1865

It appears that Sherman's army is to be mustered out as soon as possible. I suppose it is to put Sherman out of the way—I cannot find out the feeling of the government. But by the terms of agreement being published in such a way, it is evident that there is much opposition to him in the army. It is charged to General Henry W. Halleck. I see that the people in the North were highly excited and indignant at Sherman's conduct. It was a bad blunder. But as Sherman is the only loser by it, I cannot see the justice in his being abused as he is.

When Lee surrendered, I said the thing is done, and every life that is hereafter sacrificed is willful murder. And with this view, he [Sherman] governed his movements. Johnston was entirely at his mercy, and he knew it. Anyone can see Sherman was fooled in the agreement. I blame Sherman to a certain extent, but little compared with many. I attribute it wholly to his desire to prevent an unnecessary sacrifice of human life. Jeff Davis was there, and Johnston would have fought us if we had pushed him. Has he [Sherman] ever tried to save his men when it was necessary to use them? It appears to me that he could see that there was nothing to be lost by it and chose to risk his own reputation to save his men.

I sent you lilies from Richmond. The regiment was formed in six companies, and as there were six captains senior to me, I had nothing to do, so I went into the city ahead of the corps and saw them as they passed through. Then, I walked around the city, stopping occasionally for ice cream and strawberries.

Friday the 12th, we continued the march. We passed Spotsylvania Court House and encamped one night on the Chancellorsville battleground. Very many rumors about the time and place and manner of our being mustered out. But one thing is certain, that there will be work enough to do.

Federal troops finally caught up with Booth, killing him in a shootout in rural Virginia on April 26. At the same time, Lincoln's remains were being taken from one city after city in a two-week series of public funerals. And as families began looking forward to the return of their soldiers, no homecoming was more deeply anticipated than that of those who had survived being prisoners of war. They brought with them tales of their suffering. This **unknown woman** shared with her daughter the ordeals that her son experienced.

New London, Connecticut
May 1, 1865

We have been having great victories. It seems the war is about over, and a great calamity the murder of our good President. Indeed, it is a very sad affair. It's a good thing they have caught the murderer Booth. It seemed to be a plot to kill the President and Seward and all the heads of government. The secretary is recovering. There has been a great deal of pain taken to let the people see the President's body in the different cities. They were in great crowds. It would be difficult to see anything.

I was waiting to hear from William before I wrote so to give you an account. He came home last Tuesday. He sent us a letter from Washington when he was on the road. It took him several weeks before he got through. He gives some distressing accounts of prison life. He was at Andersonville Prison for five months. No shelter but his blanket. From there, he was sent to Florence, South Carolina. He found it no better there. The Rebs got some of them to put up some hospitals for our sick soldiers on parole or honor outside the pen, Will among the rest. They were given better rations. The rations in the prison, one pint of corn meal ground cob and all, and one ounce of bacon per day per boy.

He was glad to get in God's land, he said. He made his escape, him and 15 others. They had the bloodhounds after them. They caught all except him and two others. They were 7 days getting in Sherman's lines. He said they fared well there. He said the darkies was their best friends. They helpt them along. He said he wasn't sick a day all the time he was among them in prison. That was 11 months.

He looks better than I expected to see him. He was inquiring about you. Perhaps Will will get off to see you when he gets home and gets recuperated. He complains of pains in his limbs. He said he had a touch of scurvy. I think he will have to be very careful. He has lived so bad for so long. He said they were dying in prison all the time. Sometimes, a dozen a day.

Hundreds of recently released prisoners perished when the deadliest maritime disaster in American history occurred. In the predawn hours of April 27, the steamboat *Sultana*, dangerously overloaded with Union soldiers heading home from the war, exploded on the Mississippi River. Among the estimated 1,800 fatalities were men who had survived captivity in Andersonville and a smaller prison in Alabama.

To many Americans, it was finally one tragedy too many in a month that witnessed more than its share of horrors, as **Hamilton McClurg (1840–1867)**, a private in the 102nd Ohio Volunteer Infantry, wrote to a friend at home.

Decatur, Alabama
May 1, 1865

Our last sorrow is the loss of so many of our boys on the ill-fated Sultana, *which blew up above Vicksburg. Something near one hundred of our boys [in the 102nd Ohio] were on board. But you have a better chance of knowing the result than we.*

For some time back, our joys and sorrows have been alternate. One day, we are rejoicing over a great victory achieved by some general in the field. The next, we, with the whole nation, mourn the untimely death of a beloved President. The great statesman, the unyielding patriot, the glorious magistrate is no more. The silent tomb will soon contain all that is earthly of President Lincoln. The army weeps, and a mighty nation mourns—yes, friend and foe! The thundering cannon that guards the entrance of Decatur Landing [on the Tennessee River] has of late been often brought into requisition in honor of some great victory. But Hark! what means the solemn sound that now breaks in upon our slumbering sensitivities? It is a minute gun, fired every half hour from sun till sun in honor of the departed hero. It is a national honor. But still, every deafening sound seems to say, "Vengeance is mine, and I will execute."

Hurrah for Ohio! We will soon be there. The war is about over, Gertie.

Federal troops occupied Selma, Alabama, the site of a major Confederate arsenal and supply depot. Northern horsemen had swept through the city after a sharp battle on April 2 and moved on. **Caleb Glick (1843–1924)**, a private in the 114th Ohio Volunteer Infantry, was part of the force that arrived later. He told his family about conditions there.

Selma, Alabama
May 7, 1865

We have made another move and are now lying in the city of Selma. We came up here on the transport on the Alabama River. When we reached this place, there was no opposition. General James Wilson had been in here a few days before we came, and as soon as we had landed our boats, the news was soon spread around that there was an armistice between the Rebel and Union forces in this department to make some terms of surrender.

Yesterday, the first train came within one mile of the city, which was as close as it could get on account of a bridge that was destroyed by the Rebels but is now being repaired. This railroad, I believe, runs through Mississippi to Vicksburg. We have also telegraph communication to almost all parts of the Confederacy. There is a rumor now going the rounds that General Edmund Kirby Smith has surrendered his army. If this is true, the war is certainly at a close.

Now I will try and give you a little description of the city. This place is about as large as Circleville, Ohio. There are scarcely any large buildings left standing as Wilson destroyed all of the public buildings, the arsenal, and the ironworks. I tell you, they made cannon and small arms and munitions fit to kill. There are a great many citizens living here at present who seem to be very glad that there is a prospect for the war to be brought to a close. We are waiting next to hear of peace being declared. Then we want one grand order issued, and that is to go home. We all believe that we will be home by the Fourth of July. At least, I hope so.

On May 10, Jefferson Davis was captured in southern Georgia. The morning was cool and drizzly, and as he was leaving his tent to meet his captors, he pulled his wife's dark shawl over his shoulders to keep warm. (Lincoln frequently wore a shawl himself in cold weather.) That led to a wildly erroneous—and widely circulated—report intended to humiliate the former Confederate president, claiming that he was disguised in women's clothing.

Although the fighting was rapidly winding down in the East, Confederate forces remained in the field in the Trans-Mississippi Department. An Ohio woman identified as **A. S. Root (unknown)** was worried that her soldier son might be sent to Texas if the war was prolonged.

Austinburg, Ohio
May 19, 1865

Our government has a great work before them to try the conspirators and traitors. Jeff Davis was caught last week in the Georgia town of Irwinville. He was so hardly pressed he put on his wife's dress and run for the woods. Perhaps you will hear all about it before this reaches you. One hundred thousand dollars are offered for his arrest.

I have indeed been wondering if you were alive and if I should hear from you again. I have read in the papers of some of the troops going from Mobile up the Alabama River to Selma and Montgomery but could not guess whether you was there. Do you have enough to eat and wear? Have you received your pay? When you do, keep it very close. Perhaps it would not be safe to send it home if you have any to send where you now are.

I hope the time is not far distant when you will come yourself. The papers state that all the troops east of the Mississippi have surrendered on the same terms as Lee. There has been no formal declaration of peace. The general feeling is that there will be no more fighting. We read of General Kirby Smith talking as though he would not surrender but fight on. He is west of the Mississippi. I hope you will not have to go over the river to subdue them. I also hope you will not go into the regular army. It would be, I think, better to return to rural occupations as soon as consist. Better for body, mind, and morals.

We all look forward to the time when "Johnny will come home" with the deepest interest. Write as often as you can and turn your face homeward as soon as U.S. will let you.

The seven men and one woman charged with involvement in Booth's conspiracy went on trial in Washington on May 1. Three weeks later, President Andrew Johnson enjoyed the triumph that Lincoln had not lived to see. Grant's and Sherman's victorious armies rendezvoused in the capital for a final parade past their commanders and their commander in chief.

Lafayette Lunan Bennett (1840–1865), a private in the 5th Pennsylvania Heavy Artillery (also 204th Pennsylvania Volunteer Infantry), wrote to his parents about the massive processions. (He died of typhoid fever less than 90 days later.)

Annandale, Virginia
May 22, 1865

The trial of the assassins goes on daily at Washington and is drawing great interest here. The capture of Jeff Davis puts the finishing strokes to rebellion and the Southern Confederacy. I want to see them get [Confederate Secretary of War and General John C.] Breckinridge, [General] Wade Hampton, and a few others before they give it up.

The armies of Meade and Sherman are gathering around Washington. You have very little idea of the number of men in our armies. You hear of fifty or a hundred thousand men, but when you come to see them, when you look at the immense wagon trains which accompany them, you will begin to realize the immensity of the thing. Sherman's and Meade's armies have passed right by our camp on their northward march to Washington—that is, a large part of them have. All around Alexandria and Washington, the troops are gathering as thick as bees. Camps are seen everywhere, and men are moving in every direction.

There is to be a Grand Review of all the troops of Sherman's army and also that of the Potomac tomorrow and the next day. They will pass through the main street of Washington, pass the White House and War Department, and so pass out of the capital.

Thousands of people lined Pennsylvania Avenue to witness the two-day procession, including **Sallie Witherow**, a young schoolteacher who had traveled to Gettysburg with her sister Mary as volunteer nurses following the battle there. She wrote this to an **unknown Union army captain**.

Washington, D.C.
May 31, 1865

I do think we more than half expected to see either you or Major Waters here last week. Why were you not here to see the Grand Review of our Armies? I assure you, you missed the most glorious sight the world has ever beheld.

Pennsylvania Avenue was one dense crowd, extending from the Capitol quite a distance beyond the President's House. The roofs of many buildings were occupied, and in almost every square, stages were erected. Brother was fortunate enough to procure tickets for us to the Connecticut Stage, which was in front of Lafayette Square, just opposite the President's Mansion. Just across the street—on an opposite stage—sat President Johnson, Secretaries Edwin Stanton and Gideon Welles, Grant, Sherman and wife, Generals Edgar Gregory, Oliver Howard, George Meade (our dear Meade, whom everyone in Gettysburg loves), Winfield Hancock, Henry Slocum, and ever so many other dignitaries. With the aid of an opera glass, we could see every one of them distinctly. Oh, but we did enjoy even looking at them. The columns moved at nine, precisely, and continued to pass until three. Oh, how weather-beaten some of our poor soldiers do look. We waited impatiently for the 10th New York and watched it with unusual interest, but not one familiar face did we see. We somehow feel attached to that regiment.

Last evening, we attended a prayer meeting of the chaplains who have been connected with the army. Generals Howard and Gregory were present and delivered two splendid addresses. Oh, what noble men they are. Is it any wonder our army triumphed with such men at the head?

I see by the papers they are anticipating quite a grand time at Gettysburg on the "Fourth." They intend laying the Cornerstone of the National Monument. The President, Generals Grant and Howard, and a number of other celebrities are expected to be present. Of course, as they are all to be there, Mary and I will be on hand, too. I wonder if we shall meet any of our old friends there?

For many Federals, it was the first chance to see the famous city they had heard about throughout the war. Experiencing it in person made a strong impression on some. At the same time, their thoughts turned to being reunited with their loved ones, as this **unknown Union soldier** in Sherman's army told his wife.

Washington, D.C.
May 31, 1865

We marched all through the capital of these United States and were reviewed yesterday. It is a beautiful place, Emma. The White House is very nice indeed. If it should be my lot to stay in the service very long and stay at this place, I will have you come and see me. It will not cost a great deal to come. Would you do so if it is my request? But I hope I will be able to go home and see you soon. The talk is that Sherman's army will be furloughed soon.

With the fighting finished, Northerners impatiently awaited their release from the army. The delay was especially intolerable for soldiers serving in less-than-idyllic locations. **Riley Leroy Thatcher (1843–1865)** had been a private in the 96th New York Infantry for only 27 days, and he was already desperate to leave the military prison at Elmira, New York, where he was on guard duty. (He would die of "congestive intermittent fever" at Warrenton, Virginia, five months later.)

Elmira, New York
April 19, 1865

My health is good for the fare we have, but <u>damn</u> the stuff. The rest of the boys are in the same fix, and you needn't write anymore until I leave here, and I think that will be soon. There was 22 from Ontario, New York, here, and they took all but 8 this morning. I think we shall go in 2 or 3 days. I hope so, at least, for I have got sick of this damned Hell Hole.

There is something wrong about the damned thing, and it [the war] is all through, and this Union might go to hell. If I was out of it [the army], I would keep out. We can't go out of our yard down to the city, nor they won't let anybody in here. There is a fence about 12 feet high, a tight board fence, and we can't see out nor get out. There has been a Millet boy down here to see his brother, but he could not get in.

I will be glad if we should get out of this today. We are nothing but dogs and shan't be for the year to come. But it will soon wear off, and then they can go to hell for all I care.
R. L. Thatcher
Government dog

General Richard Taylor surrendered the last Confederate troops east of the Mississippi River on May 4. People in the defeated South now contemplated their future. With the region's economy in ruins, some chose to start over in another country. One of the closest options was Mexico, which was ruled at the time by Emperor Maximilian, whose reign was propped up with French soldiers sent by Napoleon III.

Adam Turney Kreps (1842–1919), a first lieutenant in the 67th USCT, hinted at the uncertainty he felt about his own post-army future to his father.

Bayou Sara, Louisiana
May 10, 1865

There are a good many men returning to their homes from the Rebel armies—some who were paroled when Lee's army was captured. There is no regular band of Rebels east of the Mississippi River now as the last army under Taylor surrendered a few days ago to General Edward Canby. I have been told that a great many of Lee's men are going to Mexico to fight the French. I have heard some say that they would go and join Emperor Maximilian, but the private soldiers in the Rebel army are as much opposed to the French as we are.

Where we are stationed at now, there is quite a village. Before the war, it was a summer resort and has been a very pleasant place. A great many of the houses have been destroyed by the shells from the vessels in the river. It has been a noted haunt for guerrillas and bushwhackers. There is no danger of the river drowning us out here as we are on high bluffs.

I am not as well contented since I came back from furlough as I was before. I think something of coming home next fall.

It is estimated that as many as 10,000 former Confederates fled to Mexico, including General Jo Shelby, whose Missouri Iron Brigade sank its battle flag in the Rio Grande rather than surrender. Another 20,000 migrated to Brazil. Others went to Canada, Cuba, and England. (Although the vast majority of those émigrés returned to the South within a few years, a sizable contingent stayed in Brazil, where their descendants, called Confederados, remain to this day.)

Taylor's surrender left General Edmund Kirby Smith's sprawling Trans-Mississippi Department with the last large-scale Confederate armed forces still in the field. **Nicholas Belveal (1839–1926)**, a private in the 33rd Iowa Infantry, passed along camp scuttlebutt about what could come next in a letter to his wife.

Mobile, Alabama
May 14, 1865

There is strong talk of us having to go to Texas to clean old Kirby Smith out, but the general opinion is that we won't have to go, for they think Smith will surrender as soon as our forces get to the state, and I understand there is an army gone from Little Rock under General Frederick Solomon and another from Memphis under General George Thomas, besides a lot of cavalry. I also understand that Smith and Grant is negotiating, and the general opinion is that Kirby Smith will come to terms. If he don't, one thing is sure, they will wish they had, for the boys all swear they won't show them much mercy either in person or property.

I understand the government has opened free trade with south Alabama. There is regular communication both by rail and on the Alabama River. The citizens of Mobile have again resumed their business. Business seems to be lively, though at pretty high prices. There is ripe watermelons for sale and many other articles, but they didn't grow here. I understand they was brought from Cuba.

Well, Mary, you needn't send me any more stamps as I can get them now and don't think we will need but a few more for I think we will be at home by the 4th of July if everything works out right. But don't look for us until you see us, for it is just as uncertain we will get home as it is about the wind blowing two days from the same direction.

Kirby Smith eventually reached an agreement on May 26 and surrendered on June 2. General Stand Watie signed a ceasefire agreement with the Federals on June 23, thus becoming the last Confederate general to capitulate. Several smaller, independent commands never surrendered—they simply went home.

While soldiers on both sides yearned to take off their uniforms for good, it was still too soon for many Northerners to tell when that would happen. But to **Woodburn Hardy (unknown),** a private in the 95th Illinois Infantry, it was quickly becoming obvious that Reconstruction would not be a smooth road.

Montgomery, Alabama
May 21, 1865

I am more anxious than ever to be at home. I think more about it, at any rate, and often fancy myself there.

We are all here at Montgomery yet, that is, I mean all of our division. There is some talk now that we will go home before a great while, but it is only a rumor, I guess. I don't put much confidence in it, for there has got to be some troops left here and quite a good many in order to keep everything straight. Hundreds upon hundreds of soldiers are coming in here on their way home, and a good many of them live in and around here. To be sure, they have no arms nor any organization as an army, but there will be a good deal of bushwhacking going on, and even now, a good many cases are reported out back in the country, and there would be mobs and riots between the whites and blacks. The white people, soldiers and all, I mean the Reb soldiers, have a most bitter hatred of the Negro, or rather hate to have them free and have to think themselves on a level [equal] with them. A good many threaten they will kill them, and even some of the masters of the Negroes have even shot at some of them because they were coming away, and so it will be for a good while, and there has got to be a force kept sufficient to keep the planters and soldiers in awe of our soldiers and compel them to submission. It is a going to take a good while here before the people, citizens, and soldiers, too, will be reconciled to the condition in which they now find themselves, although they had to give up.

The soldiers are coming in here and going through on their way home, as many as five hundred and over some days, and mostly from Lee's and Johnston's armies, and I suppose a good many go by way of Chattanooga, too. General Pierre G. T. Beauregard came through here and went on to New Orleans where he used to live, and it is reported that Johnston is on his way here. It is also reported that the 4th Michigan Cavalry captured old Jeff Davis out toward Macon, Georgia, and I suppose they will take him to Washington, where he will be tried and perhaps hung.

All the officers here have their arms draped in mourning on account of the death of the President. A piece of crepe is fastened to their coat sleeve, and I suppose it is so there.

Not every soldier shared a rosy view of the war's conclusion. Consider **Lewis M. Foster (1846–1912).** He had lied when swearing under oath that he was 18 (he was actually 16) when he enlisted in the 138th New York Infantry on September 1, 1862. With the summer of 1865 approaching, his regiment was back inside the fortifications around Washington. In the following two letters to his cousin and his mother, we see that Foster had transformed from an eager recruit into a cynical combat veteran—at age 18. He also displayed a nervous anxiety about returning home that some veterans still experience today.

Arlington Heights, Virginia
June 14, 1865

Nothing of importance has happened here since I wrote to you before except the Grand Review of our corps, and that was the most shameful thing I have seen in a long time. The day was very hot, and a great many was struck, a great many of which died. One of our company was sunstruck, but he got over it. I come through alright, but there was not a dry thread in my clothes.

Fort Sumner
Washington, D. C.
June 17, 1865

We are in the defenses once more, as the boys call it, and have been very busy cleaning out the barracks and mess houses and washing our clothes. It is rumored here that our regiment will get transportation home in ten days from today. I hope it is so. The government offers to let us take our guns home by paying $6 for them [about $225 in modern dollars], but I don't think I will give a cent for it. If Uncle Sam cannot afford to give me a gun after using one so long, I don't want one.

The weather is very warm here now. We had a pretty hard march the day we came here. We was ordered first to go to Fort Stevens, and we got almost there when up come an orderly with a different order, and we had to march to Fort Sumner, which made a 20-mile march and about half of the way over the paving stones of the city. We are here now, and I hope our marching is played out, but I presume they will give us one or two more trials before they discharge us. There was a man of Company B of our regiment drowned this morning in the Washington Canal.

Well, I have wrote all that I have the patience to write. I cannot sit down and write a long letter for some reason or another. I suppose it is because I expect to get home before long. I almost dread to go home, there will be so many questions asked, and everywhere I go, they will be urging me to stay with them. But I can fix them; I won't go anywhere. Well, I must close as it is after Taps.

With the fighting over, hundreds of thousands of men began making the transition from military to civilian life, even as hundreds of thousands of blacks began transitioning from slavery to freedom. The path wasn't always easy, especially for the latter.

In March, Congress had created an agency to assist newly freed slaves. For one **unidentified former Union soldier**, that agency also provided an avenue to begin a new life of his own.

Fortress Monroe, Virginia
July 11, 1865

Wilson has been very busy mustering out soldiers for some time, but the rush is nearly over, and thousands of our soldier laddies have abandoned the sword for the plow. I myself have the honor to be one of Uncle Sam's free and private citizens, having been mustered out of service about two weeks ago. I am, however, in Uncle Sam's private employ in the new Bureau of Refugees, Freedmen, and Abandoned Lands with a good salary and ample accommodations. I feel, my dear Devereaux, that you would be glad of anything that would enhance my interest as I positively assure you your welfare would and does afford me infinite pleasure.

You must not think because of my manner of musing on South Carolina by way of fun that such were my sentiments. No, my sentiments are equality of all the states and people in all things. I am glad that the old Palmetto State is as firmly anchored in the union as you say, and I hope she will never again think of seeking a home out of that glorious union.

Although the guns were finally silent by the end of summer, much healing remained to be done. Consider the lingering bitterness in the words that **P. L. Johnson (unknown)**, whose sons had fought in the Union army, penned to a friend.

Miami, Ohio
August 28, 1865

Well, the rebellion has closed, and we are all glad of it; old Jeff Davis is tasting prison life these days, the poor old scamp. He ought to have the same kind of food he gave to our poor boys [Union prisoners of war] until he gets so poor we can see daylight through him. What is there too bad to do to him? The devil will be ashamed to own him. Where he will have to go, must he not be a suffering the torment of Hell every day? I think he must. What poor wretches the Rebs must be. Nothing but their hands to depend on for their bread. Oh, won't it be death for them to go to work, but they have got to come to it. They must earn their bread by the sweat of their brow! I have no sympathy for them.

Our boys have all got home except Lute; his time is not out. My boy got home on the 17th of July. He was in Troy, New York, in the hospital for three months, and his leg has got well.

The hardest, most difficult healing came within fractured families. It had been a war of brother against brother after all. That was literally true for **Marcus Miles Bowers (1828–1904)**. Born in Ohio, he had moved to Richmond, Virginia, as a young man and had fought in the 12th Virginia Infantry. Wounded at Chancellorsville, he was captured in August 1864 and spent the war's final months in the Federal prison camp at Point Lookout, Maryland. In this first postwar letter to his brother in Geneva, Ohio, it was obvious that ill feelings still lingered.

Richmond, Virginia
September 3, 1865

I received your letter of Aug. 2nd in due time. I was surprised and had not dreamed that you held such sentiments. All our New York state and Pennsylvania friends have looked upon it as a cruel war and unnecessary on the part of the U.S., and their love for their friends in the South has not abated at all. Mrs. Bowers has a little niece from Jersey City, New Jersey, who had been with her a year or more before the war broke out. We heard from her about two years ago. She said she had been going to school, and one day, the teachers closed it and took the whole school down to the docks to see several thousand soldiers sail for the South. Little Emma told the teacher she wished to go home and not go to the docks. He wanted to know why. She told him she did not want to see the men who were going South to kill her uncles, aunts, and cousins.

You speak of being sore [angry] and charge it to our [the South's] responsibility. If you had stayed at home (the North), you need not have been sore, but your congressional majority laid violent hands on the institutions of the South and began to prescribe the laws that the South should have and every one of the Northern states enacted laws that made the U.S. Constitution of no effect or protection to the South. But you had the majority and so could not be called to account for it. Consequently, the South sought to protect herself by separation, and if you had been here, you would have done the same. But you have other views now because you have not had the experience of only one side of the struggle.

Brother, I did not mean to bring this subject up again, for it has no business to stand between us. And I thank God it don't stand between me and my sisters. I felt like death when this thing first broke out for to be separated from you, or to be cast as it were in a foreign country from you was hard for me to bear. I sought to avoid being a party of the war, but you don't believe it, so I will say no more.

With time, people moved on. The country was growing, business began booming, and more immigrants were constantly arriving. New wars were fought, and new heroes arose. As the twentieth century dawned, the conflict began receding into America's past.

Yet for some—those who had lost a loved one—the Civil War never truly ended. Time may have marched on, but their hearts remained permanently frozen in the blood-drenched 1860s—people like **Genevieve Byrne Runyon (unknown)**, for example. Her husband, an officer in the 26th Iowa Infantry, died aboard the hospital ship *City of Memphis* in 1863. Writing to his brother more than two years after her husband's passing, she was still entombed in a grief almost too painful to bear.

DeWitt, Iowa
August 8, 1865

I suppose you would like to know how I am getting along. I had my father move into my house, and I am keeping house for him. I was so very lonely that I could not live in the country. I feel a little better contented now, as my mind is taken up with household duties, yet I feel like a wanderer looking for someone that I'll never see again. It feels foolish to be ever complaining, but I cannot help it. I could write forever on the subject. Every tree and bush reminds me of the loved one. It was such a cruel stroke for us. How I felt when his regiment returned without him I cannot describe. I felt then that I had lost him forever on this earth.

Now that the cruel war is over, and I look back and see the many lonely homes, I wonder what it all meant.

Epilogue

"Forever free"

TEN MONTHS AFTER THE LAST GUNS FELL SILENT, A FORMER SLAVE PENNED the following letter to her former owner. Identified only by her first name, it is not known who the recipient was, where she lived, or where the letter originated (though it most likely was written in Canada).

This short piece, little more than a note, carries a powerful message. Lizzy simultaneously displays contradictory feelings, showing concern for her former owner while, at the same time, getting in some digs. Likewise, the fact that the owner chose to save the letter and did not burn or discard it suggests a level of feeling on her part as well.

Together, they remind us just how complex and complicated slavery and the Civil War itself actually were—and how we still live with the war's consequences to this very day.

[Location unknown; presumably Canada]
March 11, 1866

Dear Mistress

It has been quite a few years since I last wrote to yourself and the master in hopes that the two of you will also rejoice as I do for my brethren that have been freed by Mr. Lincoln's proclamation. Colored by the thousands have found their way to Canada. The master and yourself will be happy to know that I have been doing my part in helping as many as I can get established at their new home.

Mabel and Jobe have joined me here at the school. They have asked that I write you and let yourselves know that they are well. In all, thirty-four of your former captives reside here with me. They hold no ill will toward you and the master. We all worry that you will soon starve like we servants have in your keep. We shall write again soon.
  Forever free,
  Lizzy

Major Events Described by the Witnesses

1860

November 6   Abraham Lincoln elected president of the United States

December 20   South Carolina becomes first Deep South state to secede from the Union

December 26–27   Major Robert Anderson evacuates Fort Moultrie and shifts command to nearby Fort Sumter in Charleston Harbor

1861

February 11   Lincoln departs Springfield, Illinois, for Washington, D.C.

February 18   Jefferson Davis inaugurated president of the Confederate States of America

March 4   Lincoln inaugurated president of the United States of America

April 12   Confederate batteries fire on Fort Sumter

April 14   Fort Sumter evacuated after surrendering the previous day

April 15   Lincoln calls for 75,000 90-day volunteers; triggers secession in Mid- and Upper South

April 17   Virginia, the most populous Southern state, secedes

April 19   Baltimore Riot leaves 16 dead and more than 100 injured

April 20   Massive Gosport Navy Yard near Norfolk, Virginia, burned by retreating Federals

May 10	Camp Jackson Affair, immediately followed by St. Louis Riot, leaves 28 people dead and nearly 100 wounded
May 24	Federals seize Alexandria, Virginia; Colonel Elmer Ellsworth killed
May 29	Confederate capital moved to Richmond, Virginia
June 10	Confederate victory in Battle of Big Bethel, Virginia
June 17	Federals defeat Confederate-aligned Missouri State Guard in Battle of Boonville, Missouri
July 5	Confederate-aligned Missouri State Guard victorious in Battle of Carthage, Missouri
July 21	Federals routed in Battle of First Bull Run/Manassas, Virginia, war's first major engagement
July 26	General George B. McClellan named Union commander in the East; creates Army of the Potomac
August 10	Federals defeated, General Nathaniel Lyon killed in Battle of Wilson's Creek/Oak Hills in southwestern Missouri
September 4	Confederate General Leonidas Polk seizes heights overlooking Mississippi River at Columbus, violating Kentucky's neutrality
September 6	Federal General Ulysses Grant seizes Paducah, Kentucky, in retaliation
September 18–20	Confederate-aligned Missouri State Guard ends siege of Lexington, Missouri, with victory in the "Battle of the Hemp Bales"
Autumn 1861	Federals build seven city-class ironclads at St. Louis for use in upcoming Western Rivers Campaign
October 21	Confederate victory in Battle of Balls' Bluff, Virginia; Federal victory in Battle of Camp Wildcat in eastern Kentucky
November 7	Confederate victory in Battle of Belmont, Missouri, on Mississippi River; Federals take Port Royal, seize Beaufort and Hilton Head, South Carolina, providing important southeastern Atlantic base for naval blockade of Southern ports

November 8 · USS *San Jacinto* stops RMS *Trent* on open seas, and two Confederate emissaries bound for Europe are forcibly removed; resulting crisis almost causes war between the United States and Great Britain.

December 11–12 · Great Fire of Charleston, South Carolina

1862

January 11 · Secretary of War Simon Cameron resigns amid corruption claims, named U.S. ambassador to Russia; replaced by Edwin Stanton

January 19 · Federal victory in Battle of Mill Springs/Logan's Crossroads in eastern Kentucky

February 6 · Federal bombardment compels capture of Fort Henry in Tennessee

February 8 · Federals capture Roanoke Island, North Carolina, providing a second important southeastern Atlantic foothold

February 14–16 · Unsuccessful Federal naval bombardment of nearby Fort Donelson followed by unsuccessful Confederate counterattack; fort surrenders in Union's first major victory

February 23 · Confederates evacuate Nashville, Tennessee

February 28– April 8 · Federal victories in Siege of New Madrid/Battle of Island Number 10 in Missouri result in capture of upper Mississippi River defenses

March 7–8 · Federal victory in Battle of Pea Ridge/Elkhorn Tavern, Arkansas, securing Union control of Missouri

March 8–9 · Battle of the Ironclads between USS *Monitor* and CSS *Virginia/Merrimack* results in a draw after serious Federal warship losses at Hampton Roads, Virginia

March 9 · Confederate General Joseph E. Johnston withdraws from Manassas line, leaving large amounts of supplies and equipment behind

March 17 · McClellan begins moving 117,000-man Army of the Potomac by water from Washington, D.C., area to Fortress Monroe, Virginia

March 23 · Federals victorious in Battle of Kernstown, Virginia, start of Shenandoah Valley Campaign and one of Stonewall Jackson's few defeats

April 6–7	Federal victory in the Battle of Shiloh/Pittsburg Landing in Tennessee
April 10–11	Federals capture Fort Pulaski outside Savannah, Georgia, after 30-hour bombardment, proving rifled artillery's effectiveness
April 11	Federals capture Huntsville, Alabama, severing important Memphis and Charleston Railroad
April 16	Lincoln signs District of Columbia Compensated Emancipation Act, ending slavery in Washington, D.C.
April 24–25	Union fleet runs past Forts Jackson and St. Phillip on lower Mississippi River; New Orleans captured
April 29–May 30	Siege of rail junction at Corinth, Mississippi, ends with Confederate retreat
May 7	After inconsequential action at Williamsburg and Yorktown, McClellan moves up the Virginia Peninsula in earnest
May 9	USS *Monitor* bombards Confederate batteries at Sewell's Point, Virginia; CSS *Virginia/Merrimack* appears; though a second duel looks likely, the ironclads don't engage; Confederates abandon nearby Norfolk, Virginia, the next day
May 11	CSS *Virginia/Merrimack* destroyed in James River
May 20	Lincoln signs Homestead Act
May 31–June 1	McClellan's advance halted in Battle of Seven Pines/Fair Oaks; severe wounding of Johnston results in General Robert E. Lee assuming command of Army of Northern Virginia
June 9	Confederate victory in Battle of Port Republic, Virginia, ends Jackson's Valley Campaign after pushing back three Union armies
June 25–30	Lee summons Jackson from the Shenandoah Valley, launches Seven Days counteroffensive, forcing McClellan to retrace his steps
July 1	Federal victory at Battle of Malvern Hill, Virginia, enables McClellan to safely retreat to Harrison's Landing

July 2	Lincoln calls for 300,000 three-year volunteers
August 5	Federal victory at Battle of Baton Rouge, Louisiana; CSS *Arkansas* destroyed to prevent capture
August 18–September 26	Nearly 500 civilians and soldiers, plus 150 warriors, killed in Sioux Uprising/Dakota War in Minnesota
Late August	Lee dispatches Jackson to go after General John Pope's Army of Virginia to the north; follows with the rest of his army later
August 28–30	Confederate victory in Battle of Second Bull Run/Manassas
August 29–30	Federals defeated in Battle of Richmond, Kentucky
September 1	Inconclusive Battle of Chantilly, Virginia; Union General Philip Kearny killed
September 3	Lee launches first invasion of the North
September 15	Jackson captures more than 12,000 Federals after artillery bombardment of Harpers Ferry, Virginia (modern-day West Virginia)
September 17	Federal strategic victory in Battle of Antietam/Sharpsburg, deadliest single day in American history
September 19	Federals victorious in Battle of Iuka, Mississippi
September 22	Lincoln announces Preliminary Emancipation Proclamation, effective January 1, 1863
September 29	As Confederates invade Kentucky, General William "Bull" Nelson murdered by General Jefferson C. Davis at Federal headquarters in Louisville, Kentucky
September 30	Confederates rout Federals in Battle of First Newtonia in Missouri; withdraw to Arkansas days later
October 4	Federals victorious in Battle of Corinth, Mississippi
October 8	Federals strategically victorious in Battle of Perryville, Kentucky
November 4	Despite Democratic gains, Republicans retain control of U.S. Congress
November 5	McClellan relieved as commander of Army of the Potomac; replaced by General Ambrose Burnside

December 7	Federal victory in Battle of Prairie Grove gives Union control of northwest Arkansas
December 13	Confederates victorious in Battle of Fredericksburg, Virginia
December 20	Confederate General Earl Van Dorn leads cavalry raid on Grant's supply base at Holly Springs, Mississippi, destroying more than $1 million in materiel
December 29	Confederates victorious in Battle of Chickasaw Bayou, Mississippi, Federals' first attempt to take Vicksburg
December 31	Battle of Stones River/Murfreesboro, Tennessee, begins; USS *Monitor* lost in storm off Cape Hatteras, North Carolina
1863	
January 1	Emancipation Proclamation issued
January 2	Inconclusive Battle of Stones River/Murfreesboro, Tennessee, ends
January 10–11	Federals victorious in Battle of Arkansas Post, Arkansas, capturing Fort Hindman on Arkansas River
January 20	CSS *Alabama* arrives in Kingston, Jamaica, after sinking USS *Hatteras*
January 20–22	Army of the Potomac bogged down in "Mud March"
January 25	Burnside relieved as commander of Army of the Potomac; replaced by General Joseph Hooker
February 2 and 13	USS *Queen of the West* and USS *Indianola* run past Confederate batteries at Vicksburg
March 9	Confederate partisan rangers led by Captain John S. Mosby capture Union General Edwin Stoughton in bed at his Fairfax, Virginia, headquarters
March 13–14	Two Union warships pass Confederate batteries at Port Hudson, Louisiana; USS *Mississippi* runs aground and explodes
April	Confederates conduct "Bacon Raid" for food supplies in southeastern Virginia and northeastern North Carolina
April 1–20	Food shortages prompt bread riots in several Confederate cities

April 7	Confederates defeat Federal warships attacking Charleston Harbor; USS *Keokuk* sinks
April 16	Federal river fleet runs past Confederate batteries at Vicksburg, Mississippi
April 29–May 7	Federal General George Stoneman's cavalry raid fails to hinder Lee's movements or to enter Richmond
April 30	Grant's army crosses Mississippi River and moves on Vicksburg from the rear
May 2–3	Confederates victorious in Battle of Chancellorsville, Virginia
May 3	Federals victorious in Battle of Second Fredericksburg, Virginia
May 7	Adulterous Confederate General Earl Van Dorn murdered at Spring Hill, Tennessee; General Nathan Bedford Forrest replaces him
May 10	Stonewall Jackson dies of pneumonia after being wounded at Chancellorsville
May 22	Federals defeated in assault on Vicksburg's fortifications; Grant begins siege
May 22–July 9	Federals conduct siege of Port Hudson, Louisiana
June 3	Lee begins second invasion of the North
June 7	USCT in combat in Battle of Milliken's Bend, Louisiana; gunboat support prevents Confederate victory
June 9	Horsemen under Stuart and Pleasanton fight an inconclusive battle at Brandy Station, Virginia, in the war's largest mainly cavalry battle
June 11–July 29	Confederate General John Hunt Morgan's 2,500 horsemen head north of Ohio River in large-scale raid
June 24	Federal General William Rosecrans begins Tullahoma Campaign to maneuver Confederate General Braxton Bragg out of Tennessee
June 27	Hooker relieved as commander of Army of the Potomac; replaced by General George Meade
July 1–3	Federals victorious in Battle of Gettysburg, Pennsylvania

July 4	Confederates surrender Vicksburg, Mississippi; Confederate attempt to retake Helena, Arkansas, repulsed
July 9	Confederates surrender Port Hudson, Louisiana
July 10–September 8	Union naval and land forces assault Confederate defenses in Charleston Harbor, including Fort Wagner
July 11	Federals begin drawing names in first nationwide military draft
July 13–16	New York City Draft Riots
July 18	Second Union attack on Fort Wagner, South Carolina, defeated with heavy casualties
September 6	Bragg evacuates Chattanooga, Tennessee
September 8	Fifty Confederate defenders hold off 5,000 Federals at Sabine Pass on Louisiana–Texas line
September 10	Federals capture Little Rock, Arkansas
September 18–20	Confederates victorious in Battle of Chickamauga, Georgia, war's second-bloodiest battle; siege of Chattanooga begins
October 16	Rosecrans relieved as commander of Union forces at Chattanooga; replaced by Grant
November 19	Lincoln delivers Gettysburg Address
November 24–25	Federals victorious in Battles of Lookout Mountain and Missionary Ridge at Chattanooga, Tennessee
November 29	Federals repulse Confederate attack on Fort Sanders, ending siege of Knoxville, Tennessee
December 2	Bragg relieved as commander of Army of Tennessee; replaced by General Joseph E. Johnston

1864

February 17	Confederate experiments with naval technology (including semisubmersible "Davids") culminate in sinking of USS *Housatonic* and submarine CSS *Hunley* in Charleston Harbor
February 20	Federal invasion of Florida ends with defeat in Battle of Olustee/Ocean Pond

March 2	Grant promoted to lieutenant general (first to hold that rank since George Washington) and named Union general-in-chief; personally directs Army of the Potomac; Sherman replaces Grant in the West; Federal Colonel Ulric Dahlgren killed in failed raid on Richmond; papers found on body instruct him to kill Davis and top Confederate leaders
March 10	Federals under General Nathaniel Banks launch Red River Campaign to capture Shreveport, Louisiana
April 4–23	"Metropolitan Fair" in New York City raises $1.3 million for U.S. Sanitary Commission; similar fairs follow around the North
April 8–9	Confederates victorious in Battle of Mansfield/Sabine Crossroads, Louisiana; Federals withdraw after Battle of Pleasant Hill the next day, ending Red River Campaign
April 12	Outrage follows when black soldiers are killed in Battle of Fort Pillow in Tennessee
April 30	Federal tactical victory in Battle of Jenkins' Ferry, Arkansas; Union General Fredrick Steele prevented from assisting Banks
May 4	Grant sets Federal forces in motion, starting Wilderness/Overland Campaign
May 7	Sherman sets Federal forces in motion, starting Atlanta Campaign
May 5–6	Confederates hold off Federals in inconclusive Battle of the Wilderness
May 10–13	Confederates again hold off Federals in inconclusive Battle of the Spotsylvania Courthouse
May 12–16	Federal forces turned back in the Battle of Drewry's Bluff; Confederate counterattack leaves General Benjamin Butler's command bottled up at Bermuda Hundred
May 14–15	Battle of Resaca, Georgia, Atlanta Campaign's first major engagement. Sherman's attacks blunted, forcing him to flank Confederate lines

May 25–June 3	Heavy fighting in Battles of New Hope Church, Pickett's Mill, and Dallas as Confederates resist Sherman's drive into Georgia
May–June 1864	Russian fleet concludes wintering in New York Harbor and visits Boston on return home
June 3	Federals defeated with staggering losses in Battle of Cold Harbor; Grant acquires nickname the "Butcher"
June 8	Lincoln wins presidential nomination for second time at Republican National Convention in Baltimore, Maryland
June 10	Confederate General Nathan Bedford Forrest routs Federals in Battle of Brice's Cross Roads, Mississippi
June 12	Grant begins shifting Army of the Potomac across James River to Petersburg area below Richmond
June 14	Confederate General and Episcopal Bishop Leonidas Polk killed by artillery shell atop Pine Mountain near Marietta, Georgia
June 18	Lee shifts bulk of Army of Northern Virginia to Petersburg; siege begins that will last almost 10 months, the war's longest
June 19	CSS *Alabama* sunk by USS *Kearsarge* off coast of Cherbourg, France
June 27	Federals defeated with heavy loss in Battle of Kennesaw Mountain, Georgia
July 2	Confederate General Jubal Early begins moving toward Maryland to relieve pressure on Shenandoah Valley
July 9	Confederates victorious in Battle of Monocacy, Maryland
July 11	Confederate attacks on Washington, D.C., defenses repulsed as Lincoln watches fighting; Early begins withdrawal to Virginia
July 17	Johnston relieved as commander of Army of Tennessee; replaced by General John Bell Hood the next day
July 20	Confederate attack defeated in Battle of Peachtree Creek, Georgia
July 22	Confederates again defeated in Battle of Atlanta, Georgia; Union General James McPherson killed

July 30	Federals defeated in Battle of the Crater at Peterburg, Virginia
July 31	Federal cavalry raid to liberate Andersonville Prison thwarted; Union General Stoneman captured near Macon, Georgia
August 5	Federals secure control of Mobile Bay, Alabama, in naval battle
August 31– September 1	Federals capture railroad line from Macon in Battle of Jonesborough, Georgia
August 31	George B. McClellan wins presidential nomination at Democratic National Convention in Chicago, Illinois
September 1	Hood withdraws Confederate army from Atlanta via last route open to him
September 2	Mayor James Calhoun surrenders city; Sherman enters Atlanta
September 16	Confederates conduct "Beefsteak Raid," stealing nearly 2,500 head of cattle from Grant's army
September 19	Confederates under Native American General Stand Watie capture $1.5 million in supplies in Battle of Cabin Creek in Indian Territory (modern-day Oklahoma)
September 25–26	Confederate President Jefferson Davis visits Hood's army at Palmetto, Georgia, to boost morale
October 19	Federal victory in Battle of Cedar Creek, Virginia, gives Sheridan control of Shenandoah Valley; Confederate operatives from Canada rob three banks in St. Albans, Vermont, of $208,000
October 23	Confederates defeated in Battle of Westport, Missouri, largest battle west of Mississippi River
November 8	Lincoln reelected president of the United States
November 15	Sherman commences infamous March to the Sea through Georgia
November 29	Federal troops march past Confederate troops in the dark near Spring Hill, Tennessee
November 30	Confederates defeat Federals in Battle of Franklin, Tennessee, with heavy losses

December 15–16   Federals destroy Confederate Army of Tennessee as an effective fighting force in Battle of Nashville, Tennessee

December 21   Savannah, Georgia, falls to Sherman

December 24–25   Federal land–sea assault on Fort Fisher near Wilmington, North Carolina, fails

1865

January 12   Francis Blair Sr. meets with Jefferson Davis in Richmond trying to mediate a settlement; makes second trip at Lincoln's urging

January 15   Federals capture Fort Fisher in second, better-executed attack

January 23   Hood relieved of command of Army of Tennessee at his request

February 3   Peace conference headed by Lincoln for Union and Vice President Alexander H. Stephens for Confederacy held at Hampton Roads, Virginia

February 6   Robert E. Lee named general-in-chief of Confederate army

February 17   Most of Columbia, South Carolina, destroyed by fire

February 23   General Joseph E. Johnston takes command of all Confederate forces in the Carolinas

March 13   Confederate Congress approves allowing slaves to serve in army

March 19–21   Federals victorious in Battle of Bentonville, North Carolina

March 24   Lincoln arrives at City Point, Virginia, to visit Grant's army

April 2   Grant attacks Petersburg defenses; Lee informs Davis that Richmond can no longer be held; capital evacuated that evening

April 3   Federal troops enter Richmond

April 4   Lincoln visits Richmond

April 9   Lee surrenders to Grant at Appomattox Courthouse, Virginia; Federal victory in Battle of Fort Blakeley leads to the surrender of Mobile, Alabama, three days later

April 11	Lincoln makes last speech from White House window
April 14	Lincoln shot at Ford's Theatre
April 15	Lincoln dies at 7:22 a.m.
April 19	Lincoln's funeral held at White House; remains then displayed around the North over two weeks
April 26	Johnston surrenders to Sherman in North Carolina; John Wilkes Booth killed by Federal soldiers in Virginia
April 27	Steamboat *Sultana* explodes on Mississippi River; estimated 1,585 victims, mostly Union soldiers returning home
May 4	General Richard Taylor surrenders all remaining Confederate troops east of Mississippi River; Lincoln is laid to rest in Springfield, Illinois
May 10	Jefferson Davis captured near Irwinville, Georgia, and taken into custody
May 23–24	Grand Review of the Armies held in Washington, D.C.
June 2	General Kirby Smith surrenders Confederate Trans-Mississippi Department

The Witnesses

John Quincy Adams	60th Illinois Infantry
Freeman E. Aldrich	Civilian, farmer
George Benton Aldrich	48th Ohio Infantry
Judith Alexander	Civilian
J. N. Alvord	2nd Massachusetts Infantry chaplain
Thomas Andrae	Civilian, businessman
Benjamin H. Anthony	11th Virginia Infantry
Henry W. Arnold	13th Virginia Infantry
Edwin Wallace Atwood	8th Missouri Infantry (Federal)
William Atwood	Civilian, clerk in U.S. War Department
Dr. Thomas Bailey	10th South Carolina Infantry surgeon
Albert Henry Bancroft	85th New York Infantry
Hetty A. Barclay	Civilian
Albert Jenkins Barnard	116th New York Infantry
Cyrus Bates	Civilian, teenager; later served in Union army
Mamie Bates	Civilian, husband at war
Samuel L. Beck	Union assistant adjutant general
Edward Bell	Civilian, U.S. marshal
T. John Bell	69th Pennsylvania Infantry
Nicholas Belveal	33rd Iowa Infantry
C. F. Bennett	Union soldier; regiment unknown
Lafayette Lunan Bennett	5th Pennsylvania Heavy Artillery/ 204th Pennsylvania Infantry
William H. Bennett	5th Wisconsin Infantry

Elias Cornelius Boudinot	Civilian, Cherokee Nation delegate to Confederate Congress
Marcus Miles Bowers	12th Virginia Infantry
Henry Bowman	126th Pennsylvania Infantry
John W. Boyd	Civilian
Robert Boyd	16th Ohio Infantry
David Breed	Civilian, teenage student; brother in army
J. H. Briscoe	14th Texas Cavalry (Dismounted)
Joseph A. Briscoe	14th Texas Cavalry (Dismounted)
Aaron Brown	3rd Iowa Infantry
Albert Church Brown	16th Maine Infantry
Francis G. Brown	2nd Massachusetts Light Artillery (Nim's Battery)
George A. Brown	Civilian, son in the army
George Washington Brown	68th Ohio Infantry
Sylvester H. Brown	22nd New York Infantry
Frank C. Brownell	Civilian, businessman
Thomas Franklin Brownell	Civilian, U.S. Christian Commission volunteer
Lewis Buckley	68th Ohio Infantry
Dexter E. Buell	27th New York Infantry
Thomas Burriss	4th South Carolina Infantry
Hannah Burrows	Civilian, friend killed in war
George W. Burt	Civilian, father in army
Robert P. Bush	12th New York Infantry
Egbert B. Buzby	138th Pennsylvania Infantry
Leander Calfee	54th Virginia Infantry
George Warren Campbell	Veteran Volunteer Engineering Corps
Norton W. Campbell	12th Illinois Infantry
Charles Darwin Carpenter	20th Ohio Infantry
Thomas P. Carver	98th Ohio Infantry
Josephine Brownell Chase	Civilian, U.S. Christian Commission nurse
Edgar B. Clark	Civilian, teenager

James Henry Clark	3rd Vermont Infantry
William T. Clark	79th Pennsylvania Infantry
George Clay	2nd U.S. Sharpshooters
John Clayton	39th Alabama Infantry
Lewis Morris Cleaver	140th Pennsylvania Infantry
Calvin Hopkins Cleaves	9th Maine Infantry
John W. Cleland	111th Ohio Infantry
Mary Jane "Jennie" Cleland	Lived at home with parents
Arthur Clemmair	Union staff officer
Edwin Cobb	5th Maine Infantry
Charles S. Cockett	70th New York Infantry
Andrew Beach Coffinberry	1st Michigan Engineers and Mechanics
Leanna Compton	Civilian, teenage student
Archibald Brown Cook	Civilian, clerk in U.S. War Department
Lewis S. Coryell	Civilian, businessman
James B. Cox	29th Mississippi Infantry
S. B. Crane	Union soldier; regiment unknown
Margaret Creath	Civilian, banished from Missouri
Phillip J. Crewell	34th New York Infantry
William Jere Crook	13th/154th Tennessee Infantry
J. C. Cross	Civilian, slave trader
E.W. Curtis	88th Illinois Infantry
Dr. William Johnson Dale	Surgeon general of Massachusetts
DeWitt Davis	Civilian, lawyer and Republican activist
Ephriam C. Dawes	53rd Ohio Infantry
James Delenbaugh	38th Ohio Infantry
Insert Anna Clementine Dennington	Civilian, teenager
Leona Dickson	Civilian
John Downer	7th Iowa Infantry
Amos Downing	6th Maine Infantry

Walter Guppy Duckett	138th New York Infantry/ 9th New York Heavy Artillery
Samuel Durant	81st New York Infantry
William Harrison Dunham	8th New Hampshire Infantry
John Boultwood Edson	27th New York Infantry
Charlotte Temple Elliott	Civilian, boyfriend in army
Edson Emory	2nd Vermont Infantry
Philo Emory	2nd Vermont Infantry
Francis Farout	16th Indiana Infantry
William A. Ferguson	8th Confederate Cavalry
George W. Fernald	82nd New York Infantry
John Flannery	72nd Illinois Infantry
John Wesley Folsom	Civilian
Elizabeth A. Foster	Civilian
Lewis M. Foster	138th New York Infantry/ 9th New York Heavy Artillery
Perrin V. Fox	Captain, 1st Michigan Engineers & Mechanics
John B. Freeman	13th Michigan Infantry
Warren A. Friend	3rd Maine Infantry
Frederick Gallup	8th Connecticut Infantry
Amy Galusha	Civilian, textile mill worker
Hugh Garland	1st/4th Missouri Infantry (Confederate)
Leonard A. Gay	4th New Hampshire Infantry
Mary Cross Gayer	Civilian, widow
James Giaque	30th Iowa Infantry
Polly Giddings	Civilian
Quincy Adams Gillmore	Union general
J. D. Gilman	Civilian
Mollie Gilmore	Civilian
Caleb Glick	114th Ohio Infantry
Willis D. Golin	Union staff officer

Amos Gorrell	18th Ohio Infantry
John Gray	101st Indiana Infantry
Joseph Green	30th North Carolina Infantry
Katherine Pinckard Greenleaf	Civilian
Lorraine Walker Griffin	16th North Carolina Infantry
Columbus Griffith	2nd Kansas Cavalry
James W. Griffith	Civilian; later served in 117th Ohio Infantry
Robert Guyton	139th Pennsylvania Infantry
Sarah Ann Bowers Haffer	Civilian, husband at war
L. N. Halbert	Confederate officer; regiment unknown
Isaac Hamilton	Civilian, former slave
John William Hamlett	21st Virginia Infantry
Rebecca Hand	Civilian, teacher
Isaac Hardaker	32nd Iowa Infantry
Elisha Q. Harding	Civilian, railroad contractor
Woodburn Hardy	95th Illinois Infantry
Frank Haynes	1st Maine Veteran Infantry
G. L. Haywood	1st Minnesota Artillery
John L. Hebron	2nd Ohio Infantry
Constantine Hege	48th North Carolina Infantry
Friedrich William Charles Heldman	3rd Missouri Infantry; 17th Missouri Infantry (Federal)
William Henry	8th New York Cavalry
Charles Henthorn	77th Illinois Infantry
Sabina Hiatt	Civilian, Quaker, brother at war
Robert Hill	Union soldier; regiment unknown
Warren B. Hill	Civilian, clerk at an insurance company
Eleanor Beanes Mullikin Hilleary	Civilian
Winfield Scott Hills	Union sailor
Thomas Hine	39th Ohio Infantry

Charles William Hobbs	13th New Hampshire Infantry
John W. Hodges	Civilian, later Confederate officer
William Holiday	3rd Missouri State Militia Cavalry (Federal)
John Holmes	14th Veterans Reserve Corps
John Holt	13th Massachusetts Infantry
William Hooper	62nd Tennessee Infantry
Daniel Hicks Hopping	24th New York Cavalry
Morgan Horfius	211th Pennsylvania Infantry
William Addison Hosford	2nd Connecticut Heavy Artillery
John W. Houtaling	95th Illinois Infantry
Charles Howe	36th Massachusetts Infantry
Louise M. Howe	Civilian, war widow
Ada Hubbard	Civilian
Robert Alexander Hubbel	14th New York Infantry
Jesse Hughes	1st Pennsylvania Cavalry
Joseph Bovee Hughes	38th Mississippi Infantry (Mounted)
William Taylor Humphreys	2nd Kentucky Cavalry (Confederate States)
Edwin Imes	83rd Ohio Infantry
George Waterman Jackson	4th Independent Battery, Indiana Light Artillery
Alvah Jay	102nd Illinois Infantry
John Hancock Boyd Jenkins	40th New York Infantry
Andrew Wallace Johnson	Union naval officer
Calvin R. Johnson	14th Wisconsin Infantry
Hannibal Augustus Johnson	3rd Maine Infantry
P. L. Johnson	Civilian, son was a soldier
William L. Johnson	116th Illinois Infantry
David C. Jones	26th Missouri Infantry (Federal)
William Ferrand Keys	143rd Pennsylvania Infantry
Isaac H. Killmer	Civilian
Joseph Edward Kimball	1st Massachusetts Infantry
William Kimble	31st Ohio Infantry

Flavius Franklin Kimbrough	6th Alabama Infantry
John Evans Kinder	131st Ohio National Guard
Margaret Barclay Kirby	Civilian, brother at war
Mary Barclay Kirby	Civilian, son at war
George Dwight Knox	3rd Minnesota Infantry
Adam Turney Kreps	67th USCT
Henry Stoner Kupp	Civilian, railroad engineer; later Union officer
Daniel Lamb	West Virginia Unionist
Austin Lamonte	Civilian, college student
Andrew Lane	32nd Massachusetts Infantry
Solon Langworthy	27th Iowa Infantry
Charles A. Lawrence	7th New Hampshire Infantry
Edwin Lawrence	77th New York Infantry
Dr. Joseph Rodney Layton	Union naval surgeon
Silas Leach	52nd Pennsylvania Infantry
Enoch Leavitt	2nd Ohio Cavalry
Adolph M. Leve	38th Massachusetts Infantry
Cyrus Liggett	166th Ohio Infantry
William Line	81st Pennsylvania Infantry
Martha A. Lingrell	Civilian, brother-in-law in army
T. B. Lisle	Union soldier; regiment unknown
David T. T. Litchfield	134th Massachusetts Infantry
Mary A. Little	Civilian
John Lobdill	117th New York Infantry
John Caleb Lockwood	30th Iowa Infantry
Richard Thomas Lombard	16th Massachusetts Infantry
Stephen Long	2nd South Carolina Infantry
John M. Lovejoy	121st New York Infantry
William Henry Luse	18th Mississippi Infantry
Leonard Lusted	3rd Independent Battery, Wisconsin Light Artillery
Cornelius J. Madden	102nd Ohio Infantry

Jacob F. Mader Jr.	61st Ohio Infantry
Edward S. Manley	14th Vermont Infantry
Peter Marchant	47th Tennessee Infantry
Henry Lane Markham	2nd Illinois Cavalry
Israel Markham	7th Illinois Cavalry
Thomas Marple	91st Pennsylvania Infantry
David M. Marsh	12th Arkansas Infantry
George C. Marsh	1st Michigan Sharpshooters
Daniel Marston	16th Maine Infantry
Henry C. Martha	10th Pennsylvania Infantry
Edwin Matherry	9th Pennsylvania Reserve Infantry
John A. McAllister	Civilian, businessman
J. N. McBee	Civilian, Board of Enrollment (draft board)
Ebeneezer Hudson McCall	80th Ohio Infantry
Hamilton McClurg	102nd Ohio Infantry
Alexander McFarland	Civilian; previously imprisoned for desertion
James McFarland	Civilian
John McGee	Civilian
Francis J. McKee	16th Ohio Infantry
William Shakespeare McKinley	1st Indiana Heavy Artillery
Lycurgus Mechling	53rd Ohio Infantry
Marcellus Ovando Messer	19th Ohio Infantry
Charles Miller	140th New York Infantry
Anson Mills	23rd Ohio Infantry
Joanna Mills	Civilian
Edwin M. Misner	145th New York Infantry
James H. Mitchell	47th Illinois Infantry
Sarah Monfort	Civilian in Gettysburg, Pennsylvania
John F. Moore	10th Kentucky Cavalry (U.S.)
Edward Mott	5th Connecticut Infantry
Albert Greenleaf Mudgett	11th Maine Infantry

Thomas Munhall	11th Illinois Cavalry
Henry Scott Murray	8th New York Independent Light Artillery
Samuel Myers	49th Illinois Infantry
Don Carlos Newton	52nd Illinois Infantry
James Nicholas	118th Ohio Infantry
George Granville Nichols	42nd Massachusetts Infantry
J. W. Norris	1st South Carolina State Troops
Henry Hall Northup	49th Massachusetts Infantry
Benjamin Franklin O'Bryan	140th Pennsylvania Infantry
Henry Harrison Orendorff	103rd Illinois Infantry
William H. Orr	47th Ohio Infantry
Robert Ould	Confederate States prisoner-of-war exchange commissioner
Isham C. Paine	4th Virginia Infantry
Luther Lee Parks	13th USCT
Hiram Paulding	Union naval officer
Peter Pryor Perkins	1st Mississippi Battalion
Warren E. Perkins	2nd Massachusetts Infantry
Frank Phelps	10th Wisconsin Infantry
Albert Phillips	Union naval officer
Almon Gowing Pierce	Civilian, later Union army
Enoch Franklin Piper	4th Maine Infantry
Samuel Prior Jr.	Civilian, contract steamship pilot
Mary Margaret Pugh	Civilian
John D. Reamer	Civilian, businessman; falsely accused conspirator
Charles Kramer Reppert	Civilian
William A. Rice	Civilian, pharmacist
Reuben Rich	Union naval officer
Joseph Richards	Civilian, son died as a prisoner of war
August Josiah Robbins	2nd Vermont Infantry (Medal of Honor)
Lucinda Rockwell	Civilian, brother killed in war

Louisa Rogers	Civilian, husband at war
A. S. Root	Civilian
Sylvester "Sly" Rounds	7th Connecticut Infantry Veterans Reserve Corps
Jacob D. Row	17th Indiana Cavalry
Isaac Rowe	Civilian
W. O. Ruddock	23rd North Carolina Infantry
Genevieve Byrne Runyon	Civilian, war widow
Martha Russell	Civilian, husband at war
Thomas Rutledge	33rd Missouri Infantry (Federal)
George W. Saner	45th Illinois Infantry
Jesse A. Sargent	6th Massachusetts Infantry
John P. Schuyler	160th New York Infantry
Rogena Almira Scott	Civilian, schoolteacher
T. J. Scott	Civilian, teenage student
Ann M. Sears	Civilian
Peter Collins Sears	33rd Massachusetts Infantry
Reverend Lyman W. Seely	Civilian Baptist minister
George Setszer	18th Virginia Infantry
Benjamin Shaw	Civilian, Quaker, clerk in U.S. War Department
Emma Graves Shaw	Civilian
James S. Shaw	8th New York State Militi
Joseph W. Shaw	5th Pennsylvania Reserve Infantry
George Washington Sheldon	47th Ohio Infantry
Lewis Capet Shephard	11th New York Infantry (MOH)
Charles M. Shipley	29th Pennsylvania Infantry
George Sifleet	127th Illinois Infantry
James Sifleet	36th Illinois Infantry
David M. Simpson	4th South Carolina State Troops
Hiram Smedly	Civilian, son killed in war
Charles W. Smith	1st Connecticut Heavy Artillery

Cornelius Smith	107th Pennsylvania Infantry
William Nathan Harrel Smith	Civilian, Confederate States congressman
Frank Smitt	Civilian
John Sneed	Civilian, former Tennessee attorney general
George A. Spencer	7th Rhode Island Infantry
May Humphreys Stacey	12th U.S. Infantry
Marietta Comey Stearns	Civilian, brother in Union army
George P. Stetson	Civilian, postmaster
James A. Stewart	98th Ohio Infantry
James H. Stewart	39th Ohio Infantry
Robert Bell Stewart	15th Ohio Infantry
Arthur M. Stone	34th Massachusetts Infantry
Charles W. Strickney	1st Illinois Light Artillery (Taylor's Battery)
Georgia Anna Tucker Stubbs	Civilian, husband at war
Samuel Swats	11th Virginia Cavalry
Daniel Joseph Taft	82nd Pennsylvania Infantry
James J. Tarleton	Civilian, businessman
Addison W. Tarr	19th Veterans Reserve Corps
Abby L. Taylor	Civilian, mother who lost her son
Isaac Taylor	3rd Minnesota Infantry
Francis Teear	24th New York Infantry
Mary Ellen Teeter	Civilian
Riley Leroy Thatcher	96th New York Infantry
Alfred A. Thayer	96th Ohio Infantry
George H. Thomas	13th Indiana Infantry
Asahel W. Thompson	6th/7th Arkansas Infantry
George Tracy	Civilian
Charles A. Tripp	4th New York Heavy Artillery
Franz Trouts	11th U.S. Artillery
Gilbert A. Tucker	10th New Hampshire Infantry
Cyril H. Tyler	7th Michigan Infantry

Theodore Frelinghuysen Vaill — 2nd Connecticut Heavy Artillery

William Van Marten — Civilian, attorney

Mary Van Nest — Civilian, husband at wa

Charles Van Waggoner — 141st New York Infantry

Dr. James Vandervort — Civilian, doctor; later Union surgeon

Rev. William H. Vernor — Civilian, Presbyterian minister; later Confederate States chaplain

Edward H. Wade — 14th Connecticut Infantry

Charles Walbridge — 100th New York Infantry

A. B. Walker — Union staff officer

Edward Walker — Civilian, Board of Enrollment (draft board)

William Walker — 17th Illinois Infantry

William Washburn — 35th Massachusetts Infantry

Alexander T. Weaver — 37th Illinois Infantry

John M. Weidemeyer — 6th Missouri Infantry (Confederate)

Samuel Welch — 51st Ohio Infantry

Hiram Weller — 6th New York Cavalry

Reuben T. Wells — 115th New York Infantry

Erwin Welsh — 67th Ohio Infantry

Benjamin Wendover — 126th New York Infantry

George Westfall — 17th New York Infantry

Edwin Martin Whipple — 23rd Illinois Infantry

Ansel Lothrop White — 19th Maine Infantry

Otis Whitney — 27th Iowa Infantry

Henry Wilkins — 123rd New York Infantry

John Danforth Wilkinson — 1st Missouri Infantry (Federal); 1st Missouri Light Artillery (Federal)

R. J. Willevy — Civilian

Cyrus Willis — 58th Massachusetts Infantry

Morton Willson — 93rd Indiana Infantry

John B. Wilson — 2nd New Jersey Infantry

Luther Winship — 27th Indiana Infantry

Sallie Witherow	Civilian, schoolteacher
Robert Hancock Wood	22nd Tennessee Infantry
L. A. Woodcock	Civilian, missionary in West Indies
George T. Woodward	8th Wisconsin Infantry
Charles S. Woolston	3rd Pennsylvania Cavalry
Lawrence B. Worth	7th Iowa Infantry
Franklin S. Wright	33rd Massachusetts Infantry
Henry E. Wrigley	Independent Pennsylvania Engineers
Henry Silas Wyman	8th Indiana Infantry
Thomas Zahniser	57th Pennsylvania Infantry

Additionally, there are several dozen other witnesses whose names are either unknown or only partially identified.

In all, 432 witnesses are cited in this work.

Acknowledgments

IT TAKES A LOT TO TURN AN IDEA INTO A BOOK. COUNTLESS PEOPLE PLAY CRU-cial roles in transforming a concept into a finished volume.

My editor, David Reisch, first saw promise in this unique approach to telling the war's story. His talented hand guided this project from inception to publication, and for that, I am deeply grateful.

It is impossible to compliment production editor Felicity Tucker too highly. Not only was working with her a joy, but her patience with this technology-challenged author and her remarkable attention to detail transformed a manuscript into a finished volume.

For more than 40 years, Michael Graham has been not only my best friend but also my biggest booster. His relentless encouragement kept me going through rough patches of road more times than I can count, and I can never repay the immense debt I owe him.

Likewise, Will Folks, a good friend of many years (and also one of my many bosses), has been equally supportive, as has my longtime comrade in arms (and frequent employer) Dustin Olson.

My cherished friend, Donna Kelly, reminded me time and time again that I could do it. She helped keep me focused on my mission, just as she has throughout our 40-year friendship. There are at least 2,500 reasons why I am forever in her debt.

My fellow CNN veterans from long ago and dear friends of today, Bill Bulger (who generously shared his legal expertise) and Anna Hovind, were always there when I needed a word of encouragement.

The extraordinarily caring friendship of Sherry Connor, Furman Creamer, and Todd Smith is more precious than gold or silver.

My friendship with Dr. John and Sara Carter is savored with an appreciation usually reserved for rare fine wine.

Jerry Bellune's avid support of my writing shepherded me in the direction that eventually led to this work.

Rick Harding's decades of work preserving our shared past through the 3rd Louisiana Historical Association are an inspiration.

J. Troy Massey graciously gave of his remarkable genealogical research talents, for which I am indebted.

Rick Renshaw has buoyed me up and rooted me on each step of the way over the past two decades. The same holds true for Claire Brady, Cousin Laurie Rose Bruffey and Jim Hunter, Simon and Patricia Graham, Chris Goodman, Pete Knutson, Kimberly McLeod, Kevan Ramer, Sean Thomas, Kevin Vander Weide, Matt Williams, and Eric Wynne.

Wes Franklin, while a relatively new passenger aboard the Powell Crazy Train, offered the enthusiastic encouragement only a fellow writer and friend can give.

Two people in particular deserve special mention.

John Condra not only cheered me on throughout the long process of curating, assembling, identifying, and documenting the hundreds of letters used in this work, but he did so during an immensely challenging time in his life. My respect and admiration for him are immeasurable.

And the English language simply doesn't contain enough words to fully convey my gratitude to my brother in all but blood, Scott Senft. We became acquainted through our mutual love of Civil War letters and, from there, forged a friendship reminiscent of David and Jonathan in the Bible.

Finally, this book simply would not exist without Robert Serio. He is in a category all unto himself.

Half a century ago, a scrawny 15-year-old kid unexpectedly showed up at the door of his family's home in Pea Ridge, Arkansas, one steamy afternoon in July 1976, inquiring about Civil War reenacting. Robert had recently graduated from college with a degree in history and was a dedicated living historian. He possessed an encyclopedic knowledge of the war, coupled with a limitless curiosity about all aspects of the period. He took me under his wing that day, and I am still learning from him 50 years later. Having lived in seven states and met hundreds of Civil War enthusiasts and experts over the years, none ever came close to rivaling his unmatched expertise in even the most arcane corners of the conflict. He is the gold standard of Civil War scholarship.

Robert taught me not only factual details about the War Between the States but also—more important—how to examine them within the context of the people and their time and then interpret those findings on a personal level. In short, he taught me not only the importance of the past but also how to truly understand it. My reverence and passion for history would not be the same without him.

To all, I offer a simple yet heartfelt "Thank you."